D1707929

LAND COMBAT

LAND COMBAT

FROM WORLD WAR I TO THE PRESENT DAY

MARTIN J. DOUGHERTY

amber
BOOKS

First published as *Land Warfare* in 2008

Copyright © 2008 Amber Books Ltd

This edition published in 2016

All rights reserved. No part of this publication may be reproduced, stored in a retrieval system or transmitted, in any form or by any means, electronic, mechanical, photocopying, recording or otherwise, without the prior written permission of the copyright holder.

Published by
Amber Books Ltd
74–77 White Lion Street
London
N1 9PF
www.amberbooks.co.uk
Appstore: itunes.com/apps/amberbooksltd
Facebook: www.facebook.com/amberbooks
Twitter: @amberbooks

ISBN: 978-1-78274-334-7

Project Editor: Sarah Uttridge
Design: Brian Rust
Picture Research: Terry Forshaw

Printed in China

Contents

The Industrial Age

The twentieth century saw the fastest, most profound changes in the nature of warfare in the history of humanity. Some of those upheavals began in the preceding 50 years, but it was not until the twentieth century that their implications were perceived.

During this period, powered warships reached maturity, came to dominate the oceans and then changed beyond recognition in the face of new challenges from aircraft and submarines. The first flying machines wobbled into the air and almost immediately began trying to shoot one another down. By the end of the century, this technology had achieved maturity, with bombers striking from thousands of kilometres away and missile-armed fighters trying to stop them.

Strategic warfare, too, never really existed before this period. Previously there was a war zone and usually a fairly well defined front line. Raiding parties, ranging outside the immediate area and laying waste to the countryside, could be considered a form of strategic warfare but this was hardly significant compared with the modern capability to devastate a city anywhere in the world. Long-range weapons, such as missiles and aircraft, and fast-moving ground combat units, can now bring the war to anyone in an enemy nation, often at very short notice.

The nature of war has also changed dramatically. Where once troops could be equipped with basic weapons, camp gear, and perhaps some personal protection relatively cheaply, today's highly mechanized warfare requires widespread support in terms of logistics and equipment production. Ironically, armies have grown huge and then shrunk in size again, but the massive involvement of the civilian population has remained. Today's armies require

Warfare on an industrial scale: previously, artillery had either fired at targets within line of sight or lobbed shells over an obstruction nearby, but by the early twentieth century the big guns could reach targets at distance.

Local soldiers often fought alongside European troops during the colonial wars of the late nineteenth Century. Here Sudanese infantry await attack by Dervishes at the Battle of Omdurman.

enormous economic and industrial strength to raise and maintain them.

It is not entirely possible to ignore the other dimensions, especially air power, but this is a history of land warfare and thus the changes that have occurred will be considered in that context. The main characteristics of warfare in the twentieth century are increases in the reach of weaponry, the intensity and destructiveness of combat, and the pace at which everything occurs. It has been said that a week is a long time in politics, and also that war is simply a form of politics continued by other means.

> The characteristics of twentieth century warfare are increases in the reach of weaponry, the intensity and destructiveness of combat, and the pace at which everything occurs.

In that context, in the modern era, a week is a very long time indeed.

THE STATE OF PLAY

In 1900, armies were primarily made up of infantry armed with rifles, supported by field artillery. Early machine guns were available and had proven their value in action, but they were bulky and heavy, which limited their tactical capabilities. They were also new, and there were conflicting opinions about how to use them.

Infantry firepower had increased quickly since the middle of the nineteenth century. Muskets were supplanted by percussion-cap rifle-muskets and then by all-in-one cartridge weapons. These gradually increased in range and firepower, gaining an internal magazine that gave the user the ability to put out several rounds in rapid succession if necessary.

Every infantryman was capable of delivering accurate fire out to several hundred metres, if his marksmanship was up to the task, and his weapon was deadly at this range where muskets' lethality fell off rapidly. The implications of this change were not immediately apparent, but they were profound.

Three major conflicts, the Crimean War, the American Civil War and the Franco-Prussian War, took place in the second half of the nineteenth century.

The end of the nineteenth century saw the last of wars fought in the style of the *Boy's Own Paper,* with squares of red-jacketed infantry standing firm amid a sea of brave but outmatched tribal warriors.

These, as well as smaller conflicts such as the war between Prussia and Austria in 1866 and the Boer War of 1899–1902, demonstrated a number of important concepts.

LIABILITIES IN BATTLE

Most importantly, it was becoming apparent that brightly coloured uniforms and tight formations were a liability on the modern battlefield. Bright red and blue jackets made an excellent target, and officers whose status was obvious tended to attract fire that was altogether too concentrated and accurate to be merely ignored.

There were, however, other incidents that implied – at least to those who wanted to believe – that the old way of doing things still worked. British troops formed volley lines at the Battle of Omdurman and defeated a much greater number of Mahdist warriors, inflicting huge losses while taking very few casualties. In the same action, the lancers delivered a successful, if costly, charge.

Of course, this was 'colonial' warfare against an enemy who did not have access to large quantities of firearms. Those who advocated the bayonet as the tool of decision might have done well to note that the Mahdists, who were accounted among the most aggressive and tenacious enemies the British had ever fought, were usually stopped well short of the volley lines. European troops were unlikely to do any better.

Overall, the situation in 1900 was that huge changes had already occurred but had not made themselves apparent. Doctrine had not yet caught up with technological capability. Planners and commanders did not yet know that they could no longer achieve decisive results by manoeuvring in the old style. This lesson would be bitterly learned in the years to come.

TRADITIONS DIE HARD

The increased reach and deadliness of infantry formations also meant that cavalry were liable to be shot to pieces before they could get close enough to achieve anything. Infantry needed to adopt skirmishing tactics and to make use of cover or else entrench themselves in order to avoid crippling casualties.

However, change was coming slowly. Many armies still dressed in showy, highly visible uniforms and espoused close-quarters 'shock' tactics emphasizing bayonet assaults. Cavalry clung to their traditional high status and cited rare incidents in recent wars where horsemen had managed to close with the enemy as proof that they could still get the job done.

World War I
1914–1918

The early years of the twentieth century were marked by rapid expansion in population and wealth in many nations. Overseas investment and the building of colonial empires were an important part of the economic activity in many nations. It was widely believed that a major war was impossible since the economic disruption it would cause would be intolerable.

However, the web of political alliances and commitments, plus the souring of relations between various nations due to various events, meant that war was increasingly likely. Nor could it be contained if it did break out; if almost any nation became involved in conflict with another, Allies would be inevitably dragged in.

The end result of this was a long and bloody war between the Central Powers (chiefly Germany and Austro-Hungary but also Turkey and Bulgaria) and an alliance of Britain, France and Russia and, later on, Italy and Romania.

ORIGINS OF THE CONFLICT

The early twentieth century was a time of mistrust and suspicion. France and Germany had recently fought a major war, and German overseas ambitions worried the existing colonial powers. Britain and Germany were at odds over the rapid expansion of the German High Seas Fleet. Crises in Morocco and small wars in the Balkans created opportunities for vigorous differences in opinion.

Artillery had a huge impact on World War I. Along with machine guns and poison gas, artillery guns played a prominent part in the trenches especially at battles such as the Somme and Verdun.

Field Marshal Alfred von Schlieffen put forward his plan to defeat a Franco-Russian alliance in 1905. He feared the consequences of trying to fight a war on two fronts against major powers and wanted to knock France out quickly.

The atmosphere of mutual mistrust in Europe led to a build-up of forces as each nation sought to guarantee its security by military superiority. However, one lesson that had been learnt from the wars of the late nineteenth century was that it took a great deal of time and effort to get large numbers of troops into position, and that large numbers were needed to achieve results.

Thus mobilization for war became a major issue, and a nation which mobilized too late faced a significant risk that it might be overwhelmed before troops could be brought into action. Complex timetables were drawn up, using the railways to get troops to their assembly points as quickly as possible. The problem with this approach was that it created something of a juggernaut. Once mobilization was ordered, it was a case of all or nothing; it was not possible to change the plans on the fly.

The most famous of the war plans extant in Europe at this time was the Schlieffen Plan, named for its architect. Schlieffen's war plan was purely military in nature; it disregarded political considerations almost entirely.

The most likely opponent for Germany was an alliance of Russia and France. It was not possible to stand on the defensive between these two powers, so Germany would have to take the offensive. France had good fortifications on her German border and Russia was too big to be quickly put out of the war, so Schlieffen proposed to rapidly defeat France by bypassing her border fortifications, using a sweep through Belgium and Luxembourg. German troops would then return eastwards by train and fight the Russians.

The political implications of violating Belgian neutrality did not concern Schlieffen, though he worried that the German army was not strong enough to carry out his plan. Despite this, the plan was amended rather than being reconsidered, and when war loomed in 1914 it was the only one available.

Other nations all had their plans, of course, and given the time frames involved it was not possible to create a new one and implement it in the middle of a crisis. If war broke out in Europe, the response of each nation would be directed down a path marked out by secret and open treaties, railway and mobilization timetables. It was a situation with a certain inevitability.

The flashpoint was the assassination of Archduke Franz Ferdinand, heir to the throne of Austro-Hungary, by Serbian terrorists. It could have been almost anything else; Europe, and especially the Balkan region, was rife with conflicts of interest and potential incidents.

Initially the assassination was a matter between Austria and Serbia, but Austria delayed her response a little too long. By the time the official demands were made, Russia, which had been acting as the protector of Serbia, began to call up troops and make threatening noises.

From this point, matters slid out of control. Serbia, which had decided to accept the Austrian ultimatum, changed its mind as a result of Russian support. Germany told Russia that it felt threatened by Russian troop movements, and would have to mobilize in response if these were not curtailed.

The final straw was the demand by Germany that Belgium allow the use of its territory in the coming war against France. Belgium declined and came under attack. A British ultimatum that Germany must cease operations against Belgium was ignored, and as of midnight on 4 August 1914, Europe was at war.

MANOEUVRING TO STALEMATE

Once the vast war machines had been set in motion, there could be no

If war broke out in Europe, the response of each nation would be directed down a path marked out by secret and open treaties, railway and mobilization timetables.

Although this was the dawn of the technological age of warfare, logistics and mobility still depended largely on the leg muscles of men and horses. Here, troops and horses struggle to manhandle a wagon across a ford.

turning back. The Schlieffen Plan was already laid out and the troops were on their way to the borders. The communications of the day were too ponderous to make alterations to the plan on anything more than a very localized level feasible.

And so vast numbers of men and horses, accompanied by their artillery and supplies, reached the Western borders of Germany and dismounted from the troop trains, which ran back for more. The brigades, divisions and corps formed up and began their march. There were, however, two flaws with the Schlieffen Plan.

Firstly, there was the distance involved. The army was to sweep in a great arc across France. This meant that units at the far right-hand end of the line had much further to go than those closer to the pivot point. If some elements of the army failed to make the appointed advance, the front would become disjointed and gaps would appear. This could unravel the whole enterprise.

Secondly, there was the not-so-trivial problem of French opposition. The advance across France to capture Paris was easy enough to plan on a map, but in reality the French army could be expected to resist vigorously. Prussian victories in the short wars

STRUGGLES TO PREVENT THE INEVITABLE

There was a point where all-out war might be averted, and certainly attempts were made. Frantic discussions between Germany and Russia resulted in the Tsar cancelling Russian mobilization at the last possible moment. Peace had been given a chance, and there was a brief opportunity to find a diplomatic solution. However, both Germany and Russia decided that the risk of being caught mid-mobilization was too great. The orders to mobilize were given and with gigantic, inflexible plans in place on all sides there was now no chance now to avoid conflict. Britain and France joined the general lurch towards war, but especially in Britain there were reservations and an unwillingness to commit to anything. It may well have seemed to those involved that general war could still be avoided. Efforts were made in various quarters and some of the national leaders had their own opinions about what others would do, and these in turn unrealistically influenced their own actions.

Left: Archduke Franz Ferdinand of Austro-Hungary with his wife. His insistence on visiting the victims of an earlier attempt on his life in hospital gave the assassins their chance. They were mortally injured by close-range pistol shots.

against Austria and France in the late nineteenth century had led some observers to believe that a rapid knockout was possible, but having long considered his great plan, even Schlieffen himself had been forced to concede that 'we are too weak'.

And yet now the plan was in motion. The German army was well trained and confident of repeating

Below: The main problems with the Schlieffen plan were that it required the right wing of the army to move faster than was possible on foot, and required extremely powerful forces to break French resistance in the path of the advance.

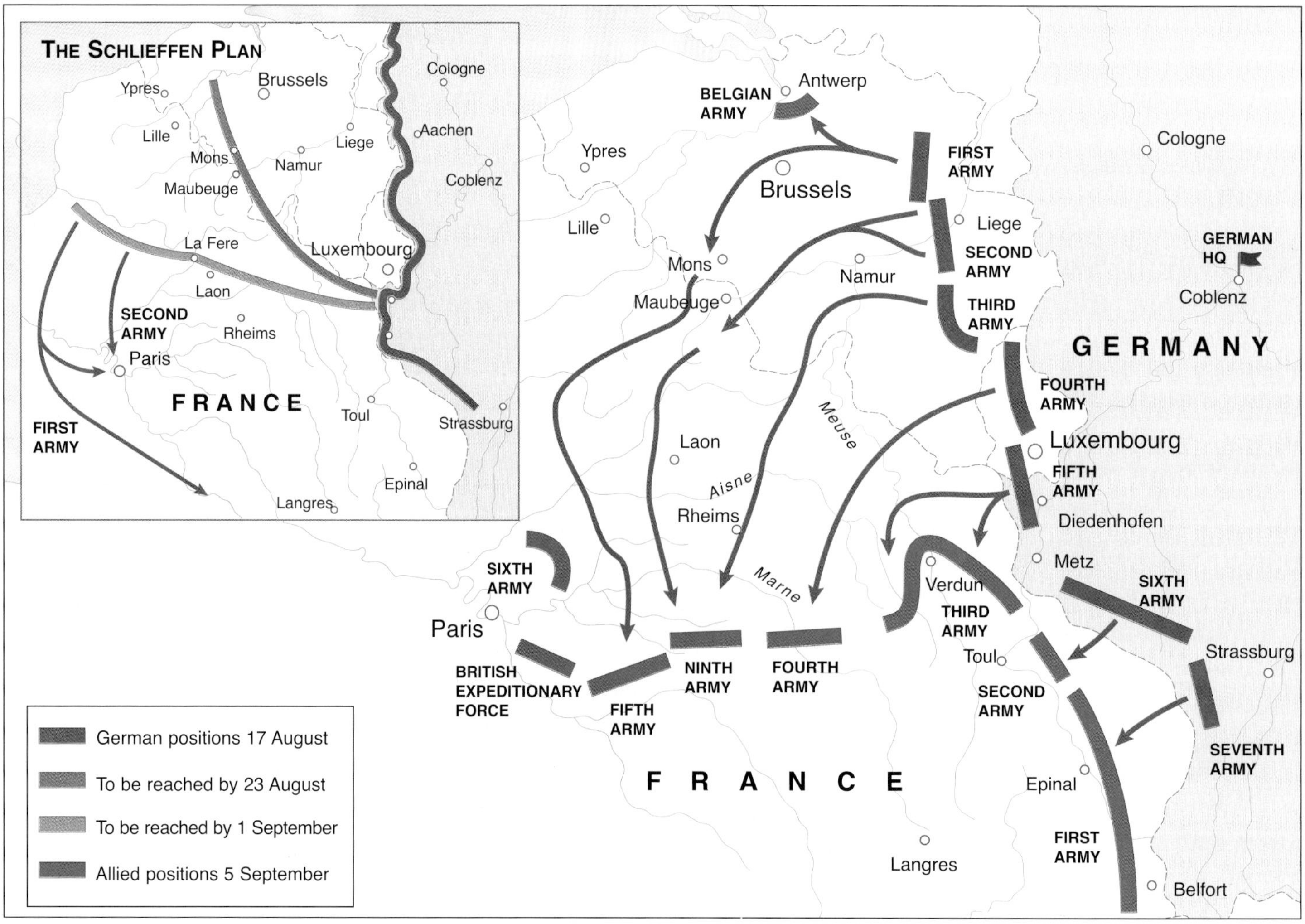

THE SCHLIEFFEN PLAN

German positions 17 August
To be reached by 23 August
To be reached by 1 September
Allied positions 5 September

Motor transport put itself on the map with the 'Miracle of the Marne', when Paris taxis and other vehicles ferried troops to the battle zone. It was not the decisive moment of the battle but it established the use of motor vehicles in war.

its previous victories, and at first the prospect of success seemed very likely.

Liège was the next obstacle. Its fall was inevitable once heavy guns were brought to bear, and the Belgian army lacked the manpower to prevent this. Nevertheless, the forts around Liège and the hastily dug-in force before them inflicted serious delays before being compelled to surrender. Meanwhile, the French army had begun a counterattack with the available forces, even though the bulk of the army was not yet in position. Hesitancy on the part of the French commander resulted in a stalled operation, and prompted the Commander-in-Chief, Marshal Joffre, to embark on a policy of dismissing commanders he considered to be insufficiently capable or energetic.

Elderly officers, as compared to their German counterparts,

UNEXPECTEDLY HEAVY RESISTANCE IN BELGIUM

The first setback was the tenacious fight put up by Belgian troops. It had been expected that Belgium would comply with the demand to allow German forces passage, or that the small and backward Belgian army would be quickly brushed aside. In the event, the Belgians blew up the Meuse bridges, which the Germans had hoped to use, and began a determined resistance. Belgian cavalry and troops mounted on bicycles rushed to the front and slowed down the invaders, though there was never any chance of stopping them at the border.

VICKERS Mk I

Type: medium-support machine gun

Calibre: 7.7mm (0.303in)

Weight: 18.15kg (40lbs)

Dimensions: length 1156mm (45.5in)

Rate of fire: 450–500 rounds per minute

Magazine: 250 round fabric belt

commanded the French army of the day. Command styles erred on the side of ponderous and hesitant, which contrasted unfavourably with the energetic and aggressive style of the enemy.

Trying again, the French army advanced into Lorraine and drove back the German forces arrayed against it. At first the operation went well, but in due course the elements of the advance became disjointed from one another. The operation slowed and was halted, then driven back by an unexpectedly heavy counterattack. This benefited from a streamlined command structure and good staff work, where the French command system was fragmented.

The Schlieffen Plan had already come somewhat unstuck, but finally the northern forces were able to advance into and across Belgium while those further south were pushing their opponents back into France.

Initiative and aggression served the German army well during this advance, with troops of the Imperial Guard seizing an opportunity to get across the River Sambre unopposed. A counterattack was beaten off, forcing the French into retreat. The French line was now badly dislocated, and contact was broken with the British Expeditionary Force (BEF) located around Mons.

The BEF had just reached Mons when the German advance guard arrived and tried to cross the canal there. In their defensive position, the British were outnumbered but did have several advantages. The BEF was no conscript force but an army of long-service regulars who thoroughly knew their business. Lessons learnt in the Boer War now served well, as the British soldiers dug in and concealed themselves.

> A tough battle turned in the favour of the French when the reserve commander, Franchet d'Esperey, personally led his corps into action.

With 10 rounds in the magazine of his Lee-Enfield rifle, the infantryman of the BEF was able to shoot both accurately and fast out to a very respectable range, and the neat blocks of German infantry advancing towards the British positions offered an easy target. A goal of 15 aimed rounds per minute was set in training, and most men could match it.

CASUALTIES FROM RIFLEMEN

Several German accounts of the action at Mons claim that the British used machine guns. There were indeed some available, but it was the rapid fire of riflemen which caused such heavy casualties among the attackers that they could make no progress.

However, with the line in tatters and the flanking French units already in retreat, the BEF could not stand for long. It began to retreat, harried by the German advance guard. Things did not look good, but even amid the general retirement Joffre was planning how the German advance would eventually be halted and how the British and French could then take the offensive. The retreating Allies fought several delaying actions, both large and small, and at times struggled to avoid being cut off and surrounded. There was a danger that the British might decide to seek the safety of the Channel ports and swing away northwards, leaving their French allies in the lurch, and this prompted the French to make a stand at St Quentin. A tough battle turned in the favour of the French when the reserve commander, Franchet d'Esperey, personally led his corps into action.

'Desperate Frankie' as the British admiringly christened him, rode at the head of his troops, with bands playing and banners flying, like it was 1814 and not 1914. His aggression was rewarded with a clear victory that bought time for the Allies to reorganize themselves and restore their equilibrium.

It was during the retreat from Mons to Paris that the British artillery deployed for the last time in Napoleonic fashion, with field guns wheel to wheel firing directly at the oncoming enemy. Artillery used in this manner no longer outranged the infantry's rifles, and the open-country battles where this tactic was useful were about to become a thing of the past.

Meanwhile, the German commanders had their own concerns. The 'Problem of Paris' had never properly been answered in any of the versions of the Schlieffen Plan. The city, with its fortified military zone and large garrison, would be difficult to subdue yet it could not be ignored

PARIS – THE HIGH WATER MARK

The battle hung in the balance for some time before the German army finally began to retire. During those fraught days, there were two important firsts in the history of warfare. The Allies used reconnaissance aircraft to find gaps and weak points in the German dispositions. Motorized transport also played a part, as several hundred Paris taxis rushed reinforcements to threatened areas. The importance of the 'Marne Taxis' may perhaps have been overplayed but their contribution was undoubtedly useful and showed what could be achieved with a motorized mobile reserve.

A Krupp 420mm (16.53in) howitzer with the muzzle elevated for extremely high-angle fire. Moving monstrous weapons like this one, and even just keeping them supplied with ammunition, required a massive logistics effort.

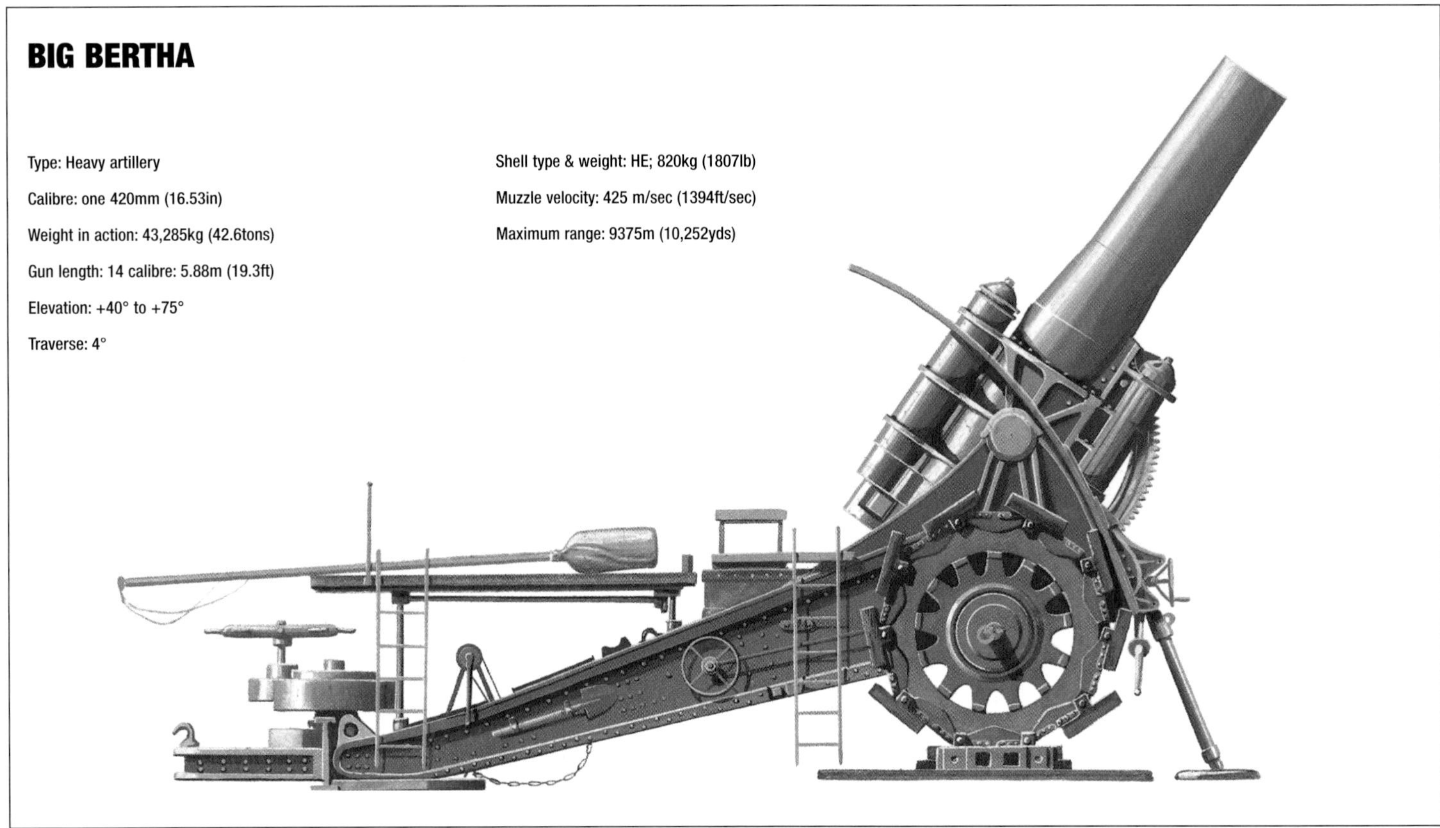

while the field armies were chased down. The garrison would be able to operate against the flank of any army that tried to bypass the city. Now, with the situation unravelling, it was necessary to come up with something that would bring decisive victory.

Time was pressing. German plans had been made on the assumption that the Russian rail system could not bring sufficient troops to the borders for an offensive until Day 40 of the war. That day was fast approaching and, according to the Schlieffen Plan, France was to have been defeated by then.

Von Moltke, commanding the German forces, responded to the situation by departing from the original plan. His intention was to encircle the French armies facing him with an attack in a south-easterly direction. However, the French commander correctly predicted this move and launched a counter of his own. The result was a bloody seven-day battle that fought the German offensive to a standstill.

The Allies attempted to drive the Germans out of France with a counter-offensive, which precipitated the Battle of the Aisne, and when this failed a series of attempts by both sides to outflank the other ensued. The succession of hooking movements to the north has become known as the Race to the Sea. Attempts were made to cut the British off from their source of supply, the Channel ports, but these were blocked.

German high command tried to make a breakthrough with cavalry, using their mobility to get into the Allied rear in Flanders. However, despite the best efforts of six divisions

SIEGE WARFARE ON A NATIONAL SCALE

As 1914 came to a close, each side was effectively dug into a giant fortress, with trenches and barbed wire protecting the artillery positions further back. Defence had triumphed for the time being. Any attack had to cross wire-strewn ground blasted by artillery and churned to mud, all the while under fire from riflemen who could barely be seen. The machine guns of the day, too clumsy for field operations, were entirely adequate for defensive purposes.

The manoeuvre period was over. Now stalemate would reign until a means could be found to break it. In the meantime, the war became a gigantic siege in many respects. Offensive operations were limited to small parties launching raids in the night, snipers and, of course, the endless shelling. It was obvious that breaking the great fortress would be a massive undertaking, and in the last months of the year both sides prepared for the large-scale attacks that would be necessary.

General Joseph 'Papa' Joffre was instrumental in rallying the battered French armies for the stand before Paris. He led the French armies through the first half of the war before being sent to assist in other theatres of war.

of horsemen, the operation was a failure and the last chance for cavalry to contribute to the war on the Western Front was lost. Gradually the hasty positions thrown up to fend off each flanking attack solidified into a line of field fortifications that stretched from the Swiss frontier to the Channel coast.

German high command then tried for a breakthrough at Ypres, throwing large forces at the town, which was held by the BEF. The resulting battle became known as 'the massacre of the innocents' as many units were made up of very young volunteers whose inexperience was matched only by their eager courage. These units, backed up by the veteran Imperial Guard, advanced into the teeth of the BEF's rifle fire and came close to breaking through.

The First Battle of Ypres ended in late November 1914. Casualties were high on both sides; it has been said that 'the BEF died at Ypres'. But there was no decisive German breakthrough, no restoration of free manoeuvre and no quick end to the war.

UNASSAILABLE POSITIONS

It suited the German war plan to remain on the defensive in the West while attending to the problem of Russia. This was a departure from the original strategy of eliminating France and then taking on Russia, but there was no alternative once the Schlieffen Plan had failed. The Russians were going to attack and the effectiveness of the Western defensive positions had already been demonstrated. Britain and France could be contained for the time being.

The British and French shared a different opinion. Both were determined to undertake offensive action, even if it were on a very small scale, such as prisoner-snatch raids into No-Man's Land. Larger offensives were planned. There was no choice really – the enemy was entrenched on French and Belgian soil and had to be ejected as soon as possible. Some sectors of the line were unsuitable for launching an attack due to their terrain or logistical difficulties. These became 'quiet' or 'inactive' sectors, though the terms were distinctly relative. Sniping, raiding and shelling went on in the quiet sectors, along with minor operations intended to

Gradually the hasty positions thrown up to fend off each flanking attack solidified into a line of field fortifications that stretched from the Swiss frontier to the Channel coast.

Above: A crowded troopship heads for the Continent. World War I required manpower on previously unimaginable scales, taking men away from the farms and factories whose output was needed to maintain the armies in the field.

gain a local advantage. The armies involved developed trench-survival skills. Even in a quiet sector, there was always danger from snipers or riflemen who fancied their chances. The adage that it is bad luck to be the third to take a light off a match stems from the observation that a sniper could spot the flare at night and set up a shot while the first two were lighting their cigarettes; the third man was a likely target.

Close combat occurred in trench raids or out in No-Man's Land at night, where reconnaissance and wiring parties did their stealthy work. The standard rifle was found to be too long and unwieldy for this kind of work. A variety of knives and clubs as well as bayonets and revolvers were pressed into service. Pump-action shotguns were sometimes used as 'trench brooms' and the need for high firepower at close range spurred the development of machine pistols and submachine guns.

The art of building trenches developed quickly. Wet conditions and enemy shellfire collapsed a lot of trench walls, sometimes burying men alive. Techniques for reinforcing a trench included using wattle to retain the walls and wooden duckboards to make a floor.

The side facing the enemy had a raised, protective front termed a parapet and included a firing step raised above the trench floor. This allowed troops to move safely along the bottom of the trench or find cover there from heavy fire, which would not be possible if the whole trench were shallow enough to stand and shoot out of. At the rear of the trench was a second raised area named the parados, which protected anyone on the firing step from fragmentation caused by shells exploding behind the trench. Sometimes the parados was omitted, which meant that an enemy who captured a section of trench could not benefit from its protection so readily.

NEW DEVELOPMENTS FOR A NEW COMBAT ENVIRONMENT

Snipers made observation difficult. Anyone sticking his head out of the trench to see what was going on was liable to be spotted and targeted for a deliberate shot even if the usual random shelling did not get him. Machine-gunners were another constant threat to anyone showing himself. Loopholes were left in the trench front for this purpose, sometimes protected by a metal plate. Trench periscopes quickly became common, allowing observation without the need to leave the protection of the trench.

A number of specialized weapons began to appear. Snipers were issued armour-piercing ammunition to shoot out the breech blocks of enemy machine guns. This was more effective than shooting the crew; another man could take over a working gun, but a smashed breech required replacement, and this took much longer. Protection took a step forward as well; gas masks lay in the future but the realization that many wounds were caused by fragmentation from shells bursting overhead promoted the introduction of steel helmets.

British infantry move up to the front line past a rural landscape. The soldiers wear the peaked cap issued early in the war. All combatant nations soon began replacing soft headgear with steel helmets because of head injuries.

Troops had to live in the trenches for extended periods, and so dugouts were constructed. These were essentially underground living areas with a thick layer of earth above to protect the occupants. Direct hits would still wreck a dugout, and conditions within were extremely unpleasant, but troops in a dugout were better protected than in the trenches. German dugouts tended to be deeper and more solid than the British equivalent, and offered good protection from artillery bombardment. One reason for this was that the German army was on the defensive and intended to be in position for a long time while the Allies had an offensive mindset and intended to move forward as soon as possible. The conventional trench was thus a deep ditch, created by digging down from above (entrenching) or along from an existing section of trench (sapping), with some of the excavated material forming the parapet and parados, often with sandbag reinforcement. However, in low-lying damp areas it was not possible to build in this fashion and many positions were actually above ground, formed of sandbags faced with packed earth.

Trenches were rarely straight but were dug in angled sections. This meant that the blast and fragmentation of shells landing in one section of the trench would be confined to a smaller area. It was also more difficult to clear an angled trench of defenders; each corner might potentially hide more enemies.

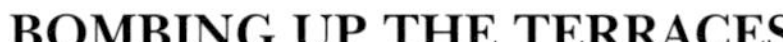

BOMBING UP THE TERRACES

One technique developed for trench clearance was 'bombing up the terraces'. 'Bombing' meant throwing grenades, and the technique involved lobbing a grenade over the intervening earth so that it came down in the next section of trench. Troops would then rush around the corner or scramble over the open ground into the next section under cover of the exploding grenade.

This was possible only if infantry could get into the enemy trenches, and although capturing a section of the defences was a victory of sorts, more was needed. Otherwise the enemy could simply retire up his communication trenches back to the next line, containing the incursion. In order to be decisively successful, an attack had not only to get into the enemy trenches and drive the opposition from them, but also to provide a breakthrough, which could

This depiction of British lancers overrunning a German artillery position is more wishful thinking than reality. Cavalry played an important part in the early actions of the war, but was soon relegated to sitting around behind the lines.

be exploited by cavalry or infantry forces moving up in support of the attacking units. This meant funnelling a lot of troops through a fairly narrow area.

The best chances for such a breakthrough were found in the Somme and Champagne regions. The locations chosen for attack were also dictated by the availability of railway links to bring in the men and supplies that would be needed. The railways of both sides were a consideration. It was necessary to attack in a place where adequate supplies and reinforcements could be assembled in a realistic time frame, and also to break the enemy's logistics chain if possible.

RAILWAY STRATEGIES

The Austro-Prussian war of 1866 was the first European conflict in which railways were strategically important. They had been vital in the American Civil War, too, with the loss of critical rail junctions having serious consequences for the combatants. Thus the Allied planners wanted to break through at a point where they could cut the rail links supplying the German army. It was thought possible that the enemy might have to make a general withdrawal if the supply chain were severed. These factors affected the choice of target. However, the formidable capabilities of a modern army on the defensive had already been demonstrated. Getting into and through the front lines of trenches represented a major undertaking.

German infantry advancing in the early days of the war. Close-order infantry tactics had proven costly but effective in recent wars. However, by 1914, these tight units simply made an easy target for rapid rifle fire.

Artillery was seen as the answer to the problems posed by wire and trenches. Heavy bombardment would cut the wire entanglements, collapse trenches and cause massive casualties among the defenders. Some planners thought that if enough artillery were brought to bear the infantry would be able to simply stroll across and take possession of the wrecked enemy positions.

The first large-scale British offensive of the war, at Neuve-Chapelle, illustrates the problems faced by the attackers. The plan was to attack on a frontage of about 8km (5 miles) and to try to isolate the target area with a curtain of artillery fire. This would prevent the area under attack from being reinforced, or so the planners hoped.

In the event, the attack achieved surprise and the initial barrage was extremely successful. The wire was indeed cut and the front trench line badly damaged, with the defenders heavily suppressed. The attacking infantry were able to make a rapid advance and soon entered the first trench line.

However, things soon began to go wrong. Behind the broken line was a series of strong positions designed to contain a breakthrough, and the stunned defenders had fallen back to these as soon as they collected their wits. The situation was not what had been expected and the pre-planned artillery support was no longer well suited to the situation. Moreover, communications with the rear were extremely difficult, and relied on runners going back and forth across No-Man's Land.

The German army had planned, in general terms, for this sort of situation. Standing orders were for the flanks of a breakthrough to be held with great determination – there was to be no retreat – while reinforcements were brought up to counterattack. Resistance firmed up as

'Bombing' meant throwing grenades, and the technique involved lobbing a grenade over the intervening earth so that it came down in the next section of trench.

German staff officers early in the war. The days of direct leadership from the front had passed; senior officers might observe part of a battle from a vantage point, but theirs was a war of maps and reports rather than combat commands.

more and more British troops became stuck in what was effectively a human traffic jam in No-Man's Land.

The attack stalled for lack of command and control on the British side. Junior officers were not permitted to use much initiative and, in any case, deviating much from the plan would have been hazardous since the artillery was still following the original orders; the attackers might have run into their own barrage.

The delay while reports went back to high command and new orders were sent forward meant that while at 9 a.m. the situation was favourable to the British, by the time permission was granted to exploit the initial success – six hours later – the advantage no longer existed. A renewed attack the following day was unsuccessful; the opportunity had been lost.

The German counterattack was delayed by the need to get reserves into position, and by the time it went in the attackers had consolidated their positions. The counterattack was beaten off with heavy losses. The eventual result of the attack at Neuve-Chapelle was an almost equal exchange of casualties for no significant gain. Some lessons were learnt about defensive operations, but overall nothing much changed.

THE EASTERN FRONT/ BALKANS

The situation developed somewhat differently in the East. There,

The capture of Ypres would have provided the German army with a forward base from which to advance on the Channel Ports, making a pivotal location for the entire Western Front campaign. The attack was ultimately unsuccessful.

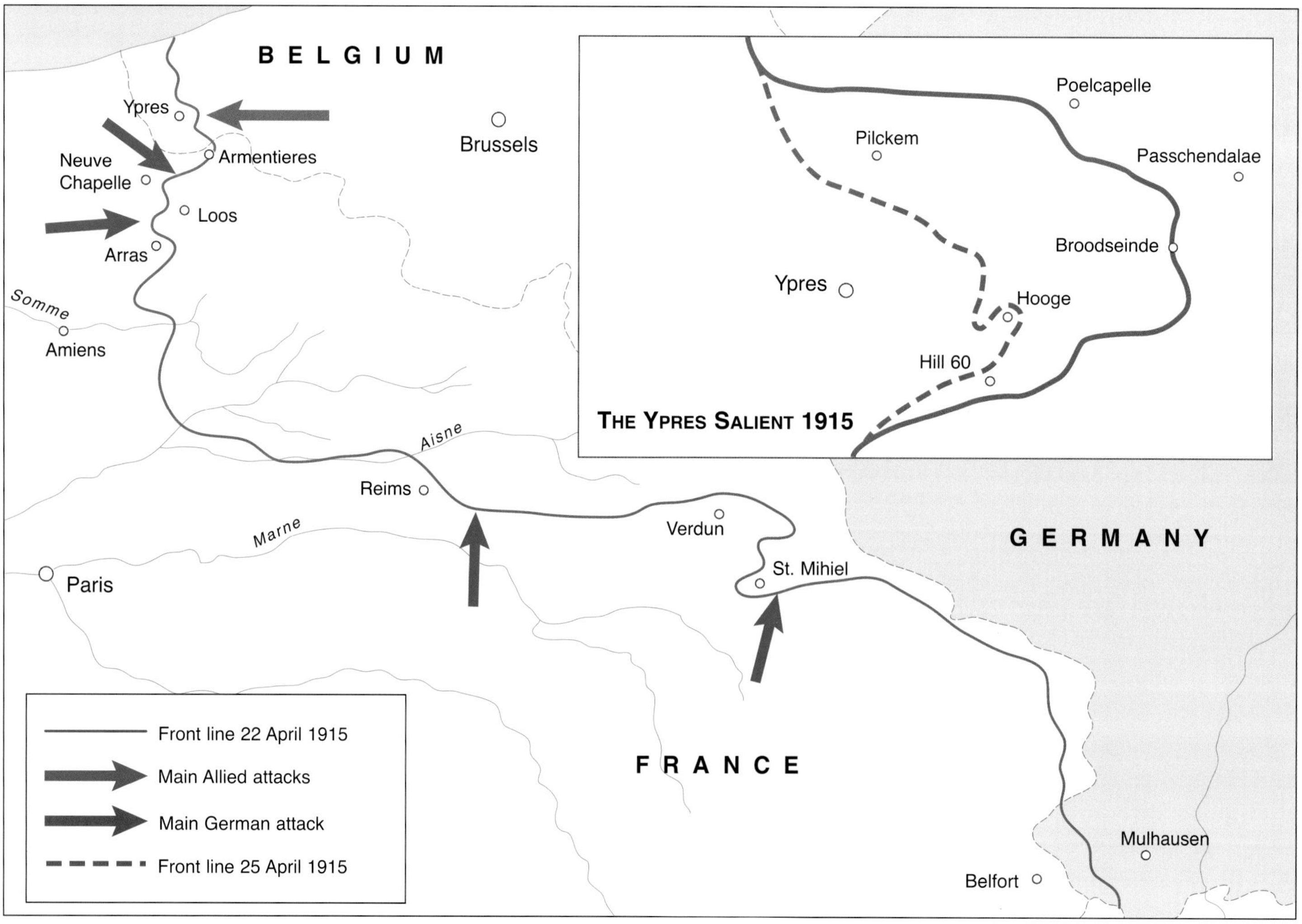

BELGIUM
Ypres
Neuve Chapelle
Armentieres
Brussels
Loos
Arras
Somme
Amiens
Aisne
Reims
Marne
Verdun
St. Mihiel
Paris
GERMANY
FRANCE
Mulhausen
Belfort
THE YPRES SALIENT 1915
Poelcapelle
Pilckem
Passchendalae
Broodseinde
Ypres
Hooge
Hill 60
Front line 22 April 1915
Main Allied attacks
Main German attack
Front line 25 April 1915

Artillery was seen as potentially decisive in the new style of warfare. More and bigger guns would surely be able to blast a hole through the enemy trench lines. In the end, artillery was just one more factor in the deadlock.

Germany and Austro-Hungary faced Russia, and Austro-Hungary was also fighting the Serbs. Most of the available German force had gone west – seven out of eight armies – and even when reinforced with reservists the army left facing Russia was greatly outnumbered.

Fortunately for Germany, the Russian field commanders did not coordinate well with one another and made some tactical mistakes, unnecessarily weakening their forces to reinforce flanks that were not threatened and lines of communication that the Germans

In the event, the attack achieved surprise, and the initial barrage was extremely successful. The wire was cut and the front trench line badly damaged.

NEUVE-CHAPELLE: A FAMILIAR PATTERN

Neuve-Chapelle was typical of offensive operations in the trenches. Attacks often succeeded in reaching at least the front line of enemy trenches, though usually at great cost. However, the attacking troops soon outran their communications and the ability of artillery to provide anything but preplanned fire support. Defence in depth and the availability of reserves to counterattack the penetration prevented any meaningful breakthrough and exploitation.

In time, this would lead to a policy of attrition, with attacks made to inflict casualties and wear down the enemy rather than in the hope of a decisive result. However, the situation was not the same everywhere.

TACTICAL MISTAKES ON THE EASTERN FRONT

Poor reconnaissance on the part of the Russians caused them to misinterpret a position change as a retreat, and as they moved in pursuit, Eighth Army used railway transport to move units onto the flanks ready for an encirclement. The Germans, for their part, benefited from radio intercepts that gave an insight into the Russian dispositions and plans.

Despite some misgivings about the situation, the Russians were sucked in until their weary and ill-fed troops, who had outrun their supply line, collided with much fresher German units. They were handed a sharp defeat, and the following morning the reinforced German flanks began their pincer movement.

could not reach. Further dispersion of effort was forced by terrain. The Masurian Lakes were an obstacle that had to be circumvented to north and south, and German strategists had studied the situation for many years.

Their solution was the obvious one. The geographical situation would allow the German army to make use of the classic strategy of operating on interior lines of communication. It would engage whichever force was most advanced, defeat it, and then fall on the other.

Thus as the Russians advanced, the German Eighth Army became aware that their two forces were divided in time as well as space; the army moving around the Masurian Lakes to the north was almost a week ahead of the one taking the southerly route. Eighth Army accordingly deployed north of the lakes and attacked the advancing Russians.

Boldness was required if the Germans were to throw back the northern arm of the pincer in time to intercept the southern one. However, the commander of Eighth Army, von Prittwitz, was prone to be cautious. After some initial successes, his mishandling of the action resulted in a reverse for Germany. He soon announced his intention to pull back behind the Vistula, abandoning the best chance the German army had of inflicting a defeat on the Russians. Prittwitz then changed his mind but

A rare aerial photograph shows the destruction at Ypres. Urban areas made natural strong points, which required bitter fighting to capture them. Fire was a major cause of destruction, especially in towns that had been abandoned.

A German propaganda image of infantry advancing in open country. It was not until late in 1914 that even those involved in the war realized how inaccurate this kind of image was.

was relieved before he could do anything. In his place, General Paul von Hindenberg was appointed, with General Erich Ludendorff as his chief of staff. The partnership between the two men would become legendary; they were very different individuals who together made an extremely effective team.

The Russians attacked in the centre despite the pressure on their flanks, but after a short time the assault disintegrated. Bad blood among the Russian commanders resulted in a total lack of cooperation, and requests for assistance were ignored. Tired, hungry and demoralized by their earlier defeat, the Russians collapsed. The Eighth Army took more than 92,000 prisoners and 500 pieces of artillery in addition to inflicting about 30,000 casualties. This first great victory became known as the Battle of Tannenberg, site of a much earlier battle in which the Teutonic Knights were defeated. News of the victory was released in Germany to distract the populace from the defeat at the Marne. Tannenberg was a massive victory, and it was unusual in that successful double-envelopments (or pincer attacks) of this sort were very rare on the Eastern Front during World War I. These would become almost standard practice during World War II, but the feat was not repeated until then.

The first attempt at another encirclement victory, or 'cauldron' battle, was made less than two weeks after Tannenberg. The German Eighth Army turned its weight against the second Russian force in accordance with long-established plans. The plan was to encircle the Russian army as it moved between Konigsburg and the Masurian Lakes. However, this force was already

> The geographical situation would allow the German Army to make use of the classic strategy of operating on interior lines of communication.

A British sniper waits for a victim. Snipers could cause disruption out of all proportion. A false alarm, and the subsequent frantic search for snipers, led to the destruction of the University of Louvain and many surrounding buildings.

pulling back to avoid being flanked. Making a fighting retreat and launching local counterattacks in some areas, the Russians were able to escape from the trap. Losses were considerable, but the Russian army was big enough to absorb them and continue fighting. That said, Germany did not face a significant threat of defeat in the East after this encounter.

Germany's ally, Austria, was engaged with the Russians as well as her own war against Serbia, which put up a much better fight than expected. Attempts to draw the Serbian army out and encircle it failed; the Serbs were experienced enough from their recent Balkan wars to spot the trap. Badly battered by Austrian artillery, they launched several attacks and inflicted a number of defeats that eventually drove the Austrians out of Serbia. They even penetrated Austro-Hungary for a time.

Meanwhile, Russian forces were also operating against the Austrians. Here, as elsewhere, there were plans for a double envelopment that would lead to large-scale annihilation of the Austrian army. However, the aggressive Austrians got the better of early engagements. The tide was eventually turned and a sharp reverse inflicted on the Austrians, who fell back to shaky and strung-out positions that might have been shattered by a determined Russian offensive.

The Russians did not realize how badly they had defeated their enemies and were reluctant to advance against what seemed to be strong positions held by determined opponents. The Austrian commander, meanwhile, had managed to convince himself that he was on the brink of victory and was trying to attack.

The result was a fluid and at times very confused situation on the Eastern front. Russian forces were able to push deep into Austrian territory and there was no repeat of the situation in the West where static lines were drawn. The war remained mobile and in many ways reminiscent of an earlier era. At times, classic cavalry engagements took place, with brigades charging at one another with sabre and revolver.

THE RUSSIANS ADVANCE

The string of defeats suffered by Austria in the East allowed the Russians to advance through Poland and to threaten even Germany. This was a major crisis. The war in the West required all the available manpower, and diverting units to shore up the crumbling Eastern front was an unwelcome distraction. Nevertheless, the Austrians were in desperate trouble and something had be done; without them, the whole flank would be open.

A new army, designated Ninth, was formed and reinforced with units from the Eighth. Rather than try to react to Russian movements, the Ninth Army would take the initiative by attacking towards Warsaw. This drew a Russian response in the form of a plan to allow the Germans to advance until their flanks were exposed, then grip their front with a stubborn defence while other forces hooked around into the flank.

This necessitated a shifting of units into position and took some of the pressure off other sectors. In turn, the Austrians were able to advance somewhat but became strung out and vulnerable. Some of the units for this operation came from further afield, brought all the way from

> The war became reminiscent of an earlier era. At times, classic cavalry engagements took place, with brigades charging at one another with sabre and revolver.

A British machine-gun team with a reliable but bulky Vickers gun. These guns could not move fast but they were excellent on the defensive, giving another advantage to the defenders of entrenched positions.

Siberia. Others, such as the Russian Tenth Army, were able to go back on the offensive in their own sectors. Tenth Army was opposite the German Eighth, which had been thinned out but remained over-confident after its victories at Tannenberg and the Masurian Lakes. It had not entrenched despite the lessons learned in attacking even hastily constructed defences, and suffered needless losses before stabilizing the situation. Manoeuvre and counter-manoeuvre resulted in mutual attempts to outflank one another. The Germans realized that they were not going to succeed and pulled back; the Austrians pushed on and were badly defeated. The Russians were proving highly adept at making large-scale manoeuvres although they again did not succeed in obtaining the intended encirclement.

The fortunes of both sides ebbed and flowed during the first months of the war, with neither gaining a decisive advantage, although losses were high.

The fortunes of both sides ebbed and flowed during the first months of the war, with neither gaining a decisive advantage. Losses, especially among long-service officers and NCOs, were high and the quality of the armies involved began to drop to an extent. This was especially true of the Austrians, who were already running short of replacements.

By April 1915, with the advantage tipping first one away and then the other, and with repeated attempts at

A Lewis machine-gun on a fixed mount. Relatively light and fed by a top-mounted drum, the Lewis gun could be used for tactical support on the advance where heavier weapons simply could not keep up.

encirclement battles failing or resulting in only local success, Austria was facing a manpower crisis. More than two million men had already become casualties. No other nation was any better off, but Austria was struggling to find replacements.

REPLACING CASUALTIES

The Austrian and Russian method of replacing casualties was much the same. More men were conscripted, given what was often a very sketchy basic training, and sent off to join the fighting units. The German system was more sophisticated. There, the policy was to split seasoned divisions to create a core for new formations, which would then be filled out with second-line and newly raised units. This avoided totally raw formations being sent into battle; the experience of the seasoned men provided a steadying influence and a source of vital knowledge for the newer arrivals.

Russia, too, was suffering from shortages. In this case, it was not manpower for the army but munitions and supplies that were difficult to obtain. The industrial and logistical problems faced by Russia have at times been referred to as 'shell-shortage', but the problem was wider and deeper than that. All manner of equipment was missing or inadequate – factories turned out thousands of shells and rifle sights, only to find they were all defective – and the shortages were beginning to really bite.

There were other problems within the Russian army too. These reflected the increasing problems in society 'back home', which in turn had a bearing on the ability of Russian industry to support the war. Troops

Trench systems gradually became more sophisticated as the war went on. Here, wickerwork supports keep the side of the trench from falling in while a roadway of 'duckboards' provides a level surface to move around on.

Above: Railway guns were extensively used during the war. Some were truly gigantic, and even the 'average' gun was a 280mm (11 in) weapon capable of throwing a huge shell for many kilometres.

Left: British infantry repairing wire in front of a trench. Cutting enemy wire and maintaining the wire defending friendly positions was a constant task. In active sectors, it had to be done stealthily at night – a dangerous occupation.

were not yet 'voting for peace with their feet' but were increasingly disaffected. The gulf between soldiers and their officers grew ever wider and both lost faith in one another.

Officers and NCOs were in desperately short supply in the Russian army, and the measures needed to create them were alien to the regime of the time. The result was that segments of the army, which was largely made up of poorly trained and undisciplined troops at best, were more or less without supervision. The consequences were serious. For example, it was not uncommon for troops to chop down telegraph poles for firewood.

Many infantry units were unsteady at best, and tended to scatter when shelled. The infantry was most definitely of a lower social class than the artillery and cavalry, and tended to be abandoned by them in adversity. German attacks would often capture thousands of infantrymen but not a single artillery piece. It was also notable that most of these captives were quite content to be put to work behind the German lines and, so long as they were fed, were not in the least bit interested in escaping.

When forced to it, the Russian infantry were stoic and patriotic in battle, but the social divisions that would soon rip Russia apart were already hamstringing the army. The commanders' response did not help much; the usual practice was to brutalize the men for any infraction, mistake or setback. Threats were made of sanctions against the families of men taken prisoner, and upon occasion the Russian artillery shelled its own infantry as punishment for halting in an attack.

Despite these problems, the Russian army made gains at times, though there was no decisive victory to be had and their German opponents were coming out on top in most engagements. The Central Powers had established a reasonably effective joint command and were gradually pushing forwards. While the Austrians in particular suffered at Russian hands, a bungled counter-offensive resulted in more losses than standing on the defensive would have, and deprived the Russian armies of their reserve strength. The declaration of war against the Central Powers by Italy did not result in serious consequences. Local Austrian units contained initial Italian operations. The Russians had no alternative but to retreat from Galicia, exposing their forces to flanking attacks by the aggressive Germans. Casualties were heavy and large numbers of prisoners were taken. By May 1915, the Russians were holding a long salient with its deepest point about 80km (50 miles) west of Warsaw. Many Russian

The Russian army made gains at times, though there was no decisive victory to be had and their German opponents were coming out on top in most engagements.

A logistics yard, where supplies were transferred from rail cars to horse-drawn wagons as part of the immense task of keeping the field forces combat-ready. Motor transport was introduced, but horses remained a part of the logistics chain.

A trench mortar mounted on a railway car. In theory, a threat to an important rail link could be countered by running a train loaded with artillery up the line to support a more conventional response.

commanders were uneasy about the situation and even went so far as to suggest that in the event of a German attack, the most forward parts of the salient might be best abandoned.

When the offensive did come, the response was very confused. A cavalry feint in Courland on the Baltic coast should have been easily handled, but instead the Russian forces in the area fell into chaos. An aggressive German force grabbed the fortress of Libau during the confusion.

With Galicia fallen and Courland in danger, the situation looked bleak. It was obvious that the Central Powers would try to pinch off the Warsaw salient, and a retreat was the only way that vast losses could be prevented. However, with the Western Allies about to launch an offensive, it seemed that Russia could hang on to Poland.

ATTRITION AS A POLITICAL TOOL

This offensive was intended to use attrition as a political tool to try to persuade the Russians to agree a separate peace. The German commanders were unhappy about their prospects in a deep invasion of Russia, and probably correct in this. They also knew that whatever troubles were besetting Russian society and her army, an invasion of the Motherland would provoke a fanatical response. It would also require operating at the end of a long line of supply and pull troops away from the Western Front.

The alternative was to inflict such losses on the Russians that they sought peace, without pushing much further to the east. Thus the three-front offensive was fairly limited in territorial scope; its goal was the destruction of enemy armies and infliction of a defeat rather than deep penetration.

DEFENSIVE LINES

A plan was made to create several strong defensive lines and to force the Germans to fight for each one in turn – shades of the Western Front perhaps – but these fell apart in arguments over where and how to build the defences, and who was to do the work.

Although the Germans did not want to advance in the East, they needed to obtain a victory rather than simply avoid defeat. Victory was to be found in the ranks of the enemy, and it was necessary to seek it there. Thus the expected pincer attack began.

The Central Powers attacked on three fronts: in Courland; in the

Indian troops on the march. Britain's forces included large contingents recruited from all over the Empire. These extra recruiting grounds represented a huge advantage over Germany, which could recruit only at home.

region around the Narev; and in Galicia. The attack was heavily supported with artillery, which was highly effective, as the Russians had not deeply entrenched themselves. Caught in scanty protection and not allowed to make even a tactical withdrawal to avoid the worst of the shellfire, the Russian forces in the centre were battered to breaking point. Those that belatedly tried to escape through the barrage suffered heavily.

The offensive was assisted by poor Russian cooperation. The fortress of Novogeorievsk, for example, held over 1600 artillery pieces, yet these were not called upon to assist nearby troops. Reinforcements were misdirected or short-stopped by corps commanders along their route who thought they might be useful in the local sector. Orders came down to hold ground at all costs, which simply allowed the German heavy artillery to pulverize inadequately protected troops.

> Orders came down for the Russians to hold ground at all costs, which simply allowed the German heavy artillery to pulverize inadequately protected troops in place.

By 17 July, the offensive had not advanced very far at all but had inflicted massive casualties, which was the goal. Finally the Russians decided that some backwards movement might be in order, and a withdrawal to the Narev line was undertaken. There, supported by archaic and virtually useless fortresses, sketchily entrenched behind a river that was too shallow to make much of an obstacle, the miserable Russian infantry were once again ordered to die in place.

German over-confidence resulted in excessive casualties in some areas; artillery was not prepared for counter-battery fire and infantry blundered

into areas swept by machine guns. The defence, inadequate as it was, actually held. However, the bigger picture concerned the Russian high command, where the Central Powers were making gains in several areas. Permission was given to retreat behind the Vistula, which meant abandoning Warsaw, and the Russian army conducted a fairly orderly retirement to its new positions. German forces took Warsaw on 4 August.

A LONG RETREAT

The retreat went on longer and further than it need have, due to a lack of confidence on the part of Russian commanders, who were unnerved by the shortage of ammunition and supplies, coupled with the perceived unreliability of the infantry. This shortened the Russian lines by greatly reducing the salient, which was considered desirable, as it would free some troops to stabilize the situation in Courland.

The German pursuit was less than vigorous. The normal pattern was for the Russians to fall back about 5km (3 miles) a day, throw up a feeble defensive line and then abandon it the next morning. The advancing German army in the centre, which was suffering increasingly acute supply problems, followed rather than pursued. Minor actions were fought but there was no real attempt to force the issue. Nor was there much of an attempt to slash around the flanks of the salient and encircle the retreating armies, even though sufficient forces were available.

However, in the north there was a more determined push in Courland. Some commanders wanted to try for a decisive victory in the region, but the

On the Eastern Front, the war was more mobile than in the West. Harsh weather conditions hampered operations by both sides. River crossings were actually made simpler by the cold, as the men standing on the ice show.

terrain and the weather were such that a limited tactical victory was all that was realistically possible.

The offensive in Courland occurred at a particularly bad time for the Russians, who were trying to reorganize their command structure and move units about to counter threats that were, in many cases, entirely imaginary. The Russian armies in the region did not support one another and the imposing fortress of Kovno, containing over a thousand guns, was little use. The defence of Kovno was a fiasco. The aged commander lacked initiative and gave confusing orders. Forts in Russian hands fired on one another instead of those the Germans had captured. The garrison, which included second-rate regulars, and *Opolchenie* (territorial troops, or militia), began to desert.

The fall of Kovno caused a radical shake-up of Russian command, and more seriously in the long term, prompted the Tsar to assume personal command of the army. This was a dangerous move since the blame for subsequent reverses could be laid directly at his feet.

The offensive in Courland gradually ran down, due to terrain and a shortening of the Russian lines. It did push forward but there was no realistic chance of a great drive up the Baltic coast on St Petersburg. Faced with a need to send troops to help in France and with further gains being unlikely, the order was given for the German army to dig itself in, forming a permanent front with extensive trench defences much as in the West.

The corresponding Austrian advance also stalled, with extremely heavy losses that could not be replaced, and movement in the East slowed to a halt. Austria was busy with Serbia, and Germany with France, while Russia was busy dealing with internal problems. It was some time before the Eastern Front became active once again.

BESIEGING THE GREAT FORTRESS

By the winter of 1914–15, the trench lines of the Western Front ran from Switzerland to the coast, and were well established with dugouts, wire, machine-gun nests and deep layers of supporting fortifications. Troops in the trenches quickly became aware of the weak points of their own defences, such as where a section of trench was

A German sniper position, with a rifle set up on a rest and spare weapons nearby. Note the observer located slightly apart from the shooter. This position seems to be a long-term proposition.

Trench life rapidly became a fact of life, and troops adapted as best they could. Where conditions were not too wet, life in a dugout was not too different from being part of the garrison of a more permanent fortification.

overlooked by high ground, and the main features of the enemy works. Thus soldiers developed a sort of trench-wisdom, knowing where they were most exposed to fire and from which areas it might come.

However, it was not the defences alone that made it impossible to achieve a decisive breakthrough. It was possible to get into the enemy trenches and even to push through to the second and third lines. What made major success elusive was the time.

It took time for an assault to fight its way into the enemy trenches, and to grind forwards into the successive lines, eliminating points of resistance as the troops went. Movement forward was at a very slow pace.

Movement behind the lines, however, was much faster. Reinforcements could be brought into the threatened area by train and then marched up over open country much more quickly than the enemy could force his way forwards. Unless the enemy commanders made a serious mistake, any assault would be met by heavy reinforcements to halt it and then begin driving the attackers out.

These counterattacks would be made into the rear of the trench system, and against troops who were both tired and disorganized, and these were therefore far more likely to succeed than the direct frontal assault the attackers were forced to make. As a result, gains were small at best.

> It was possible to get into the enemy trenches and even to push through to the second and third lines. But what made major success elusive was the time factor.

The methodically brilliant General quartermeister Eric Ludendorff formed a highly effective partnership with the more flamboyant Paul von Hindenberg, creating an excellent command team.

Western Europe had become, in effect, two great fortresses trying to besiege one another. There was no really effective means to attack deep into enemy territory beyond the reach of heavy artillery. Air power was very much in its infancy and tanks were still on the drawing board. Thus the only option was infantry assault against defences optimized to resist such an attack.

And yet the great fortress had to be broken. There were high hopes for artillery at first, but by the spring of 1915 it was becoming apparent that bombardment, however heavy, was not sufficient to blast the enemy positions aside. The key, in tactical terms, was to remove barbed-wire entanglements and suppress the defenders so that assault troops could get to their objectives without being shot to pieces. In strategic terms, reserves had to be tied down elsewhere or eliminated to prevent a counterattack.

Artillery preparation before an attack and support during it were considered vital to success, but other means were sought to suppress the defenders and gain an advantage. In the Second Battle of Ypres in April 1915, the German army attempted to use poison gas for this purpose.

GAS WARFARE

Gas warfare was outlawed even before the attack at Ypres; this was one reason why the Allies discounted the possibility of a gas attack even though suspicious cylinders were observed and deserters brought warning. Thus on the afternoon of 22 April 1915, the release of the gas came as a surprise to the troops opposite the attack.

Gas shells had been tried earlier without success; they were perfected later. At Ypres, the gas was delivered from cylinders and carried on the wind. This was a hit-and-miss method, which favoured the Allies more than their opponents since the prevailing wind blew towards the German trenches. Shifts in the wind caused many friendly casualties during gas attacks of this nature.

FIRST USE OF CHRLORINE GAS

Experiments with lethal and non-lethal gas had been carried out previously, without success, but at Ypres the first use was made of chlorine gas. Chlorine is heavier than air and will flow into low areas, making it ideal for attacking trenches. It is a choking agent; in other words, it disables or kills the target by making it impossible to breathe. In this case, however, the gas was successfully delivered and the greenish cloud rolled ominously into the opposite trenches, accompanied by the usual artillery bombardment. Directly opposite the gas attack were French troops, who had no gas protection. Casualties were very heavy. Those who fell into or sought shelter in the bottom of a trench were doomed as the gas pooled there. Those who fled were running with the cloud and many were overcome. Ironically, the few who chose to remain on the firing step were the best off as the cloud of gast rolled quickly past them. Even so, they suffered terribly and many were killed.

Chlorine is heavier than air and will flow into low areas, making it ideal for attacking trenches. And it disables or kills the target by making it impossible to breathe.

Within an hour, a gap some 800m (0.5 mile) wide had been opened in the Allied line, with thousands of French riflemen fleeing, dead or dying. Some gas drifted into neighbouring positions held by newly arrived Canadian troops, but it was not concentrated and had much less

German infantry in a firing position dug into the floor of a building. This position combines the advantages of concealment and being dug into the ground, allowing the men within to open fire by surprise.

effect. German infantry moved up to exploit the breach and were virtually unopposed at first. Their goal was to eliminate the salient in the Allied line around Ypres with a view to a future offensive towards the Channel ports. This would have cut off the British troops on the Continent from supplies and reinforcements. Thus the German attack into the nearly deserted French section of the line at Ypres had the potential to devastate the Allied effort, thereby achieving a massive strategic result for the Central Powers.

It was imperative to halt the advance, and so the Canadian troops on the flanks and British reserves were sent in to make a counterattack. Bitter fighting ensued, in which the Allied efforts were aided by two factors. Firstly the German high command had not expected the gas to be so shatteringly successful and had provided insufficient reserves to support the breakthrough. Secondly, German infantrymen were understandably reluctant to charge into the gas and so began to dig in and consolidate their new positions in the French trenches.

Allied troops suffered very high casualties in the counterattack, but the line was shakily held at the end of the first day. The gas was identified as chlorine, and basic protection was hastily improvised from wet cloths. Thus when the attack was renewed, with more gas, the effect was not as dramatic. This was partly due to the reduced psychological effect of the gas; men who knew what they were facing and felt that they had some protection were better able to resist the temptation to flee. Indeed, close-quarters fighting sometimes took place within the gas cloud itself, and the Allies were pushed back despite costly and largely unsuccessful counterattacks. Eventually, the Allies were forced to pull back to better positions and accept a defeat at Ypres. However, it was a relatively minor one and not the huge disaster it might have been. Gas would be used throughout the remainder of the war but it would never again hit entirely unprepared troops, nor have the devastating effect it had at Ypres.

EVOLVEMENT OF GAS WARFARE

Over the next months, gas warfare evolved considerably. Crude gas hoods and masks began to appear, along with new agents, including phosgene and a chlorine-phosgene mix. Attempts were made to combine tear

The traditional cavalry role of scouting was possible for a short time on the Western Front, after which the continuous trench lines made it impossible. Aerial reconnaissance had replaced cavalry scouting by the middle of the war.

gas with a lethal gas, in the hope that the irritant gas would cause troops to tear off their masks and be exposed to the killing agent.

Mustard gas, or lewisite, was also used. This causes skin blistering and irritation of the eyes, though this may appear only several hours after contamination. More serious doses cause victims to slowly asphyxiate due to irritation of the lungs and airways. Mustard gas was used primarily as a harassing measure since it would contaminate an area for long periods and make the defenders' task a little harder.

The common image of the Great War is of miserable soldiers cowering in wet trenches under artillery and gas attack. However, this was only one facet of the war. Elsewhere, traditional military scenes like this were common.

After the Second Battle of Ypres, the Allies went over to the offensive. The British attacked at Artois and the French at Vimy Ridge. The offensives went in within a week of one another and used similar tactics. The main difference between them was the availability of large stocks of artillery ammunition to the French. The British were not able to put down such

> Gas would be used throughout the remainder of the war but it would never again hit entirely unprepared troops, nor have the devastating effect it had at Ypres.

Horses were not the only animals pressed into military service. Any source of muscle power was welcome when it came to dragging guns and supply wagons through the blasted, muddy landscape of the battle zones.

a ferocious barrage. Thus the French should, according to the theory that weight of artillery was decisive, have made much better gains. In reality, neither offensive was a success. The British were halted earlier than the French, who actually reached the crest of Vimy Ridge before being driven off by a counterattack.

Had the French offensive succeeded, it might have cut the rail lines that ran behind the German positions and made it impossible for reinforcements to reach the battle zone. Severing the supply line might even have forced a withdrawal, and without ready positions to fall back into, a period of renewed manoeuvre might have ensued. However, it was not to be. Once again, reinforcements were able to plug the gap made at such cost before Allied reserves were brought up to consolidate or increase the gains.

The Allied Spring offensives did not fail for lack of effort or stupidity. Warfare had changed radically in recent years and no one really knew what was possible. Mistakes were made and learnt from – though not always the right lessons. However, commanders on both sides were discovering new facts about this new style of warfare and creating a new doctrine to deal with the realities they encountered.

The scale of the logistics effort required in making an attack surprised both sides, and much had to be done to ensure that adequate supplies of ammunition and food were available. Artillery ammunition in particular was devoured at an alarming rate.

Communications also proved to be a serious problem. Radio sets were available but required several men to move them and, in any case, they were not very reliable. Field telephones were highly useful but prone to having their wires cut by shelling – and that was when they could be laid at all. This was less of a problem in prepared positions, since wires could be buried

A poignant image of war; a lone sentry stands silhouetted against the wreckage of civilisation. To some extent, the sacrifice and destruction already endured made it even more imperative to fight through to victory.

There was no glamour in this kind of war. The next troops to occupy this trench and dugout will have to clear and bury the bodies, repair the trench as best they can and try to forget the possibility that they, too, will end up like this.

> Communications also proved to be a serious problem. Radio sets were available but required several men to move them and, in any case, they were not very reliable.

to protect them, but such precautions were obviously not possible during an attack. And so, runners carrying messages back and forth across No-Man's Land were often the only means available.

Other options were to use flares for prearranged signals or to take carrier pigeons forward with an attack. These, naturally, were a one-way system but at least a report could be sent from an advanced position – providing someone had time to write a message and the bird arrived where intended. The only way around these problems was to use a rigid timetable for attacks and hope that everything went according to plan. Of course, it never did, resulting in attacks being held up by their own supporting fire or a barrage running ahead of bogged-

ADVANCES IN DEFENSIVE TECHNIQUES

One trick the German army used to great effect was to build a secondary position on the reverse slope of a defended terrain feature such as a ridge. Such a position could not be reconnoitred or accurately shelled unless spotter aircraft were available, which was not common at the time. An assault that broke through the front position would find itself facing another line of dug-in troops protected by wire, with machine guns ready. This position would have been spared the worst effects of preparatory bombardment and would be in good shape to repel the disorganized and tired attackers.

Other defensive measures included the use of artillery to bombard assembly areas for an assault, which could often be observed from high ground occupied by German forces. An assault could be severely disrupted by artillery before it began, and once underway would be forced to move through a defensive bombardment. Close defence was a matter for machine guns and riflemen. The effectiveness of the defensive fire – both direct and artillery – was enhanced by the difficulty of getting forward across no man's land. Shell holes, mud and wire slowed down the attacker and broke up his formations, reducing his effectiveness while giving the defenders more time to shoot at the attackers. Wire, of course, did not defend positions. It was an obstacle and according to the old adage 'an obstacle not covered by fire is not an obstacle'. In other words, wire alone could be circumvented or cut. Its role was to impose delay, not to halt an attacker all on its own.

down troops who ceased to benefit from its effects since they were not advancing behind it on schedule.

Both sides tried various measures to deal with wire. Artillery tended to move it around rather than cut it, which was not very effective. Another option was to send out parties at night to snip the wire with cutters. This was a risky occupation but less hazardous than trying to do it in daytime as an assault formed up. Wiring parties also worked during the night to repair and replace wire, and small-scale fights sometimes broke out between opposing parties. More often, a party was spotted, flares went up, and the party would have to flee or take cover under fire.

GAS ATTACK AT LOOS

Now that gas had been used, the Allies also began deploying it. During the Autumn Offensives of 1915, the British used gas to support an attack at Loos in the Artois region. The gas was blown about by the wind, at one point coming back into the British trenches. As stated earlier, this was a major problem with delivering gas from cylinders – it originated close to friendly troops and would endanger them if conditions were not perfect.

The British attack at Loos was made in close order, impaired by its own gas, and was driven home with great determination despite everything the defenders could do to stop it. Eventually the attacking units became stalled by unbroken wire and, machine-gunned at relatively short range, lost hope. Of the 15,000 attacking troops, some 8000 were killed or injured.

Gas-masked German infantrymen manning a machine-gun. The ammunition belt is made from canvas. Water-cooled guns like this one could keep up sustained fire through thousands or even tens of thousands rounds.

Casualties might have been much higher but for the fact that the defenders ceased fire as the British fell back. German soldiers afterward spoke of being overtaken by a feeling of compassion and mercy, being sickened by the sight of the 'corpse field of Loos'. With their own survival no longer in doubt, the defenders allowed their defeated foes to retire more or less unmolested. The British battered away at Loos for three weeks but made very slight gains. The same happened with the French offensive in Champagne. Despite the support of gas and a thousand heavy artillery pieces, the French army made only the slightest headway. The year 1915 was, in many ways, the year of stalemate, when the Great Fortress resisted all efforts to break through its walls and achieve a decisive result.

At the very end of 1915, a joint conference was held among the Allies with a view to establishing a joint plan for 1916. It had been realized that the movement of reserves was the key to defeating an attack, and since the Central Powers were able to operate on interior lines they could quickly transfer reserves from one theatre to another to counter Allied attacks. The answer was to coordinate offensives so that the Central Powers were under attack from several points and could not concentrate against one and then another.

The field telephone was a significant step forward in command and control technology. It was vulnerable to having its cables cut and was quite bulky. As a result, troops making an advance often outran their communications.

Since Russia needed to reorganize its forces and rearm them, and Britain was about to introduce conscription, time would be needed to prepare for these separate but coordinated offensives. The summer of 1916 was chosen for the 'main event', with preparatory operations beginning earlier in the year.

Meanwhile, the German analysis was that Britain was the main enemy – and one that could not be directly attacked. The submarine blockade at sea offered some hope but there was no chance of successful offensive operations in the British sector of the Western Front.

France, on the other hand, might be knocked out of the war. It was thought that she was running out of the means and the will to fight. If dealt a sufficiently heavy blow in terms of casualties, France might be persuaded to give up even if a traditional field victory, complete with peace terms dictated from the enemy capital at the point of a bayonet, could not be won.

Thus it was that on both sides the main consideration at the end of 1915 came down to manpower – how to obtain enough of it and how to use casualties as a political lever to force a surrender.

NEW RECRUITMENT PRACTICES

At the outbreak of war, the British Army was a small, all-volunteer force, with considerable experience of

Cutting wire during the hours of darkness. Preparations for an attack often included stealthy reconnaissance of enemy wire, and wire-cutting expeditions were a common activity even between major operations.

small-scale colonial operations. British units had been involved in combat all over the Empire, usually outnumbered though possessing better equipment than the enemy. Thus the BEF of 1914 was a seasoned and well led force at the company and battalion level, but with little experience of large-scale operations. These skills had to be rapidly gained as the army learnt how to conduct warfare on a grand scale. Where previously companies and perhaps battalions had undertaken operations, now the tactical units were divisions. Even without the heavy casualties taken early in the war, a larger army was needed if the Central Powers were to be defeated. This New Army was the brainchild of Lord Kitchener, then Secretary of State for War. He originally called for an army of 100,000 men to serve in the war. Many times this number volunteered.

The Autumn Offensive of 1915 was the first major attack to be undertaken by the New Army, which took heavy losses for little gain. This was one reason why the queues to enlist shrank rapidly as 1915 turned to 1916. Conscription was introduced in Britain in 1916 to ensure adequate numbers of troops.

Enforced military service, especially in wartime, is rarely welcomed, and large-scale conscript armies are inevitably of lower overall quality than professional volunteers. Training was also truncated in order to get men to

THE PALS BATTALIONS

One of Kitchener's innovations was the creation of so-called 'Pals' battalions, formed from men of the same town, workplace or other associations who were permitted to serve together. Many of these units were allowed to elect their own non-commissioned officers, as there were not enough experienced men to provide the proper quota.

The Pals system encouraged enlistment, but it had serious consequences for many communities. When a Pals battalion took heavy casualties, this meant that a large proportion of the young men of a particular town or institution were killed or injured. The effects of this phenomenon would be felt for many years after the war.

The Pals and other volunteer battalions formed Kitchener's New Army and began to arrive in France after basic training. Most of these new units had been created from the ground up and had no core of long-service professionals to pass on experience. This was gained rapidly and at a high cost in casualties when the New Army reached the front lines.

New recruits being fitted with uniforms. Finding men to fight was not much of a problem early in the war. As time went on and war-weariness increased, voluntary recruitment had to be replaced by conscription.

the front in numbers, causing a drop in troop quality. Many commanders believed that the new conscript army was incapable of more than the simplest tactics, and this influenced military thinking of the time. However, there was no alternative. Manpower was needed, and quickly.

Conscription was already in force in the larger armies of the Continent. Both Germany and France had been using it for many years and had an established system in place. More importantly, their military establishment was ready to process and train conscripts; in Britain, the system had to be developed when conscription was introduced.

The usual system in nations where conscription was used was for certain segments of the population to be exempted and for the remainder to be divided into 'classes', from whom a proportion of men were called. Exactly who was exempted depended upon the needs of the nation and the prevailing conditions. Workers in key industries, married men, men over a certain age, and so on, were usually exempted, but these boundaries were eroded as casualties rose and more troops were needed.

In Russia, virtually the entire male population was theoretically eligible for conscription, but the army could never handle so many men. There were many reasons for exemption, with the result that the vast majority of men eligible for conscription were exempted. It was no coincidence that there were a huge number of sudden marriages in the villages of western Russia when war broke out – heads of families were safe from army service.

THE MEATGRINDER

While the Allies planned their offensives, the German army was quietly getting ready to launch its own. The plan was simple; a target would be chosen that the French simply had to defend, which would force them to fight at a place of the Germans' choosing and at a disadvantage. The target was Verdun, a fortress city that French pride would demand to be held. Tactically, it provided what the Germans needed as well; the city was located in a loop of the River Meuse with limited access from the French side. They would be forced to feed reinforcements in down a single narrow road (which became known as the Voie Sacrée) while the city and the positions around it were subjected to a massive artillery bombardment, which would create a 'meatgrinder' effect.

Abandoning Verdun would be a political blow to the French, which might force them to consider an armistice. Defending it would result in the loss of their reserves, which might enable an offensive elsewhere to succeed even if it did not force France to the peace table.

So many fortresses had fallen earlier in the war – and much more

One of the most iconic images of the Great War was that of Lord Kitchener making his appeal for men to join up. Many times more volunteers than had been hoped for signed up as a result of this appeal.

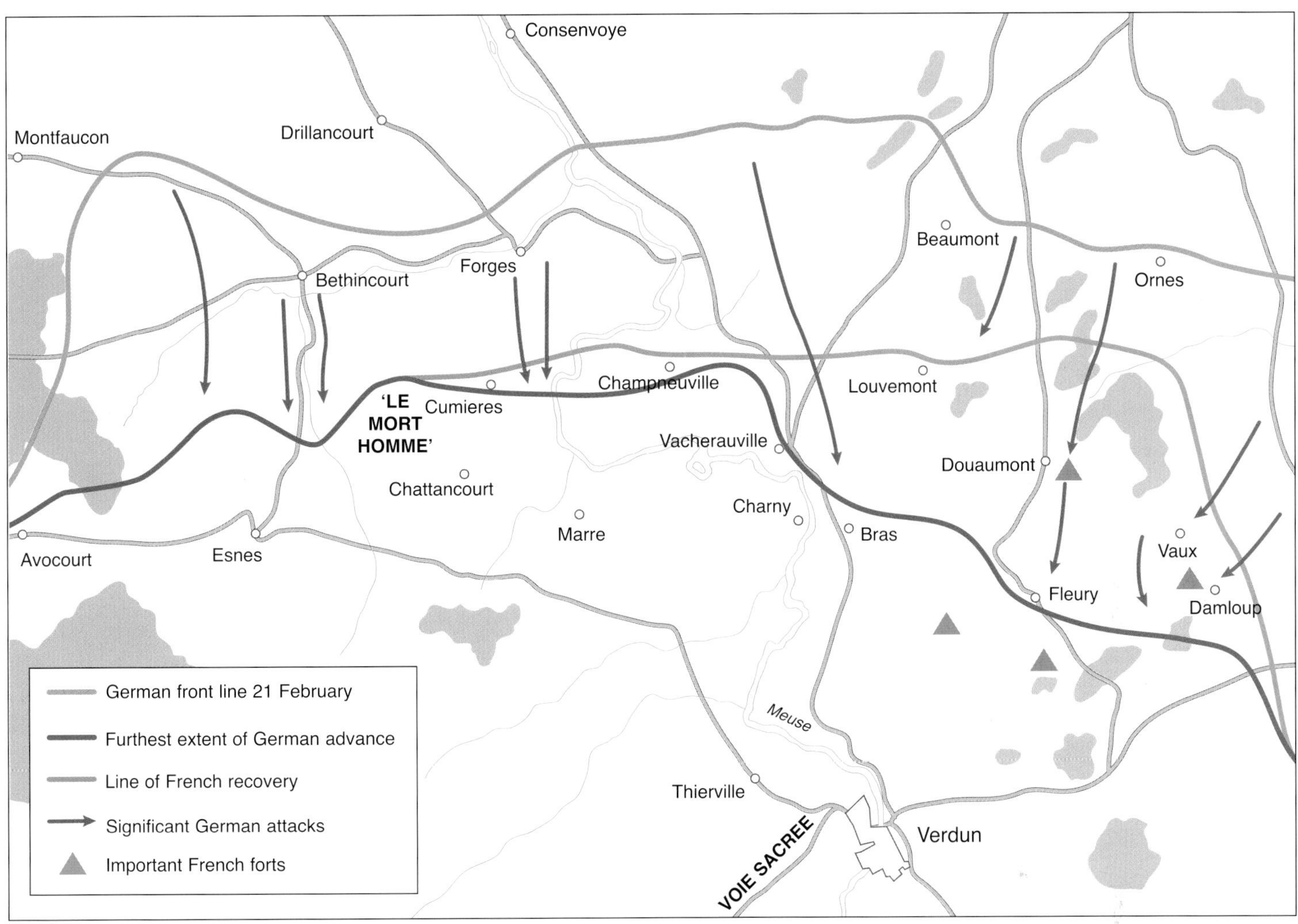

Above: Starting as a deliberate attempt to draw the French into a 'meatgrinder', the battle for Verdun resulted in massive casualties on both sides. By the end of the battle, the tactical situation was little changed.

easily than expected – that the French no longer placed great faith in them. Many of Verdun's guns had been removed for use elsewhere and the sector, which had previously been quiet, was lightly held. Preparations were made in secret and when the attack opened on 21 February 1916, it came as a shock to the defenders. The bombardment was huge and, due in part to its suddenness, succeeded in driving the unprepared defenders from their positions. It is possible that a determined attack at that point might have smashed right through and taken the city.

German infantrymen are showered with earth by a nearby shell explosion. In previous wars, battles had been short and sharp, which was less damaging than extended exposure to miserable conditions and the chance of sudden death.

ASSAULT TACTICS

Getting into the enemy positions was a tough task, and not made any easier by the fact that the British force was receiving large numbers of quickly trained conscript soldiers. It was decided to throw in the assault force as a series of waves, with standing orders to maintain a general forward movement in all sectors. This was considered more likely to succeed than trying to control raw troops as they made complex evolutions under fire.

Some units, however, were given extensive training in fire-and-manoeuvre tactics and trained to advance as the French did, in short rushes from one position of cover to another. The enduring image of World War I is of long lines of men walking slowly forward to be machine-gunned, but this tactic was by no means universal. It was most commonly used when poorly trained troops were deployed, as there was a general feeling that they could not be trusted to do anything more complex and if close control broke down the attacking force might simply disintegrate.

French troops rest as behind them supplies move up the Voie Sacrée towards Verdun. This single road was the city's lifeline, bringing enough supplies in to keep the garrison fighting for the long months before the tide finally turned.

However, that was not the purpose of the exercise. What German high command wanted was to make a series of local attacks, methodically encroaching on the city. This would draw in French reserves and force them to fight at a disadvantage or defend positions within reach of the massive artillery concentration. Taking ground was not the objective; destroying the French army was.

The outer defences were taken by 24 February, and soon afterwards Forts Vaux and Douaumont were attacked. These protected high ground overlooking Verdun and the bridges through which French reinforcements had to enter the city.

Abandoning Verdun would be a political blow to the French, but defending it would result in the loss of their reserves, which might enable an offensive elsewhere.

If German forces held these areas, the supply line would be exposed to artillery fire. Fort Douaumont fell quickly, but Vaux held out.

Although the city was more or less taken at this point, the French commanders now made the decision for which their German counterparts had hoped. They began to funnel troops into Verdun along the Voie Sacrée while pioneers worked to widen the road. The shaky defence

Field Marshal Sir Douglas Haig with military and civilian dignitaries. Much criticism has been levelled at Haig's methods but in reality his tactics were largely dictated by the political situation and the military technology available at the time.

began to stiffen, though casualties mounted rapidly.

FRENCH TENACITY

Although German high command got the battle it wanted, the tenacity of the French came as an unpleasant surprise. The ruins of villages changed hands many times and the scope of the operation widened as German forces tried to outflank the defenders. The new attack found limited success but was then counterattacked and driven off – yet again, the movement of reserves had prevented a local victory from becoming decisive.

As the battle for Verdun went on through March and into April, the French brought ever more artillery into the sector and pounded the German positions as hard as their own were being hit. They also began the practice of rotating units through the Verdun sector and then out again to recuperate. Their German counterparts stayed in the line and received reinforcements instead.

By the end of April, it was obvious that the strategy was going awry; Verdun was costing huge numbers of German casualties as well as French, and as an objective it was simply not important enough to merit this. However, the struggle had by now taken on a life of its own; winning at Verdun had become important for its own sake rather than being part of an overall strategy.

The French gradually got the better of the artillery fight, though the outcome was in doubt as late as 11 July. By then, Fort Vaux had fallen and the assault was still grinding forward. The fort's defenders halted a final attack directed at Fort Souville,

In some areas, it was possible to build extensive concrete fortifications, though most fortresses dated from before the war. Layers of earth and concrete protected the personnel within from anything but a direct hit by the largest of shells.

Field Marshal Sir John French commanded British forces at the beginning of the war. His career had been distinguished but he struggled with the realities of the new situation, alternating overconfidence with what amounted to despair.

just 4 km (2 miles) from Verdun itself. This was the last gasp of the Verdun offensive. Afterward, the German army went over to the defensive.

The sector then quietened down until late in the year when a French counteroffensive retook what was left of the lost ground. The area was so thoroughly shelled that the local geography had been rearranged beyond recognition and the soil was poisoned by explosive residue. The Verdun offensive was a workable idea that was allowed to run away with its creators. The original aim of the operation was forgotten somewhere along the line, until it became a brutal slogging match serving no directly useful purpose. Verdun did pull in the French reserves, and did eliminate large numbers of them, but the casualties were not one-sided, as had originally been planned.

Verdun was not a total failure, however, in that it forced the Allies to launch an offensive of their own to try to take the pressure off the French at Verdun. The Allies had already agreed to make large offensives in 1916, though there was some debate as to exactly where the effort was to be made.

THE SOMME

In the end, Douglas Haig, who had recently replaced Sir John French as the British commander-in-chief, decided that the effort should be made on the Somme. The attack was mostly a British effort, but one reason for choosing the Somme as the location was to be able to include a French contingent.

Haig's plan was not very different from the one in use by the Germans at Verdun; a large-scale infantry assault would follow an enormous artillery preparation. However, Haig's intent was to break through the enemy lines and disrupt his logistics chain in the rear, which was a more classical strategy than the deliberate meatgrinder at Verdun.

The Somme had been a quiet sector since the first weeks of the war, and the German army held high ground that overlooked the Allies' positions. They had spent the past two years improving their positions; notably the German troops were

British infantry leave their trench to begin an attack. Going 'over the top' was dangerous. However miserable life in the trenches was, it was preferable to moving around in the bullet-swept wasteland of No-Man's Land in daylight.

provided with deep dugouts that could withstand the heaviest barrage. The attackers' concentration areas could be seen from the heights and in many cases could be brought under direct machine-gun fire.

Shelled and shot at before they had even reached No-Man's Land, the attackers would then have to get through the wire before advancing uphill in the face of well dug-in opposition. There were high hopes that the week of artillery preparation, during which the defenders would be targeted by upwards of a million shells, would cut the wire, shatter positions and enable the attackers to take possession of the enemy positions with ease.

In the event, the wire was not cut. Some commanders stated that it had been smashed when in fact it could be seen to be intact. Nor were the enemy positions shattered, though the defenders were roughed up somewhat. And as the assault kicked

AN OPPORTUNITY LOST

Some of the 36 tanks involved in the attack got stuck (or 'ditched'), some were hit by artillery and some poisoned their crews with carbon monoxide. Most broke down sooner or later. Yet they were able to advance some 3.2km (2 miles) with infantry in support, making their attack one of the most successful operations of the war. However, the British were unprepared to follow up this success, so the victory remained a strictly local one.

The landscape alone was a significant obstruction. Advancing across this sort of shell-torn and muddy terrain was a slow and arduous task, which gave the enemy more time to shoot at the attacking troops.

off on 1 July 1916, German troops emerged from their dugouts and opened fire.

The difficulty of coordinating artillery support was countered by a fire plan that dropped a 'creeping barrage' onto the enemy positions. The target zone was 'moved up' towards the enemy rear at intervals, supposedly to cover the infantry as they advanced. However, the infantry were nowhere near where the planners had hoped. Stalled by thick masses of intact wire in No-Man's Land, the assaulting divisions were savaged by direct fire and artillery called in upon them by observers. So confident of stopping the assault were the defenders that some did not fire on the troops directly in front of them, instead machine-gunning the concentration areas of units waiting to go in as part of subsequent waves. Some battalions took heavy casualties even before they crossed their start line.

> So confident of stopping the assault were the defenders that some did not fire on the troops in front of them, instead machine-gunning the units waiting to go in.

Twelve attacking divisions were stalled in No-Man's Land and shot to pieces without ever getting close to the enemy, but by dogged and sustained effort elements of five others actually managed to reach the enemy trench line and put in an attack. This was contained and repelled, and by the end of the first day the attackers had achieved nothing of significance.

The casualty figures were frightening. Close to 100,000 men had taken part in the assault. Some 20,000 were dead and twice that number had been wounded in just one day of action. It might have been worse but for the fact that, as at Loos, many of the defenders ceased fire as the assault troops broke off. Failure on the first day of the Somme presented the Allied commanders with a difficult choice. Something had to be done to relieve pressure on Verdun, and that meant a major offensive. But building up for an attack took time, and the Allies did not have months to prepare for an offensive somewhere else. There was no option – the attack had to be continued.

Subsequent attacks were costly but began to make some gains. These were small successes – a position gained here, a section of trench cleared there – and by the end of July the Allies had advanced only 5km (3 miles).

The battering went on through August and into September, when a new idea was tried. Armoured fighting vehicles – tanks – made their combat debut in the region around Flers and Courcelette. Mechanically unreliable to start with, the tanks struggled to cope with terrain they were not suited for but nevertheless managed to win a spectacular victory. Enemy troops fled at their approach – the first recorded instance of 'tank terror'.

General Aleksei Brusilov, architect of the 'Brusilov Offensive'. Despite violating several military principles, notably the need for concentration of force, Brusilov's operation was highly successful.

Below: The battle at the Somme achieved what was needed in a strategic sense. It drew German reinforcements away from Verdun and the Eastern Front and helped stabilize the situation.

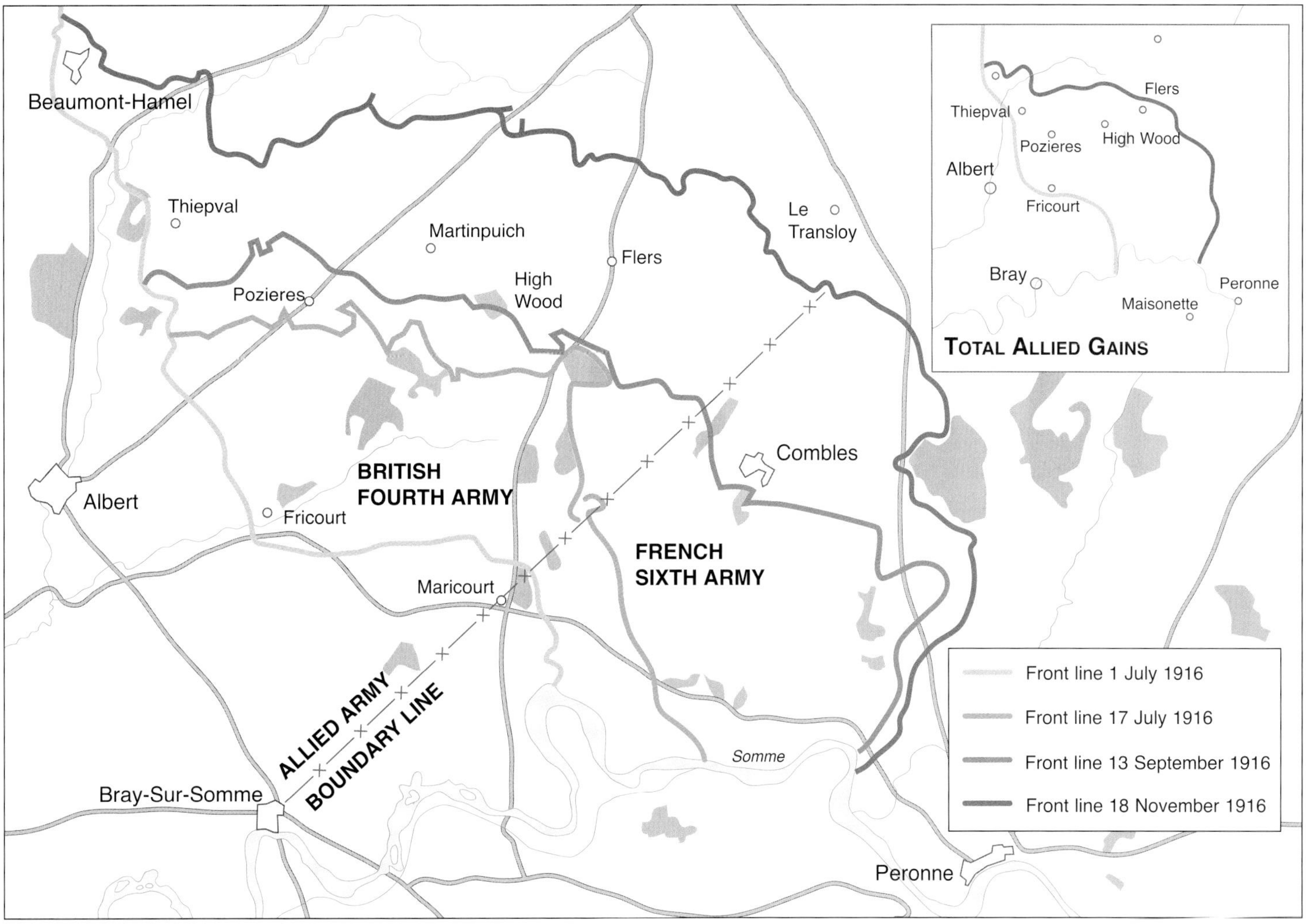

Beaumont-Hamel
Thiepval
Martinpuich
Le Transloy
Flers
Pozieres
High Wood
Combles
Albert
Fricourt
BRITISH FOURTH ARMY
FRENCH SIXTH ARMY
Maricourt
ALLIED ARMY BOUNDARY LINE
Somme
Bray-Sur-Somme
Peronne

TOTAL ALLIED GAINS
Flers
Thiepval
Pozieres
High Wood
Albert
Fricourt
Bray
Maisonette
Peronne

Front line 1 July 1916
Front line 17 July 1916
Front line 13 September 1916
Front line 18 November 1916

The Russian army suffered from supply shortages and a variety of internal command and control problems, most notably a breakdown of confidence between officers and enlisted men.

After this, the Somme offensive struggled on through increasingly bad weather until it was called off in the middle of November. There was no decisive breakthrough, but in some ways the attack had succeeded in its main strategic objectives. It had pulled in German reinforcements that otherwise would have been sent to Verdun, and taken the pressure off the defenders there. It had worn down the German army and, as would become apparent later, caused a general reduction in its quality.

Casualties on each side were about 600,000. In the light of stark numbers, this favoured the Allies, who had more men of military age than the Central Powers. The Allies were better able to replace the casualties and keep fighting, and so in the end the 'meatgrinder' concept invented by the German high command worked against them.

THE LATER WAR IN THE EAST

During the winter of 1915–16, the Russian army made good much of its shortage of ammunition and weaponry and began trying to undertake offensive operations once again. However, although material deficiencies could be set right, there were deep-rooted problems in the Russian army. Men totally unfamiliar with conditions at the front wrote many of the manuals detailing how to conduct the business of war.

The result was that basic and foolish mistakes were being made as late as 1916, such as trenches being dug where they were overlooked by

Cavalry remained useful in the Eastern theatres, where the war remained mobile. Occasionally, cavalry brigades would encounter one another and then engage in an old-style fight with sabres and revolvers.

enemy positions, or along the skyline. There was still an assumption that if enough artillery firepower could be delivered – one heavy shell per square metre of the enemy line was the benchmark – then victory was assured.

This was proven not to be the case in a series of attacks that went awry for all kinds of reasons. Artillery and infantry did not cooperate and the handling of reserves was inept. On one occasion, a night attack was made with the support of searchlights, which were supposed to dazzle the enemy. Instead, they silhouetted the attacking infantry and made them easy targets.

Although lessons were learned, these were not always implemented, and internal problems beset the Russian army right to the end of its involvement in the war. Political intrigues and the use of influence by high-ranking officers who wanted to disadvantage a rival did little to help a situation that was already very difficult.

In early 1916, Russia had made something of a recovery from the battering of the previous months, but had also lost heavily in a gallant but mismanaged series of attacks designed to take the pressure off the Western Front. A renewed campaign in June 1916, which became known as the Brusilov Offensive, was launched to try to restore a situation that was becoming desperate at Verdun and on the Italian frontier.

Brusilov, commanding the southern Russian army group, went about his preparations for attack in a fairly bizarre fashion. He dispersed rather than concentrating reserves and made preparations for attack at many different places. Somehow convincing his superiors that he could

> There were deep-rooted problems in the Russian army. Men unfamiliar with conditions at the front wrote many of the manuals on the business of war.

succeed despite trying to attack with a dispersed force that was merely equal in numbers to the concentrated defenders, Brusilov was given permission to proceed.

The attack achieved total surprise, as Brusilov had hoped, and what began as a reconnaissance in force became a runaway success. The Russian Eighth Army smashed through the Austrian defensive lines and drove between their Fourth and Second armies, taking tens of thousands of prisoners. The success continued on subsequent days as other attacking forces punched through the stunned Austrian lines and rounded up yet more captives.

Brusilov now had a chance to execute a double-envelopment of the remaining Austrian forces; he had already broken both flanks and the way lay open. However, a lack of support from other commanders delayed the operation, which meant that German reinforcements, coming to the assistance of the recovering Austrians, were able to launch a counterattack into the flank of Brusilov's forces.

The attack was stalled for a time, and renewed in July. By then, however, resistance had firmed up and there was no significant gain to be made. In some ways, the campaign did achieve its grand-strategic aims, in that large

Russian infantry in the forest of the Eastern Front. Despite the neglect of their superiors and poor training, Russian troops were able to meet the Germans on equal terms and could usually beat an equivalent number of Austrians.

numbers of German troops were pulled away from the Western front, where they had been mustering to counterattack the British advance on the Somme. However, the campaign had been carried on too long and the losses incurred were simply too great. Over a million men became casualties, and the effect on the fighting power of the Russian army was critical.

One other result of the Brusilov offensive was that Romania was induced to enter the war. She declared against the Central Powers, whom she was most certainly unprepared to fight. The Romanian army was small and badly equipped. It was also poorly led.

The Romanian offensive against Austro-Hungary was halted within two weeks. Although the Germans tended to look down on the Austrian military, it was more than capable of throwing back the Romanians. Soon after, reserves were transferred to the Romanian front and the destruction of the country began. Bulgaria also declared war on the Romanians, seeking among other things to regain territory lost in earlier Balkan wars.

Late in 1916, the German army constructed a chain of fortifications and dugouts named the Hindenberg Line, falling back to occupy them in early 1917. The work was done behind the current front line, which formed a salient.

More than a million men became casualties of the Brusilov Offensive, and the effect on the fighting power of the Russian army was critical.

Although Russian offensives were ongoing, these had returned to the more usual Russian practice of attacking en masse on a narrow front with huge artillery support rather than continuing Brusilov's strategy of using surprise and thrusts at various points on a wider front. Such attacks were halted without undue difficulty and so did nothing to detract from the Romanian campaign.

It may be that there was little alternative. Brusilov's methods required extensive preparation, and there was no time for this, not if the pressure was to be maintained. Russian high command felt that with the Western Allies pushing forwards, Russia should mount an attack at a point where the Germans would be forced to stand and fight, draining their reserves. This would also prevent more troops being sent to Romania.

There was also the fact that the Russian army of the time was made up largely of raw conscripts who could not, high command believed, carry out any more complex evolution than to walk forward in a long thin line towards the enemy. Sent forward as 'waves', they made easy targets for enemy machine-gunners.

Meanwhile, the Austrians were displaying a new resilience and fighting power. This had much to do with the practice of supplying German NCOs and command staffs to the Austrian army, in a bid to stiffen its resolve.

> The Austrians were displaying a new resilience and fighting power. This had much to do with the practice of supplying German NCOs to the Austrian army.

While the Russians made a series of brave but ultimately ineffectual attacks, Romania was overrun. Russia sent what troops could be spared, but rail links between the two countries were so bad that only a fairly small force of some 50,000 men could reach

Execution by firing squad. The Russian army inevitably became involved in the political troubles besetting the nation as well as its own internal problems. Those accused of being rebels or traitors were given short shrift.

The battle for Messines Ridge was treated as a siege on a grand scale rather than a field battle. After months of preparation, the explosion under the German lines stunned those defenders it did not kill, and wrecked the defensive positions.

their new allies in time. Joint operations did not start well, with Romanian troops mistaking the Russians for advancing Bulgarians and trying to surrender to them.

Continued Russian attacks elsewhere did not distract the Central Powers from their advance through Romania. The Romanian army tried to undertake offensive operations but these broke down rapidly for lack of planning. The defensive forces in Transylvania were deployed as isolated units without any hope of mutual support or even much cooperation and were defeated in detail.

Elsewhere, the defence was a fiasco, with Romanian units falling back without informing their Russian allies. The result was a loss of what little confidence existed and the general collapse of the front. It was by now apparent that Romanian intervention, rather than being an asset to the Allied cause, was a liability. The occupation of Romania would

THE MUTINY OF 1917

Despite the successes gained by their British allies, morale collapsed in the French army. The men had been promised a great victory if they made a sufficiently heroic effort, and they had given their best. All they got for it was another massive casualty return and a continuation of their squalid trench existence.

Thus began what has been described as a mutiny in the French army but which in many ways resembled industrial action rather than outright mutiny. The troops of no fewer than 54 divisions made it known that they were willing to defend their positions but not to launch large-scale attacks. Several demands were made, including improvements in the troops' food and living conditions, increased leave allowances and, of course, an end to the war.

British infantry amid the wrecked Western Front landscape of the later war. The trenches are no longer tidy with supports for the walls, and are quite shallow, suggesting that they may be temporary or that deeper digging is not practical.

give the Central Powers a new route into Russia and access to vast amounts of supplies. This had to be prevented, and a new Russian force was assembled to make the attempt.

Logistics difficulties prevented the Russians from making much impact, though they did manage to halt Bulgarian advances along the Black Sea coast. It seemed for a time that Romania still had a fighting chance, especially when French advisors arrived and put together what seemed like a workable plan.

A counteroffensive was launched in December with every unit that could be scraped together. It was, predictably, a disaster. Entirely outclassed, the Romanians were quickly put to flight. This effectively destroyed the last reserves available to Romania. Russian troops delayed the enemy advance as best they could and the encroaching winter brought the campaign to an end. The Central Powers benefited from Romania's entry into the war. For relatively light losses, they shattered the country's unprepared army and captured large quantities of useful materials. Without this booty, Germany might have had to agree to an armistice in 1917 rather than a year later.

As 1917 dawned, the internal troubles in Russia were intensifying, but her armies were still able to prosecute the war. The prospects looked good at times – American intervention was expected and the Allies were apparently gaining the upper hand in terms of manpower and matériel.

However, after the outbreak of revolution in March, Russian attention was mostly directed inwards. Those offensives that took place were minor, and so were the Central Powers' operations. The Eastern Front gradually quietened down until the November coup in Russia and subsequent peace treaty took Russia entirely out of the war.

BREAKING THE GREAT FORTRESS

At the beginning of 1917, it may well have seemed that nothing had changed since late 1914, but this was not so. A great deal had been learnt about modern industrial warfare, and moves were afoot to create new technologies and doctrines that would finally break through the trench lines and allow a decisive victory to be won.

However, war-weariness was taking its toll and the abysmal conditions on the front line, coupled with massive casualties among combat troops, were draining the morale of the troops to a dangerous degree. Once again, the Allies had met near the end of the previous year. Then they planned a massive joint campaign for 1917, just as they had for 1916. Although the Italians and Russians would apply pressure, it was agreed that Britain and France were to throw the knockout punch. The British would assault Vimy Ridge and Arras on the northern edge of the Somme salient, while the French would launch an attack on the Aisne.

The Eastern Front gradually quietened down until the November coup in Russia and subsequent peace treaty took Russia entirely out of the war.

Strategically the plan had some merit, but there were problems, not the least of which was the fact that the French sector faced the toughest defences in the Western Front and would have to be launched from concentration areas overlooked by enemy positions. In the event, the salient was much reduced before the attack began, as the German army pulled back into a new set of positions named the Hindenburg Line. This straightened their line and reduced its vulnerability as well as the number of men needed to hold it. The intended targets lay outside the sector covered by this new line, but if the intent was to 'bite off' the salient and encircle the forces within, this was now less likely to be possible.

New defensive tactics were emerging on the German side. Front-line trenches were lightly held, with the main force kept back out of reach of enemy artillery. This reserve was to advance and repel the assault once the enemy artillery support had become disorganized – as it inevitably did.

The new doctrine was a success on the French sector. Their artillery support, in the form of a creeping barrage, ran ahead of the advancing infantry and so was of little assistance. The first trench line was penetrated, but then the attackers ran into a maze of machine-gun-armed strong points,

Tank Mk V

Type: tank

Crew: 8

Powerplant: one 112kW (150hp) Ricardo petrol engine

Maximum speed: 7.4km/h (4.6mph)

Range: 72km (45 miles)

Weight: 29,600kg (65,120lb)

Armour: 6–14mm (0.24–0.55in)

Armament: two 6-pounder guns, four Hotchkiss machine guns

Dimensions: length 8.05m (26ft 5in)
width over sponsons 4.11m (13ft 6in)
height 2.64m (8ft 8in)

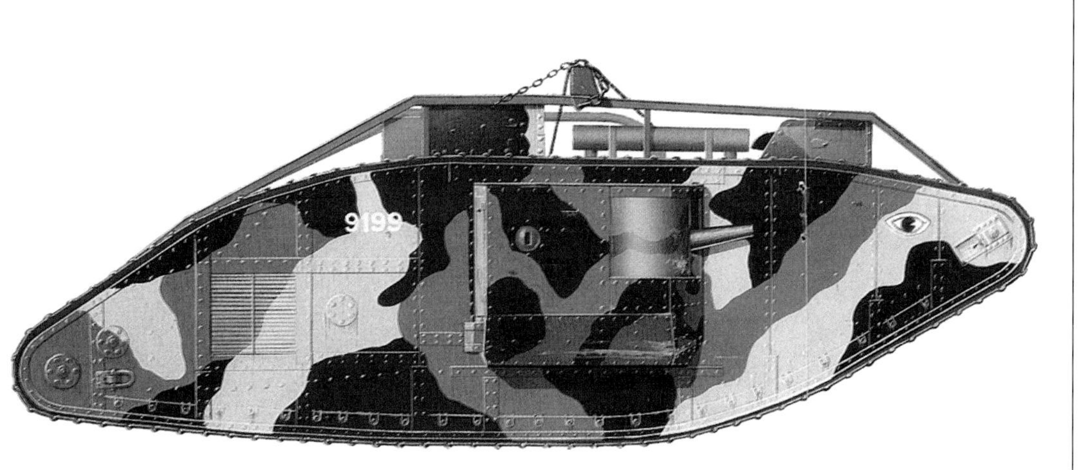

which brought them to a halt with heavy casualties. The main body of troops, kept out of harm's way during the barrage, then counterattacked the exhausted French and pushed them back. However, things did not work out quite according to plan on the British sector. The usual massive bombardment prepared the way for the assault. This drove the defenders under cover and, unusually, smashed up the wire badly enough that the British could advance quickly. Better than usual fire planning resulted in the defenders still being pinned in their dugouts when the assault infantry arrived. Those who did not flee in time or surrender promptly were eliminated with grenades thrown down the steps.

A TURN OF EVENTS

The 'Mutiny of 1917' was an alarming turn of events. Not only was there a wave of civil unrest sweeping across Europe but Russia was beginning to collapse into Revolution. There were fears that a similar situation might arise elsewhere, and rapid action was needed. A mix of conciliation and harsh measures put down the mutiny. Civilian anti-war agitators and some of the military ringleaders were arrested; some were executed. Meanwhile, leave entitlement was increased and other improvements were made wherever possible. Offensive operations were suspended for a time.

It may be that the single most important factor in restoring the morale of the French army was that their commanders and the government were keen to listen to the grievances and to do what they

In low-lying areas, excavations rapidly filled up with water, creating a problem for troops trying to fortify themselves into a position. The only solution was to build upwards, creating earth ramparts rather than digging down.

A 'ditched' British tank. There were limits to what these vehicles could cope with, especially in wet soil. Becoming stuck in No-Man's Land was extremely dangerous, as the enemy could drop artillery fire onto the ditched vehicle.

could about them. Soon the French army was back on the offensive, albeit on a limited scale. The French army did not make any major attacks from June 1917 to July 1918. Small operations eliminated dangerous enemy encroachments, but overall the French army played little more than a holding role for the next year.

It thus fell to the British to carry on the struggle. Tanks offered some hope of achieving a decisive breakthrough but few were available and there was considerable debate about how they were to be used. In the meantime, offensive operations had to be undertaken somewhere.

British high command had for a long time wanted to attack in Flanders, in the region around Ypres. In order to do this, it was decided that flank security had to be established, which meant capturing the high ground of Messines Ridge. Bitter experience had shown that trying to undertake an offensive on ground overlooked by the enemy was extremely costly. Messines had to be taken for Ypres to stand a chance of success.

> Bitter experience had shown that trying to undertake an offensive on ground overlooked by the enemy was extremely costly, but Messines Ridge had to be taken.

However, an assault on a well defended position located on high ground was not something to be taken lightly. The solution was to resort to mining, a tactic used for centuries in siege warfare. In previous centuries, it was not uncommon for the attackers to build a tunnel, or 'mine', under the wall of an enemy castle or other stronghold, and then collapse it to weaken the structure's foundations. Undermining a wall in this manner could bring down a section of wall. With the advent of explosives, mining gained a new dimension. If a tunnel could be driven into enemy positions and packed with explosives, they could be destroyed from a safe distance. British forces began digging 20 mines towards the German positions on Messines Ridge, from a distance of 8000m (5 miles) or so away. Some of the mines were detected and an attempt at countermining was made, but only one was successfully intercepted. The remaining 19 were detonated on 7 June. About 600 tons of explosives were used, blasting a huge gap in the trench lines and stunning the surviving defenders.

MASSED TANKS AT CAMBRAI

The attack at Cambrai was the first offensive to use tanks en masse. Previously they had been sent forward in small numbers, and usually in terrain that was not well suited to their use. The results were uninspiring, and it had taken the pro-tank faction among the British commanders considerable time and effort to obtain agreement for the operation.

Nevertheless, almost 400 tanks were assembled for the attack. They were great lumbering monsters, difficult for the crew to operate and prone to break down. They were also tremendously hot inside and tended to slowly suffocate their crews with carbon monoxide poisoning. However, despite these drawbacks they could get across trenches and were more or less proof against enemy small arms and machine-gun fire.

Had the defenders followed the new doctrine of using a light screen in the forward positions and larger forces in reserve, the outcome might have been different. However, local commanders were firmly wedded to the old system of creating a solid, heavily defended front and fighting for every inch of it. Thus large numbers of troops were needlessly exposed to the mine explosion and the bombardment that followed.

Pounded by artillery at the same time as the mines were blown under them, the German forces on Messines Ridge put up little resistance at first, but gradually recovered their wits and began to fight back. However, the assault troops were well trained and supported by an artillery barrage that, for once, was well timed to support the attack.

Although they faced a tough fight later in the attack, the Allied troops assaulting the ridge were able to achieve their objectives, and were quickly supported by infantry reinforcements and a few tanks. Defences were thrown up and proved sufficient to beat off the inevitable counterattack. Indeed, after repulsing the attack, the British forces (which included large numbers of Irish and New Zealander troops) were able to advance a little more.

Messines Ridge was never intended to create a decisive breakthrough, so the fact that the German army was able to create new positions and resume a solid front was of no consequence. The flank had been cleared; the way was open for the main assault.

About 600 tons of explosives were used in the British mines, blasting a huge gap in the trench lines and, perhaps more importantly, stunning the surviving defenders.

Now, at the very end of July 1917, began what became known as the Third Battle of Ypres. One of the critical problems the offensive faced was that the region was poorly drained and prone to flooding. The war had destroyed most of the artificial drainage system, and observers, notably from the Tank Corps, now warned that extensive bombardment would wreck the rest and turn the whole area into a swamp.

The propensity for flooding caused problems for the defenders too. The usual trench system was not a viable option in Flanders, where any hole would quickly fill with water. The Germans solved this problem by creating a defensive system of pillboxes and strong points whose

The light cruiser *Konigsberg* made a raiding cruise before being trapped in the delta of the Rufiji River in East Africa. Subsequent attempts to eliminate her involved small vessels, aircraft and ground forces acting in concert.

fire interlocked. Troops advancing through the wet ground would be vulnerable to the fire of these machine gun-equipped strong points and any gains they made could be reversed by the intervention of fresh troops held back in reserve.

German high command was well aware of the preparations for an assault going on near Ypres, and prepared accordingly. Mustard gas was used for the first time, fired in shells into likely concentration areas and to harass artillery units. Realizing that the enemy was bound to be moving reinforcements into the area, Haig ordered the start date for the offensive to be advanced, and the preparatory bombardment began on 22 July. Ten days later, the attack opened. Some gains were made despite the conditions, which were made worse by heavy rain, but these could not be followed up. The ground soon became impassable to tanks and then infantry, holding up the next phase of the attack until 16 August. This made even smaller gains than the first attack, and at heavy cost.

The attack was again held up by bad weather and preparations until 20 September. Supported by a massive weight of artillery, a new attack was made on a slightly shifted front. This was surprisingly successful, partly due to the heavy artillery support available and partly because of the tactics used. Rather than going all-out for a decisive breakthrough, the assault troops made a series of short attacks, each aimed at securing a position and consolidating it. This approach was more often used in sieges than field battles and was entirely appropriate to the situation.

Another important asset was the successful use of aircraft to spot for artillery and to report on enemy concentrations. Several counterattacks were disrupted by artillery fire in this way, while the Allied advance worried German commanders enough that

CAMBRAI: ALMOST A STRATEGIC SUCCESS

Cambrai was an opportunity for a decisive victory at last, and indeed the German high command thought one had occurred. Their logistics chain was threatened and there was a huge hole in the line. Reinforcements could not be deployed in time to seal the breach; things were desperate and orders were drafted for an emergency retreat. However, the British advance came to a halt and the moment passed.

By the end of the first day at Cambrai, many tanks were out of action. Most were broken down or ditched rather than the victims of the enemy. The crews of surviving tanks were exhausted and the infantry were not in much better shape. Subsequent days saw only relatively small gains and the enemy strength gradually increased until the situation was stabilized.

Paul von Lettow-Vorbeck led a successful guerrilla campaign against the British in East Africa. Though badly outnumbered, his force of European and African riflemen avoided defeat and hit at their enemies throughout the war.

The battlecruiser *Goeben,* with the light cruiser *Breslau*, evaded pursuit and reached Constantinople. This helped convince Turkey to join the war on the side of the Central Powers, bringing large reserves of manpower into the war.

they began packing men into the front lines. This strengthened the front, but at the price of increased casualties from bombardment, since artillery could get at them more easily.

British commanders and their staffs became convinced that the Germans were now tottering on the brink of defeat and that there were no reinforcements to be had. In fact, they had already begun to arrive, but no account was taken of this as the British tried to exploit the imaginary weakness of their opponents. More attacks were made in October, despite the never-ending rain. These were predictably repulsed with heavy casualties, though some tiny gains were made here and there. The Third Battle of Ypres finally came to a close with the occupation of what was left of

British commanders and their staffs became convinced that the Germans were tottering on the brink of defeat and that there were no reinforcements to be had.

'Johnny Turk', as the Turkish infantryman became known to the Allies, was a tough and tenacious but honourable fighter. Allied troops involved in the Gallipoli campaign acquired a respect for their opponents.

the village of Passchendaele. The attack had achieved virtually nothing at the price of using up most of the British reserves. Their lack was felt just weeks later when the British army won a victory near Cambrai but could not follow it up.

TANK ATTACK

There were two types of tank available. 'Males' were armed with 6-pounder guns while 'females' had machine guns for anti-personnel work. The tanks were deployed in three-tank groups, with a male and two females to each. Previously, tanks had been deployed in support of infantry, and considered as infantry weapons. They thus went forward under the normal conditions of an infantry attack – i.e. after a lengthy bombardment. For the Cambrai attack, it was decided to treat tanks as a weapon in their own right, and to create conditions suitable for their employment. The Cambrai attack therefore dispensed with the usual massive bombardment, since the mud and shell holes thus created would impair the tanks' advance. This precaution had the additional advantage of not alerting the enemy that an attack was imminent. Preparations undertaken in secret meant that when the tanks began their advance on 20 November 1917, surprise was achieved.

Being attacked by surprise was bad enough; being attacked by large numbers of terrifying monsters that apparently could not be stopped or even harmed by the weapons at hand was more than the defenders could bear. Many defenders fled before the tanks got into range, and those who stood and fought were unable to do much to the armoured vehicles.

The tanks carried fascines – bundles of sticks – to drop into enemy trenches and facilitate a crossing, and

> The battle ended with the occupation of the remains of the village of Passchendaele. It had achieved virtually nothing and had used up most of the British reserves.

some carried hooks to drag away enemy wire. Infantry followed in close support except in one sector, where the local commander had his own ideas. There, the tanks went on ahead and outran the infantry, who were then stopped by machine guns bypassed by the armour.

Elsewhere, however, the attack was an astonishing success, punching through the enemy's lines and gaining sight of the open country beyond. However, the problem was that the attack was a little too astonishing. Adequate preparations had not been made to follow up a breakthrough since nobody could really believe that one would be made. In any case, there were few reserves available as a result

The landings at Gallipoli did not go well for the Allies, and the initial gains made were not great. As a result, the attackers were pinned against the sea with no depth to their positions.

WITHDRAWAL FROM GALLIPOLI

The withdrawal from Gallipoli was a masterpiece. Thinning their lines while maintaining the illusion of normal activity, the defenders were able to re-embark and slip away before the Turks realized what was happening. The whole campaign had been an ill-conceived gamble but at least the final act went smoothly.

In order to avoid a repeat of the Turkish advance against the Suez Canal, the British army deployed a large force in Egypt and constructed defences across the only practicable axis of attack; the Sinai Peninsula. These defences defeated a second thrust, launched in August 1916, and the decision was taken to launch an offensive into Palestine.

of the Third Battle of Ypres. However, there were large numbers of cavalry deployed to support the attack, and here was a perfect opportunity for them to get through the enemy lines and wreak the sort of havoc they traditionally caused in an enemy's rear. But their headquarters was too far back, and communications too poor, for the horsemen to advance in time and so the opportunity was lost.

The counterstroke came on 30 November, and in its own way was as innovative as the British attack. Instead of a lengthy preparation, the German artillery delivered a short but intense bombardment, which included gas and smoke shells, and their infantry used infiltration tactics rather than trying to storm the entire line. Units were pushed through weak points in the British lines, bypassing centres of resistance instead of trying to reduce them.

This attack, too, achieved surprise despite some warning signs that it was being prepared, and for a time the situation was very serious. The British tanks were out of the line by this point, but a mobile counterattack by infantry helped restore the situation while all the available tanks were rushed back up to the line to help.

The German counterattack was an unpleasant setback to the British, and at the time attracted more attention than the original strike. However, the fact remained that armoured vehicles had achieved great things when used correctly. For the first time in the war, Allied troops had seen the open country on the far side of the enemy lines.

THE WAR IN OTHER THEATRES

World War I was mainly a European conflict, though the fighting did spread to the German colonies. Most German overseas territory lay in Africa but there were Pacific holdings too.

In Palestine and the Middle East, camel-mounted troops made long-range raids, sometimes supported by aircraft and armoured cars. In this region, small forces operated over long distances, often improvising their supply train.

Late-war German infantry equipped with flamethrowers, light machine guns and rifles. These are most likely stormtroopers, elite infantry trained to lead an assault using the new infiltration tactics rather than smashing head-on into the strongest enemy positions.

The latter were quickly taken by Japan, New Zealand and Australia.

Only at Tsingtao, on the Chinese coast, was there any serious fighting outside Africa. There, a joint British and Japanese force, enormously outnumbering the defenders and equipped with 28cm (11in) howitzers, bombarded the position and launched an assault. The defenders surrendered after a stubborn but hopeless fight.

There was some hope in Germany that the African colonies might not be involved in the conflict, especially in the light of a prewar agreement dividing up the continent among the European powers. However, the Allies thought it necessary to oust Germany from her colonial empire and thus landed troops.

The distances involved, along with difficult terrain, enabled the garrisons of German territories in Cameroon and South-West Africa to avoid defeat for many months, though they had no hope of achieving anything beyond tying down Allied troops. By mid 1916, the only remaining German territory in Africa was what is today Tanzania. This area, 'German East Africa', had been left largely alone up to this point.

Among other factors, one reason for the outbreak of hostilities in the region was the arrival of the German light cruiser *Königsberg*. She had been commerce raiding and had attracted the attention of powerful British forces, which chased her into the River Rulfiji. There, she hid for many months, forcing the British to exert a great deal of effort to get at her before she was finally sunk. Her crew then joined the German forces fighting on land in the region.

Most German overseas territory lay in Africa, but there were Pacific holdings too. The latter were quickly taken by Japan, New Zealand and Australia.

The latter were commanded by Colonel von Lettow-Vorbeck and were mostly made up of Askaris, who were troops raised from among the local population. Although he had only a few hundred men under his command, von Lettow-Vorbeck defeated an attempt to land British and Indian troops from India, though

T.E. Lawrence 'Of Arabia' acted as liaison between the British government and the Arab tribes, inciting an Arab revolt against their Turkish overlords. This distracted Turkish troops from operations against the British in the region.

they did get ashore elsewhere. He conducted a brilliant guerrilla campaign against enormously more powerful forces and was still fighting when Germany surrendered at the end of the war.

Turkey also played a relatively minor part in the war. Friendly with Germany and with a long history of hostility towards Russia, she entered into active hostilities in late 1914. The opening move was an advance into the Caucasus, accompanied by a bombardment of Russian Black Sea ports by the battlecruiser *Goeben* and the light cruiser *Breslau*, both on loan to Turkey from Germany.

Launched in winter at the end of a shaky supply line, the Caucasus campaign was a disaster that started with casualties from frostbite and ended in total defeat at the hands of a Russian army.

Turkey's entry into the war forced the British to consolidate their holdings in the region and created a complicated situation in the Middle East. Egypt had long been a Turkish possession but had been administered by the British for 30 years. Britain declared Egypt a British protectorate and closed the Suez Canal to enemy shipping. This prompted the Turks to launch an offensive against the canal region. The Turkish force was spotted crossing the Sinai Desert by a French reconnaissance aircraft and driven off. However, the continued threat to the canal tied down British troops that could have been used elsewhere. Turkish involvement also prompted one of the great follies of the war – the attempt to force passage of the Dardanelles and reach the Russian Black Sea ports.

THE NAVAL WAR

The naval campaign started out well enough, with British and French capital ships engaging and destroying the forts commanding the narrow passage as they reached them.

Turkey's entry into the war forced the British to consolidate their holdings in the region and created a complicated situation in the Middle East.

However, losses due to mines and shellfire became too great and the naval operation was called off. It was decided instead to flank the forts on land.

On 25 April 1915, a joint force of troops from France and the British Empire landed at various points under cover of naval bombardment. In many areas, the landings were entirely unopposed, but on some of the beaches there was determined resistance, though by relatively small numbers of enemy troops. Although they succeeded in getting ashore, the Allied troops were boxed into a small area overlooked by enemy positions and received several counterattacks as Turkish reinforcements came up. After making some small gains, the Allied troops could gain no more headway and remained in place, clinging to their positions with their backs to the sea, for several months.

An attempt to flank the Turkish positions with new landings was met with vigorous counterattacks, and at the end of the year the decision was made to withdraw. The campaign was never going to succeed and was simply tying up men needed elsewhere. There had been hopes that the operation might deter Bulgaria from entering the war, persuade Greece to throw in her lot with the Allies or take some pressure off Serbia. Having failed in all these things, it was time to stop wasting lives on the enterprise.

In early 1917, the British were repulsed at Gaza, twice, by Turkish troops. As had already been demonstrated at Gallipoli, 'Johnny Turk' was a tough but honourable opponent, and German troops were sent to assist.

PALESTINE

Palestine was a wholly different environment to the Western Front. Operations in the Middle East were conducted over large distances and in a fluid environment where aircraft and armoured cars were employed alongside horsed cavalry and camel-mounted troops. There were long-range strikes and penetrations into enemy territory and even charges by sabre-armed cavalry.

The British made alliances with local tribesmen, whose forces were able to badly disrupt Turkish operations and who took part in the decisive victory at Megiddo in 1918 as well as the capture of Damascus and Aleppo. It was in conjunction with these irregular but highly effective tribal forces that T.E. Lawrence (1888–1935) became a national hero, earning the sobriquet 'Lawrence Of Arabia'.

Defeat in Palestine was a major factor in Turkey's request for an armistice in October 1918. Perhaps equally important was the fact that German defeat was now inevitable. Turkey would get better terms if she

Erwin Rommel made his name in World War I. His aggressive and effective leadership at the junior-officer level brought him recognition and rapid promotion. He was thus an obvious choice for the command of armoured troops.

RENAULT FT 17

Type: tank

Crew: 2

Powerplant: one 35hp (926kW) Renault four-cylinder petrol engine

Maximum speed: (road) 7.7km/h (4.8mph)

Range: (road) 35.4km (22 miles)

Weight: approx 30,480kg (30 tons)

Armour: 16mm (0.63in)

Armament: one 37mm (1.46in) gun or one machine gun

Dimensions:		
	length	5m (16ft 5in)
	width	1.71m (5ft 73in)
	height	2.1m (7ft)

THE U-BOAT CAMPAIGN BACKFIRES

The U-boat campaign was effective and there was a real risk that Britain might be starved into surrender. However, when American ships were attacked the United States had no choice but to declare war in response. The mood was already in favour of war, ever since Germany tried to recruit Mexico to its side with the promise of Texas and New Mexico.

sought peace before the final defeat of her major partner in the war.

Meanwhile, after being repulsed from Serbia in the early months of the war, the Austrians had failed to make much headway against their supposedly backward and militarily weak opponents. A period of what amounted to standoff went on until September 1915, when Bulgaria agreed to join the Central Powers in destroying Serbia. Greece decided to remain neutral but the Allies landed large forces at Salonika (many of these troops came from Gallipoli) and began moving into Serbia. Serbia was now under heavy attack from multiple sides. Belgrade fell and what remained of the Serbian army was forced into retreat, fighting where it could and then pulling back to avoid being overwhelmed. The survivors managed to cross the mountains into Albania and were evacuated to Corfu while Serbia was overrun. Those Allied troops that had managed to reach Serbia arrived too late to help and were forced to pull back to Greece.

Late in 1917, with Russia out of the war, the Central Powers achieved a spectacular victory over Italy. Italian troops had been grinding slowly forwards against the Austrians, often at great cost, in the difficult terrain of the Alps. However, the Italian army was at the end of its collective tether. Subject to harsh discipline and suffering massive casualties for no gain, its troops were demoralized and weary.

The Austrians facing them felt the same, and were not confident of

After years of clawing their way forward through difficult, mountainous terrain, Italian forces met with a serious defeat at Caporetto and were driven rapidly back before they were finally able to establish a new defensive line.

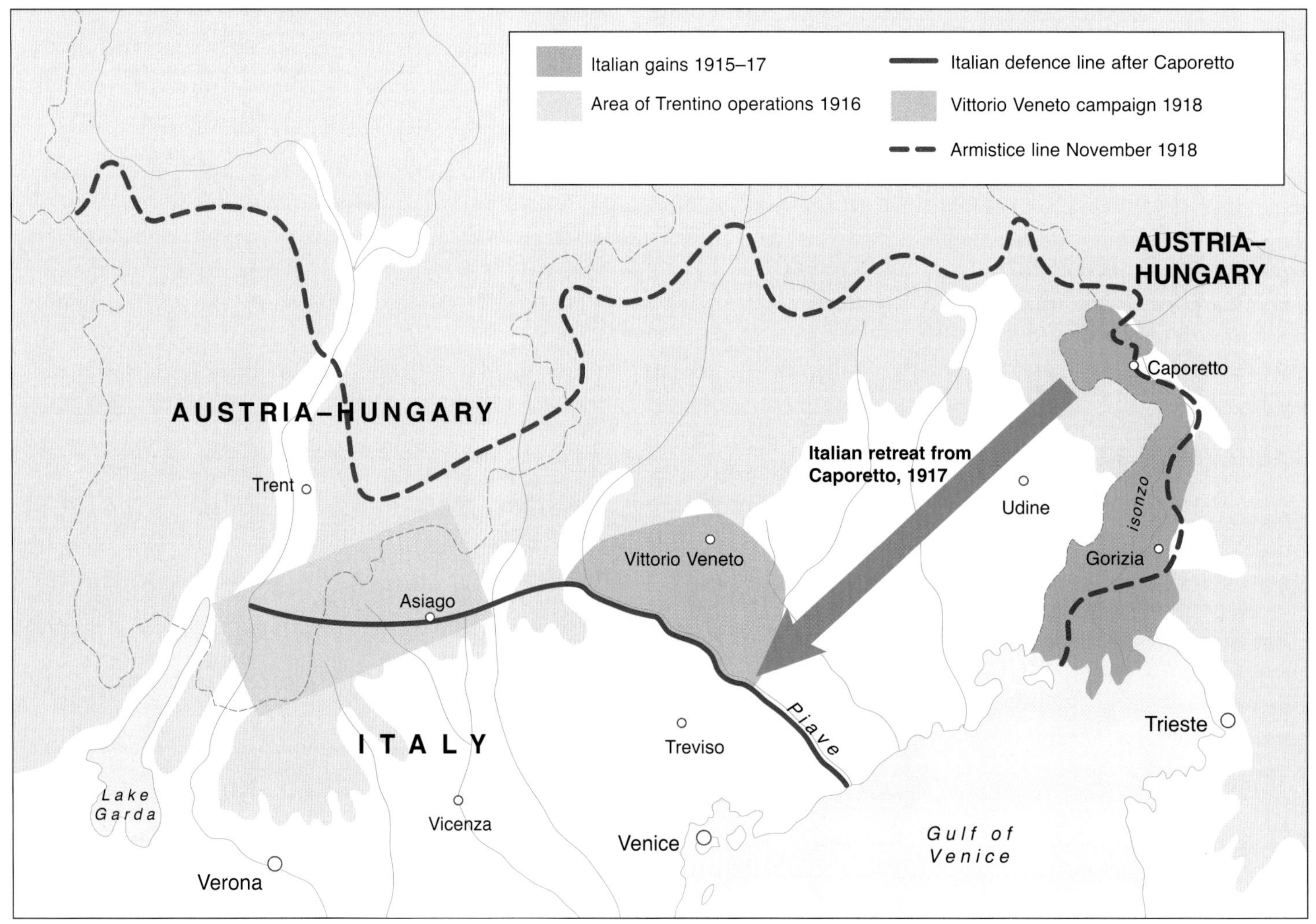

A7V STURMPANZERWAGEN

Type: tank

Crew: up to 18

Powerplant: two Daimler-Benz, 4-cylinder petrol engines, each delivering 74.5kW (100hp)

Maximum speed: (road) 12.8km/h (8mph)

Range: (road) 40.2km (25 miles)

Weight: approx 30,480kg (30 tons)

Armour: Maximum, 30mm (1.18in)

Armament: one 57mm (2.24in) gun; six or seven 7.92mm (0.312in) MGs

Dimensions: length 8m (26ft 3in)
width 3.05m (10ft)
height 3.3m (10ft 10in)

winning their next battle with the apparently indefatigable Italians. Assistance from German troops was requested, and among those sent were elite alpine troops and a young lieutenant by the name of Erwin Rommel. A joint Austro-German force was formed and sent into action near Caporetto. In this action, Rommel displayed the sort of reckless dash and aggression that would become his trademark in his later career as a Panzer commander. Leading his small force of about 200 men from peak to peak, he was able to overwhelm several positions, taking most of them by surprise.

Rommel was not the only one operating in this fashion. Rapid advance and extreme aggression allowed the alpine troops, who were something of an elite, to eliminate those positions they could not bypass and to get into the Italian rear. There, they caused confusion and disrupted the response to the main offensive to such a degree that a sector of the front collapsed.

As the Italian army began to retreat, it was pursued aggressively. A Prussian commander of an earlier age had remarked that in pursuit brigades are not necessary; battalions will do. Here, forces as small as a company were able to chase brigades and divisions down the river valleys.

The retreat went on for almost a fortnight before the Italian army was able to collect itself and establish new positions. Attempts to restore morale by executing large numbers of soldiers for various infractions predictably failed, so a more conciliatory approach was taken. Even so, the Italian army was unable to contribute much for the remainder of the war.

THE RETURN OF MANOEUVRE

At the beginning of 1918, things were changing. The British and French were deploying increasing numbers of tanks, and although these were primitive by modern standards they were able to do their job of breaking into the enemy trench system and destroying strong points. Germany was working in tanks of her own and developing advanced infantry tactics to achieve the same results.

With Italy more or less out of the picture and Serbia overrun, Russia in the throes of the Revolution and also out of the war, things were not as bad as they might have been for the Central Powers. The survival of Austro-Hungary had been in doubt at times. It was now assured, and the supplies captured from Romania helped keep troops few and industry going.

However, the British sea blockade of Germany was causing severe shortages. The other side of that coin was the use of unrestricted submarine warfare by the Germans. This had been tried in 1915 and found to be far more effective than the practice of following traditional commerce-raiding procedures and warning targets before they were attacked. In 1917, the U-boats returned to a policy of unrestricted warfare despite American warnings that this could lead to war.

> Although German manpower was an issue, the collapse of Russia partially solved that problem, freeing 50 divisions to be transferred westwards.

The United States had only a small national army, backed up by the National Guard forces of the member states. What troops could be mustered – one army division and two brigades of marines – were sent to France as quickly as possible. The vast resources of US industry were brought to bear, but an army capable of intervening in Europe took time to create.

Many German commanders were sure that the US could not get significant forces past the submarine blockade. However, the arrival of fresh troops from a nation not already war-weary, was a ticking clock that drove the search for a means to end the war quickly and on favourable terms.

Although manpower was an issue, the collapse of Russia partially solved that problem, freeing 50 divisions to be transferred westwards. The problem was how to use them. Work was underway to create a tank force but the German model, the A7V, was a clumsy monster of even lower reliability than the British Mk 1 had been, and a bigger target to boot. They were slow to build and there was simply no way to get enough of them ready for offensive operations before American manpower tipped the balance irrevocably. A few captured British tanks were available, but not enough of them.

INFILTRATION TACTICS

So in the end it came down to the infantry once again. However, they were to use 'infiltration' tactics that had shown promise previously. Instead of attacking the strongest points of an enemy position and seeking a wide breakthrough, the infantry would move forwards in small groups, making short rushes between positions of cover, and bypass centres of resistance. By breaking deep into a position, they would – hopefully – cause it to crumble and collapse rather than trying to batter the defences to pieces head-on.

To assist in their task, these 'stormtroopers' were issued a range of weapons, including flamethrowers, submachine guns and lightweight machine guns. They were supported by a vast weight of artillery, which were to make a 'hurricane' bombardment lasting just a few hours. The idea was to saturate the defences with a combination of explosive and gas shells, then go in while the defenders were stunned. The short bombardment would not give time for large reserves to be brought up into the rear to contain the attack.

Late in 1917, German high command decided on how best to use these new forces in the hope of finally achieving victory. Some wanted to smash France and put her out of the

A LAST GERMAN EFFORT

Operation Michael was called off on 5 April, but this was not the end of the German offensive effort. Switching axis northwards, a new attack was opened near Ypres, which was accompanied by an effective bombardment. The British came under very heavy pressure but Foch, now in overall command, refused to send reinforcements. He was correct; the offensive was fought to a stop by the end of April. German tanks were involved in this attack but proved ineffective in the face of Allied machines.

German infantry rush forward during Operation Michael in 1918. New tactics allowed the German forces to achieve a significant breakthrough before exhaustion and stiffening resistance finally dragged the operation to a halt.

war, but in the end it was decided to make the effort against the British. One reason for this was that Britain was seen as the cornerstone of the alliance against the Central Powers. Another was that British dispositions were vulnerable to infiltration attacks.

There had been a gradual move towards a more elastic defence over the course of the war, with forward positions held relatively lightly and reserves kept back to counterattack. However, the British were still using the 'hard crust' strategy of trying to hold the line strongly at all points. This resulted in smaller numbers of reserves close to the battle area and consequently a reduced capability to respond to a successful attack.

OPERATION MICHAEL

The campaign, named Operation Michael, opened on 10 March 1918, with diversionary operations against Verdun, Rheims and the Champagne region. Since a bombardment always preceded an attack, artillery could be used as a diversionary measure; heavy shelling would attract the enemy's attention to the region.

The attack began on 21 March with a five-hour bombardment. This was then switched into a creeping barrage, intended to cover the advance of some 38 divisions and another 28 in support. Opposite them the British, already spread fairly thin, were thrown into chaos by the artillery attack, their communications severely disrupted.

'Stormtrooper' tactics worked well, with many pockets of resistance cleared out from the rear after being bypassed. Here and there, the defenders stood their ground and fought, including artillery crews, but there was no coherence to the defence, and segments of the front simply collapsed.

Having punched a hole, German forces began to fan out north and south, trying to push the Allies apart. The British were most concerned about the Channel ports and their supply line to England while the French needed to protect Paris. These aims guided the deployment of reserves and prevented a well coordinated counterblow. In some areas, British and French troops put up a good, if disorganized, fight but in others the advancing German units were able to run somewhat wild. In fact, they outran their supplies and

HOTCHKISS Mk I

Type: Machine gun
Calibre: 8mm (0.3in)
Weight in action: 11.7kg (25.8lb)
Gun length: 1190mm (46.8in)
Muzzle velocity: 740m/sec (2428ft/sec)
Maximum range: 3800m (4156yds)
Cyclical rate: 500rpm
Feed: 30-round metallic strip

were forced to forage. Units also became completely exhausted and were unable to continue the advance, and in some cases discipline broke down as troops found stocks of liquor and food in the towns they overran.

It was now that the first American troops entered combat, as part of a cobbled-together response that fought the advance on Amiens to a standstill. The achievement was particularly significant in that it was rear-echelon troops, including supply and engineering detachments, who did most of the fighting.

The runaway advance eventually ran out of steam in the face of piecemeal but stiffening resistance. Operation Michael had penetrated deeply into the Allied rear and caused a great deal of damage, though at a high cost in casualties. The German army was exhausted and desperately short of manpower after the great effort it had made. Even so, a number of renewed attacks were made, and the Allies responded with counterattacks of their own.

A UNIFIED COMMAND

Changes were made on the Allied side in the wake of Operation Michael. Most notably, a unified command was finally created, with the French Marshal Foch placed in overall command. This would allow a much more organized response to a renewed German assault, though the time when that would be most useful had now passed.

In May, the Germans attacked again, this time against the Chemin Des Dames ridge. Capturing it was a difficult undertaking that would

The long barrel of a railway gun such as this one needed to be braced in much the same manner as a suspension bridge, using cable stays to prevent the barrel from sagging. Barrels wore out quickly under the huge pressures of firing.

require the crossing of marshy ground and water obstacles. The only chance was to do so by surprise, so the build-up for the offensive was undertaken with great care. Elaborate measures were taken to conceal the strength of the preparations and despite warnings from the intelligence community surprise was indeed achieved.

The ridge was lightly held and had been used for some time as a place for raw troops to gain experience and wounded to recuperate. On top of that, the defence was disposed as a rigid crust with light reserves. The result was heavy casualties from the preparatory bombardment, which blasted wide holes in the defences.

The assault went in on 27 May 1918. It was a huge success, with German troops not only taking their objectives but capturing the Aisne bridges intact and exploiting into the Allied rear. Many Allied units disintegrated and Paris was once again threatened, as it had been in 1914. As at the first Battle of the Marne, Allied troops motored quickly to the battlefield. This time, they included American units.

The first US division into action was a totally raw formation, which nevertheless advanced to contact and fought its attackers to a bloody standstill. More Allied units came up and the Germans suffered the first setbacks of the campaign. Soon afterward, the order came down to halt the advance.

Switching axis again, back to the salient created by Operation Michael, the German army lunged again at Paris. Progress was good at first but by this time the Americans had truly arrived. Their fresh, if very green, troops were instrumental in halting the advance. US troops played an increasingly important part in the fighting that went on through June and into July.

THE PARIS GUN

Type: Field gun

Calibre: 210mm (8.26in)

Weight in action: 750,000kg (7378 tons)

Gun length: 176 calibre: 37.0m (121.4ft)

Elevation: 0° to +55°

Traverse: 360°

Shell type & weight: HE; 119.7kg (264lb)

Muzzle velocity: 2000m/sec (6560ft/sec)

Maximum range: 122,000m (75.8 miles)

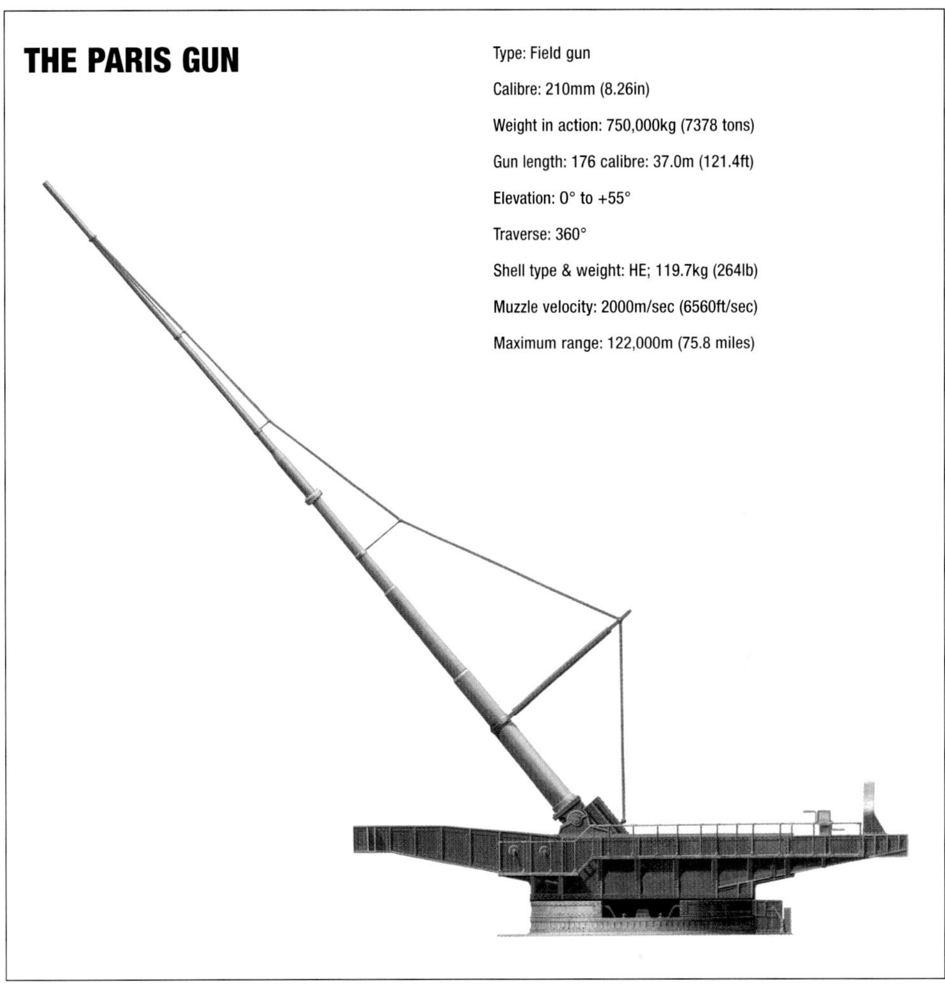

In the meantime, Paris was bombarded by a huge railway gun (actually three guns in succession), which caused numerous civilian casualties but achieved nothing of strategic significance. A final attack was made in the direction of the French capital, starting on 15 July. This was the last chance for a German victory, but was driven back by a well prepared French counterattack with heavy American support.

However, the fighting was not over. The new German line was held against attempts to dislodge it, and on the Allied side plans were being made for great tank offensives in 1919. Most observers thought there was at least a year of war left, but this did not mean that there should be any let up in attempts to force an ending.

There were now three large salients in the German lines. These made obvious targets for offensive operations, which would also allow the recapture of rail links lost to the recent German offensives. American manpower and large numbers of tanks

> A final attack was made in the direction of Paris. This was the last chance for a German victory, but was driven back by a French counterattack with heavy American support.

Allied wounded behind the lines during the later stages of Operation Michael. Although the offensive caused large Allied casualties, these were no longer so critical since American manpower was already arriving.

(which were of improved designs over the original Mk 1), plus an improvement in morale that came with the arrival of reinforcements, all contributed to a new offensive spirit.

The Allied offensive began on 18 July 1918 and was extremely successful. Despite stubborn resistance the German army was driven back and away from Paris, ending both the threat of invasion and bombardment by the Paris Gun. First the Aisne-Marne salient was driven in, then that around Amiens. The latter attack dispensed with the usual preparatory bombardment, relying instead on tanks, and gained surprise. The tactic worked well and resulted in an advance of 14.5km (9 miles).

The third salient, around Saint Mihiel, had been held by German troops since 1914. It was here that the American army in France conducted its first operation under US command, rather than as part of a mixed force under a senior European officer. The defenders realized that they were about to be attacked in overwhelming force despite attempts to keep the attack secret, and began to pull back.

However, the move was not complete when the attack went in, and large numbers of troops were captured by the extremely rapid pincer movement that bit off the salient and surrounded those trapped within. One contributory factor was American ingenuity, which provided some useful solutions to defensive obstacles. Wire was crossed by using chicken wire flung over it to push it down, while in other places Bangalore Torpedoes (hollow poles filled with explosives) were used to blast holes in the entanglements.

By now, German commanders, notably Ludendorff, were certain that Germany would be defeated. They recognized too that there was not much chance for a favourable treaty. The Allies in their turn realized that they could end the war in just a few weeks and so they now began to make preparations for a final offensive in September. The target was the Meuse-Argonne region.

Signatories of the Treaty of Versailles outside the railway carriage where the ceremony took place. The terms of the treaty were harsh, and were forced upon an exhausted Germany as an alternative to naval blockade of her ports.

COMPAGNIE
2419 D

CHAOS AFTER THE WAR

Europe in general and Germany in particular were in a terrible state at the end of the war. Exhaustion was made worse by the blockade of German ports by the Royal Navy, and large segments of the army and navy joined a general uprising. An epidemic of influenza claimed millions of lives across Europe even as the former combatants tried to create some kind of peace.

The operation took the form of a pincer movement, with British and French troops forming the northern arm and a Franco-American force the southern. As with many operations during the war, railways were an important consideration. A successful attack would not only drive a wedge into the enemy positions but would sever the rail links between them, dislocating any response.

The German army constructed powerful defensive positions, making use of high ground and forests. However, its units were under strength and demoralized. There was little chance of reinforcement since the Allies were attacking in other sectors as well.

The offensive opened on 26 September 1918, the same day that Bulgaria requested an armistice. The troops went in after a short bombardment and were highly successful, driving forward until 1 October, when the situation stabilized for a time. The offensive was resumed days later but did not clear the Argonne forest until 31 October. Although US troops were militarily inexperienced, they were highly effective in the forest, both as snipers and in close quarters assaults where sawn-off shotguns were used despite German protests.

The Influenza epidemic that broke out at the end of the Great War killed millions. The response was hampered by the need to prosecute an all-out war with the resources of entire nations.

The Treaty of Versailles took the form it did in the hope of preventing another war by keeping Germany weak. The policy might have succeeded had the treaty been aggressively enforced by the Allies.

THE END

The German army could do nothing now but fall back, fighting rearguard actions as it went. The war was once more one of manoeuvre, but this was obviously the endgame. Turkey sought an armistice on 30 October; Austro-Hungary was breaking up as its member states declared independence. Hungary became independent from Austria on 1 November and both nations surrendered to the Allies on 3 November. The collapse continued until 11 November, at which point an armistice was agreed. The final terms of the peace were harsh, and were rammed down the throats of Germany's people by the blockade that continued unabated until the Treaty of Versailles was signed. Huge war reparations, limits on the size of her military and other terms were forced on Germany. The intent was that she would never again be able to threaten European security, and had the terms been enforced as harshly as they were imposed, this would have been achieved. However, there were other problems to deal with after World War I, and when the Allies' attention was elsewhere, Germany would begin to regain her power. Instead of crippling her, the Treaty of Versailles created a rallying cry for German extremists and so paved the way for the war it was intended to prevent.

> A successful attack would not only drive a wedge into the enemy positions but would sever the rail links between them, dislocating any response.

The Inter-War Years

1919–1939

World War I was an immensely traumatic experience for all nations involved. Much has been written about the 'Lost Generation', but the vast numbers of casualties incurred in combat were only part of the problem. Many of those who came home physically intact were never quite the same, and the cost of looking after the injured and maimed was astronomical.

The influenza epidemic that began in the latter years of World War I killed millions across Europe, further debilitating the economic strength of the nations affected. The result of all this was a feeling that the world did not want and could not afford another war. This sentiment guided military thinking in some nations long after it had become obvious that another war was coming.

REARMAMENT

In some ways, the forcible demilitarization of Germany worked in her favour. Other nations entered the inter-war period with large stocks of 'legacy' equipment left over from the huge armament programmes of World War I. With little money for arms of any sort, this gear remained in service long after it had become obsolete, and there was so much of it that it cost a great deal to maintain. Thus there was little impetus to design new and improved weapon systems, especially on land, and

The Spanish Civil War broke out in the middle of 1936 after a coup against the government. Here, Spanish Falangists at Irun in Northern Spain search the houses for hidden Communists.

Sailors from a visiting Italian warship form an honour guard as Japanese naval infantry move in to occupy Hankow in September 1936. The troops were deployed in response to the killing of two Japanese policemen a few days before.

thus no real need to evolve new doctrine and methods to make use of the new technologies that were becoming available.

The end result was that British and French tank development languished for many years, while Russia did not begin developing a tank arm until the late 1920s. When new tanks were developed, they were an evolution of World War I designs rather than a new generation.

Germany, on the other hand, was able to create both a doctrine for the use of armoured troops and the vehicles to implement it, more or less to order. Ironically, it was the ideas of British tank advocates that drove German thinking in terms of armoured forces.

Armoured forces were not the only new development. Several nations began to experiment with airborne troops and aircraft for close support on the battlefield. It eventually became apparent that ground forces needed air defence weapons.

One other development occurred, which seems to be a retrograde step. Despite the generally poor performance of fortresses in World War I, several nations built new fortifications with ever-bigger guns in them. The French constructed their Maginot Line, and to face it the Germans constructed the Siegfried Line, a chain of defences protecting the Franco-German frontier.

Other forts were built or strengthened, even though the manuals of various nations stressed offensive action. There may have been an element of the security blanket in the fortress-building that went on across Europe. Nobody wanted a war and with strong enough defences in place perhaps one could be deterred. As events would show, this was a forlorn hope.

ARMOURED WARFARE

Japan's emergence onto the world stage after centuries of isolationism necessitated the creation of a powerful modern army, navy and air force. Industrial developments created a need for resources not found in

Georgy Zhukov became a Hero of the Soviet Union. His armoured tactics at the Battle of Khalkhyn Gol were ahead of their time and, despite a period in eclipse, he returned to head the Soviet drive to Berlin.

Two Russian soldiers congratulating themselves on the victory in Khalkhyn Gol, where Soviet troops routed the Japanese forces, taking many prisoners and artillery. The wording on the flag says 'From the soldiers girlfriends in 1939'.

Japanese territory, and this led to an aggressive policy of territorial acquisition.

In the early 1930s, China, with its large resources, was in political turmoil and ripe for conquest. Its fragmented forces were outdated and lacked heavy weapons that could deal with even the lightest of tanks.

Japanese tanks were indeed light; most were more properly termed tankettes and virtually useless in battle against an opponent equipped with anti-tank weapons. Since the Chinese lacked them, these small, lightly armoured vehicles, often armed with nothing more than a machine gun, were a potent force on the battlefield.

Between 1931 and 1937, a series of 'incidents' took place, stopping short of open war but resulting in a gradual encroachment of Japanese forces into China. Full-scale warfare began in 1937. The Chinese could not stop the advance of mechanized Japanese forces, however weak they were by European standards. Beijing was taken and the Japanese advanced quickly across northern China. This resulted in a border clash with the Soviet Union in 1938, known as the Changkufeng Incident. Japanese attacks spearheaded by tanks and other armoured vehicles were met by an armoured counterattack.

> Japan's emergence onto the world stage after centuries of isolationism necessitated the creation of a powerful modern army, navy and air force.

A few years later, this sort of thing would become commonplace in Europe, but at the time it was a very new form of warfare. A year later, in 1939, another incident resulted in a large-scale conflict between Japan and the Soviet Union. The latter sent

General Georgi Zhukov to take command of its forces in the region. After a period of build-up, characterized by raids and skirmishes, the Japanese launched a classic double-envelopment operation. One arm of the attack was spearheaded by tanks.

The resulting action, today known as the Battle of Khalkhyn Gol, was an initial success for the Japanese, and for a time it was possible that they would complete the encirclement and destruction of very large Soviet forces. However, the Soviets used armour to counterattack, without waiting for infantry support, and were eventually able to drive off the Japanese.

The German Panzer generals are normally considered to be the pioneers of fast-moving armoured warfare, but it was the Soviet commander, Zhukov, who now demonstrated the classic armoured attack. After beating off another Japanese assault, Zhukov launched his operation. To do so, he had to contend with severe logistical difficulties.

In the centre, the Soviets advanced to contact and 'grip' the enemy front, then hooked armoured forces around both flanks, encircling a Japanese division, which was then reduced by air attack and artillery bombardment. Heavily defeated, the Japanese agreed to a peace treaty with the Soviet Union, which was signed on 15 September 1939. This secured the Russians' flank and enabled them to take part in the carving up of Poland a few days later, while the Japanese retained their conquests in China and were able to turn their attention to the conquest of Southeast Asia.

Although the Soviet tanks taken into action in 1938–39 were not good, they were better than their Japanese opponents, which in turn were entirely adequate to deal with infantry that did not have many machine guns, let alone anti-tank weapons. The Japanese army actually told the tank design bureaus that it did not want heavier tanks, so satisfied were its commanders with the performance of their light tanks and tankettes against the Chinese. This was one reason why the Japanese did not introduce a

Street fighting was common during the Spanish Civil War, as possession of the cities was seen as an indicator of who was winning. The many different factions on each side, and the confused situation, made target identification difficult.

PANZER I

Type: Light tank
Crew: 2
Powerplant: one Krupp M305 petrol engine developing 45kW (60hp)
Weight: 5500kg (12,100lb)
Armour: 6–13mm (0.2–0.5in)
Armament: 2 x 7.92mm (0.31in) G13 machine guns
Performance: maximum road speed, 37km/h (21mph); fording, 0.85m (2ft 10in); vertical obstacle, 0.42m (1ft 5in); trench, 1.75m (5ft 9in)
Dimensions: Length: 4.02m (13.2ft)
Width: 2.06m (6ft 7in)
Height: 1.72m (5ft 7in)

satisfactory medium tank until very late in the war.

THE SPANISH CIVIL WAR

The Spanish Civil War broke out in the middle of 1936 after a coup against the government, and fighting continued until April 1939. The turbulent politics of the time meant that various nations were drawn in, supporting one side or the other. The Nationalists were supported by Portugal and the Fascist regimes in Italy and Germany, while the Republicans received assistance from the Soviet Union and Mexico. Many individuals from various nations also went to join the fighting, joining whichever side suited their personal politics.

Both Germany and Italy used the Spanish Civil War as a testing ground for their forces and doctrines. Perhaps 75,000 Italian troops and 20,000 Germans went to fight in Spain, though not all at once. Both nations sent armoured troops. The German contingent were mostly equipped with PanzerKampfwagen (PzKpfw) I light tanks. These were never intended as combat vehicles, being an interim measure to gain experience and train troops while more powerful designs were developed.

The Panzer I was effective enough in an anti-personnel role. Mobile, able to resist small-arms fire and equipped with a pair of machine guns, it was a useful little combat vehicle, but badly outmatched by the Soviet-provided BT-5 tanks on the opposing side. These were armed with a 45mm (1.77in) gun that could easily kill a PzKpfw I while their own armour was proof against return fire.

Similarly, the large numbers of tankettes sent by Italy allowed their forces to gain experience and were useful in some circumstances. Overall, however, the Spanish Civil War showed how ineffective these little vehicles could be on the modern battlefield, especially against true combat tanks.

Gradually, the Nationalists gained control of more and more of the country until their leader, General Franco, received recognition from Britain and France as the legitimate ruler of Spain. Fighting went on until the end of March 1939, when Franco's Nationalists took Madrid and Valencia, which more or less ended Republican power.

General Francisco Franco became head of state after the Spanish Civil War. He could be said to have started the war by launching a coup against the government, though by that point conflict was probably inevitable in an unstable situation.

World War II
1939–1945

World War II was much more widespread than World War I, with large-scale combat taking place in Africa and the Far East as well as Scandinavia and Western Europe. The characteristics of these different theatres of war dictated rather different styles of combat.

In Western Europe and the Eastern Front, the general pattern was of large-scale conventional combat, with offensives generally spearheaded by armoured divisions or supported by smaller armoured forces. In the deserts of North Africa, it was discovered that infantry could not operate against enemy forces including even a few tanks unless armoured support was available. Large-scale combined-arms operations were the order of the day here, too.

This was not possible elsewhere – for example, in the jungles of the Far East. While tanks were used in the island-hopping campaigns of the Pacific and in the fighting in Burma, these were mostly light units operating in support of infantry formations rather than acting as the arm of decision. In such close terrain it fell to the infantry, with artillery and naval gunfire support where possible, to close with the enemy and fight it out.

There was, however, much more to the war than this. It is not possible to entirely disregard the strategic bombing campaigns or the naval dimension to the war since these had an effect – which was at times profound – on the logistical and industrial efforts necessary to carry on the war. The efforts of partisans and resistance fighters in occupied countries from the

Motorized transport was not universal in the German army in 1939, but there was enough to equip many units. These could move further and faster than more traditional foot and horse-drawn units.

Philippines to Norway also disrupted enemy activity and tied down large forces. While individually not very significant, these pinpricks added up to a serious drain on the resources of the occupying powers and at times contributed greatly to Allied successes.

The Poles were not as overmatched as is often supposed. Most of the German tanks that went into Poland were PzKpfw Is, armed only with a pair of machine guns.

THE INVASION OF POLAND

Nazi Germany had already made significant gains when war broke out. Union with Austria had been achieved, bringing in more manpower and industrial output; other territories had been annexed without a fight.

The next target was Poland, which had been divided with Russia in a secret agreement guaranteeing that there would be no clash between the two powers when the attack took place. After engineering a number of incidents as a pretext, the German army invaded.

The invasion of Poland was not a Blitzkrieg. The term had not yet been coined and, in any case, it was actually a conventional and indeed cautious operation. The Poles were still mobilizing for war when the attack began, and in truth they never had a chance from the outset. However, they were able to put up a much better fight than anyone had expected.

Poland's long frontier was not defensible against a superior force, but there was no choice but to try. Some armoured forces were available, but these were mostly armed with tankettes; the heaviest tanks in Polish service were British light designs. Nevertheless, they fought back hard and inflicted heavy losses on the Panzer divisions.

The Poles were not as overmatched as is often supposed. Most of the German tanks that went into Poland were PzKpfw Is, armed only with a pair of machine guns. These could be killed by the 20mm (0.78in) gun fitted to many Polish tankettes.

However, the German army had large numbers of tanks, including Panzer IIs with a 20mm (0.78in) gun and much more powerful battle and fire support tanks in the form of Panzer III and IVs. These could withstand heavy fire and brush aside most opposition. More importantly, the Germans had good and well rehearsed tactics for armoured and combined-arms combat plus heavy air support, which was also well drilled in close cooperation with the armoured forces.

On 17 September, all hope of Polish survival was dashed when the Soviet Union declared war and began

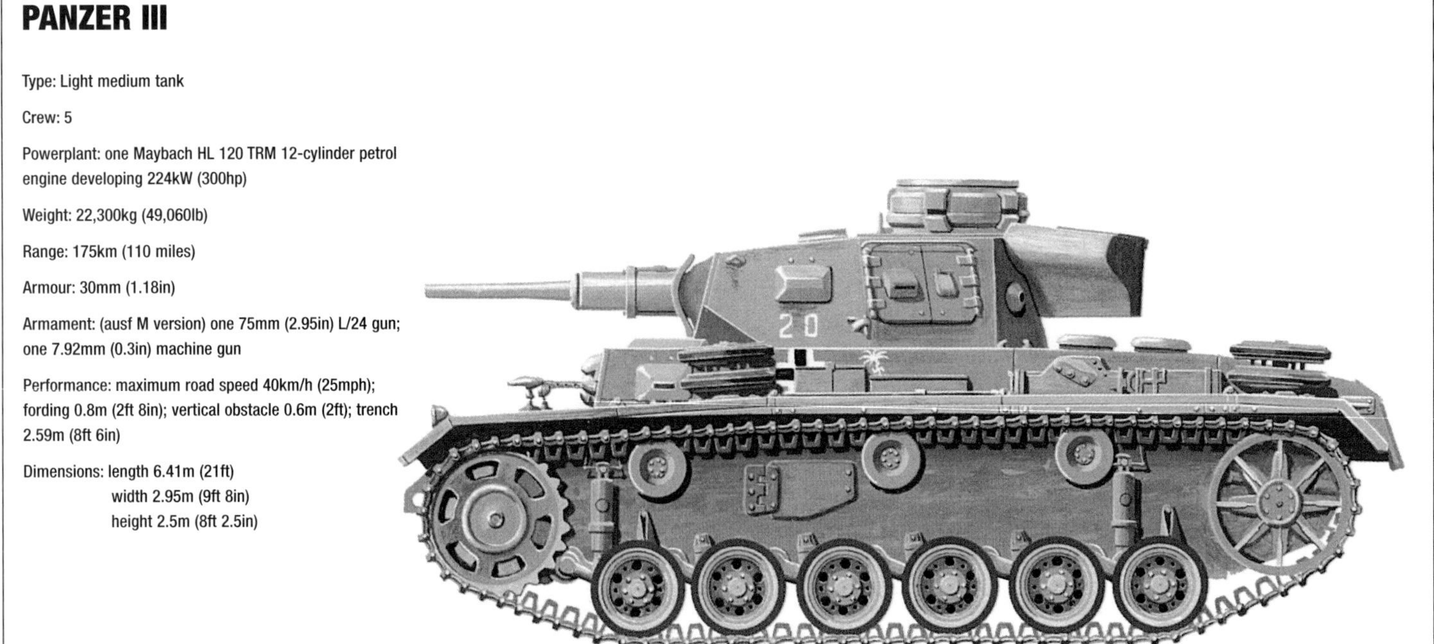

PANZER III

Type: Light medium tank

Crew: 5

Powerplant: one Maybach HL 120 TRM 12-cylinder petrol engine developing 224kW (300hp)

Weight: 22,300kg (49,060lb)

Range: 175km (110 miles)

Armour: 30mm (1.18in)

Armament: (ausf M version) one 75mm (2.95in) L/24 gun; one 7.92mm (0.3in) machine gun

Performance: maximum road speed 40km/h (25mph); fording 0.8m (2ft 8in); vertical obstacle 0.6m (2ft); trench 2.59m (8ft 6in)

Dimensions: length 6.41m (21ft)
width 2.95m (9ft 8in)
height 2.5m (8ft 2.5in)

to advance. Already under attack from several directions, Poland simply could not deal with this new onslaught, which made the establishment of a new defensive line impossible. Some areas held out for a time, and elements of the Polish forces were able to escape to join the Allies, but Poland was more or less conquered by early October.

Poland's treaties with Britain and France required a response, and both nations declared war on Germany. However, there was nothing that could be done in time, and little enough to do it with. Preparations for the defence of France and Norway were

Although half-tracked trucks are an iconic image of the war, the German army made extensive use of ordinary wheeled vehicles too. Some could be built with either wheels or half-tracks.

NO BLITZKRIEG IN POLAND

Six Panzer divisions were deployed for the Polish campaign, which began on 1 September 1939. There was no breakthrough followed by Devil-take-the-hindmost exploitation; conventional tactics were used with the armour as a spearhead or fast-moving flanking force. Successive Polish positions were broken in this manner, driving the defenders gradually back.

The Winter War was an unpleasant experience for the Soviets, who had thought that the Finns would be easy to overrun. The lightly equipped but highly mobile Finns made good use of camouflage and their knowledge of the land.

put in place, and consideration was given to defending the British Isles if it came to that. The outbreak of war was something of an anti-climax at first, leading to the use of the term 'Phoney War' to describe this period.

THE WINTER WAR

Soviet Russia had already attracted international condemnation for what was seen as her betrayal of Poland. Further censure was earned by the attempted subjugation of Finland in a campaign that became known as the Winter War. This was preceded by a series of demands for territory, which were refused by the Finnish government, and a border incident was then engineered.

With a pretext in place, the invasion opened at the very end of November 1939. It began with a Soviet push up the neck of land

GUERRILLA WARFARE, FINNISH STYLE

Although outmatched in terms of numbers and equipment, the Finns were very good at guerrilla fighting in the arctic forests that characterized the combat zone. Camouflaged in white and experienced at operating in the conditions they encountered, bands of Finnish irregulars moved swiftly about the countryside on skis, attacking targets of opportunity. A favourite tactic was to sneak up on a field kitchen and snipe at the troops there before slipping away.

German infantrymen rush forward to the next position of cover. Although much has been made of the Panzer divisions, the German army was still a predominantly infantry force and its riflemen were vital at the beginning of the war.

between the Gulf of Finland and Lake Ladoga along with other drives into Finnish territory.

The Finns were woefully underequipped, especially in terms of equipment with which to fight tanks. Several weapons were improvised but these performed very poorly. Even though most Soviet tanks were poor or obsolete designs, and some were multi-turreted monstrosities that did not work very well to start with, the Finns had trouble stopping them.

One method that worked, though it required getting dangerously close to the tank, was to use a Molotov Cocktail, an improvised incendiary bomb made from petrol and oil in a breakable glass container, with a rag as a fuse. Soviet tanks burned readily and many were lost.

Being attacked in this manner was demoralizing for the Soviets, who often struggled to even find their opponents in the forests. When they did, they came under fire from weapons stolen from their supply depots; the Finns used the same weapons as the Soviets and raided their enemies for war matériel.

The Red Army suffered from over-confidence at the beginning of the Winter War, largely due to recent victories over the Poles and the Japanese. Purges of competent but politically suspect officers by the Soviet leader Josef Stalin had greatly reduced the leadership capabilities of the army. On top of this, individual initiative was discouraged by a practice of executing officers who deviated from 'the book' and who were unsuccessful. The result was a hidebound army whose officers had little skill or experience and dared not deviate from conventional practices even when it was obvious that these were inappropriate. The intervention of political commissars made this even worse. These political officers often had no military knowledge but could veto orders they felt were inappropriate, such as a necessary retreat.

As a result, the Soviet army blundered around incompetently in appalling conditions for which it was insufficiently equipped to deal, suffering casualties from frostbite and constant equipment breakdowns, while its supposedly inferior enemies flitted about, chopping up formations with ambushes and launching strikes in 'safe' areas before disappearing into the snow once again.

Some assistance was received from overseas, including individuals who came from other countries to fight for Finland, and the Allies considered plans to send more substantial aid. This was not possible, given events elsewhere, and in the end it was not necessary. The Soviet Union, suffering large losses for no gain and losing international prestige as a result, decided that nothing was to be gained from continuing the campaign.

After some negotiations, a peace treaty was agreed and signed in March 1940. Finland ceded a considerable amount of territory considering how poorly the war had gone for her enemies. The peace was short-lived, however. Finland attempted to recover the lost territories by joining the Axis cause in 1941, resulting in renewed hostilities with the Soviet Union.

THE INVASION OF DENMARK AND NORWAY

The Allies considered the possibility of sending troops to Denmark and Norway to prevent German occupation. This was desirable for several reasons. Norway's northern ports could be used by German naval units to effectively bypass the Royal Navy's attempts to pen them in their ports, as had happened in World War I. Occupation of Norway would also

Soldiers of the Dutch army during the German invasion of 1940. The Dutch never stood a chance of repelling the much more powerful German army, but resisted as best they could until forced to surrender.

make it much easier for Germany to receive shipments of iron ore from Sweden. Air bases in Norway would make strikes at Britain more effective as well.

To prevent the Allies from establishing heavy forces in Denmark and Norway, thus making an invasion impossible, German high command decided to launch a rapid attack to capture key points and gain control of the two nations. Denmark could be easily accessed by land, but a naval invasion was required to reach Norway. Rather than use slow transport ships, the invasion troops were mostly carried aboard warships.

The operation began on 9 April 1940. Denmark's small army did not stand a chance, but put up what resistance it could. A threat to bomb Copenhagen resulted in a negotiated surrender on fairly generous terms; Germany did not really want much to do with Denmark other than to keep the Allies out.

British and French forces attempting to hold the port of Narvik were evacuated on 9 June, but Norwegian resistance to the occupation continued throughout the war. By this time, German armoured divisions were rolling across France.

GERMAN PARATROOPERS IN NORWAY

When Norway came under attack, she was no pushover. The Norwegians put up a stubborn fight, enabling the king and parliament to escape. The legal government of Norway never surrendered, even though the last organized resistance was suppressed by the middle of June.

In addition to landing troops on the shore, paratroops were used to capture some objectives. Although several nations had developed a parachute arm, this was the first time they had been used in action. The paras were successful and thus established their credibility as a combat force.

THE APOTHEOSIS OF ARMOUR

The German army in 1940 was primarily an infantry force, and used mainly horsed transport. However, the spearhead was an armoured force, which could cover ground rapidly and bring heavy firepower to bear at the destination. Initial doubts about the effectiveness of armoured attacks were dispelled by success in Poland, and by the time France was invaded the Panzer commanders were inclined to launch deep penetration attacks rather than using armour to support more conventional operations.

The main obstacle to invasion was the formidable fortress chain of the Maginot Line. It was possible to bypass this to the north by going through the Low Countries, but such a move would inevitably be met by British and French mobile forces. However, these were not formidable.

On 10 May 1940, the drive westwards began with the invasion of the Low Countries. Paratroops landed ahead of the advancing ground invasion. A notable first was achieved when glider-borne troops assaulted the fortress of Eben Emael, defending the Meuse crossings. This was the first of many fortresses that failed to resist attack. Built in the 1930s, it was well designed, modern and apparently formidable but could not withstand modern methods of warfare.

French troops were sent to assist Holland and Belgium, but were turned back. Meanwhile, the small and inexperienced Dutch army put up a fight until 14 May, when surrender became the only option. German forces were then able to turn west and advance into Belgium from the flank. The Belgians did not surrender until 27 May, though by then most of the country was firmly in German hands.

This opened the way into Northern France, and the armoured spearhead began its advance. Meanwhile, other armoured forces had outflanked the Maginot Line by moving through the Ardennes forest, which the Allies considered 'untankable'. This threatened to cut off any forces moving to assist the armies of the Low Countries and drove a wedge deep into the unprepared Allied forces facing the attack.

With heavy close air support, the armoured divisions led the assault. Tactics were intelligently aggressive. Heavy resistance was bypassed and left for infantry, artillery and air units to reduce while the armoured forces struck at headquarters, logistics and communications centres, dislocating an already confused response.

The 'miracle of Dunkirk' was a prodigious achievement that saved a large proportion of British manpower at the cost of abandoning transport, artillery and heavy equipment, although many men were killed by shelling.

ALLIED ARMOUR DOCTRINE

Britain had neglected her tank arm until it was almost too late, but was now finally beginning to field modern tanks. There were not nearly enough of them, however. The French, on the other hand, possessed more tanks than their German opponents. Most were of obsolete designs, some dating from 1917. Worse, French doctrine also dated from World War I and dispersed tanks as infantry supports rather than concentrating them as an arm in their own right. The result was excessive dilution of fighting power and limited mobility.

The Allies did fight back, launching counterattacks with available forces. Many of these were not very aggressive or were hamstrung by a lack of mobility. What was needed was a rapid counterpunch with tanks. But most of the French tank strength was embedded in infantry formations, and these could not move quickly, so the counterattacks tended to be too small, too slow or too late.

Some counterattacks were more successful than others. An armoured thrust from Laon and another in the region of St Quentin on 17–19 May hit the flanks of the advancing Panzer force and slowed it somewhat. Others, at Cambrai and Amiens on 22–23 May, failed. A British counterthrust at Arras, made by a small number of British tanks and supporting infantry, achieved excellent results and badly frightened German high command, who increasingly demanded that the Panzers proceed more cautiously.

The Panzers were slowing for other reasons. They had charged ahead of their logistics 'tail' and left their supporting infantry behind. High command were becoming concerned about the vulnerability of the armoured forces and wanted to halt and regroup. The Panzer

Horse-drawn German artillery in Paris. Most of the artillery of the Wehrmacht was pulled by horses. Horse-drawn or even vehicle-towed guns could not keep pace with the armoured spearheads, necessitating self-propelled guns.

Foreign tanks in the streets drove home to the French population that their armies had defeated. Many French tanks were co-opted into German service for 'occupation duties', keeping down the population they were built to protect.

commanders had other ideas and interpreted their orders rather freely, continuing the advance over the objections of headquarters.

Although the term 'Blitzkrieg' had not yet been coined, the rapid German advance was succeeding in doing what a similar campaign in 1914 had failed to achieve. The British and French were being pushed apart and the British driven towards the Channel ports. Had the Panzer divisions continued their headlong advance, the entire British force might have been pinned against the Channel and crushed. However, aided by a halt ordered by German high command and an increasingly stubborn defence, the British were able to reach the port of Dunkirk and begin an evacuation.

The Dunkirk evacuation was over by 4 June. The British army lost most of its heavy equipment but was able to salvage almost 340,000 troops from the disaster in France. They would be sorely needed as the nation tried to rebuild its military strength.

FRENCH RESISTANCE

Meanwhile, the French continued to resist as best they could. The Panzer divisions turned southwards and began advancing on Paris. This renewed drive was undertaken by two main forces, which began their offensive operations on 5 and 9 June respectively. The French, assisted by some cut-off British units, resisted valiantly but Paris was taken on 14 June. Two days later, France began negotiating surrender terms, though not before elements of her government escaped to London and declared their continued resistance.

The armistice between Germany and France took effect on 25 June. Elements of the French armed forces were still resisting even after the armistice was requested on the 19 June, but by this time overall command had broken down and the final acts of defiance were undertaken in a manner both piecemeal and ad-hoc.

Italy declared war on France on 10 June, just in time to make

> Although the term 'Blitzkrieg' had not yet been coined, the rapid German advance was succeeding where a similar campaign in 1914 had failed.

The Fall of France: Hitler insisted that the surrender be signed in the same railway carriage used for the signing of the Treaty of Versailles, which was humiliating for an already defeated France.

an opportunistic grab for territory against an already defeated opponent. In fact, Italian troops made no real headway before the armistice took effect, though Mussolini was rewarded with an occupation zone in France.

France was divided into the German-occupied area, a small Italian zone and an unoccupied French state with its capital at Vichy. Some French forces located overseas, notably in North Africa, remained loyal to Vichy France. Some declared for the Allies and fought on.

The war had begun very badly. Other than resistance forces in various nations and some organized units that had escaped the fall of their parent nations and joined the British, there was little to stop the Axis powers. Britain itself had started out under-prepared and been severely defeated in Europe. An invasion was entirely likely, and there was doubt that it could be successfully resisted.

Britain itself had started out under-prepared and been severely defeated in Europe. An invasion was entirely likely, and there was doubt it could be successfully resisted.

DESPERATE MEASURES: HOME GUARDS AND PARTISANS

Britain had always maintained a relatively small army for overseas service, backed up by the Territorial Army. The size and prowess of German forces were such that Britain could not resist invasion with the troops she had available. The Royal Navy promised that it could stave off invasion 'for a time' and there was reason to hope that the Royal Air Force might be able to play a

LOCAL DEFENCE VOLUNTEERS

In Britain, the Local Defence Volunteers, which had originally been formed unofficially in February 1940 to defend Dover, were now established nationwide, to counter the threat of invasion. Tens of thousands came forward, bringing whatever weapons they possessed.

Gradually, the LDV got organized. Weapons were still in short supply, as the regular army had to be re-equipped and expanded. A collection in the United States yielded thousands of privately held firearms sent by ordinary citizens, and gradually proper small arms became available. By late July 1940, the LDV had been renamed the Home Guard and was receiving uniforms, weapons and training.

part in preventing a successful Channel crossing.

As events would show, the RAF was indeed able to prevent the enemy from attaining air supremacy, which was necessary for an invasion. However, it was a close-run thing, and in the summer of 1940 the situation looked bleak. Frantic preparations were undertaken to resist an attack. The Home Guard fulfilled two roles. Firstly, it was important to British morale at a time when things seemed very bleak indeed. In a more material sense, it also freed regulars and territorials from routine local security and 'tripwire' duties.

As the Home Guard came into its own, its members watched the coasts for invasion and scoured the countryside for enemy parachutists or downed airmen. These functions could be carried out by older men and those too young to be called up for service; without the Home Guard, these tasks would have absorbed

Volunteers receive basic instruction in rifle handling. Many of those who came forward had military experience as veterans of World War I. Although long in the tooth perhaps, these men had fought before and emerged victorious.

manpower that was needed in the formations which would eventually win the war.

On top of all this, there was one other thing the Home Guard could do. Its members might be too young, old or infirm to serve in an infantry division, but they could defend their homes. Had the Panzers come to Britain, the part-time soldiers of 'Dad's Army' would have fought them with everything that came to hand.

Extensive fortifications were put in place to resist a landing and to contain enemy movements if one were successfully made. These included anti-tank obstacles and pillboxes as well as less permanent infantry positions. The Home Guard also acted as a cover for a 'stay-behind' force, which would hide until bypassed by the invaders, then emerge to conduct a campaign of sabotage. In some areas, these forces were equipped with quite elaborate hidden bunkers.

Ironically perhaps, many of the British preparations made for invasion in 1940 were echoed in Germany a few years later, with units composed of invalids, old men and boys equipped with whatever weapons could be obtained. These *Volksturm* soldiers fought hard to defend their homes and perhaps showed how their British equivalents might have performed had they been called to do so.

Meanwhile, in the occupied territories of Europe, partisans and resistance forces did all they could to harass and disrupt the invaders' plans.

PARTISANS AND RESISTANCE

Meanwhile, in the occupied territories of Europe, partisans and resistance forces did all they could to harass and disrupt the invaders' plans. They rescued Allied aircrews, gathered intelligence and tied down large numbers of troops that might have been deployed on the front lines. Partisan groups also conducted raids and ambushes, particularly against railways.

The impact of the partisans is difficult to estimate, but it is certain that they did have an effect on the outcome of the war. For example, German operations in Russia were

It was possible to hold down the major cities with troops and tanks, but rural areas required too much manpower to be properly garrisoned or swept for insurgents.

French resistance fighters dream of a free France during the occupation. The resistance in occupied countries was a significant problem for the Axis. Most operations were minor in scope, but they collectively resulted in a drain on resources.

hampered by partisan activity in Poland, where trains were frequently derailed or damaged by guerrillas. The already over-stretched logistics chain was thus further disrupted. Resistance forces also fulfilled the vital function of keeping hope alive; even the most minor of nuisance operations were preferable to just accepting the occupation. The largest partisan force in Europe was in Yugoslavia, where an estimated 800,000 people actively resisted the occupation. Poland fielded about 400,000. Numbers are hard to establish, of course, since resistance groups had to be compartmentalized for security purposes.

In the dark days of 1940, there was little the British could do to help the resistance forces in Europe and elsewhere. The Special Operations Executive (SOE) was one such measure. Created with the aim of 'setting Europe aflame', it existed to coordinate and support local resistance groups. SOE agents made contact with resistance groups and arranged for supplies of arms and ammunition to be delivered, usually by airdrop. Although the effects of SOE and the various resistance movements cannot be accurately measured, they were significant in that the enemy took them seriously and had to deploy personnel and resources to deal with them. Just as importantly, SOE was a sign that Britain had not forgotten the people of the occupied countries at a time when more direct support was simply impossible.

Later in the war, the partisans and resistance groups provided vital information to assist the Allies in their liberation of Europe, and in some areas orchestrated uprisings to coincide with the Allied advance. Information on enemy strengths and dispositions, plus diversionary operations, was extremely valuable to the Allies as they advanced across Europe.

DESERT OFFENSIVES

With the creation of Vichy France, Britain and the Free French were faced with a distasteful problem. France held large territories in Africa and strong land and naval forces were deployed there. These might be forced to join the war on the Axis side.

This was something the overstretched Allies simply could not afford, and so it was necessary to force the issue. This was especially important in the case of major warships; they had to be kept out of German hands. The result was an

ultimatum – come over to the Free French, go to a neutral port and be interned, or be destroyed. Some units came over, but the bitter task of neutralizing the others had to be undertaken.

Some land units and minor colonies came over to the Free French, but operations to gain control of other areas were repulsed. However, the British forces in Africa soon had a more serious problem to contend with.

Hitler was not really interested in Africa, but his ally Mussolini was. Italy had large territorial holdings in Africa whereas Germany had lost hers in the World War I. Even later in the desert war, when German forces had taken over the main combat role in the theatre, Hitler saw North Africa as the southern arm of a giant pincer attack against the Soviet Union rather than an important objective in its own right.

For the British, whose main strength was in Egypt, Africa was of critical importance. The fleet base at

The deserts of North Africa were a harsh fighting environment with little cover to protect the units operating there. However, collateral damage was rarely an issue when using artillery since there was usually no civilian population nearby.

Hitler was not really interested in Africa, but Mussolini was. Italy had large territorial holdings in Africa whereas Germany had lost hers in the World War I.

Alexandria allowed the Royal Navy to project force into the Mediterranean and protected the Suez Canal, greatly shortening the transit time for supplies and forces moving to and from the Far East, where a worsening situation suggested that war with Japan was likely. On top of that, defeat in Egypt might mean the loss of the Middle East oilfields and a subsequent reduction in the ability of the Allies to fight the war.

The southern force made some gains and then became largely inactive. However, the presence of Italian troops in the region tied down British forces and required that actions against the army coming in from Libya be conducted with one eye on the flank.

ITALIAN ASPIRATIONS IN NORTH AFRICA

Mussolini had big plans for Africa, and decided that it would be possible to drive the British out. His main forces were in Libya, Ethiopia and Eritrea. Attacks on British Somaliland and part of Kenya were small sideshows to the main event, the invasion of the Sudan and Egypt. Italian troops from Ethiopia pushed northwards into the Sudan as troops from Libya advanced on Egypt, threatening the British from two sides.

THE INVASION OF EGYPT

The invasion of Egypt began on 13 September 1940, and by 18 September the Italians had advanced some 96km (60 miles). They now began building a forward base at Side Barrani to support subsequent operations. However, no further advances took place and on 8 December the British launched a counterattack.

The Italian forces in North Africa were very numerous but possessed

In some ways, the desert was excellent tank country; in others, it made operations a nightmare. Dust clogged air filters and increased mechanical wear, while the long distances ate up fuel and spare parts at an alarming rate.

little armour. Most of what they had was made up of tankettes and light vehicles unsuited to a heavy combat role. The supply situation was also less than ideal. The heavily outnumbered British forces had more and better tanks than the Italians. These included Matildas, which were slow but more or less impervious to the Italians' tank and anti-tank guns.

The British attack achieved surprise against the complacent enemy, and was able to hook into the enemy rear through a gap in the line. Good reconnaissance and operational security thus contributed to the stunning victory that followed.

The Italian forces were not expecting an attack and had been encamped for some time. Their response was slow and disorganized, and the camps of successive units were overrun one by one. Tales of Italian cowardice were a propaganda invention; even caught off guard, individual units resisted as best they could. There was no overall plan and each piecemeal defensive effort was shattered as it was encountered until eventually the whole Italian position collapsed. The overmatched armoured force was brushed aside, in many cases destroyed before the crews could even mount up. Anti-tank gunners fought to the muzzle in some cases but could not penetrate the attacking tanks. As later events in the war would show again and again, infantry in the open without tank support were unable to do much against an armoured attack.

> It was over quickly, with tens of thousands of stunned Italian prisoners in Allied hands and the remains of an army of 200,000 reeling westwards in total disarray.

It was over quickly, with tens of thousands of stunned prisoners in Allied hands and the remains of an army of 200,000 reeling westwards in total disarray. The counterattack had achieved far more than the British had intended, and now they had the opportunity to exploit the victory further. Despite having to detach troops to send southwards, the British were able to pursue the retreating Italians.

DIFFICULT DESERT TERRAIN

The pursuit took place along the coastal strip between the Gulf of Sirte and the approaches to Alexandria. The coast road there was vital to logistics, and while some forces did hook inland to get around a flank, the difficult desert terrain made wide-ranging operations impossible. Smaller forces, such as the Long-Range Desert Group, which launched raids and gathered information deep inside enemy territory, could bypass forces in the coastal region, but major formations had to use the coast road.

The British advance across North Africa was spearheaded by armoured

MATILDA

Type: Infantry tank

Crew: 4

Powerplant: two Leyland 6-cylinder petrol engines each developing 71kW (95hp) or two AEC diesels each developing 65kW (87hp)

Weight: 26,926kg (59,237lb)

Range: 257km (160 miles)

Armour: 20mm–78mm (0.78in–3.1in)

Armament: one 2-pounder gun; one 7.92mm(0.3in) Besa machine gun

Performance: maximum road speed 24km/h (15mph); maximum cross country speed 12.9km/h (8mph); fording 0.914m (3ft); vertical obstacle 0.609m (2ft); trench 2.133m (7ft)

Dimensions: length 5.613m (18ft 5in)
width 2.59m (8ft 6in)
height 2.51m (8ft 3in)

troops in what could become classic fashion. Minor opposition was simply brushed aside by a combination of aggression and firepower, and the Italians were too off-balance to mount any serious defensive operations. Had an armoured rearguard been available, things might have been different. But it was not. As a result, the Italians were unable to turn and fight, and were bundled westwards by the advancing allies.

Some Italian formations became cut off and were reduced by forces following up the spearhead. Meanwhile, a stand at Bardia was smashed, Tobruk was taken on 22 January 1941 and the *coup de grâce* delivered by a masterstroke at Beda Fomm on the Gulf of Sirte.

The coast road followed the coastline of North Africa, which bulged northwards and then swung south around the Gulf of Sirte. The retreating Italians and the main pursuing force had to follow this route, but a more direct track ran through difficult terrain somewhat inland of the coast.

BLOCKING POSITION

Although the going was very bad, a force of light armoured vehicles with infantry and some artillery was able to get ahead of the Italians and establish a blocking position near Beda Fomm. Although vastly outnumbered and short of supplies, this force was able to cling to its positions against determined attempts to break through. From 4 to 7 February, the Italians struggled to break out of the trap, coming close but never quite achieving a breakthrough.

Extremes of temperature were a problem for both sides. The desert could be cold at night but daytime temperatures were very high. Troops operating independently, such as raiders and scouts, had to go equipped for all conditions.

Finally, after a shocking defeat, weeks of aggressive pursuit and then finding itself trapped between two apparently powerful forces, the encircled Italian army reached the end of its endurance. About 130,000 troops surrendered. Indeed, there were so many of them that the Allies counted prisoners by the acre rather than trying to be precise.

The British and Allied forces in North Africa found themselves at the end of a long supply line, however, and the advance was now halted at El Agheila on the Gulf of Sirte. Troops were urgently needed to assist Greece,

The coastal region of North Africa is huge but the war was confined to a relatively small area where there were roads and water. Soft sand, rugged mountains and arid regions pushed the combatants into a narrow strip along the coast.

which was under heavy pressure. Greece could not be saved, which was obvious to some observers, but it was politically necessary to try.

THE BALKANS AND THE MEDITERRANEAN

Hitler had not intended to open a campaign in North Africa, but his Italian allies had dragged the Axis into one. Similarly, he had intended to gain control of the Balkans by diplomacy, albeit of a strong-arm sort. Having persuaded Romania and Hungary to side with the Axis in 1940, German diplomats began working on Bulgaria. Although they were eventually successful – in March 1941, Bulgaria signed a pact with the Axis – Italian intervention in the Balkans disrupted the plan.

Italian troops marched over the border from Albania on 28 October 1940, expecting the Greeks to cave in almost immediately. However, they put up a stiff fight and pushed the Italians back into Albania. By March 1941, the Italians had been soundly defeated and it was necessary to commit German forces to restore the situation. Hitler could not afford the political consequences of leaving an ally – even a disobedient one – unsupported.

As German plans to invade Greece were advanced, Yugoslavia's cooperation was demanded. When the government gave it, a coup was staged, which in turn prompted German invasion. Although organized resistance ended fairly quickly, a large segment of the Yugoslav population continued the fight. Yugoslavia became the site of the largest of all anti-German partisan movements.

Meanwhile, Greece came under attack from the Bulgarian and Yugoslavian frontiers and could not resist. Allied troops coming to help arrived too late and had to be evacuated, resulting in heavy shipping losses. Many of the survivors were sent to Crete.

By 30 April 1941, Greece was in enemy hands, along with those Balkan nations that were not active members of the Axis. It was deemed necessary to capture Crete from the Allies. A seaborne invasion was possible but might be costly. The alternative was for the main offensive force to arrive by parachute. Thus the invasion of Crete was undertaken as an airborne operation. This was a first; previously, airborne troops had been used to

The original Axis intention was to conquer the Balkans by diplomacy rather than invading. But seeking an easy victory, Mussolini committed the alliance to an unnecessary conflict that drained manpower and derailed diplomatic initiatives.

The MG-34, and its later replacement the MG-42, was a versatile weapon that could be tripod-mounted for air and ground defence or could be dismounted and used with the integral folding bipod, increasing tactical mobility.

seize strategic objectives ahead of an advance by conventional forces. The ability of paratroops to capture and hold an objective in their own right had not been proven.

Crete was held in some strength, having been reinforced by troops evacuated from Egypt. However, invasion by sea was expected and this guided the defenders' thinking. After the airborne landings began, an attempt was made to bring in additional forces by sea. It was roughly handled by the Royal Navy, but this was not decisive. For the attackers, the key was to capture airfields into which supplies and reinforcements could be flown.

Resistance was heavy, and it was two days before an airfield could be secured well enough to fly reinforcements into, and then only at some risk. However, this sealed the fate of the Allied forces on Crete. As German strength on the island grew, it became obvious that the Allied troops would have to be evacuated before they became trapped and forced to surrender. The evacuation was completed by 31 May. Those forces remaining on the island were compelled to surrender.

The airborne invasion of Crete was a success, but at such a high cost that

CONFLICTING AXIS AGENDAS

Political control of the Balkans was important to Hitler's goal of invading and destroying the Soviet Union, and this could (he believed) be achieved without military force. However, Mussolini wanted a victory of his own; Italian participation in the fall of France had been unimpressive and Mussolini decided that a rapid invasion of Greece was necessary to restore his prestige.

no further operations of this kind were mounted. Nevertheless, the Western Allies had been ejected from mainland Europe and their prestige further dented by defeats in Greece and Crete. There had been some hope that Turkey might be persuaded to join the fight against the Axis, but this was greatly diminished by events in Greece.

REVERSALS IN THE DESERT

Dismayed at the hammering received by his Italian allies, Hitler decided that German forces must become involved in the battle for North Africa. Two armoured divisions were set up, forming what would become famous as the Afrika Korps, under the command of Erwin Rommel.

Rommel was an extremely aggressive commander; indeed, he had a tendency to ignore his orders and attack regardless, and to run out of control. He also achieved spectacular results, as he had shown in command of Panzers in France and light troops during World War I.

Rommel was an extremely aggressive commander; indeed, he had a tendency to ignore his orders and attack regardless, and to run out of control.

The British had established a defensive line at El Agheila on the Gulf of Sirte. The need to detach troops to Greece had weakened the position, and in addition the British were not really expecting an attack. Rommel's

British troops with the ubiquitous Bren gun in a sandbagged strongpoint. Although the term General-Purpose Machine-Gun had not yet been coined, it described the Bren very well. This weapon was used for everything.

A rooftop position in a North African town. Urban combat was rare in the desert war compared to Europe, but towns tended to be found where there was a road and water, offering natural strongpoints to base a defence.

forces were not fully ashore when he began offensive operations for which he was, on the face of it, too weak.

The El Agheila position was forced on 30 March 1941 and Rommel began an advance along the coast, disregarding his orders, which were far more cautious than he liked. Using a reversal of the British tactic at Beda Fomm, Rommel sent elements of his force around the British rear using difficult desert tracks while the rest of his command advanced up the coast road. The British tried to make a stand on a line from Derna on the coast to Mekill inland, but after a short battle they were forced to retreat once again.

The Allies were pushed back past Tobruk, which was besieged from 11 April onwards, and fell back eastwards until a new line was established on 15 April. Rommel wanted to smash this line and drive on Egypt, but Hitler sent the rather more cautious von Paulus to rein Rommel in. Thus the Afrika Korps and its Italian allies were ordered to establish a defensive line facing the British and to reduce Tobruk.

The situation in the desert was now critical, and the British desperately needed more tanks. The decision was made to rush a convoy carrying 300 tanks straight down the Mediterranean despite the Italian fleet, U-boats and anything else that might get in the way, rather than to take the safer but much longer route

Left: German infantry and tanks in Eastern Europe, summer 1941. The Wehrmacht entered Russia unprepared for the weather conditions. It was expected that they would defeat the Soviet Union before the onset of winter.

around the southern tip of Africa and into Egypt via the Suez Canal.

The operation was a success despite the grave risks, and the increased tank strength enabled the British to launch an attack on 15 May 1941. Although an initial success, the operation ran into difficulties caused by well sited anti-tank guns, which halted the tanks. An armoured counterattack then drove them off with heavy casualties. A second British attack on 15 June was also unsuccessful, leaving Tobruk cut off far behind enemy lines.

Meanwhile, Iraq had joined the Axis side after a coup, and German forces were also active elsewhere in the Middle East. Syria was controlled by Vichy France and had begun receiving German troops. This threatened the Allies' oil supplies and necessitated a campaign to restore the situation.

A combined force of British, Indian, Australian and Free French troops entered Syria on 8 June and took Damascus within a fortnight. Elements of this force then drove on Baghdad and forced an armistice by the end of May.

Meanwhile, German attention was on the invasion of Russia, which brought the Soviet Union into the war on the side of the Allies. To Hitler, North Africa was a sideshow that was important only as a possible means to open up a southern flank into Russia. For the Allies, however, the region was much more important. Clearing Iraq allowed a line of communications between the British in Egypt and the Soviets via the Middle East, and did away with the distraction in the rear. Offensive operations in the desert would not, however, resume for some time.

OPERATION BARBAROSSA

Hitler made treaties of non-aggression with the Soviet Union, but he always considered that it would be an enemy at some point in the future. Now, worsening relations, partly caused by tensions in the Balkans, prompted

> Hitler made treaties of non-aggression with the Soviet Union, but he always considered that it would be an enemy at some point in the future.

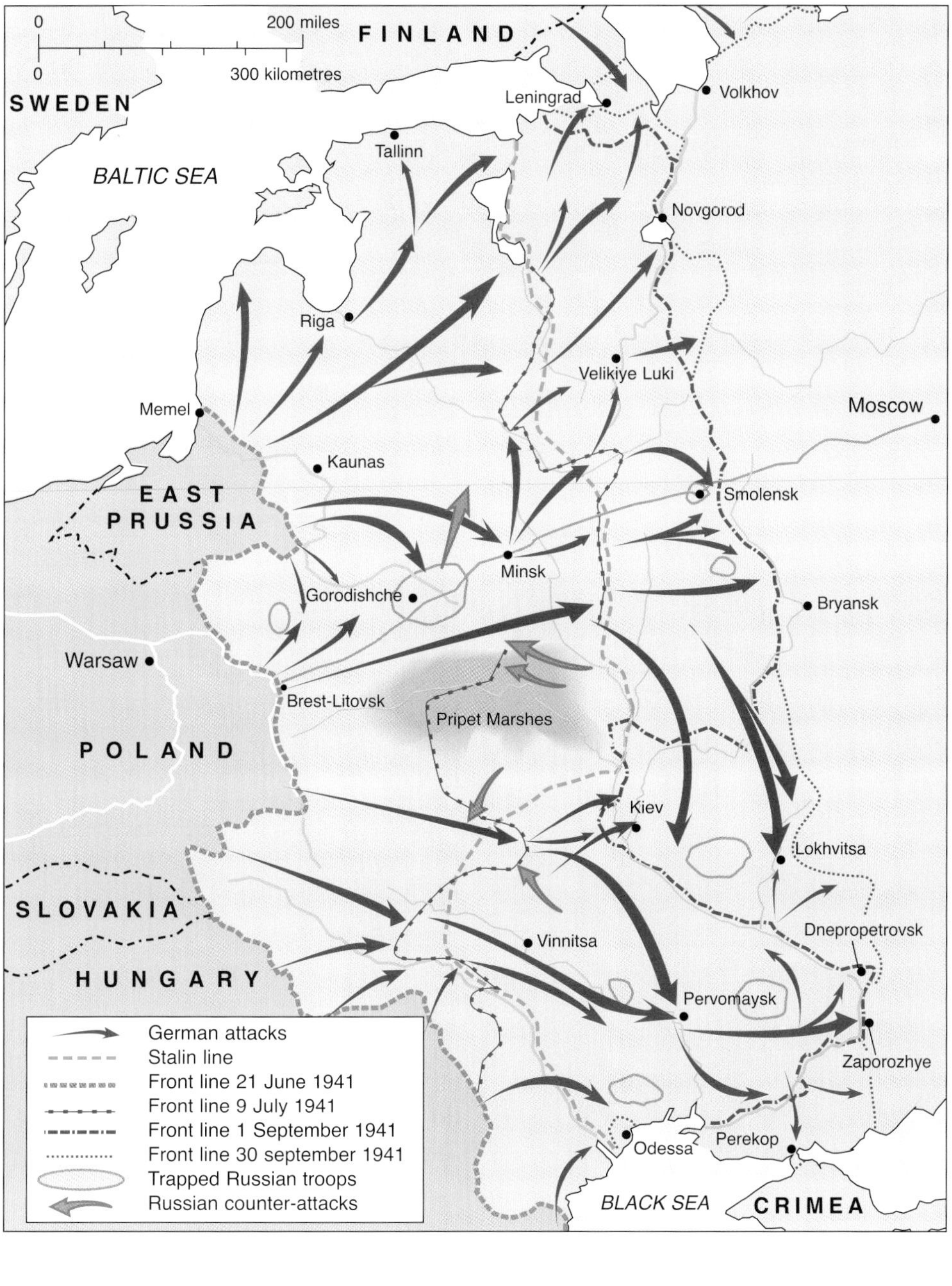

Above: In the first weeks of Operation Barbarossa, the situation on the Soviet side was very confused. Coherent and up-to-date orders were rare, and it fell to the ordinary soldiers of the Soviet Union to fight back as best they could.

Hitler to bring forward his plans for an invasion of the Soviet Union.

Previous armies to advance eastwards had been largely defeated by the great distances involved, but Hitler was confident that the mobility of his Panzer forces would enable them to cover the ground swiftly and overturn the defence wherever it was encountered. Codenamed Operation *Barbarossa*, the invasion had a chance of success and, indeed, came close to reaching its objectives.

The frontier was split by the vast expanse of the Pripet Marshes, which more or less divided the offensive into two theatres. To the north of the marshes lay the Baltic coast and the road to Moscow. The latter was critical not only as a political symbol but also as the logistics and transport hub of

Left: Operation Barbarossa was essentially an advance on a front the width of Europe. Early successes suggested that the plan might actually work, but even for the mighty Wehrmacht, the undertaking was simply too large.

A German infantry gun team. Support weapons of this kind were essential to combined-arms combat and were used for direct fire against enemy strongpoints when tanks and assault guns were not available.

the region. The loss of Moscow might or might not have shaken the Soviets badly enough to force a surrender, but it would certainly have deprived them of major industry and made the task of fighting back much harder.

To the south of the marshes lay the Ukraine and the industry of the Donetz basin and, further east, the oilfields of the Caucasus. Possession of these would be of immense benefit to the German war effort.

The plan was for Army Groups North and Centre, deployed north of the marshes, to break through and destroy immediate opposition, then support each other as they pushed on to their objectives. Army Group North was to drive up the Baltic coast and take Leningrad while Army Group Centre attacked along the Minsk-Smolensk-Moscow axis, taking the capital and major cities before the summer's end. This arm of the campaign would be aided by operations on the northern flank. German and Finnish forces were to attack into the former Finnish territories ceded after the Winter War. This would threaten Leningrad from the north and distract Soviet attention from the main thrust. South of the marshes, Army Group South was to use its armoured troops for a rapid envelopment of Soviet forces in the Ukraine, while other formations advanced from Romania to pin and distract the enemy. Next, Army Group South (AGS) would drive rapidly eastwards across the Ukraine towards the Donetz Basin and the Caucasus.

LOW READINESS IN THE RED ARMY

The Soviet Union had large forces available, but these were in a poor state of readiness. Many senior officers were inexperienced as a result of the recent purges, and although the army possessed the arms and equipment of a modern force it was lacking in many of the factors that make an army work – communications, logistics and general organizational ability. This made it difficult to respond coherently to a threat and made the consequences of defeat more severe.

The forces committed were enormous – about three million men on the German side alone – but there was insufficient Panzer strength for the task at hand and most infantry formations were unable to keep up with the lead units' advance. Logistics would also become a major problem before long.

Nevertheless, Hitler was sure that the Soviets would quickly cave in. He announced that the racially inferior Slavic soldiers could not withstand the Aryan onslaught, and in any case the average Russian soldier was unwilling to fight for the communist regime. There was also a feeling that the Soviet army was incompetent. This was a not unreasonable assumption, given its performance in the Winter War, but the worst effects of Stalin's purges were now over and the Red Army had learnt from its mistakes.

Operational reconnaissance was sketchy, where it existed at all. This was perhaps necessary, as it was hoped to achieve strategic surprise and a sudden increase in overflights would signal that something was afoot. However, it did mean that the German forces had at best a vague idea what they were about to face.

Stalin himself received warning from the Allies and his own reconnaissance units that the German frontier was active. However, he refused to allow his commanders to mobilize or prepare for attack and even denounced some of the warnings as Allied trickery.

Although the Soviets possessed many tanks, the vast majority of these were light vehicles or poor designs that were not up to direct combat with German Panzers.

Although the Soviets possessed large numbers of tanks, the vast majority of these were light vehicles or poor designs that were not up to direct combat with German Panzers. The T-34 and KV-1 were both entirely capable, but these were a minority. Tank forces suffered from disorganization, as they were then in the process of being remodelled into German-style mechanized formations, and logistics arrangements were also rudimentary.

DELAYED LAUNCH

The invasion was launched on 22 June 1941, instead of May as originally planned. Initially the German spearheads made excellent progress against disjointed and relatively ineffectual resistance. Rapid pincer attacks resulted in the encirclement of large forces, which were then forced to surrender. The Red Army haemorrhaged men and matériel in the first weeks of the campaign.

Orders emanating from high command indicate just how confused the situation on the Soviet side became. Formations that had been

KV-1 HEAVY TANK

Type: Infantry tank

Crew: 5

Powerplant: one V-2K V-12 diesel engine developing 448kW (600hp)

Weight: 43,000kg (94,600lb)

Range: 150km (93 miles)

Armour: 100mm (3.94in)

Armament: one 7.62mm (0.30in) gun; four 7.62mm (0.30in) machine guns

Performance: maximum road speed 35km/h (21.75mph); fording not known; vertical obstacle 1.2m (3ft 8in); trench 2.59m (8ft 6in)

Dimensions: length 6.68m (21ft 11in)
width 3.32m (10ft 11in)
height 2.71m (8ft 11in)

A PanzerKampfwagen II. Early in the war, these light vehicles had to fill in for battle tanks, but by 1941 sufficient numbers of heavier tanks were available and the PzKpfw II could revert to its intended armoured reconnaissance platform role.

shattered or were retreating in tatters were ordered to counterattack and destroy the enemy. Other forces might have been able to comply had they possessed sufficient supplies or received their orders in time; communications equipment was insufficient and the situation was exacerbated by poor procedures.

Progress was less rapid in the south, where the Panzer spearhead suffered heavy losses from an armoured counterattack involving more than a thousand Soviet vehicles. The battle raged for four days before the attacking force was eliminated. However, even where resistance was strongest the invasion forces kept moving eastwards.

By the middle of July, the German army had driven deep into Soviet territory and destroyed several entire armies, taking hundreds of thousands of prisoners. The Baltic states were 'liberated' and some forces were raised from them to fight against the Soviets. However, German supply lines were becoming dangerously stretched. Foraging was made difficult by the traditional Russian policy of 'scorched earth'.

More than just distance conspired to make the logistics task difficult. Soviet railways ran on a wider gauge than in Europe and many German locomotives lacked the range to travel between water and fuel stops in the vast countryside. Partisans in Poland, together with the remnants of Soviet military units that had been bypassed, attacked the logistics tail and inflicted a steady drain on its capacity to supply the units at the front.

The Panzer forces, spearheading the advance, had to be halted at times to allow the supply chain and supporting infantry formations to catch up. This invited counterattacks, which further drained ammunition and fuel supplies, imposing further delays. The worst problem was the terrible state of the Russian roads,

Many of the anti-tank guns available to the Soviet army were outdated short-barrelled weapons that produced a low muzzle velocity and could not penetrate the heavier German tanks.

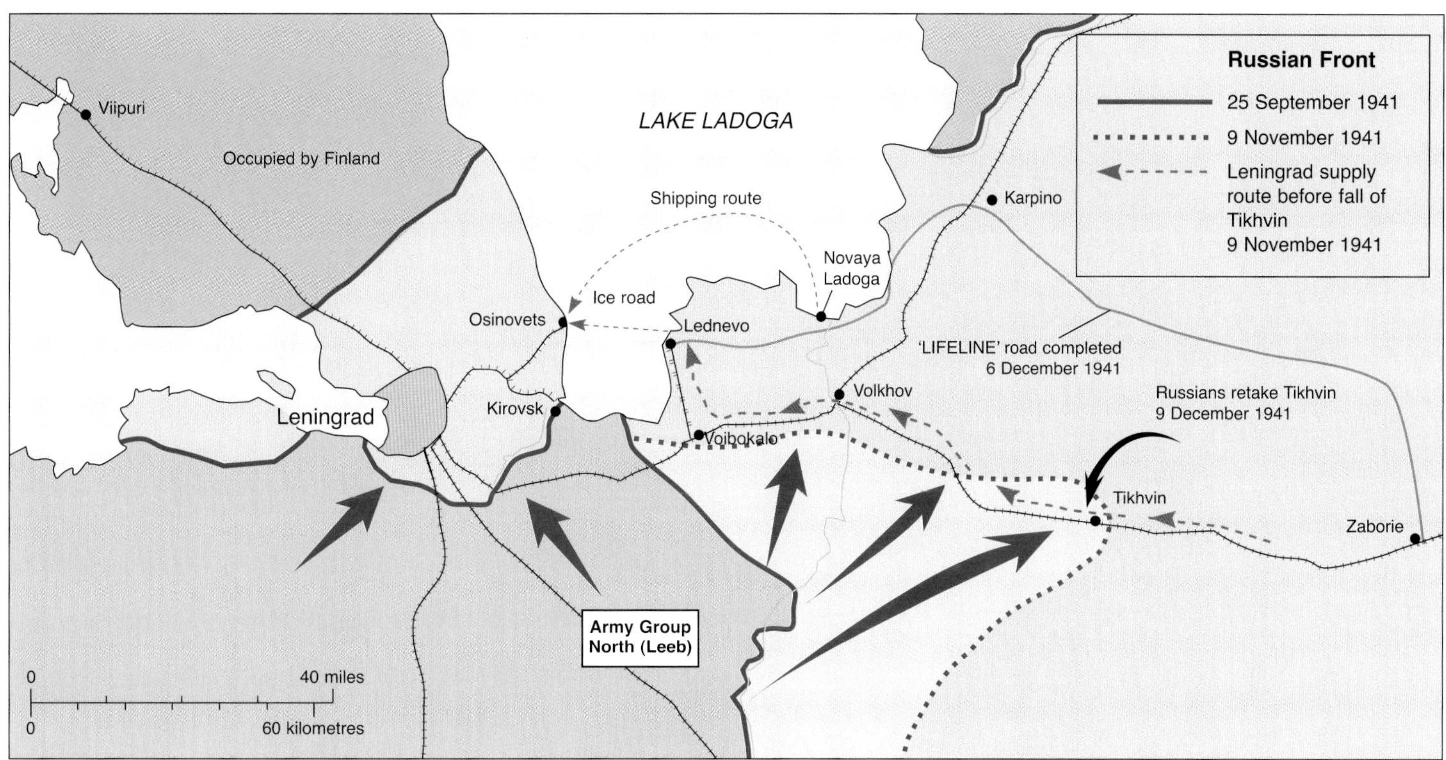

Leningrad was the first of the great city-sieges of the war. Although the German advance reached the city and all but cut it off, a tenuous supply line running across Lake Ladoga enabled the defenders to hold out.

which took a heavy toll on tanks as they pushed forward. The need for repairs took more Panzers out of action than the enemy.

The situation was not improved by Hitler's interference. He disagreed with his army commanders about whether or not Moscow should be the main objective, and pulled Panzer formations out of the advance to assist elsewhere at a time when the concentration of force was of critical importance.

> By the middle of July, the German army had driven deep into Soviet territory and destroyed several entire armies, taking hundreds of thousands of prisoners.

However, the advance got moving again and further gains were made despite stiffening resistance. Early in August, the port of Odessa on the Black Sea was surrounded, though it was not taken until October. On 19 August, the first German forces reached Leningrad. Rather than assault the city, it was decided to besiege it and starve the defenders out while pounding them with artillery and air attacks. A Finnish offensive in the region should have completed the encirclement, but a small corridor was kept open to supply the city across Lake Ladoga. The siege of Leningrad began in earnest on 15 September and would continue for most of the rest of the war.

Meanwhile, Army Group Centre continued its advance on Moscow despite being delayed by having its armoured forces continually retasked elsewhere. The going got harder as the autumn *Rasputiza*, or 'Season of Mud', began and the advance slowed down still further. Yet still the Germans were able to advance, driving Panzer forces into the enemy to create gaps and then following up with infantry formations.

MOSCOW UNDER SIEGE

On 19 October, the Soviet government declared that Moscow was under a state of siege. Josef Stalin remained in the city, whose defence was now in the hands of Georgi Zhukov. Although the Germans ground their way into the outer limits of Moscow, the nearest they got was a point some 19km (12 miles) from the city centre. This was on 30 November; less than a week later, further attacks on Moscow were put on hold. The Russian winter then began to close in, creating a new problem for the German army. The plan had been for

In the early days of Operation Barbarossa, confidence was high. The Wehrmacht had overrun all its enemies and were led to believe that the Russians would collapse if pushed hard. It was some time before reality intruded.

the Soviet Union to be conquered by the onset of winter, and a relatively small garrison to remain there. Instead, the German army was forced to try to live and fight in conditions for which it was wholly unprepared.

There were other problems, too. Confident now that Japan was not about to attack the Soviet Union, Stalin was able to call in large reserves from Siberia, which could be used on the European front. The level of competence in the Red Army was also rising fast, its leaders and personnel having served a bloody apprenticeship since the invasion began. The armoured forces were already being reorganized when Operation *Barbarossa* began. Now the Red Army created strategic reserves of artillery and air units, which could be deployed where concentration was most necessary. Logistics, communications, and command and control procedures were all tightened up. The effects would take some time to show results, but the days of the Red Army as a large but clumsy blunt instrument were over.

A Soviet counteroffensive was launched on 6 December. This used a new formation, the Shock Army; a formation about the size of a German Corps optimized for highly aggressive short-term operations. The offensive did a lot of damage but was fought to a stalemate. However, the situation

> Hitler demanded a policy of holding ground at all costs while his commanders asked permission for a more elastic defence, making tactical withdrawals were necessary.

caused problems at the highest level on the Axis side. Hitler demanded a policy of holding ground at all costs while the commanders at the front asked permission to adopt a more elastic defence, making tactical withdrawals were necessary. The resulting arguments resulted in the sacking of all three Army Group commanders and the assumption of direct command by Hitler himself.

On Hitler's orders, his units in the Soviet Union stood their ground and fought wherever they were. On the line of communications, garrisons that would otherwise have been pulled in and amalgamated into parent units were left out in the wind. Soviet forces getting into the German rear overran some, but others were able to hold out and repel Soviet attacks that were too weak and poorly supplied to break them.

As far as Hitler was concerned, this validated his policy. If only his soldiers would have courage and stand their ground, the *Führer* believed, they could beat off any attack. This delusion would cost many thousands of lives before the end of the war.

By the end of 1941, a state of stalemate existed in Russia although Stalin was planning a grand offensive to drive the Germans and their allies out. Meanwhile, war had broken out in the Pacific. On 7 December 1941, Japan attacked the US fleet base at Pearl Harbor in Hawaii, inflicting heavy damage. This was part of a plan to establish a defensive buffer zone in the Pacific and prevent American interference in the Japanese expansion that was taking place in Southeast Asia.

THE DRIVE ON SINGAPORE

Japan was able to gain control of much of Southeast Asia by a combination of threats, diplomacy and rapid, aggressive military action. Some nations agreed to ally with

A supply column moves through the Russian landscape. Mobility was not much of a problem in summer or in winter when the ground froze solid. In between the two, the land turned to a sea of mud and made movement very difficult.

Japan or become client states, fearing that they could not resist Japan's effective army. Others put up a fight and were overrun.

This expansion threatened the British fleet base at Singapore. The plan to defend it – scattering forces all over the Malay Peninsula in order to protect the airbases there – was rather poor. However, there were few aircraft available to use the bases, which made the deployments pointless.

Attempts to resist the Japanese drive down Malaya towards Singapore were dislocated by aggressive advances through supposedly impassable terrain that placed Japanese troops in position to attack unprepared units.

When war was declared on Japan by Britain and the United States in December 1941, Japanese forces were already in position to drive on Singapore.

The result was a piecemeal defence, which was further hamstrung by '1917 thinking'. Far too much emphasis was placed on forming a neat defensive line and establishing contact with flanking units. There was also a tendency to fixate on roads and to assume that the jungle was impassable. Yet, as the Japanese army had demonstrated time and again, it was possible to move significant forces through the jungle, bypassing tough positions to attack from the rear or to force a retreat, which could then be ambushed.

When war was declared on Japan by Britain and the United States in December 1941, Japanese forces were

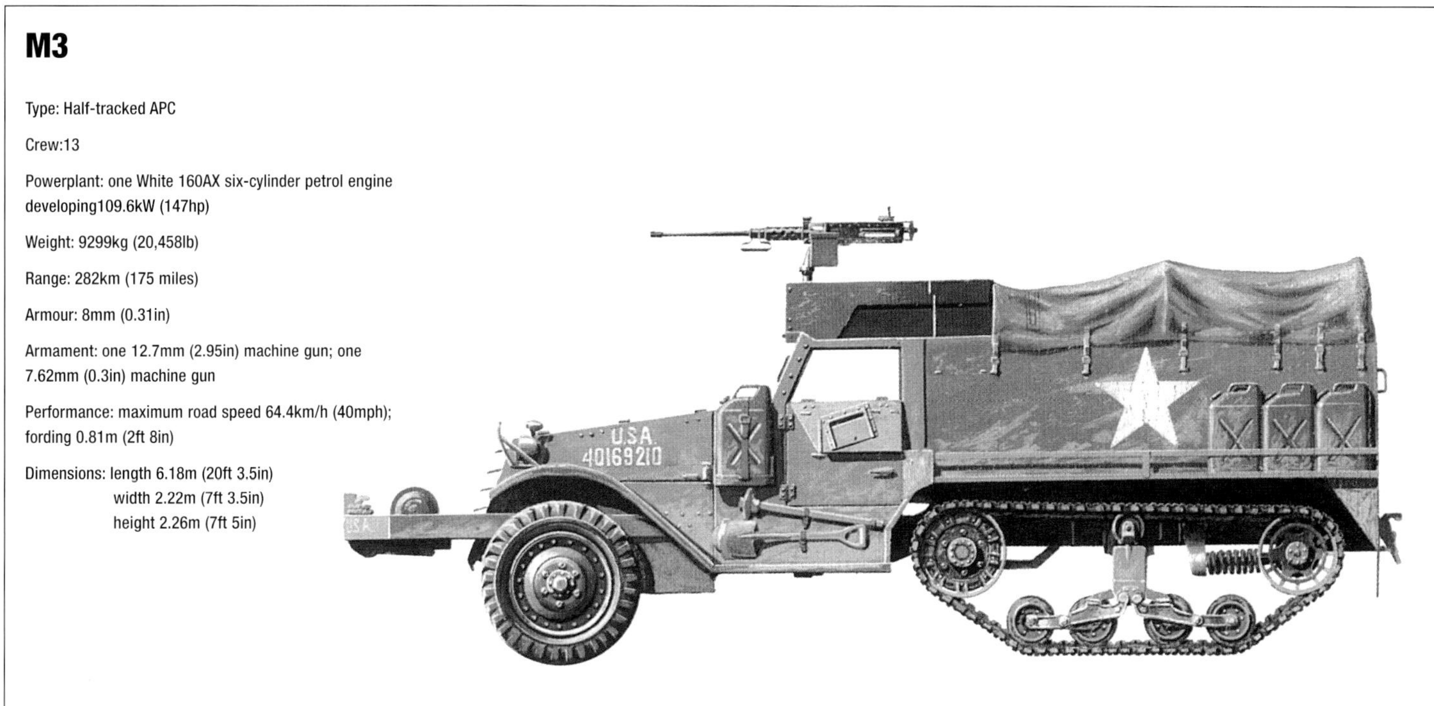

M3

Type: Half-tracked APC

Crew:13

Powerplant: one White 160AX six-cylinder petrol engine developing109.6kW (147hp)

Weight: 9299kg (20,458lb)

Range: 282km (175 miles)

Armour: 8mm (0.31in)

Armament: one 12.7mm (2.95in) machine gun; one 7.62mm (0.3in) machine gun

Performance: maximum road speed 64.4km/h (40mph); fording 0.81m (2ft 8in)

Dimensions: length 6.18m (20ft 3.5in)
width 2.22m (7ft 3.5in)
height 2.26m (7ft 5in)

already in position to drive on Singapore. Some formations came overland, advancing around the northern end of the Gulf of Siam and down the Isthmus of Kra. However, the majority of forces landed on the east coast of the peninsula.

An attempt by the Royal Navy to interfere with the landings led to the loss of the capital ships *Prince of Wales* and *Repulse* for no gain, while land forces achieved little against most of the amphibious operations. Once established ashore, the Japanese advanced quickly, using further amphibious landings to turn the flanks of successive positions.

Eventually, the British and Imperial troops were pushed back onto the island of Singapore itself. The Japanese made a difficult amphibious assault across the narrow channel to the mainland, and after heavy fighting on the island the defenders were forced to surrender on 15 February 1942. The loss of Singapore had significant consequences for the course of the war, as it opened Australia to attack and deprived the Royal Navy of its forward base in the Far East. The consequences for the British Empire reached even further.

Meanwhile, other British Empire forces were able to retreat through Burma in the direction of India. Their rearguard actions were better handled than the defence of Singapore, and the Japanese armoured forces in particular became wary of aggressive advances after being mauled by British troops operating American-made M3 Stuart light tanks. The Allies were able to establish a defensive position at Imphal on the India/Burma border. Here, they built up their strength until an attack into Japanese-held territory became possible.

THE NEW YEAR IN RUSSIA

The German army had gone into Russia assured of a quick victory like those in Poland, Denmark and France. It was entirely unprepared for the savage conditions of the Russian winter. The Soviets were properly equipped, but were struggling to overcome other difficulties caused by inefficiency in the army.

THE DEFENCE OF MALAYA COLLAPSES

Conventional wisdom said that tanks could not be used in the jungle, but the Japanese were able to do so. Their armour was light and not very good, but against British and Imperial troops unprepared for armoured attack it was decisive in several actions. The Japanese advance, especially that of the small tank force, was aggressive to the point of recklessness, keeping the defenders off balance and demoralized.

The result was a steady collapse of the British positions as one hurried defensive line and then the next was broken through or forced into retreat by flanking forces. There were a few stubborn actions, but for the most part the defence of Malaya was badly handled and had all the hallmarks of being an attempt to stave off the inevitable rather than a serious attempt to defeat the advance.

At the beginning of 1942, the Soviets launched their winter offensive. Stalin hoped to drive the Germans straight back out of his country, and wanted a massive campaign leading to decisive victory. The Red Army was not in any condition to deliver this, though initially it seemed like it might be possible.

The German forces had been ordered to hold their positions, no matter how exposed, and were thus dug in as well as was possible in the frozen ground wherever their advance had ended. Russian counterattacks in November and December had been beaten off, but the Germans were in a difficult position.

Army Group Centre, facing Moscow, adopted a system of defensive 'hedgehogs' (also used elsewhere) and struggled to cling to its positions. Although some penetration of the German line was achieved by the Soviets, the situation remained largely unchanged for some time.

In the southern sector, a major Soviet counteroffensive got underway on 1 January, attacking the invaders near Kursk. Although a hole was punched in the German lines and a penetration of some 32km (20 miles) was achieved, the German response was efficient and effective. Formations on the flanks of the breakthrough held their positions, attempting to prevent a collapse of the front while that penetration was contained. The Soviet advance now ran out of momentum and the situation was stabilized.

The first winter in Russia was a time of great suffering for the German army. Amid extremely low temperatures, the Soviets struck back, forcing the invaders to fight in unfamiliar conditions.

Army Group North continued to besiege Leningrad throughout this period. The city was entirely cut off for a time and starvation killed tens of thousands every month.

Late in 1941, the Soviets managed to get large numbers of troops across the Straits of Kerch, which separate the Black Sea from the Sea of Azov. This gave them a foothold in the Crimea, from which to try to relieve Sevastopol. The heavily fortified port was under siege and far behind the main German lines. Unable to reach it by land through the Ukraine, the Soviets took the indirect route.

Heavy fighting took place over the next two months, and the port of Feodosiya changed hands twice. Red Army elements from Sevastopol tried to break out and join the fighting but were contained, and by March the offensive had wound down into stalemate. German troops retook the Kerch peninsula in May, dashing hopes of relieving Sevastopol, and returned to the task of reducing the fortress.

A monstrous 800mm (31in) railway gun nicknamed 'Dora', one of two built to destroy the Maginot Line, bombarded the forts around the city. These were the largest guns of all time, and the defenders had no reply. In the middle of July, Sevastopol fell.

By this time, German forces were pushing eastwards again, launching a summer offensive towards Stalingrad and southward into the Caucasus. This was intended to secure Russian grain and oil production for German use and to threaten the Allied position in the Middle East. It might also convince Turkey to join the war on the Axis side.

Army Group North continued to besiege Leningrad throughout this period. The city was entirely cut off for a time and starvation killed tens of thousands every month. A road was forced through the forests to the edge of Lake Ladoga, but from there supplies could reach the city only on barges or, if the lake were frozen, trucks moving over the ice. This thin lifeline kept the city alive, though just

Japanese air strikes at the beginning of the Pacific war gained them air superiority for a time, and this was used both to permit further air strikes and to make amphibious assaults against Allied bases.

Above: Early in the Pacific war, the Japanese seemed unstoppable. The Allies were driven from Malaya and Singapore, from the Philippines and other islands. There were fears the Japanese flag might be raised in Australia and New Zealand.

barely, and resistance continued as best the defenders could manage. German forces shelled Leningrad steadily. However, with its seaward flank covered by the fortress of Kronstadt and the Russian Baltic Fleet, and with insufficient forces available to storm the city, all the invaders could do was to try slowly to crush the life out of Leningrad.

JAPANESE IN THE PACIFIC

Just hours after the strike on Pearl Harbor, Japanese aircraft savaged the US air forces in the Philippines, catching them on the ground and wholly unprepared for attack. Having thus gained air superiority, the Japanese began to land ground forces on 22 December 1941. The main targets were Luzon and

Mindanao, the largest and most important islands of the Philippines, but several other islands were also secured at the same time. The Japanese intent was for the main US force to be trapped in a pocket around Manila on Luzon, and the assault was based on the assumption that US troops would try to defend the capital. However, large numbers of US and Filipino troops escaped from the trap and reached the nearby Bataan peninsula.

During the delaying actions covering the retreat, elements of the US 26th Cavalry made what may have been the last cavalry charge in history, getting in among surprised Japanese infantry and causing havoc with their hard-hitting .45 calibre semi-automatic handguns. US forces were able to hold out in the Bataan peninsula until early April and the fortress island of Corregidor lasted until 7 May. All remaining US forces in the Philippines surrendered along with Corregidor, though segments of the Filipino army went into hiding and began a guerrilla campaign against the occupiers.

> The outbreak of war in the Far East had diverted Allied attention, while the Axis had been overwhelmingly concerned with the invasion of Russia.

Having already more or less driven the Allied navies from the southwest Pacific, the Japanese had quickly overrun the Dutch East Indies and by early March 1942 were fairly secure in that region. With the Philippines as a base, they were also able to take several islands that had previously been out of reach, with much of New Guinea in Japanese hands and bases being developed in the Solomon Islands.

Trucks move along the Coast Road in North Africa. The fighting went back and forth along this road as first the Allies and then the Axis forces were driven back only to regroup and push forward again.

Japanese advances in the Pacific theatre were ultimately curtailed by a sea battle – the carrier action of the Coral Sea – but it would be some time before the pendulum swung the other way. In the meantime, fighting continued in New Guinea and along the Burmese frontier.

NORTH AFRICA

A period of relative quiet had existed in North Africa since the middle of 1941, for various reasons. The outbreak of war in the Far East had diverted Allied attention, while the Axis had been overwhelmingly concerned with the invasion of Russia. Both sides had tried to build up their strength and had to overcome different problems.

The Allies were operating at the end of a long supply line through contested seas, while the Axis supply chain was much shorter but ran past Malta. Air and sea units operating out of the island were at times able to cripple Rommel's supply lines, though on other occasions the island was so heavily beset that its defenders could do nothing but try to survive the latest onslaught. Finally, the British achieved a slight superiority in North Africa and opened an offensive in late November 1941. Codenamed Operation *Crusader,* the attack achieved surprise and made good initial gains. However, the forces in Tobruk, ordered to break out and link up with the advancing Eighth Army (as the British force in the region had been renamed), were unable to do so. The operation then stalled for a time.

The Eighth Army got going again before the end of the year and drove through to Gazala by 7 December 1941. By the end of the year, they were back at El Agheila. However, the British position was tenuous. At the very end of a long supply line, weary and with many of its vehicles down for maintenance, the Eighth Army was vulnerable to a bold counterattack.

Rommel, who by now had richly earned his nickname of 'The Desert Fox', was just the man to launch one. He succeeded in driving the British all the way back to Gazala by 4 February. The front line remained stable until 12 May, at which point Rommel launched a renewed offensive. Although outnumbered and equipped mainly with inferior Italian tanks, Rommel sent his armoured forces

> Beating off repeated attacks, Rommel forced the logistics corridor wider open and was able to re-supply his armour sufficiently to launch an attack of his own.

General Erwin Rommel, the 'Desert Fox', preferred to command from the front. He moved from one unit to another and saw the situation for himself. This was almost his undoing on more than one occasion, but most of the time it was a highly effective command method.

The Wehrmacht made extensive use of motorcycles, for reconnaissance purposes and as light weapons carriers. A sidecar could carry only a machine gun, but this created a fast-moving reconnaissance unit with reasonable fighting capability against infantry.

hooking into the rear of the British positions and achieved considerable initial success.

At that point, the attack came unstuck, with the Axis armour trapped behind the main British line and under attack from several directions. The only avenue for supplies was a narrow corridor though the main line. Beating off repeated attacks, Rommel forced the logistics corridor wider open and was able to re-supply his armour sufficiently to launch an attack of his own.

The Gazala line collapsed in the face of this offensive, and Rommel gave chase all across North Africa, driving the British all the way to El Alamein on the Egyptian border. Tobruk was swept up more or less in passing; its fall owed a lot to the suddenness of the Axis breakthrough.

By the end of June 1942, Egypt was under severe threat. The Eighth Army was dug in between El Alamein on the coast and the impassable Qattara Depression inland. This was an extremely strong position that would be impossible to flank. Rommel needed to build up his strength for renewed operations, which granted the Allies a respite. He was suffering from severe logistics problems caused by operating at the end of a long supply line, much as the Allies had at El Agheila.

Rommel attacked the Alamein line on 1 July, but ran into heavy Allied resistance. The next day, the renewed attack was met with a largely unsuccessful Allied counterattack. However, the strength of the opposition caused Rommel to go over to the defensive while he waited for reinforcements.

The Allies launched an attack of their own on 10 July 1942, ushering a period of to-and-fro fighting on a fairly local level. This wore out the British strength, and operations were ceased on 31 July. Efforts were made to shore up the Allies positions in case Rommel attacked again, but in the

Aircraft could strike over great distances and sink ships. However, aircraft required bases and the carriers could not be everywhere. Many ground actions fought on Pacific islands were intended to secure suitable bases or deny them to the enemy.

southern sector the preparations were not completed when the Axis forces renewed the offensive on 30 August.

Rommel's armoured forces attempted a right hook around the main defensive line, but ran into unexpectedly heavy resistance. A breakthrough was achieved the next day and the armour then advanced on Alam el Halfa, where they were engaged by anti-tank guns, tanks and artillery in good defensive positions on high ground. With casualties mounting, the chance of success diminishing and the fuel situation becoming desperate, Rommel decided to break off the operation and pulled back to his own lines. The attack at Alam el Halfa was the high water mark of the Axis campaign in North Africa. They made no further progress towards Egypt and, after a period of build-up, it was the Allies that renewed the offensive.

TURNING THE PACIFIC TIDE

In the middle of 1942, Japanese hopes for the war were dealt a smashing blow at the Battle of Midway. Four aircraft carriers and their highly trained air groups were destroyed in addition to other naval casualties. This seriously affected the ability of the Imperial Japanese Navy to project power and also improved morale among the Allies, who up to that point had few victories to celebrate.

Nevertheless, the Japanese were uncomfortably close to the Australian mainland. From their regional command post at Rabaul on New Britain, Japanese commanders oversaw operations to establish air bases in the Solomon Islands and the gradual reduction of resistance on New Guinea. Victory there was the final stepping-stone to an invasion of Australia.

After a landing at Gona in New Guinea, Japanese forces brushed aside opposition and pushed inland to Kokoda, arriving on 27 July 1942. The main objective from there was to push directly south to Port Moresby. However, this proved to be a difficult undertaking, even for Japanese troops who were highly experienced in jungle warfare.

The island of Tulagi was occupied by the Japanese with the intention of setting up a seaplane base. After a damaging air raid, the island was more or less left alone until assaulted in the Solomon Islands campaign.

> The defeat at Midway seriously affected the ability of the Imperial Japanese Navy to project power and also improved morale among the Allies.

On 26 August, an operation against Milne Bay got ashore but was withdrawn in the face of Australian counterattacks by 5 September. Then, on 11 September, the Australians turned back a drive down the Owen Stanley Range towards Milne Bay.

Meanwhile, supply problems, combined with Australian resistance, slowed the advance on Port Moresby so that it was not until 16 September that Japanese forces got within 40km (25 miles) of their objective. There, they were forced to hold while

problems elsewhere distracted the attention of the commanders in Rabaul.

On 7 August, an Allied fleet landed troops in the Solomon Islands, destroying the Japanese seaplane base at Tulagi and clearing minor forces off some of the other islands. The main operation was against the island of Guadalcanal, where the Japanese were building an air base.

While other islands were held almost to the last man, the airfield on Guadalcanal fell quickly and after pushing patrols out to mop up resistance, the Allies set about getting the airfield into operation. This was not without problems. Air attacks out of Rabaul were common and a Japanese cruiser force cut up the Allied naval units covering the beachheads, forcing the withdrawal of transports that had not yet been unloaded.

The Allied campaign in New Guinea was greatly assisted by the naval Battle of the Bismarck Sea, in which a Japanese convoy was shattered.

The Japanese then began running troops into Guadalcanal from destroyers and fast light cruisers. They were not great in number but they put in a determined attack that was beaten off with heavy casualties. Another run resulted in a major naval battle and the loss of several Japanese ships. However, by using fast warships it was possible to get infantry into Guadalcanal at night, albeit without artillery or heavy equipment. Conventional transports could not make the run in time to get clear before Allied aircraft came hunting at daybreak.

JAPANESE STRENGTH

The 'Tokyo Express', as it became known, gradually built up Japanese strength on the island until there was a good chance to dislodge the US forces there. The order to attack was given on 7 September and on 12 September the attack began. The US Marines defending the airfield, now named Henderson Field, were forewarned by a patrol that found a

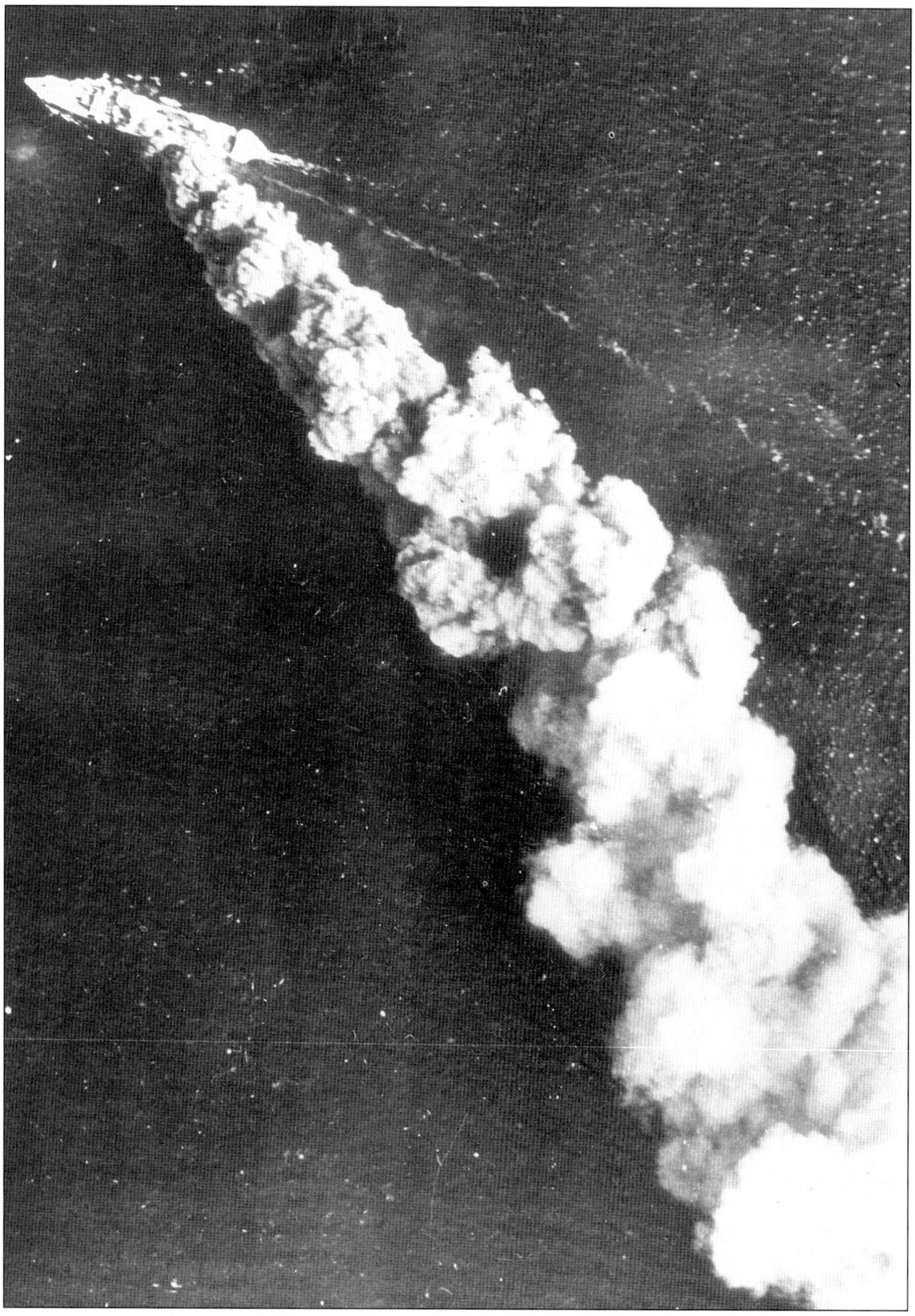

The Japanese decision to reinforce New Guinea, moving troops by sea, brought about a major effort by Allied air units to prevent the transports reaching port, in what became known as the Battle of the Bismarck Sea.

recently abandoned supply base, and they put up heavy resistance.

The main attack lasted two days, in which the fighting was extremely fierce. Some Japanese troops got past the perimeter defences and had to be hunted down, while casualties were high on both sides. The US position was not assisted by an outbreak of dysentery, which debilitated a large number of troops.

Sporadic fighting then went on for some time as more Japanese troops arrived on the island and the Allies tried to dislodge them. The Japanese build-up was completed by late October, and on 23–24 October a renewed and even more intense assault went in. This was supposed to be a concerted attack, but last-minute difficulties caused it to become disjointed. Nevertheless, some attackers got into the Allied positions once again. Japanese high command called off the offensive on 26 October, though the island was contested for some time afterwards.

In thick jungle, combat was at short range. Rifles were less useful than submachineguns and carbines. Victory often depended on spotting the enemy first and laying down intense firepower before he could react.

A German infantry gun crew during the fighting for Stalingrad. Large areas of the city were destroyed by the fire of weapons such as this one, creating a wide expanse of treacherous rubble.

Meanwhile, the Japanese forces in front of Port Moresby had been denied reinforcements and re-supply while the Guadalcanal campaign was fought out. This gave the Allies time to move more troops into Port Moresby and begin a counterattack that slowly forced the Japanese back up the Kokoda trail. The Australians retook Kokoda on 2 November 1942.

Naval action, supported by aircraft flying out of Henderson Field, dictated the fate of Guadalcanal and the rest of the Solomon Islands. The Allies were able to run men and supplies into the islands in quantity, and the Japanese were not. As a result, the Japanese on Guadalcanal were unable to undertake much in the way of offensive action and the initiative shifted to the US forces.

The first US attempt to clear the island was beaten off in the middle of November, but naval losses and the resulting inability to support or supply the troops on the island forced Japanese high command to abandon the campaign on 31 December 1942.

Having achieved naval superiority, the Allies now had the initiative. Rather than expend a great deal of effort on reducing Rabaul, it was decided that the Japanese regional HQ could be bypassed. A series of island-hopping campaigns were mounted to clear the Japanese garrisons out of the Solomons.

The Allied campaign in New Guinea was greatly assisted by the naval Battle of the Bismarck Sea, in which a Japanese convoy carrying reinforcements to New Guinea was shattered. With no additional forces available, the Japanese were gradually ground down and eliminated.

Although the Allies never took Rabaul, it played increasingly little part in the war. Naval supremacy allowed the Allies to strike when and where they chose, and forced the Japanese onto a defensive footing. There were hard years ahead, but the tide had been turned. There were no more Japanese advances in the Pacific.

STALINGRAD

Stalingrad was politically and strategically important to both the Soviet Union and Germany. The city's fate would affect morale on both sides. It was also a major transport nexus and a centre for industry, whose loss would affect the Soviet capability to prosecute the war.

The order to capture Stalingrad was issued on 19 August 1942, though the German army had been advancing in that direction for some time. Things were not going well for the Soviets at the time; Voronezh had already fallen, opening the way for an advance on the city from the northeast. On 23 August, Rostov-on-Don was taken and the northern arm of the German advance reached the Volga.

If the Soviets were pushed out of Stalingrad and across the Volga, it would be virtually impossible to interfere with the Axis advance into the Caucasus. Thus rather than blowing up what could not be evacuated, Stalin gave orders that the city was to be held at all costs.

The efforts to hold the city were prodigious, but so were those of the attackers. Coming under intense bombardment and air attack, the defending formations were rapidly reduced to wreckage and pushed back into the city. However, the newly appointed commander of the defence, General Vasily Chuikov, had not been idle. Militia units were formed from the population and hastily armed. Although of dubious value in conventional military operations, these irregulars knew their way around their home city and were capable of defending a strong position. Much of the Soviet artillery was moved across the river to the East bank, where it was out of reach of the enemy but able to shell the attackers.

Although of dubious value in conventional military operations, the irregulars knew their way around their home city and were capable of defending a strong position.

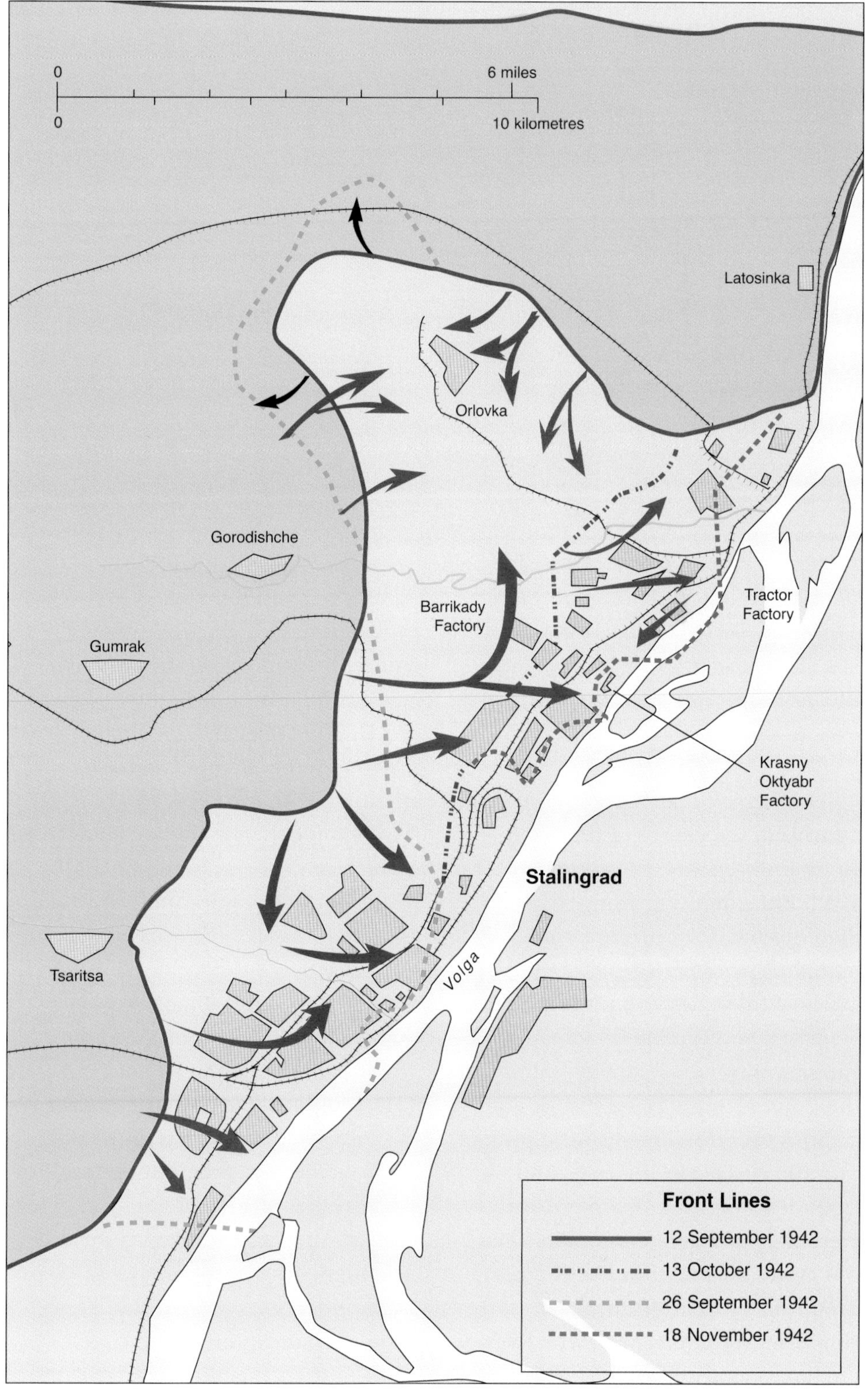

The Soviet defence of Stalingrad represented the ultimate in total warfare, with workers in non-essential industries fighting as militia while their colleagues in the war-related factories worked, sometime within the combat zone.

The Battle of Kursk. Tanks were most effective in open terrain, but were also vulnerable to anti-tank guns and artillery fire. Speed and armour protection, with rapid elimination of opposition, were the keys to survival.

The fight for Stalingrad began with a thrust at the centre of the city by German forces, on 13 September 1942. Bitter house-to-house fighting then ensued, with strong points emerging as centres of resistance. Many of these became notorious; the Soviet HQ on the hill of Mamayev Kurgan, the central railway station and the grain elevator being just three.

Soviet reinforcements were pushed into the city across the river, and the wounded evacuated the same way. German gains were counterattacked, but gradually the Soviet-held areas grew smaller. A large attack, supported by tanks, struck the Red October factory on 27 September, only to be counterattacked in force by troops moved across the Volga especially for the operation.

German units reached the Volga and by 5 October had gained control of some of the landing areas, attempting to prevent further reinforcement. The tractor, steel and armament factories in the northern sector of the city were then heavily assaulted. Most of the area was taken, but some Soviet defenders clung on in the wreckage until the offensive exhausted itself in early November.

THE FINAL EFFORT

On 11 November, a final effort was made, achieving some but not total success against the battered and weary Soviets. The supply situation for the defenders was critical; food and ammunition were desperately short and many units were down to one-tenth of their establishment strength.

> The Soviet policy of sending 'everyone who could carry a rifle' to fight was paying off. Casualties were vast on both sides, but could be better replaced by the defenders.

However, the Soviet policy of sending 'everyone who could carry a rifle' to fight was paying off. Casualties were immense on both sides, but could be better replaced by the defenders. Digging militia out of their positions resulted in casualties among well trained German troops and depleted their supplies. Worse, a powerful Soviet counteroffensive opened to the north on 19 November, threatening German forces in Stalingrad with encirclement and annihilation. The two arms of the Soviet counter-offensive met near Kalach and cut off the German troops in Stalingrad.

There had been plenty of warning that something like this could happen, but Hitler and his staff were inclined to believe that the Soviets were not in a position to launch any major offensives. Hitler had caused further confusion by forcing General List, the commander of his forces trying to advance in the Caucasus, to resign. Hitler demanded results and would not believe that List's men were trying their best in the face of difficult terrain and stubborn resistance.

General Von Manstein, commanding the German Don Army Group, warned of a threat to Rostov, which would cut off the forces in the Caucasus. A decisive stroke was needed to get the trapped German forces out of Stalingrad and restore the situation.

Hitler did not agree. He had already trumpeted to the world that Germany would never leave 'Fortress Stalingrad'. The quarter of a million Axis troops within the pocket would be maintained by an 'air bridge' provided by the *Luftwaffe*. Some *Luftwaffe* officers protested that it simply could not be done, but their chief, Herman Goering, assured Hitler that the pocket would be kept supplied by air.

Meanwhile, the Red Army consolidated its positions, facing

The T-34 came as an unpleasant surprise for the Axis powers, with its effective 76mm (2.9in) gun and good protection. In the later war years, it was outclassed by German tanks, and an upgunned version was produced.

The Red Army has always favoured mortars. Their range is shorter than conventional artillery, but mortars can drop a lot of large bombs into the target area in a short time and can be easily moved around by infantrymen.

inward to contain the pocket and outward to prevent a relief expedition. It then began the task of crushing the forces within the pocket. Von Manstein, ignoring Hitler's orders that Stalingrad would be held at all costs, began an offensive to break the encirclement and ordered the commander within the pocket, Von Paulus, to make a breakout to meet up with him.

Von Paulus was faced with a choice of obeying orders from Hitler or those from Von Manstein. In the event, his forces were not in any shape to mount a breakout battle and were forced to fight on in their positions as the Soviets ground ever further into what remained of the city.

Even pressing light bombers into transport service, the supplies flown into Stalingrad were insufficient to keep the trapped troops fed and combat-capable. Soon the German forces were limited to a few rounds per day and ordered to fire only in self-defence.

By the last week of 1942, Von Paulus knew the end was near. Requests for help, more supplies and permission to surrender were all brushed off. Hitler promoted

STALINGRAD – THE TURNING POINT

The battle for Stalingrad was the largest in history and cost the German army about one-quarter of its forces in Russia. The disaster might have been averted, but once the struggle for the city began, it served one purpose at least. Had Stalingrad fallen quickly, the Soviets might have been able to move on Rostov as Von Manstein feared, cutting off the segment of Army Group South that was fighting in the Caucasus and resulting in even more serious setbacks for the Axis.

Nonetheless, many historians consider the battle of Stalingrad to be the turning point of the war. It was not immediately apparent, but the balance had irrevocably shifted. The Axis position at the outset of the war was that they had to achieve victory through feats of arms, and had a real chance to do so. The Allies, if they could only avoid defeat long enough, would eventually win through superior production and manpower.

Von Paulus over Von Manstein's head, to Field Marshal and reminded Von Paulus that no German marshal had ever surrendered.

On 24 January 1943, Von Paulus dissolved the remaining forces under his command, ordering them to break up into groups and more or less fend for themselves. It was an admission that his command no longer functioned as an organized military force. At that time, there were two enclaves of German troops left in Stalingrad, plus scattered stragglers. On 31 January, Von Paulus and the southern enclave surrendered. Two days later, the northern group

On 24 January 1943, Von Paulus dissolved his remaining forces in Stalingrad, ordering them to break up into groups and more or less fend for themselves.

followed suit. Hitler had failed to conquer Britain, and now Russia's survival was also assured. Japan had run wild for a time but was also beginning to be turned back. The chance for Axis victory was slipping away and the Allies' time of supremacy was about to begin.

DEFEAT OF THE DESERT FOX

In the summer of 1942, having failed to break the Allied line at El Alamein, the Axis forces stood on the defensive. Rommel was expecting an Allied attack and had prepared his positions, though he himself was on sick leave when the operation opened.

The Allied forces were now under the command of Bernard Montgomery. He decided to launch a diversionary attack in the south and then drive a corridor into the enemy positions with his infantry in the north, through which his armour would then attack.

Preparations for the battle were characterized by clever deception operations and an element of double

German troops surrender at Stalingrad. Although initially there was a real chance of victory in a battle that was worth fighting, Hitler's insistence on holding Stalingrad ultimately cost the German army large numbers.

bluff, whereby dummies, which the enemy was permitted to discover, occupied positions. The real thing then replaced them. Meanwhile, tanks were disguised as trucks and trucks as tanks to give the impression of armoured build-up in a different sector.

> By the end of 2 November 1942, Rommel had less than three-dozen tanks left. He radioed for permission to retreat but, predictably, this was denied.

Bernard Montgomery believed in using overwhelming force to achieve his goals. This required meticulous planning. The British attack at El Alamein made extensive use of deception operations to increase the odds of success.

The battle opened on 23 October 1942 with a massive artillery bombardment, much of it coming from batteries previously 'revealed' as dummies. The infantry then advanced and began clearing the Axis minefields, which were very deep. The going was slower than expected and the armour was not able to push forward on the first day. To keep

Many of the British batteries at El Alamein had been deployed as dummies and then substituted once the enemy had a chance to realize what they were. The guns were therefore considered to be harmless until they opened fire.

the Axis forces off balance, a massive effort was made by supporting air forces.

On 24 October, with the Allies still not through the mines, the inevitable Panzer counterattacks came in, resulting in heavy fighting but no gains by either side. Finally breaking out of the mined zone, the Allies made a small advance before being brought to a halt once again. There ensued a period of grinding down the opposition, during which Rommel returned hurriedly from sick leave. Although hamstrung by lack of fuel, the Panzers made local attacks and responded to crises as a mobile reserve, while the Allies launched attacks of their own, which often became confused and resulted in heavy losses.

The last days of October saw bitter close-range fighting and heavy casualties on both sides. German 88mm (3.46in) anti-tank guns disabled many Allied tanks. Gradually, though, the Axis armour was expended in counterattacks to restore a deteriorating situation.

By the end of 2 November 1942, Rommel had less than three-dozen

VICTORY THROUGH SUPERIOR RESOURCES

The keys to the Alamein position were Kidney Ridge and Tel al-Aqqaqir, and here the fighting was intense as both sides attacked and counterattacked. Allied air units contributed decisively, though indirectly, to the battle by sinking tankers bringing fuel to Rommel's forces. Mobility was as important to the tanks as firepower, and their capability to manoeuvre was diminishing fast.

So was the number of tanks available to Rommel. This was part of Montgomery's strategy. Having established a large strategic reserve of armoured vehicles, he could afford to take heavy casualties so long as the Panzers were also ground down in the process. With the German and Italian armour out of the picture, the Eighth Army could replace its losses from the depots and carve up the Axis infantry more or less at leisure.

A German 88mm (3.46in) anti-aircraft/anti-tank gun on its characteristic towed carriage. The '88' was one of the finest anti-tank weapons of the war, capable of penetrating most tanks at any range.

tanks left. He radioed for permission to retreat but, predictably, this was denied. The next day, Rommel's subordinate, General Von Thoma, led his remaining Panzers into action, where they were destroyed.

Meanwhile, despite large holes in the line, the Axis infantry – Italians and Germans alike – were still trying to make a fight of it. Some units had been more or less entirely destroyed and, realizing the insanity of trying to obey Hitler's order to stand and fight, Rommel authorized a retreat.

Scraping together a handful of tanks, Rommel was able to cover the retreat of his battered army. Once again, the war moved along the Coast Road, this time heading westwards. An Allied attempt to hook past the retreating Axis force and repeat the great victory of Beda Fomm was unsuccessful, and Montgomery settled for pushing steadily after his retreating foes.

For his part, Rommel could do little but fall back. However, his tiny armoured force was masterfully used to cover the retreat. After halts at El Agheila and Wadi Zemzem, he retreated to the relative security of the Mareth Line in Tunisia.

The Mareth Line was originally constructed by the French to protect against an attack by Italian forces. Now it was occupied by Italian and German troops. Although the Panzer strength of these units was greatly reduced, the infantry formations had been salvaged in reasonably good shape and they were more than capable of putting up a fight in defensive positions.

The Mareth Line was originally constructed by the French to protect against an attack by Italian forces. Now it was occupied by Italian and German troops.

Rommel had been beaten and pursued halfway across the north coast of Africa, but he was not yet in a hopeless position. He had a short supply line to southern Europe via Tunis and a solid front in good defences. He also had secure flanks, with the Gulf of Sidra to the east and the Atlas Mountains to the west.

The British were once again suffering from the effects of being over-extended, at the end of an even longer supply line than ever before. Initial operations against the Mareth Line were beaten off easily enough.

However, Rommel faced another threat. Allied forces had landed in northwest Africa, in the Vichy French territories of Morocco and Algeria, in November 1942. By the time Rommel's men had reached the Mareth Line, American-led forces were pushing into Tunisia from the west. These formations were largely inexperienced, and suffered badly when counterattacked by veteran Axis forces that had managed to regain a little of their former tank strength.

THE KASSERINE PASS

As the Americans and Free French pushed into the Kasserine Pass through the Atlas Mountains, they began to threaten the supply chain to the Mareth Line. Something had to be done about that, and Rommel decided to remove the threat by chasing the enemy off.

The Panzers attacked the advancing Allies head-on with tremendous aggression. Many US commanders had their headquarters far back from the battlefront and could not react to the rapidly changing situation in time. An attempt at a counterattack was made, but it was clumsy and badly coordinated. The Allies then pulled

Short movements on foot were possible, but the distances involved in the desert war made motorized transport vital. Apart from anything else, it was not possible for men on foot to carry enough water to sustain themselves.

US Rangers on the march in North Africa. Inexperienced US forces initially suffered at the hands of the vastly more skilled Wehrmacht. Experience was rapidly and painfully gained, and by 1944 US troops could match the enemy.

back into the Kasserine pass, where the terrain favoured defence.

However, Rommel was willing to personally lead his Panzers into the pass and assault the hasty positions there. The few Tiger tanks available to Rommel showed their mettle. Fuel-hungry and over-complex they might be, but they were also largely impervious to Allied anti-tank guns.

Stubborn resistance by units caught in the fighting, often on the initiative of very junior officers, slowed the German onslaught somewhat, and the advance was finally halted by Allied reserves on 22 February 1943.

Rommel fell back, knowing that his supply line was not in danger of being cut in the immediate future, though the Americans advanced once again and by 3 March were back where they started. However, there was a pause while the Americans absorbed the lessons they had just been taught by the master of armoured warfare. As they began reorganizing their forces to avoid a repetition of the disaster, the British were making probing attacks against the Mareth Line.

Early in March 1943, Rommel, who now had the advantage of a short supply chain and was operating on interior lines, attacked the British. Outnumbered almost three to one in

DESERT STORM: A PILOT'S ACCOUNT

Just as the Tiger tank had come as an unpleasant surprise to the Allies, the new 17-pounder guns carried by some Allied tanks were a shock to their opponents. Capable of blowing the turret clean off a Panzer IV, they allowed the Allies to take on the best Panzers on a more or less equal footing. Given that the Allies could field more tanks than the Axis, this was a significant shift in the balance of any conflict.

Right: German prisoners being escorted to the rear by troops of the Black Watch in October 1942. Although the campaign in North Africa was by no means over at this point, Axis forces were being pushed back into Tunisia.

tanks and facing prepared positions defended by anti-tank guns, this attack ground to a halt with heavy losses.

The British then made an attack of their own, hooking a flanking force in behind the Mareth line while other formations attacked frontally. Rommel counterattacked the flanking force with the few tanks he had available, finally succeeding in dislodging it. However, this distracted attention from the frontal attack, which eventually managed to break the Mareth Line.

> With their surrender, North Africa was finally cleared of Axis forces and the Allies could think about pushing northwards into southern Europe.

The Axis forces fell back to a new line of defence at Wadi Akrit. Although a strong position, this was broken by infantry attack against the high point that was its key. Yet again, Rommel was able to fall back, taking up final positions in the Medjerda Valley. Infantry, making a night attack, again broke this line and the armour exploited the breakthrough to take Tunis and smash what remained of the Axis forces in North Africa.

What was left of the Italian forces in Tunisia surrendered on 7 May 1943.

The Germans held out until 13 May. With their surrender, North Africa was finally cleared of Axis forces and the Allies could think about pushing northwards into southern Europe.

THE GREATEST TANK BATTLE

Early 1943 saw renewed movement on the Eastern Front. Fresh from their victory at Stalingrad, the Soviets launched a new campaign to drive Axis forces from all of Russia. While other forces attacked into the rear of German forces still fighting before Moscow and then pushed northward to the relief of Moscow, a major campaign would liberate the Ukraine.

Below: Positioned in the open like this, anti-tank guns were at a disadvantage in that their position was fixed. Other than the gun shield, there was no armour protection for their crews.

A column of Soviet tanks moving up to join the Battle of Kursk. Although the best German tanks outmatched anything that could be sent against them, they were not so good that they could not be defeated by good tactics and sheer numbers.

The plan was to cut off German forces fighting in the Donetz basin and force them southwards into the Crimea, where they could be contained for destruction at leisure. Powerful forces were available for this undertaking, including large numbers of T-34 tanks and self-propelled guns that could penetrate the armour of most German tanks at a respectable range. Increasing numbers of heavy self-propelled guns that could kill even a Tiger were becoming available, though the heavy tanks still presented the Soviets with a difficult target.

> By 14 March, the city was once more a German possession and the Soviets in some places had been driven back up to 160km (99 miles).

The offensive opened on 29 January 1943. Von Manstein, commanding what was at that time designated Army Group Don, asked for permission to conduct a tactical withdrawal to avoid encirclement. Naturally permission was refused, but Von Manstein went ahead anyway, thereby saving his command from destruction, and Hitler reluctantly condoned the action.

The Soviet advance went well, with the cities of Kursk and Bielgorod falling to the Soviets. They then began driving on Kharkov. This was an important objective. It was the fourth-largest city in the Soviet Union, and Hitler gave orders for it to be held to the last man. As the Axis forces trying to halt the Soviet advance were driven in, an SS Panzer Corps moved up and for a time held up a vastly superior Soviet force.

However, there came a point where to hold on was to be encircled and destroyed. Predictably, the SS troops were commanded to stand their ground but instead fought their way out of the trap through the falling city. Hitler was furious and ordered this formation to lead an immediate counteroffensive to retake Kharkov, which was fully in Soviet hands by 15 February.

The counterattack began on 19 February and was highly successful

M4A2

Type: Medium tank

Crew: 5

Powerplant: twin General Motors 6-71 diesel engines developing 373kW (500hp)

Weight: 31,360kg (69,000lb)

Range: 161km (100 miles)

Armour: 15–76mm (0.59in–2.99in)

Armament: one 75mm (2.95in) gun; one coaxial 7.62mmn (0.3in) machine gun; one 12.7mm (0.5in) anti-aircraft gun on turret

Performance: maximum road speed 46.6km/h (29mph); fording 0.9m (3ft); vertical obstacle 0.61m (2ft); trench 2.26 (7ft 5in)

Dimensions: length 5.9m (19ft 4in)
width 2.6m (8ft 7in)
height 2.74m (9ft)

despite heavy casualties. By 14 March, the city was once more a German possession and the Soviets had been driven back up to 160km (99 miles) in some places. This created a large salient in the line, in the region around Kursk.

OPERATION CITADEL

The spring thaw turned everything to mud and halted operations from late March onwards. Both sides planned offensives in the summer. For the Germans, the Kursk salient was a chance to smash a large Soviet force. For the Soviets, it was the launch point for a renewed offensive. However, they decided to allow the Germans to attack first and launch their own countermeasures after the attack had been defeated. Given that they could predict the likely axes of attack, the Soviets were confident that the German summer offensive could, and would, be stopped in its tracks.

Thus while the Axis generals planned Operation *Citadel*, the great armoured assault on the Kursk salient, the Soviets prepared to halt it. Three belts of defences in depth were created, with the gaps in between covered by artillery and mobile forces. Combined-arms positions were created, containing anti-tank guns, tanks, infantry and engineers, all protected by mines.

These preparations took time, and had the offensive been launched in May as planned, it would have struck unfinished positions. However, it was delayed to build up supplies and allow numbers of heavy tanks and assault guns to be delivered to the Panzer formations. Here, the Germans had made a strategic mistake.

The first Tiger tanks were available in small numbers at the beginning of the year and were committed piecemeal. They caused alarm, as most Soviet anti-tank rounds simply bounced off their armour. However, in the period between first appearance and the battle of Kursk, heavier anti-tank guns were deployed that could stop a Tiger. Had they first been used in reasonable numbers at Kursk, the Tigers' resilience might have made a difference to the outcome.

Increasing Soviet strength in the Kursk salient prompted German commanders to suggest that Operation *Citadel* would fail, and Hitler considered calling it off. In the end, however, the attack went ahead, on 5 July 1943. The Soviets knew roughly when the operation was to start and had good reconnaissance of the German concentration areas, which were taken under artillery fire as the Germans began to form up.

Given that they could predict the likely axes of attack, the Soviets were confident that the German summer offensive could, and would, be stopped in its tracks.

Disrupted by shellfire, the lead formations launched their attack. Many of the new Panther tanks, developed to counter the T-34, broke down. They had been rushed into production and were still in need of further development. The remaining tanks, led by Tigers in many cases, were able to penetrate the outer defences. However, they often became detached from lighter tanks following in support as anti-tank guns that could not halt a Tiger stopped these.

The heavy tanks then ran into heavy concentrations of anti-tank guns, whose crews had been trained for this situation. Fire was concentrated on each tank in turn, halting many with broken tracks and overwhelming others. Infantry assault teams used satchel charges and other close assault weapons to disable many more.

Yet the assault forced its way forward, reducing one position after another. Progress was very slow. Rather than the expected breakthrough and exploitation, the Germans were forced to battle their way through heavy defences. In some areas, a penetration of just 13km (8 miles) was made by 10 July. Nowhere had the advanced elements of the German army covered more than 32km (20 miles).

On 12 July, the Soviet armoured counterattack began. Huge numbers of Soviet tanks advanced into the battle zone, hitting the disrupted Panzer formations and bringing about immense armoured clashes that went on for days. Losses were heavier on the Soviet side but these could be more readily made good than those of the Axis forces. In fact, few reinforcements were available to them; the Allies had invaded Sicily and were obviously aiming to push into Italy. This diverted resources from a continuation of Operation *Citadel*, and Hitler cancelled it on 13 July.

However, the fighting did not simply stop. The armoured battles along the Kursk Salient continued for some time, with the Soviets increasingly gaining the advantage. As usual, Hitler wanted his forces to stand and fight, but reluctantly agreed to a more elastic defence. This was the beginning of the fighting retreat that would end in Berlin two years later, but in the interim it saved the Axis forces in Russia from annihilation and prolonged the war considerably.

Despite brilliant defensive fighting by the German forces, which used mobility to blunt an attack and then counterattacked before pulling back, the Soviets advanced steadily. By 27 August, the front line was on the eastern edge of the Ukraine.

The Germans now established a practice of forming 'battle groups' out of whatever forces were to hand. Often thrown together from the remnants of shattered formations plus whatever reinforcements had recently arrived, these ad-hoc formations put up a stubborn fight, but they were never again able to take the strategic offensive.

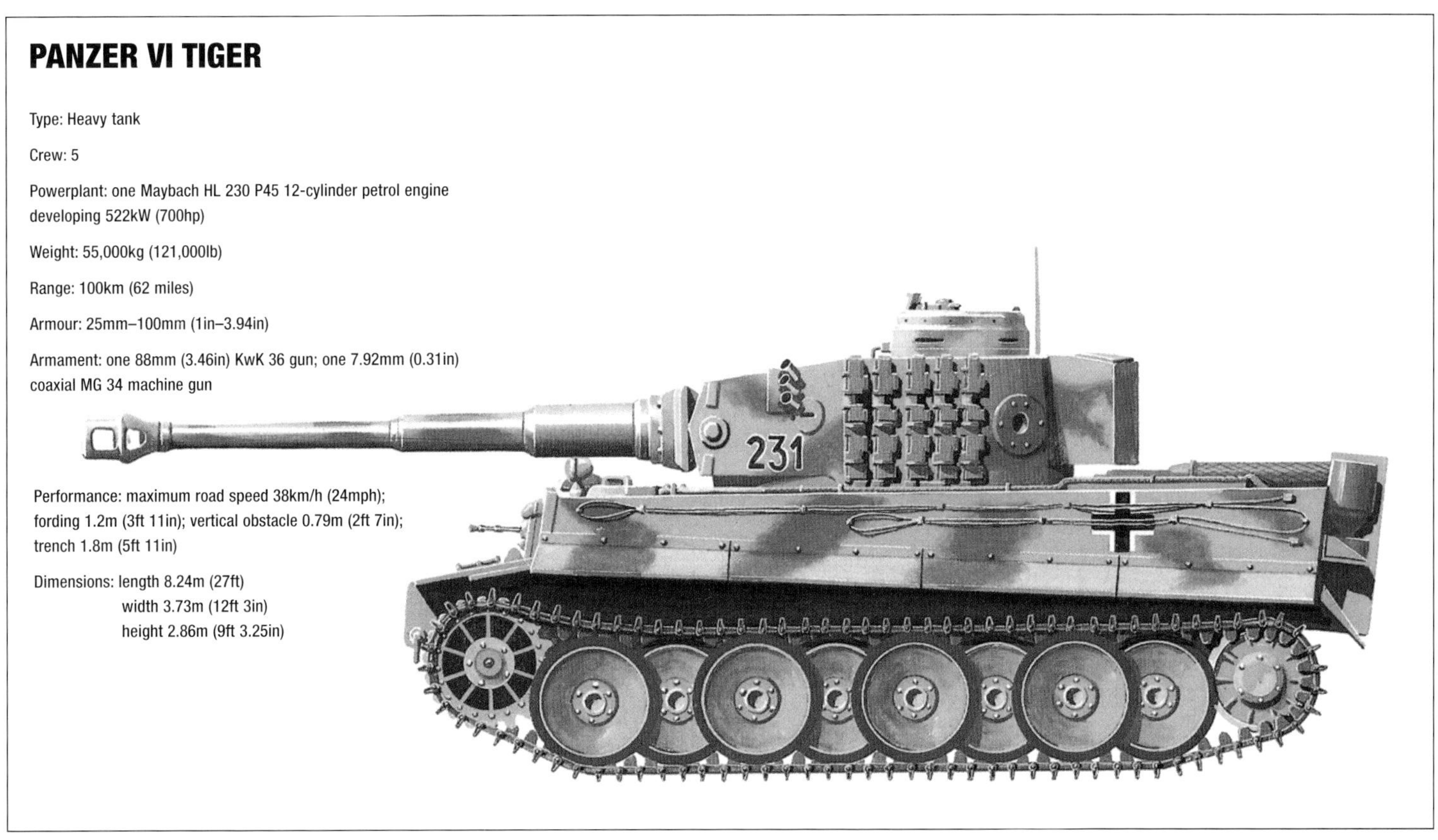

PANZER VI TIGER

Type: Heavy tank

Crew: 5

Powerplant: one Maybach HL 230 P45 12-cylinder petrol engine developing 522kW (700hp)

Weight: 55,000kg (121,000lb)

Range: 100km (62 miles)

Armour: 25mm–100mm (1in–3.94in)

Armament: one 88mm (3.46in) KwK 36 gun; one 7.92mm (0.31in) coaxial MG 34 machine gun

Performance: maximum road speed 38km/h (24mph); fording 1.2m (3ft 11in); vertical obstacle 0.79m (2ft 7in); trench 1.8m (5ft 11in)

Dimensions: length 8.24m (27ft)
width 3.73m (12ft 3in)
height 2.86m (9ft 3.25in)

THE RETURN TO EUROPE

The Soviet Union had been demanding an Allied offensive into Europe for some time, but it was not feasible to mount one before the situation elsewhere was stabilized. Once the Axis forces had been cleared from North Africa, it was possible to consider landings somewhere in Europe. Although an assault from Britain into northwest Europe was an option, it was decided that an advance across the Mediterranean into Italy made more sense.

The first stage of the campaign was the invasion of Sicily. This began with an airborne landing on 9 July 1943.

The invasion of Sicily was supported by airborne landings that prepared the way for the seaborne assault. Once the Allies were ashore, the Axis defence was hampered by Italy's preparations to pull out of the war.

Italy had quietly begun discussing an armistice with the Allies, and on 25 July Mussolini was deposed as Italian leader and his Fascist government was dissolved.

Unlike the invasion of Crete, the airborne landings on Sicily were not the 'main event' but were made in support of the next day's amphibious assault. The latter were successful despite light resistance and poor weather, and soon the Allies were advancing across the island.

German reinforcements were sent to hold Sicily, but at the same time Italian troops were being evacuated. Italy had quietly begun discussing an armistice with the Allies, and on 25 July Mussolini was deposed as Italian leader and his Fascist government was dissolved.

Mussolini was arrested and imprisoned, but subsequently freed by SS troops and installed as leader of a Fascist republic in northern Italy. However, in the meantime the legitimate Italian government began peace talks with the Allies, which led to a treaty signed on 3 September but not announced until the 8 September. As part of the peace deal, Italy declared war on her former allies on 13 October 1943.

Benito Mussolini prepares to board a light transport aircraft. It is perhaps telling that the insignia on the tailplane is German, not Italian. Hitler wanted his ally in power in Italy, or at least part of it, far more than most Italians did.

Fighting for Sicily continued until the middle of August, at which point the remaining German troops were evacuated to the Italian mainland. The advance was assisted by a series of short-range amphibious operations to outflank successive positions, and American troops under General George Patton reached Messina on 17 August.

AN AMPHIBIOUS INVASION

The logical course for the Allies was to launch an amphibious invasion across the narrow Messina straits, and this was undertaken in early September. The first landings coincided with the secret Italian surrender on 3 September.

With German attention drawn to the Messina Straits, the Allies launched an amphibious invasion at Salerno on 9 September 1943, the day after the Italian surrender was announced. This move caught the Germans off guard, though they had suspected their allies were about to defect and were moving some forces in to cover areas previously held by Italian troops. German countermeasures were thus patchy and uncoordinated, but rapidly developed into heavy counterattacks on the beachheads.

Additional Allied landings elsewhere, accompanied by a push out of the Salerno beachheads, gradually drove the German forces back, northwards and into the Apennine Mountains. Contesting high ground and river lines, the German forces slowed the Allied advance to a crawl even though Italian partisans, who made movement behind the lines a risky business, beset them. German troops were pulled out of Corsica and Sardinia to assist in the defence of Italy, and made the advance costly by contesting the close terrain of Italian villages. Infantry teams were able to destroy tanks at close range with satchel charges and Panzerfausts. These were very simple one-shot shaped-charge anti-tank weapons. Villages had to be cleared by combined-arms teams of armour, infantry and combat engineers, with artillery often unable to play much part in the close fighting.

As the Allies pushed their way slowly forwards up the spine of Italy, the Germans built and manned successive defensive lines. Emplaced

From Sicily, the logical next move was across the straits to Messina on the Italian mainland. The operation was timed to coincide with the Italian surrender, ensuring that only German units opposed the landings.

artillery and anti-tank guns, concrete bunkers and mobile forces of tanks and assault guns, often moving between pre-prepared firing positions, backed up obstacles, ditches, minefields and barbed wire. Tank turrets were sometimes set into concrete mountings to create a powerful direct-fire emplacement.

Soldiers loyal to Mussolini's new Fascist republic gradually joined the defence of the German lines, though larger numbers of Italians fought against them. However, the successive lines of defence were broken one by one and the Allies gradually advanced on Rome.

The Allies launched an amphibious landing at Anzio on 22 January 1944, attempting to outflank Axis positions. Three days later, land forces tried to force their way into the Liri Valley past the monastery of Monte Cassino. The advance was repulsed; it took two months of savage fighting before Monte Cassino was taken on 18 May. On 23 May, the Allies began to break out of the Anzio beachheads, where they had been pinned down since January. The Allies now had a chance to catch the German Tenth Army, in a double envelopment, and destroy it. The opportunity slipped away, however, amid wrangling about which of the Allies was to gain the honour of entering Rome first. The German commander, Kesselring, was able to extricate his force and fall back to a new defensive line.

US troops entered Rome on 5 June 1944, the day before the Allies landed in northwest Europe, and continued to advance until they came up against Kesselring's new positions on the formidable Gothic Line. After a pause to prepare, the line was assaulted in late August and was penetrated on 8 September. Meanwhile, the Allies were advancing across northern Europe and had landed in southern France on 15 August.

Allied strength was so great by this time that they could push on all these fronts, preventing the Germans from restoring the situation in any theatre by concentrating there. However, the Axis forces under Kesselring continued to fight hard and give ground slowly. A German counterattack in December achieved little, but as late as April 1945 the German forces in northern Italy were still putting up stiff resistance.

The Italian front collapsed in April. Allied breakthroughs flanked other sections of the line and resistance finally began to cave in. As the Allies made rapid gains, Mussolini was captured and killed by Italian partisans. The forces of his Fascist Italian state rapidly disintegrated, and at the very end of April the German forces in Italy requested surrender terms. On 2 May 1945, all German forces in Italy surrendered.

SLOW CHANGES IN THE FAR EAST

Although defeat at sea and in the Solomon Islands more or less ended Japanese expansion in the Pacific theatre of war, there was no immediate shift in the strategic situation, at least not according to the maps. In terms of fighting power and

Although defeat at sea and in the Solomon Islands more or less ended Japanese expansion in the Pacific, there was no immediate shift in the strategic situation.

strategic initiative the balance had shifted in favour of the Allies, but it would be some time before the threat of defeat even featured in Japanese military thinking.

The Japanese intent had been to create a forward defensive zone in the Pacific, facing the United States, using islands as bases for air and sea units. In the middle of 1943, the main line of defence was anchored on Saipan in the Marianas and Truk in the Caroline Islands. Bases further west were considered to be outposts and not critically important to the overall plan. Thus, when US troops landed in the Gilbert and Marshall Islands between December 1943 and January 1944, Japanese high command was not unduly worried.

The Gilberts were taken first, as a base from which to attack the Marshalls. The fighting for atolls such as Tarawa and Kwajalein was bitter, with outgunned Japanese defenders fighting stubbornly from well prepared positions.

Getting across the beaches was a significant problem. The Japanese were adept at concealing fire positions

Wherever possible, islands held by Japanese troops were bypassed rather than being assaulted. However, in many cases it was necessary to storm islands defended by stubborn and well dug-in troops.

in the thick vegetation at the shoreline and were difficult to dig out. Tanks and amphibious assault vehicles, some of them fitted for fire support missions, were of great assistance in establishing the Marines ashore.

Where possible, garrisons were bypassed and allowed to 'wither on the vine' for lack of supplies while the Marines moved onto more important targets. One such was the Marianas Islands. The Marianas were part of the main defensive line, and a determined stand was certain. However, with Japanese air power in the region crippled by carrier-borne air raids just before the assault, the defenders were at a disadvantage when the land forces began coming ashore in June 1944.

There was never anything routine about island clearance, but a flexible and effective system was developed during the advance across the Pacific, utilizing naval gunfire and air support as well as armoured vehicles to establish a lodgement and clear the beaches, followed by a drive inland to break the defenders up into isolated pockets and strong points. These were then eliminated one by one.

Meanwhile, Japanese forces were active in mainland Asia. The British had been on the defensive on the Indian/Burmese border for many months, but they had not been inactive. Raiding forces, including the famous Chindits, were causing a lot of damage throughout the region. It was also becoming apparent

Where possible, garrisons were bypassed and allowed to 'wither on the vine' for lack of supplies while the Marines moved onto targets that had to be taken.

US Marines aboard a landing craft. Troops assaulting an island were most vulnerable as they first hit the beach. With little or no cover available, they would come under fire from troops in bunkers hidden just inside the treeline.

The Imperial Japanese Army did not leave all of its artillery behind for the advance to Imphal, although the harsh terrain made it necessary to restrict how much heavy equipment was brought up.

that the British were planning to attack with regular forces. In addition, Japanese commanders were worried that US bombers could be based in China to attack the home islands.

OPERATION ICHI-GO

A major offensive, codenamed *Ichi-Go,* was planned to remove the latter threat, while eliminating the British base at Imphal would defend Burma. The Imphal operation began on 8 March 1944 and was initially successful in driving the British forward units, which had taken up advanced positions ready for the projected offensive into Burma, back towards Imphal. The city was now besieged, with its main supply route cut at Kohima. This placed the British in a difficult position, but the Japanese were not much better off. Operating at the end of a long supply line, they suffered worsening shortages of ammunition and food. Meanwhile, the British were re-supplied by air. This technique had been used a few months before to allow the encircled defenders of the so-called Admin Box to hold out and eventually emerge victorious.

The fighting at Kohima was so bitter that it became known as the Stalingrad of the East. Eventually the Japanese were pushed off the high ground that commanded the Imphal road and the siege was broken. Moreover, the Japanese before Imphal were out of supplies and were forced to pull back from 3 July. Meanwhile, Operation *Ichi-Go* began in April 1944 and was a success, establishing a large controlled zone. This linked all Japanese gains in China and prevented the United States from operating bombers from China.

The attack at Imphal and Operation *Ichi-Go* represented the last major Japanese offensives of the war. The Allies advanced into Burma and, supported by amphibious operations to flank Japanese positions, made steady progress. Meanwhile, the Japanese gains in China could not be

The Soviet Union received large quantities of war matériel from the Allies, including tanks, aircraft and artillery weapons. This Matilda MkII probably arrived in Russia via the hazardous North Cape convoy route.

maintained and after a period of occupation the Japanese army began to fall back.

THE GREAT RETREAT

As the Soviets began their great westward advance, the liberation of the Ukraine was a high priority. This began in August 1943 with an advance on four fronts. The Soviets enjoyed an advantage of about 2:1 in infantry and 4:1 in artillery, with rough parity in armour and air support.

The first objective was to clear Axis forces from the area east of the River Dneiper, which more or less bisects the Ukraine. This was not too much of a problem; after some wrangling at Axis supreme headquarters, it was agreed that the German armies in the Ukraine should withdraw behind the Dneiper, which was considered to be a major obstacle. However, the Soviets had given much thought to the need for river crossings, and prepared well. If bridges could be seized, they would be; aggressive advances straight from the march offered a chance to catch the defenders unaware and prevent destruction or reinforcement. Assault crossings were also practiced.

Thus the offensive opened on 26 August and by 22 September some Soviet forces were across the Dneiper. Some Soviet tactics worked well, such as detaching a fast 'mobile group' from an advancing formation and using it to unbalance the enemy while the main force moved up and deployed. Other gambits, such as airborne operations to expand the Dneiper bridgeheads, did not meet great success.

For most of the rest of the year, the Dneiper line was held, with the Soviet penetrations contained within bridgeheads that had to be supplied across the river. The balance tipped steadily, with Axis forces in the Crimea cut off and Kiev retaken by the Soviets. By the end of the year, the Red Army had forced the Dneiper line and could begin to resume mobile operations.

Having cut off German forces in the Crimea, these were gradually reduced until the fall of Sevastopol in early May 1944 removed the final German presence there. Odessa on the Black Sea had fallen a month before; Soviet forces in the region were established on the River Dneister and had cut German troops in Poland off from those in Romania.

While German forces in the south were being driven back towards the Danube, Operation Bagration was launched in the north. Starting on

22 June 1944, exactly three years after the invasion of the Soviet Union, the operation was assisted by increased partisan activity behind German lines and air attacks on logistics centres and rail links.

As usual, Hitler ordered many formations to stand and fight to the last man, making their encirclement and destruction certain. Mobile groups were used to cut off the retreat of units that did try to pull back. The Soviets were able to concentrate against one then another of these immobile forces and destroy them before moving on to the next, negating the strength of what was on paper still a very powerful German army. Minsk was taken by the Soviets on 3 July, having already eliminated most of the forces that could have defended it. A fortnight later, the advanced elements of the Red Army crossed the River Bug into Poland. By the end of July 1944, the Soviets were just 16km (10 miles) from Warsaw, with large German forces encircled near Brest-Litovsk.

THE WEHRMACHT IN RETREAT

The Soviet advance began to wind down. The main German forces in the region were shattered; those that remained were in full retreat. It was necessary to pause and reorganize before moving on, but there was no danger of a counteroffensive in the meantime. The German army was incapable of more than local counterattacks.

Some German forces were bypassed in the advance, mainly those along the Baltic coast. These had remained in position, protecting ports used by naval vessels that in turn used their big guns to support landward operations. However, by late 1944 these enclaves were cut off. Many troops were evacuated by sea. The remainder were trapped and forced to surrender as the Soviets moved into Estonia, Latvia, Lithuania and Courland.

Tank destroyers and assault guns, with their weapons in limited-traverse mounts rather than a revolving turret, were easier to produce than tanks. In many roles they were just as efficient, but in the later war years they were forced to fill in for tanks even where they were inadequate.

SOVIET BETRAYAL OF THE WARSAW RISING

The Poles had orchestrated a mass rising in their cities, planning to oust the Germans and re-establish Poland as an independent nation before the Red Army arrived. This would have implications for Poland's post-war status. Stalin wanted a pro-Soviet puppet government in Poland rather than an independent-minded one that had just fought for freedom, and ordered a slowdown in the advance on Warsaw.

Thus the rising was largely a success, but instead of welcoming the Red Army into their city, the Polish Home Army was left to fight alone against a savage campaign to retake the city. By the time the German army regained possession of Warsaw, there was little left of the city.

Further south, German forces were being driven west and southwest before ever-increasing Soviet strength. By now, the Germans were experts in mobile 'elastic' defence tactics. As a Soviet attack developed, the defenders would pull back so that artillery preparation hit empty positions and the advanced units found nothing to fight at their objectives. Then, as the assault inevitably became disorganized, a counterattack was put in before the Germans again pulled back to new positions.

The retreating German army made a series of stands on river lines, inflicting delay and casualties before pulling back to avoid encirclement. The Soviets used fast-moving mechanized formations to try to cut the line of retreat. Sometimes this resulted in a race between Russian and German forces trying to close or escape a pocket.

By now, the German army groups were being pushed apart, and command was devolved in some places, essentially breaking the major groupings into smaller formations. This gradual disintegration of German forces was matched by the departure of allies.

Romania, invaded by Soviet forces on 20 August 1944, defected to the Allies soon after. This came as a shock to the Axis, caught by surprise by the move. Bulgaria went next, declaring herself neutral. The Soviets invaded anyway, but there was no fighting. Hungary fought on, and was sent help from German forces.

These had to come from somewhere, and in this case it was the northern front that was weakened. However, the Vistula proved a major obstacle. Some units did manage to cross as early as the end of July, but they were mostly contained for the time being. The advance on Warsaw was halted just short of the city, ostensibly to shake out tangles in the logistics tail. However, there may have been a more sinister explanation.

The advance elements of the Red Army were just a few kilometres away from Warsaw, and it is true that the Soviets had to deal with some German attacks on the flanks. However, the halt at a point so close to the city cannot be explained other than as a cynical gambit to allow the Polish bid for independence to burn itself out,

M7 PRIEST

Type: Self-propelled artillery

Crew: 5

Powerplant: one Continental nine-cylinder radial piston engine developing 279.6kW (375hp)

Weight: 22,500kg (49,500lb)

Range: 201km (125miles)

Armour: up to 25.4mm (1in)

Armament: one 105mm (4.13in) howitzer; one 12.7mm (0.49in) machine gun

Performance: maximum road speed 41.8km/h (26mph); fording 1.22m (4ft); vertical obstacle 0.61m (2ft); trench 1.91m (6ft 3in)

Dimensions: length 6.02m (19ft 9in)
width 2.88m (9ft 5.25in)
height 2.54m (8ft 4in)

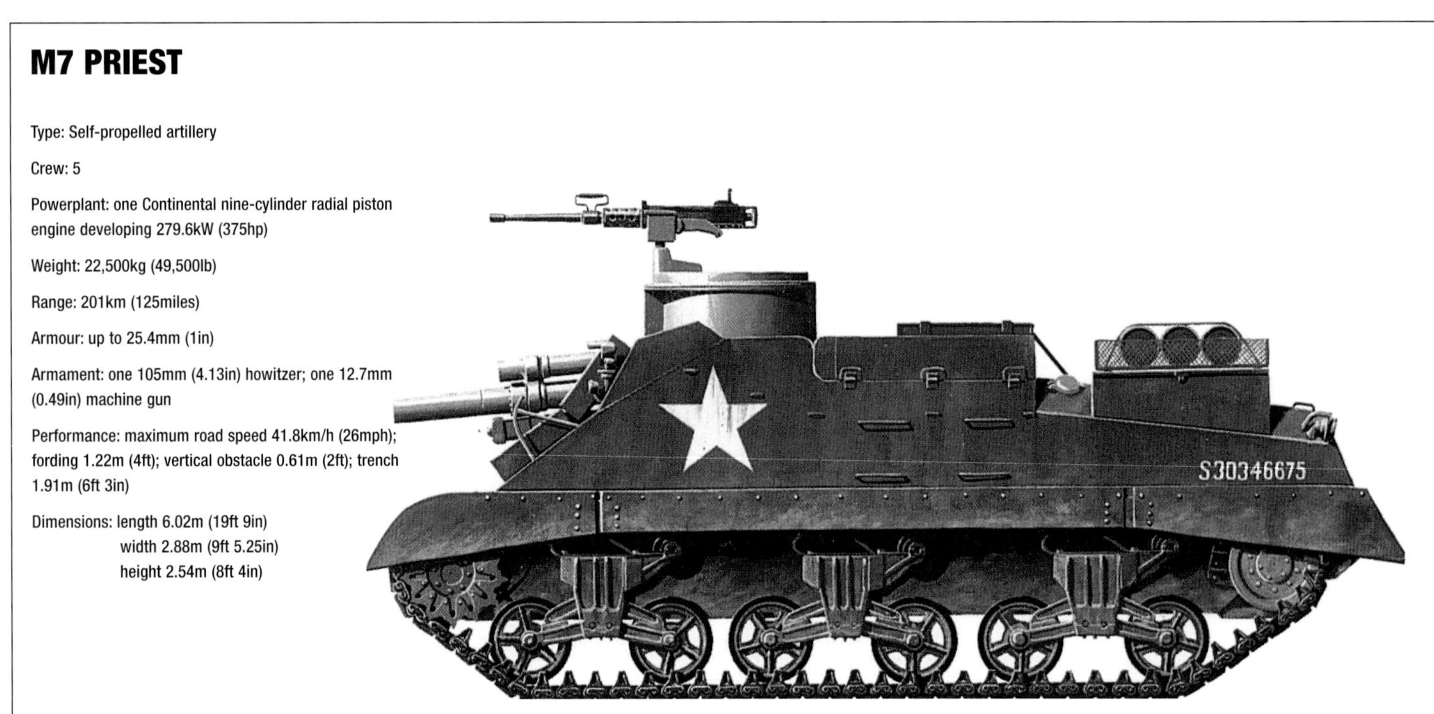

incidentally inflicting casualties the enemy could not afford.

The northern advance continued in other sectors. Riga fell to the Soviets on 10 October, just two weeks before the Red Army pushed into East Prussia. Although Konigsburg held out until April 1945, the Soviet armies were able to push westwards at a steady rate.

THE NORMANDY LANDINGS

The Allied landings in Normandy represented the largest amphibious operation in history. Even though the distance to be crossed was very short, getting so many troops across the English Channel and establishing beachheads in hostile territory was a tremendous undertaking. Supplying them once there also presented a huge challenge.

A landing somewhere in Europe was inevitable, and it was obvious to Hitler and his commanders that Britain was the logical jumping-off point for the operation. However, it was still possible to misdirect the enemy about where and when the invasion was to take place. A whole range of deception measures, under the blanket heading of Operation *Bodyguard,* were put in place to cover preparations for the assault.

Whole dummy armies were created using radio deception and a variety of fake tanks, guns and vehicles. Dummy landing craft were deployed to the coasts opposite the Pas de Calais, apparently ready to carry the army assembling there into battle. That, too, was fake. Meanwhile, troops undertook arctic and mountain training, suggesting that their destination was Norway.

Thus it was that when the invasion of Normandy took place, German reserves were scattered about Europe

The days before the Normandy invasion were difficult ones for all concerned. It was not possible to say when the weather conditions would allow the operation to be launched, and troops had to be held at high readiness.

Getting enough troops ashore to create a foothold on the continent, and enough to avoid being dislodged, was a mammoth undertaking. Even with specially designed equipment, the landings were a massive gamble.

and there was great doubt as to whether this was the real attack or simply a diversion. This delayed the counterattacks that might have driven the Allies back into the sea.

However, crossing the beaches to get inland was no easy task. The 'Atlantic Wall' may have been a white elephant, attempting as it did to defend every port and practicable beach in Western Europe. But on the Normandy beaches there were obstacles, minefields and concrete walls to contain an attack, and the troops landing came under fire from machine-gun positions and artillery sited further back. A determined Panzer attack at this point might have been disastrous for the Allies, but uncertainty tied down available units and what counterattacks were made were beaten off.

Having established a lodgement, the Allies poured supplies and reinforcements into the beachheads and began pushing inland. Local units put up a good fight, but Hitler largely denied them reinforcements because he was convinced that another invasion force was waiting

THE 'FUNNIES' PLAY THEIR PART

Even with troops dropped in by air causing confusion inland and heavy naval gunfire support, the assault troops met resistance, which in some areas was extremely determined. Amphibious tanks and specialist armoured vehicles (collectively known as 'funnies') were extremely helpful in getting past some obstacles. These forerunners of modern combat engineering vehicles cleared mines, bulldozed obstacles aside and laid tracks over areas of soft sand, all of which allowed conventional armour to get inland and help secure the beachheads.

to land on the Pas de Calais as soon as it was left exposed.

By 12 June, all the landing zones had linked up and Allied aircraft were operating from airstrips in France. German resistance was firming up, but the danger of being pushed off the continent was receding. Allied progress was certainly slow in most areas, but even stalled operations pulled in German reserves that could not be used elsewhere. Thus although Operation *Goodwood,* a renewed attempt by British forces to take Caen on 18–20 June, was halted, this drew in Panzer formations, which were then in no position to interfere when US armoured forces attacked at the eastern end of the lodgement area during Operation *Cobra.*

By the end of June, Cherbourg, cut off on the tip of the Cotentin peninsula, had surrendered and the Allies had built up sufficient forces to break out of their lodgement. This began on 25 July with Operation *Cobra.* US armoured forces burst out of their positions and drove on St Lo, intending to seize terrain features that would enable a later expansion of the Allied lodgement. Instead, the attack was a runaway success.

Just before the operation opened, heavy air attack wrecked the local Panzer reserve; no other armoured forces were available, as all had been committed to opposing Operation *Goodwood.* Meeting little resistance, Operation *Cobra* blasted open a corridor into Brittany as well as threatening the rear of German forces still opposite the Allied beachheads.

Hitler finally agreed to release forces opposite the Pas de Calais on 30 July. An armoured counterattack was put in against the flank of Operation *Cobra,* but this was defeated and by 7 August Brittany was isolated. The port of Brest surrendered in September but St Nazaire and Lorient, famous as U-Boat and surface raider bases, were simply encircled and left to rot. Both surrendered in May 1945.

US forces pushed south and then swung east while British and Canadian troops continued to push southwards against the forces containing them. Once the US hook got into the German rear, large forces became

A light howitzer recoils. Although limited in firepower and range compared to many other types of artillery, light guns of this sort could be air-dropped with paratroops, giving them a much-needed indirect-fire support capability.

Volksturm units, composed of Hitler Youth members and old men, were sent to defend the pillboxes and bunkers of the Siegfried Line facing the French border.

encircled around Falaise. The German response was an armoured thrust towards the coast, attempting to sever the US line of communications. This bold move was defeated by good intelligence work, which enabled reinforcements to be in position to counter it.

After the counterattack was defeated on 6 August, the Falaise Pocket was closed off on 20 August. Thousands of troops were captured, along with heavy equipment. A large proportion of the personnel got away across the River Seine but the matériel losses were considerable. Meanwhile, the French resistance led a rising in Paris, and Allied troops entered the city on 25 August to find that it was already free.

The drive towards the German frontier now began. Hitler had hoped to make an invasion difficult by denying the Allies use of the Channel ports. Heavily garrisoned, they were to be fortresses against an Allied advance, and without them it would be impossible to bring supplies into Europe to support the invasion. The logic here was sound, though the Allies got around the problem by creating their own mobile harbour and taking it across the channel to the Normandy coast.

Nevertheless, the ports held out for a time, and supplying the armies in France was a problem, necessitating some hard decisions about when and where to advance. Meanwhile, the

Troops disembark from gliders as transports drop 'sticks' of paratroops. Air-landed forces of this type seized strategic objectives ahead of the main advance. This was a risk; they were lightly equipped and could not hold out for long.

German army was mustering reserves to meet the advances and engaging in the same sort of desperate measures that the British had resorted to in 1940. *Volksturm* units, composed of Hitler Youth members and old men, were sent to defend the pillboxes and bunkers of the Siegfried Line, a deep chain of fortifications facing the French border. These were backed up by second- and third-rate army formations, some of which were composed of men with various illnesses. Among them were 'stomach' and 'leg' battalions, composed of men who needed similar medicines and treatments.

The Allies were able to drive into the Low Countries, but found themselves facing a series of tough positions. The Siegfried Line was strong enough that breaking it would be costly, even in the face of third-rate opposition. North of it was the Ruhr, which would also be heavily defended. The Rhine itself was a formidable obstacle.

There was, however, a chance to bypass the strongest defences by crossing the two broad arms of the Rhine (the Waal and the Lower Rhine) in the Netherlands. This necessitated a rapid advance to capture a series of bridges across major water obstacles, culminating in a grab for the Rhine bridges.

It was a bold and difficult undertaking, but there was a good chance of success. Thus Operation *Market Garden* was launched on 17 September 1944. The plan was for the critical bridges to be captured by a sudden paradrop, accompanied by glider-borne troops. Armoured forces would then rush up the corridor thus created and get across the Rhine, into the rear of the main German positions.

Although the war had turned against them, the soldiers of the German army had no choice but to keep fighting as best they could. The slow retreat into Germany was characterized by extremely stubborn resistance and hard fighting.

The operation very nearly succeeded, but unexpectedly heavy resistance held up the advance while the paras were either kept away from their objectives or dislodged from them by German counterattacks. The airborne troops in particular took very heavy casualties before the operation was declared a failure on 26 September.

LAST GASP IN THE WEST

As the winter of 1944 approached, the Allies were struggling with logistical difficulties and having trouble supplying their troops on the Continent. Hitler, ever given to grandiose plans, came up with a

scheme to cripple the Allies and perhaps force them to negotiate. An armoured thrust through the Ardennes forest and a drive to the coast would cut the Allies' supply chain and compromise their entire force in Europe.

Although his commanders were unsure and pushed for a more limited offensive, Hitler was determined that his great plan could win the war or at least prevent defeat. Given the situation, it is easy to see how a great gamble was attractive – nothing short of a spectacular victory was going to save the *Reich* now, so Hitler might as well try for one. Thus it was that on 16 December 1944, under cover of bad weather which grounded the Allies' air forces, Operation *Autumn Mist* was launched. The attack was accompanied by excellent operational security and the Allies had no idea that anything was about to happen, especially not in a 'quiet sector' like that facing the Ardennes.

The stunned US forces facing the attack fought back as best they could, managing to hold the town of Bastogne against heavy odds. The delay proved vital; the Panzer spearhead was unable to overrun and capture the Allied supply dumps that its commanders had counted on, and by 23 December many tanks were disabled for lack of fuel.

US infantry advance past a belt of anti-tank obstacles known as 'dragon's teeth'. The Siegfried Line, constructed to protect Germany's western border in the 1930s, included vast numbers of these obstructions.

Allied reinforcements then arrived and began to counterattack, relieving Bastogne on 26 December. Hitler ordered the operation to continue even though it had obviously failed, and even authorized a small diversionary attack in Alsace.

In the first week of January 1945, the Allies began to reduce the salient, or 'Bulge', created by the offensive and the German forces within were granted permission to retreat. The

> Hitler ordered the operation to continue although it had obviously failed, and even authorized a small diversionary attack in Alsace.

attack had given the Allies an unpleasant surprise and derailed their plans, but it had not altered the strategic balance in the favour of Germany. Quite the opposite; the operation had used up the last armoured reserve and most of the available fuel.

ENDGAME IN EUROPE

With the failure of the Ardennes offensive, the German capability to undertake offensive operations was largely gone. The only option now left was to create a succession of defensive positions and thereby try to delay the inevitable. One such was the 'Westwall', named the Siegfried Line by the Allies.

Long before the creation of the Atlantic Wall, Hitler had begun his bid for the title of 'greatest fortress builder of all time' with the creation of the Siegfried Line. With Axis Panzer divisions rampaging all over Europe, the fortifications covering the French-German border were all but forgotten, but as the tide turned they

The capture of an intact bridge over the Rhine was a priority for the Allies. Despite determined efforts to hold and then destroy the railway bridge at Remagen, it was taken by the US 9th Armoured Division.

OPERATION SPRING AWAKENING

Hungary and Austria fought on alongside Germany, almost to the last. Despite strong resistance that cost the Soviets dearly, Budapest was taken in the middle of February 1945. In March, a German counterattack codenamed Operation *Spring Awakening* halted the Soviet advance but did not succeed in its objective of driving the enemy back to the Danube where a solid defensive front could be established.

became once again significant. German propaganda had made much of the impenetrability of the Siegfried Line, but while it was a significant obstacle, it was by no means invulnerable. Advances in weaponry meant that tank guns could now destroy bunkers considered formidable in 1936. However, the ditches, anti-tank obstacles and prepared positions of the line enabled the troops fighting from them to hold up the Allies for a time and to inflict more casualties than might otherwise have been possible.

Although trumpeted as a great fortress, the Siegfried Line was penetrated on 9 February 1945, a little over a week after the first Allied troops reached it. Once the gaps were widened enough to get significant forces through, the Western Allies resumed their drive eastwards.

The Red Army surged forward again on 12 January 1945, driving on Warsaw. The main Axis of the attack was pointed directly at Berlin, with subsidiary operations peeling out to take secondary objectives.

The advance was made in massive strength, punching through in a deep penetration all the way to Warsaw, which fell on 17 January. Hitler had ordered that Warsaw be held to the

Hitler's refusal to surrender forced the Allies to fight all the way to Berlin, bringing needless destruction to the towns and cities of Germany, Hungary and Austria. Every scrap of land was to be held to the last, no matter what the cost.

A propaganda photograph showing the brotherly regard of US and Soviet troops for one another. The reality was somewhat different; political distrust led to a lack of cooperation and the need for strict demarcation lines.

last, but the garrison decided to withdraw rather than fight to the death, and slipped out before they could be encircled. The drive westwards then slowed as Soviet attention turned to Silesia with the intention of capturing its industrial centres intact. This done, the final push across Germany itself could begin.

The Red Army established itself across the Vistula on 27 January, and pushed on via Dresden and Poznan, taking Danzig in a subsidiary thrust on 30 March. Although the motorized and armoured units ran into supply problems, the momentum of the advance was kept up, with mobile units and cavalry ranging ahead of the main forces to gather reconnaissance and to keep the enemy off balance.

Once the *Spring Awakening* offensive was defeated, the Soviets resumed their advance, driving German forces out of Hungary in April. Fierce resistance in the mountain passes held up the drive on Vienna, but the German army was by this time in tatters. Breaking through to Vienna, the Red Army met resistance within the city limits in early April until an agreement was reached between Austria and Russia. On 13 April 1945, Vienna was occupied by Soviet troops.

On 5 March, the Western Allies reached the Rhine, with the first units getting across on 7 March after catching the defenders of the Remagen Bridge by surprise. This was the last significant terrain objective to be crossed. By the end of the month, it was obvious that the Soviets were going to reach Berlin first, and the line of advance was altered to deal with other centres of resistance.

The Allies possessed almost total air supremacy and could field vast numbers of tanks and men against the scraped-together battle groups of the German army. German movements were likely to be spotted and harassed from the air. This meant that the Allies could afford to be deliberate and careful where they applied their force. The only real time pressure was the Soviet advance; it was considered desirable that the Soviets did not end up in control of too much of Europe.

DESPERATE MEASURES

Despite desperate measures, such as arming old men and boys with nothing more than a single Panzerfaust and executing anyone found away from his designated position in the latest defended zone, the defenders of Germany were

The Allies possessed almost total air supremacy and could field vast numbers of tanks and men against the scraped-together battle groups of the German army.

Soviet soldiers raise their victory flag over the Reichstag in Berlin. Seldom in the history of warfare has a nation been defeated in the streets of its capital.

unable to prevent the Allies from driving them from one position after another.

On 1 April 1945, the Ruhr was surrounded and the reduction of the army group defending it began. The last German forces in the Ruhr surrendered on the 18 April. US forces captured Leipzig on the same day. By this time, the final assault on Berlin was well underway. The offensive opened on 16 April, forcing three main defensive lines and entering the city proper on 20 April.

Bitter street fighting ensued as the remnants of the SS forced anyone who could hold a rifle or throw a grenade to try to resist the Soviet advance. As at Leningrad during the great German siege, weapons were improvised and strong points were created out of rubble. Some of the defenders used the sewers to move around. Others tried to sneak out of the city. The skeleton of SS and regular army divisions fought to hold what remained of the city while Hitler descended further and further into delusion. While he issued orders to armies that no longer existed, the city's perimeter crumbled street by street.

> On 4 May, German forces in Denmark surrendered and Salzburg was taken by US forces, which had also pushed into Austria and Czechoslovakia.

Elsewhere, the advance continued against rapidly disintegrating resistance. US and Soviet forces met up on the lower Elbe on 25 April, having agreed where their respective advances would halt. On 29 April, Hitler refused to consider surrender at what was to be the final conference of German commanders. Hours later, he was informed that forces attempting to break the siege of Berlin had all been halted. The Reichstag building was stormed on 30 April, though holdouts remained inside up until the final surrender. Less than an hour later, Hitler killed himself. The Soviets were informed of this on 1 May and the following day the city was surrendered.

Meanwhile, the British were pushing across northern Germany, taking Hamburg on 3 May. The following day, German forces in the region, including those in Denmark, surrendered and Salzburg was taken by US forces, which had also pushed into Austria and Czechoslovakia.

Leadership of what little remained of Germany had been moved to the town of Murwick, where some of the senior leadership had taken refuge. There was little for them to do but end the madness by ordering their forces to lay down their arms. General Jodl signed final surrender of all German forces on 7 May.

The surrender of what remained of Army Group Centre took place three days after the Allies declared victory in Europe. These, the last German forces, were still fighting in the region of Prague. US troops were available to help in their reduction but the Soviets refused. A demarcation line had been agreed, dividing the Eastern and Western Allies' spheres of influence. Stalin insisted on the US keeping its forces on their side of the line.

Surrounded by overwhelming force, the last significant German field army surrendered on 11 May, though mopping up took longer and was complicated by civilian unrest and nationalist risings. With this, World War II came to an end in Europe. However, Japan was still stubbornly resisting defeat.

TOWARDS THE HOME ISLANDS

From the Marianas, US forces advanced on the Philippines, landing in October 1944. Attempts to interfere with the landings led to the naval battle of Leyte Gulf, which shattered what was left of the Japanese navy. With air and sea supremacy, the Allies could now pick and choose their targets, which could not be significantly reinforced or even properly re-supplied.

Japanese resistance in the Philippines was stubborn, but the defenders were open to defeat in detail, as the Allies concentrated against each target in turn. Lacking

US Marines armed with Thompson submachineguns in action in the Pacific. Firing a hard-hitting .45 round in full-automatic mode made the Thompson deadly in close-range combat.

STORMING IWO JIMA

Offensive preparations for the attack on Iwo Jima involved two-and-a-half months of air attack plus heavy naval bombardment. Beach conditions played havoc with the landings, and when the marines went ashore they found their opponents well dug in and waiting for them when the marines went ashore on 19 February. After dealing with extremely strong positions on Mount Suribachi, the invasion force drove the Japanese northeastwards into a final pocket, which fell on 26 March.

strategic mobility, the defenders were ground down one island at a time. Small groups continued to make a nuisance of themselves for some time, even after the region was officially cleared of organized opposition.

Manila was taken on 4 March 1945 and by late April the Philippines were more or less entirely in Allied hands. Australian forces pushed into Borneo in June, by which time the final offensive towards the Japanese home islands was being prepared.

In order to assault Japan itself, forward bases were needed. US commanders decided that Iwo Jima and Okinawa were good choices, though both would be stubbornly held. For the Japanese, these islands represented a chance to cause massive casualties and demonstrate to the Unitd States what an invasion of the Home Islands would cost, perhaps deterring the enemy or allowing a negotiated peace.

Okinawa, being larger, was held in even greater strength. The assault began on 1 April 1945, hitting the central part of the island. US forces pushing northeastwards were able to make good progress; the last opposition in that end of the island was crushed by 21 April. However, the main Japanese position was in the southwest and this proved very difficult to eliminate.

Japanese troops counterattacked strongly and, on the defensive, had to be dug out of caves or prized at bayonet point out of good positions. The assault bogged down for a time, and on 4 May the Japanese counterattacked again, using amphibious landings to outflank US positions. By 11 May, the Allies were again on the offensive, however, and

The aftermath of nuclear bombardment. At the end of the World War II, it seemed probable that this scene would be repeated in any major conflict.

The surrender of Japan was on 2 September 1945 aboard the battleship USS *Missouri*. Had the Allies invaded the Japanese home islands, the death toll among Japanese civilians and troops of both sides would have been immense.

on 13 May two key pieces of high ground were taken, compromising the Japanese line. The main Japanese position at Shuri Castle was taken on 29 May.

However, it still was not over. The defenders fell back to a last line with their backs to the sea and fought on until 17 June, when the last organized units collapsed. Mopping up took a while longer, but Okinawa was in US hands by 4 June 1945. The way was now open for the final invasion of Japan. Significant ground forces were still in action in Burma and Siam, and there were still some reserves available by pulling troops out of the captured territories in China. Preparations for the defence of the home islands included suicide troops and plans for fanatical stands by army units as well as civilian irregulars. The Allies were apprehensive about the price they would have to pay in order to end the war.

However, two events made the invasion unnecessary. One was the delivery of atomic bombs against Hiroshima and Nagasaki. The other was the declaration of war on Japan by the Soviet Union, which had enormous forces at its disposal.

JAPAN SURRENDER

The surrender of Japan became official on 2 September 1945, though it had been a fact for some time before that. The atomic bombs alone did not force surrender; the threat of Soviet invasion was also a factor. However, it was the bombs that cast the biggest shadow over the events of those days. Most observers believed that conventional forces were now obsolete, and that any future war would be fought with nuclear weapons.

Although this grim prediction did not come true, it is true to say that the end of World War II was also the end of the industrial age of warfare and the beginning of the nuclear age. Nuclear weapons might not be used in future conflicts but they would influence strategic thinking and the conduct of warfare in profound ways.

45
USA
3-64Δ

The Nuclear Age

Many people believe that the end of World War II ushered in a new era of peace and stability. To some extent, this is true. Certainly there has been no period since where so many nations were involved in conflict, nor has such widespread devastation taken place in the post-war world. Yet just as the Great War To End All Wars, as World War I was once known, did not succeed in eliminating all conflict, the 'peace' that followed World War II was both fragile and incomplete.

Thus far, we have avoided the horrors of all-out worldwide conflict, but a great many smaller wars have been fought, some of them involving tremendous upheaval and all of them causing great suffering. Many of these conflicts resulted from the political situation that arose after the end of the war. The increasingly tense standoff between the former allies in East and West, and the emergence of China as a superpower in its own right, polarized the allegiance of many nations and armed groups within them.

Meanwhile, the colonial age was truly over and its legacies crumbling. The British were shedding their former Imperial territories and colonial possessions of other nations were seeking independence. In many cases, this was achieved peacefully. In others, there was unnecessary violence as the forces of the departing colonial powers were attacked by extremist groups. Some nations fought for their independence.

On top of all this, a rash of revolutions, civil wars and low-level insurgencies broke out in the decades after the end of the war. Some resulted from the conditions mentioned above; others were due to local social, economic and political factors. Thus while large-scale conventional conflict has been relatively

At the end of the World War II, relations between the former allies cooled rapidly and the armed standoff known as the Cold War began.

SDKFZ 251/1

Type: Armoured Personnel Carrier

Crew: 12

Powerplant: one Maybach six-cylinder petrol engine developing 74.6kW (100hp)

Weight: 7810kg (17,182lb)

Range: 300km (186 miles)

Armour: 6–14.5mm (0.23in–0.6in)

Armament: two 7.92mm (0.31in) machine guns

Performance: maximum road speed 52.5km/h (32.5mph); fording 0.6m (2ft); vertical obstacle 2.0m (6ft 6.7in)

Dimensions: length 58m (19ft 0.3in)
width 2.10m (6ft 10.7in)
height 1.75m (5ft 8.9in)

uncommon since 1945, military forces have been involved in a great variety of combat situations during this period. These range from insurgencies and guerrilla conflicts through revolution and civil war to what amounts to major wars, even if they were not named as such. The following chapters attempt to distinguish between large-scale international warfare and other conflicts, which includes what might be termed 'bushfire wars', 'operations in support of peace' and internal conflicts.

There have been many conflicts since 1945, and it is not possible to detail them all here. Many low-level conflicts, while deserving of more detailed treatment for reasons of historical interest, are glossed over or omitted because their military characteristics are repeated elsewhere. To try to cover them all would be to create an immense and depressingly repetitive volume. Where there is a significant or unusual factor about the conflict, or if it had particularly important ramifications for the wider world, it is included. No disrespect is intended to those who fought or suffered in the omitted conflicts.

WORLD WAR II AFTERMATH

The changes that came about in the years 1939–45 were profound. Most of the concepts and technologies existed before the war, but it required a major conflict to allow the evolution of doctrines to make best use of them.

The most important outcome of the war, from the point of view of doctrine, was the use of fast-moving armoured formations to achieve a breakthrough and exploit it. The tank was the instrument of choice for such operations, but tanks alone could not overcome all obstacles. Support from the other combat arms and from the air was also necessary.

Thus tactical air power had become an integral part of ground operations by the end of the war. Formations needed some form of air defence, and specialist vehicles had appeared to fulfil the role in fast-moving armoured formations.

Similarly, while the concept of combined arms operations goes back literally millennia, it became ever more critical in the new age of warfare. Armoured fighting vehicles combined firepower and mobility with protection, but they could not do everything. Infantry and artillery were necessary to successful operations, and they had to be able to keep up with the tanks.

Thus self-propelled artillery became common, with the added advantage that it could 'shoot and scoot', avoiding counter-battery fire. Infantry had to be provided with

ARMOURED 'BATTLE-TAXIS' ARE NOT NEW

The APC was not a new concept; what were effectively gunless tanks were used in World War I to move troops across no-man's land. However, they became properly integrated into the mobile forces only in World War II. The original APCs were simply armoured trucks, many of them in half-track configurations, but soon purpose-designed APCs began to appear. These were generally constructed on the lines of a tank, though much more lightly armoured. Wheeled versions have always been available, which do not have such good off-road performance but are cheaper and usually faster.

mobility, too. Simple trucks were fine for strategic mobility – getting troops to a battle area – but they were very vulnerable. The solution was to create transport for infantry that could also protect them, and so the Armoured Personnel Carrier (APC) was created.

APCs were originally envisaged to act as 'battle taxis' from which the infantry dismounted to fight. Their armament, usually just a machine gun, allowed for some air defence and self-protection on the move, and could be used to support infantry as a sort of mobile emplacement.

Some APCs were fitted with firing ports to allow troops to shoot on the move, such as during an assault or encounter battle. The effect of such shooting could never be more than marginal; the occupants would be bounced about too much by a vehicle on the move. However, the concept of the APC as more than an armoured

> The most important outcome of the war, from the point of view of doctrine, was the use of fast-moving armoured formations to achieve a breakthrough and exploit it.

transport was of sufficient interest that some users began to develop infantry Fighting Vehicles (IFVs). IFVs (sometimes designated Mechanized Infantry Combat Vehicles, or MICVs) were designed to do much more than transport troops. The IFV could also support them in combat with automatic cannon or even anti-tank missiles. There are still varying opinions worldwide about how much protection and armament is best for an APC or IFV. Too much and the vehicle becomes too expensive to deploy in numbers, while at the same time reducing the number of troops that can be carried. Too little and the vehicle is of negligible combat value. Many users see the latter as wasteful – if a significant part of the defence budget has to be spent on transport for the infantry, that transport needs to contribute to the fighting power of the formations.

Once the APC concept proved itself, infinite variations became possible. The basic vehicle provided mobility and some protection while the space inside could be put to all manner of uses, creating a command post.

The APC also spawned a range of other vehicles, from field ambulances and command posts to artillery observation vehicles and mobile electronic warfare posts. Often built as a family of vehicles on the same hull, these vehicles contributed to the creation of fully integrated armoured battle groups.

To be able to carry out their roles, the armoured forces needed to cross or remove obstacles. For this reason, engineering vehicles and bridge-layers were also developed along with specialist formations to use them. The recovery and repair of broken-down or damaged vehicles proved its worth during the war, with many vehicles towed from the battlefields returning later to fight again. The sheer expense of armoured vehicles (and the desire not to allow the technology aboard to fall into enemy hands) necessitated the formation of specialist armoured recovery and field workshop units.

The final factor was to some extent dictated by this vast preponderance of vehicles and technical equipment, or more accurately by the amount of support it all needed. As the armoured formations developed ever sharper 'teeth', they also needed an increasing amount of 'tail' to keep them fed, fuelled and armed. The logistics vehicles themselves needed logistical support. Thus the task of maintaining an armoured force in the field grew ever more complex and expensive.

As the armoured formations developed ever sharper 'teeth', they also needed an increasing amount of 'tail' to keep them fed, fuelled and armed.

However, it was also necessary. World War II demonstrated that armoured forces were required for effective offensive actions and also to oppose them. Static infantry garrisons and fortresses could achieve only so much; mobility was the key to victory. Thus in the tense years after World War II the major powers engaged in a build-up of armoured forces, and it was this 'grand threat' that influenced strategic thinking most of all.

As relations between the Soviet Union and her former allies

The Churchill tank and its descendants served into the early Cold War years before being replaced by more modern vehicles. The chassis remained in service much longer as the basis for mobile bridging equipment.

The annual May Day parades in Red Square served to demonstrate the military power of the Soviet Union and remind both friendly and potentially hostile states of the potency of her armies.

deteriorated and the 'Iron Curtain' came down across Europe, what became known as the Cold War began. The formation in 1949 of NATO (the North Atlantic Treaty Organization) among mostly Western European nations, plus the United States and Canada, was countered by the 1955 Warsaw Pact.

NATO differed from the Warsaw Pact in several ways. Most importantly, NATO was an alliance of independent nations who agreed to work together in matters of defence and foreign policy, and most especially to defend themselves from Soviet aggression. Each nation remained free to obtain or produce its own military equipment as it saw fit, though technology that would not have been made available to non-allies was traded between NATO members and standardization of weapon calibres was undertaken.

However, NATO remained very much an alliance of independents, who were at times prone to disagreements. On the other hand, the Warsaw Pact was essentially a formalization of the existing treaties between the Soviet Union and her allies, tying all of them into a framework that was subordinate to Moscow.

EQUIPMENT STANDARDIZATION

Much greater standardization of equipment and procedures existed among the Warsaw pact nations, which also had far greater manpower available. Warsaw pact equipment tended to be simpler and often cruder than that used by NATO countries, not least because it was to be employed in vast numbers by conscript armies, whereas the less numerous forces of the West were generally filled by volunteers of a standard of higher education. The differences in thinking between the two alliances are best illustrated by their tank designs. Soviet tanks, used by all Warsaw Pact nations, were optimized for mobile combat in large numbers. Low, rounded turrets made a hard target and afforded good protection for tanks that expected to fight on the move. Vehicles were simple and robust in order to withstand being maintained by relatively poorly trained crews.

Western tanks, on the other hand, were far less numerous but qualitatively better. The expectation was that these vehicles might have to fight a defensive battle against a horde

The US M47 'Patton' tank was the last in a line descended from World War II designs. The M48 was the beginning of a new family, which discarded features such as a hull-mounted machine gun.

of Soviet vehicles. They were thus designed for survivability as well as the ability to fight from defensive positions. Somewhat higher turrets than their expected opponents were common, enabling the Western tank to engage from a hull-down position behind cover.

The tank was very much the weapon of decision in the years after the end of the World War II. In the Soviet army, it was considered vital that every unit, no matter what its function, must be able to fight tanks. Thus marginal weapons, like the RPG-7 grenade launcher, were issued to formations that did not possess a better anti-tank capability. The best tank country, the Soviets said, was that without anti-tank weapons, and a unit which could not fight tanks could not fight at all.

The same problem faced NATO. If the Cold War went 'hot', they would have to stop vast numbers of tanks pouring westwards. The Soviet advances at the end of the recent war indicated that they would be difficult to halt. The questions that plagued the planners were how to do it, and more importantly, whether it could be done at all.

IDEAS PUT FORWARD

Various ideas, some of them rather strange, were put forward. Belts of concealed fortifications manned by infantry with anti-tank missiles, creating a defended zone in the countryside of West Germany, were suggested several times. However, fortifications had not helped much in recent history and there was no reason to believe that the results would be any different this time around.

Other ideas included a mass civilian defence force of German citizens armed with disposable light anti-tank weapons, which would be used from concealed positions or even the sunroofs of private cars. This bizarre concept was quietly discarded, which was probably just as well.

This left only two options, one of which was already in place. At the end of the war, large Western forces remained in Germany and these would form the basis of resistance to an invasion from the East. They would be reinforced as quickly as possible but would have to take the brunt of the Soviet attack. Pre-positioning heavy equipment in Europe for the use of US troops when they arrived would speed up reinforcement, but it would still take time to establish sufficient force density to guarantee success.

The Soviets were thus in some ways in the same position in which Nazi Germany had found herself at the outbreak of World War II. There was an initial period in which chances of a knockout blow were good, after which the odds would lengthen considerably. If a crisis arose that required war to be considered as an option, the question that would be asked was this: Could the Warsaw Pact overrun Europe fast enough to prevent the reinforcement of forces – particularly US forces – stationed there?

Deterrence was achieved in another way. For a time, the United States maintained a policy of 'massive retaliation' against even conventional aggression. The key factor was that an invasion of Europe might be met with nuclear bombing of Warsaw Pact cities. Later, this policy was modified to one of 'flexible response', which did not rule out a strategic nuclear response to a conventional attack but made it far less likely.

There was the second option, to defend Europe using the threat (or actual use) of strategic weapons. The situation was further complicated by the availability of tactical nuclear weapons. These ranged from demolition charges through artillery shells to aircraft-delivered bombs and short-ranged missiles.

A range of battlefield nuclear weapons were developed in the 1950s and '60s, including atomic howitzers and even infantry weapons designed to deliver a nuclear warhead to a target just over 3km (2 miles) away. The thinking behind these weapons

CONVENTIONAL FORCES

The role of conventional forces in Europe was not just to fight off an invasion, though obviously it was hoped that they could do so, or at least to impose sufficient delay on the Warsaw Pact that reinforcement operations could be undertaken. They also had an important deterrent role. Whatever the actual capabilities of these forces, if they could create sufficient doubt in the minds of Soviet planners that a knockout could be achieved, they might serve to deter an attack altogether.

The RPG-7 gave a measure of anti-armour capability to infantry and other forces. It is a 'spigot mortar' type weapon, which launches a 70mm (2.75in) rocket-propelled grenade from a re-useable launch and aiming device.

was to make up for the discrepancy in numbers with destructive power, and to deter an attack by the threat of their use. There was always a risk that the use of battlefield nuclear weapons would escalate into a strategic exchange that would wreck all the nations involved, and indeed many observers felt that the days of conventional forces were over. Any future conflict would be fought with nuclear weapons and the only role for conventional units was as a 'tripwire' to trigger the nuclear alert.

However, as the second half of the twentieth century would show, nuclear weapons may have affected strategic thinking but they did not dominate warfare. The nuclear age began in 1945 with two detonations, and no nuclear device has been used in anger since.

Warfare in the nuclear age is influenced by the need to consider the nuclear option. Forces normally concentrate to fight but dispersal is needed to survive a nuclear attack; conventional forces train to undertake such a dispersal if the need arises and to decontaminate their equipment if they survive it.

The nuclear option also affects strategic thinking, imposing limits on military and strategic operations.

There was always a risk that the use of battlefield nuclear weapons would escalate into a strategic exchange that would wreck all the nations involved.

If war had broken out between East and West, Germany would have been the primary battleground. British, US and German armoured forces would have faced the daunting task of halting the advance of the Red Army.

A US Army atomic howitzer, capable of delivering a low-yield nuclear warhead. Nuclear weapons offered a means to offset the numerical advantages of the Red Army, albeit at the cost of using atomic munitions.

Indeed, many of the wars of the later twentieth century were fought between groups armed and supported by the superpowers. They formed part of the jockeying for position that went on during the Cold War, allowing the Warsaw Pact and NATO to further their interests without coming into direct conflict.

Other dimensions of warfare also became important. So-called 'brushfire wars' flared up all over the world, involving the conventional forces of the greater and lesser powers. Insurrection and revolution also required a conventional response – nuclear weapons are useless against a revolutionary cell in an otherwise friendly city.

The term 'brushfire war' has been applied to relatively low-intensity conflict, not least because of its tendency to flare up again after a period of apparent quiet. The term applies most correctly to insurgent conflicts in overseas or colonial holdings, but the characteristics of this kind of warfare are similar to other sorts of insurgency as well as counter-revolutionary warfare.

Conflicts of this type tend to be highly asymmetric. There is, of course, asymmetry in all conflict – only in chess are the two sides perfectly matched. A war between two major powers equipped with modern weapons, albeit of different designs and in differing numbers, is not what would be termed an asymmetric conflict, however. Only if one side fielded modern tanks and aircraft against a force of ill-armed rebels would there be obvious asymmetry.

Common sense suggests that the modern technological force should

A multiple-launch rocket system fires. Short-ranged and inaccurate, and liable to pinpoint their firing position by throwing up a huge cloud of debris due to backblast, rocket systems can dump large amounts of explosive.

win easily, and yet this has not always been the case. One side or the other will always have greater numbers, better technology, more effective training and many other potential advantages. Which side's assets will be decisive is not always apparent; good strategy is all about making use of one's own advantages while denying the enemy the benefit of his.

WAR AND POLITICS

It has long been held that war and politics are two sides of the same coin. Warfare is, after all, simply the attempt to impose one side's political will by force upon the other. However, in a brushfire-war situation, the two are even more intertwined. Guerrillas may be hidden from the authorities by the local populace or revealed to them, depending on how the two sides are perceived. A military defeat might result in a loss of popular support. Many apparently pointless military operations are therefore undertaken for their value in influencing popular opinion.

Thus while sometimes the goal of an operation is simply to kill or capture members of the enemy force, a commander who sees the destruction of enemy forces as his only goal is in danger of winning battles at the expense of the war. If insurgents can demonstrate to the populace that the government cannot protect them or even carry out its basic functions of providing services, collecting taxes and the like, then the government will lose support.

Thus there are many dimensions to such conflicts, and any given operation may have important consequences to the war as a whole. As well as attacking each other's forces, the two sides will also seek to discredit one another in the opinion of the populace. A brushfire war can be won or lost in the field or in the newspaper stands. This is also true of conflicts on a larger scale. The widespread availability of information in the modern world has changed the nature of war considerably. Many otherwise conventional wars are fought with one eye on the reactions of the friendly and enemy populations.

To some extent, this is nothing new. Many military operations have been launched over the centuries in the hope of triggering a popular rising or discrediting a ruler. However, the presence of news cameras and other means of getting reports of the conflict to people all over the world adds a new importance to this aspect of conflict. The main difference is that in conventional conflict, it is of lesser importance than the military operations undertaken against enemy forces, whereas in a lower-intensity conflict the 'living-room warfare' element of the conflict may be one side's only real hope for victory.

Despite the prediction that conventional forces had been rendered obsolete by the nuclear dimension, large-scale conventional conflict did not disappear. Just a few years after the end of World War II, the Korean conflict pitted large forces against one another. Tank battles and artillery bombardments took place much as in World War II.

Thus as the twentieth century went on, it was found that the availability of nuclear weapons did not do away with the necessity to field conventional forces. Indeed, the demands on the militaries of modern nations are perhaps wider than ever. In addition to dealing with the 'grand threat' – large concentrations of advanced Main Battle Tanks and their supporting formations – the modern army must also be able to deal with lower levels of threat, including peacekeeping, counter-insurgency and low-intensity conflict.

The nuclear dimension did change the nature of warfare, and as a general rule lowered the intensity of conflict that has taken place in the second half of the twentieth century. This in turn led to a number of changes in the way wars are fought. The 'battle space' in which an army of the twenty-first century must operate is more complex than it has ever been. The events of the second half of the twentieth century show how that came to be.

LARGE-SCALE CONFLICT IN THE NUCLEAR AGE

Other large-scale conflicts took place; the Falklands War, the Iran-Iraq War and what is normally referred to as the First Gulf War (though the Iran-Iraq conflict is also given that name in some quarters). All pitted large conventional armies against one another. Other conflicts fell somewhere between a war of this type and an insurgency, such as the US involvement in Vietnam.

Despite predictions about the widespread use of nuclear weapons in future conflict, no nuclear weapon has been used in combat since 1945. Conventional weaponry, including tanks and artillery, has developed in sophistication.

Post-War Guerrilla Conflict

1945–1960

Insurgency and guerrilla warfare were nothing new, but in the years after World War II they ceased to be a nuisance and became a real force for political change. Conventional forces that failed to adapt to the new situation risked an insidious defeat even while they seemed to be winning.

CIVIL WAR IN CHINA

By the time World War II ended, China had been troubled for many years. The last emperor abdicated in 1912, and the breakdown of central government left power in the hands of regional warlords and the leaders of political factions. Various warlords (usually whoever had control of the capital) were recognized by outside powers, but the internal situation was very confused.

From this situation arose a new power, the Kuomintang (KMT), or Chinese Nationalist Party. Its goals were to re-unify the country and implement democracy, while keeping out Western influences. Its chief opponent was the Chinese Communist Party, which was at that time very small.

The KMT attempted to ally itself with the Soviet Union and received support in its bid to bring the warlords to heel. This included military advisors and some hardware. While happy to recruit Communist Party members, the KMT was not willing to bring

The Chinese Communist Party had much to offer the workers and farmers of post-war China. Its officials largely came from among their numbers and dressed like the people they represented.

Chiang Kai-shek was a senior army officer who took control of the Chinese Nationalist movement after the death of Sun Yat-sen. He removed many Communists from the Kuomintang ranks.

the organization on board as an ally or subordinate. However, when the KMT founder, Sun Yat-sen, died in 1925 the individual Communist members of the KMT began to exert greater influence on it. This suited the Soviet Union, which preferred a communist China to a nationalist one.

The situation was not acceptable to General Chiang Kai-shek, who saw himself as rightful successor to Sun Yat-sen. He purged many Communists from the KMT before launching a military campaign that took control of most of central China from the warlords and gave the KMT control of Shanghai. More widespread purges followed, in which thousands of Communists were killed, and the Soviet advisors were sent home.

The Communists, who had grown in strength somewhat, responded by orchestrating a rising on 1 August 1927. It was quickly put down but is usually considered to be the beginning of the Chinese Civil War. Uprisings followed in several cities, but these were also suppressed. These were influenced by Soviet thinking, which had worked well enough in 1917 but failed in China. Having tried urban insurrection, the Chinese Communists looked for another means to secure victory.

The Kuomintang gradually increased its hold over the country, but was not entirely successful in removing cadres of Communist supporters from the cities, or in entirely eliminating guerrillas in remote areas. Worse, the Communists had secured control of a modest region and declared Mao Tse-tung president of it.

Now receiving German military advice, the KMT moved against the Communist-held areas with the intent of crushing them. Sure of defeat if he stood his ground, Mao took radical action. Mustering some 100,000 of his supporters, he led them westwards on what became known as the Long March, which began in October 1934.

By 1937, China was being overrun by the forces of Imperial Japan and the KMT was more concerned with repelling the invaders than fighting fellow Chinese. A deal was offered to the Communists to present a united front against the Japanese, which was accepted by Mao and his followers.

The prestige of the KMT and its credibility as a government plummeted as the Japanese inflicted a series of defeats and captured large segments of the country. The ill-armed Chinese army – in some areas, little more than militia armed with outdated weapons – could do little against even the rather poor tanks

THE LONG MARCH REACHES ITS END

Fewer than 20,000 of Mao's supporters reached their final destination, after a march through difficult terrain. Covering several thousand kilometres (claims to the exact figure range between 6000km/3730 miles and 13,000km/8078 miles), they suffered great hardship, but managed to leave the KMT forces behind. The terrain that they crossed was a barrier to a military campaign against them, allowing the Communists to set up a new capital and make preparations for the struggle ahead.

and the aircraft of the Japanese invaders. Meanwhile, the Communists actually benefited from the situation. As their opponents lost face and in some regions descended into confusion, the Communists maintained good discipline and conducted reasonably effective guerrilla warfare against the invaders, in some cases gaining control of new areas.

As the tide of war turned against the Japanese in other theatres, the United States tried to broker a deal between the Communists and the KMT, but neither group was interested in a deal. Wanting sole power, both consolidated their hold on those parts of the country where they could and began preparing for a showdown. The United States helped airlift KMT troops into the northern and eastern regions of China to counteract growing Communist influence.

Despite several attempts to facilitate negotiations and several truces, open conflict soon broke out again between the factions. Open fighting was taking place throughout China by July 1946, and by the end of the year the United States withdrew its involvement.

As confidence in the Nationalists fell, the Communist message began to reach ever-greater numbers of people. Some of those coming to hear Communist speakers would return to their homes and spread the message still further.

The Communists had named their military assets the People's Liberation Army (PLA) and were using tactics they had developed over the past few troubled years, against both the Japanese and their fellow Chinese. Mao Tse-tung had long ago abandoned the Soviet style of insurrection, which called for armed occupation of the cities as its main tool. Instead he focused on control of the countryside and the people who lived there.

As the bulk of the Chinese population were rural workers, this approach yielded the PLA vast numbers of recruits. It was here that the seeds of victory were sown, as any successful insurgency requires the support of the local population. Mao knew that friendly peasants would feed his men and give them information; hostile locals would betray them to the government. He thus set about winning over the people.

Chinese Nationalist (Kuomintang) forces in action. Although extensively re-equipped with donated US weaponry after the end of the war, the KMT failed to retrain its troops to make best use of their new equipment.

REQUIRED PRINCIPLES

To this end, Mao established certain principles that his men were required to follow at all times. In their dealings with the people, Communist personnel were required to act as friends, being respectful, polite and fair at all times. They were to return anything borrowed, pay for anything damaged, and not to cause ill feeling by damaging the peasants' crops or other means of making a living, and not to flirt with their women.

Significantly, Mao also enjoined his men not to treat prisoners badly. He believed that some could be recruited, and even those that could not be would spread the word that their enemies were not the monsters that government propaganda painted them as. The common enemy soldier, just like his brother who remained at home to work the fields, was a target in Mao's campaign to win over what would later be termed 'hearts and minds'.

Mao's intent was to present his men as no different to the peasants they moved among. They were no better off and were fighting to make things better for everyone. They were no richer and were not inclined to lord it over their peasant friends. The Nationalists were painted as corrupt, disorganized, arrogant and intent on forcing their will on the common people whether it was in their interests or not.

Communist groups living in the villages also provided supplies and information to the PLA, and recruited new members to fight or to spread the process to another village. Spies were

Communist recruits undergoing basic training before being issued rifles. The Communists did not simply train their troops to fight. Indoctrination in their political views was also carried out.

presented as enemies of the local populace, their execution described as being in the common good. By encouraging the population to be pro-Communist and eliminating the opposition, Mao hoped to turn the rural population into a 'sea' in which 'fish' (i.e. Communist guerrillas) could swim.

The KMT made no organized efforts to win over the populace in this manner, and tended to impose control in the traditional manner of a legitimate government. This made Nationalist troops and officials come over as distant, aloof and arrogant. It might not have mattered much under other circumstances, as the acceptance of governmental authority tends to become something of a habit. However, with the Communists spreading the message that this authority did not have to be accepted and actively demonstrating a more peasant-friendly form of governance, the effects on the allegiance of the rural population were considerable.

PLAYING THE LONG GAME

Mao Tse-tung was playing a long game. He was not after meaningless field victories, and did not believe that defeating enemy forces was a worthwhile end in and of it self. Instead, he believed that every action taken by his forces must be in support of the overall goal of the campaign, which was to take control of the country by gaining the support and allegiance of the people.

The military side of the campaign was to be carried out in three stages. At first, and in any area where the Communists were weak, the aim must be defensive. The goal was to establish a presence and maintain it while harassing the nationalist forces in the area. Capturing weapons, gaining information and winning over the local people were the main aims. Eliminating KMT forces in a region would not be possible in this stage.

The next stage would begin when the Communists had built up their

WINNING OVER THE POPULATION

Mao's supporters moved into many villages (or recruited representatives from among the local populace) and gradually insinuated themselves into the daily life of the people. Communist supporters helped educate the locals and protect them from banditry, and took part in necessary local projects. Meanwhile their message was disseminated, not by distant propaganda, but by friends living close by, or else was wrapped around entertainment and education.

TYPE 95

Type: Light tank

Crew: 4

Powerplant: one Mitsubishi NVD 6120 six-cylinder air-cooled diesel engine developing 89kW (120hp)

Weight: 7400kg (16,280lb)

Range: 250km (156 miles)

Armour: 6–14mm (0.25–0.6in)

Armament: one 37mm (1.46in); two 7.7mm (0.3in) machine guns

Performance: maximum road speed 45km/h (28mph); fording 1.0m (3ft 3in); vertical obstacle 0.8m (2ft 8in); trench 2.0 (6ft 7in)

Dimensions: length 4.38m (14ft 4in)
width 2.057m (6ft 9in)
height 2.184m (7ft 2in)

power somewhat. The emphasis would be shifted to securing the area and building up a conventional combat force capable of directly challenging government forces. Once sufficient forces were available, the final phase could begin.

The third stage was to engage in more or less conventional warfare, challenging the government forces directly and defeating them to gain control of strategic objectives. As well as the obvious goal of destroying the Nationalists' ability to fight, this would also send a message to the world in general that the Communists were a power to be taken seriously and perhaps to be recognized as a legitimate government. Few world powers would be inclined to recognize a gang of revolutionaries but a political group capable of fielding a conventional army was something rather different.

There was no need for the campaign to progress at the same rate in all areas at once. One region might be at Stage Three while the Communists were just moving into another to start Stage One. A major setback might force Mao to go back to Stage One in a given area, beginning the process again.

Mao formulated 10 strategic principles for the conduct of the campaign. These were simple common-sense rules that may seem obvious, but were profoundly effective. Mao's overall plan was to strike only after good preparations when victory was all but assured, in keeping with Sun Tzu's concept of winning before engaging in combat. Targets were to be carefully selected, beginning with weak and isolated objectives and moving on to better-protected areas and stronger forces when the means to eliminate them were available. Targets that yielded weapons which could be used by the guerrillas, or even prisoners who might be persuaded to switch sides, were to be chosen above purely symbolic ones.

Tactics were to favour the guerrillas' strengths and to minimize their weaknesses. Where possible, the enemy should be attacked while on the move because this was the point when he was vulnerable. Attacks should be made so as to concentrate against one part of the enemy force and annihilate it before moving on to another. This would achieve local superiority of numbers and ensure that a defeated enemy force would be unable to rally and return to the fight.

Mao formulated 10 strategic principles for the conduct of the campaign. These were simple common-sense rules that may seem obvious but were profoundly effective.

Morale was considered important on both sides. Mao enjoined his commanders to keep the enemy off balance by making small harassing attacks even when the main body of Communist forces was regrouping or resting. He urged his commanders to reward bravery and to be willing to suffer hardship and make sacrifices if necessary to achieve a goal. However, Mao's most critical strategic principle was to define the goal of every operation. The point was not to capture and hold objectives but to destroy the enemy's ability to engage in combat. Once the enemy was unable to fight, objectives could be occupied without cost. If capturing or holding a position was useful to the goal of eroding the enemy's means or will to fight, the operation was worthwhile, but Mao was not willing to be drawn into battles of attrition for possession of a meaningless terrain feature or even an important city.

WEAPONS DO NOT MAKE AN EFFECTIVE ARMY

With the surrender of Japan, large quantities of US equipment were made available to the Nationalists, giving them a considerable military advantage over their Communist enemies. However, training levels were generally low and many experienced personnel, notably senior officers, had been killed. The result was that although the rabble was now heavily armed, it had not really regained the status of a professional army. In particular, it did not know how to get the most from its new weaponry.

Mao redefined guerrilla operations to a great extent. His principles have been used as the basis for many guerrilla campaigns since that fought by Mao and his Communists. Even those fighting Mao have used them against him. Those who had no real alternative had used these methods previously, but Mao believed that a strategic result could be obtained by following such a strategy. As conflict with the KMT intensified, his theory was put to the test.

MASS MOBILIZATION

The Nationalists were not greatly interested in mass mobilization of the population. They possessed an

Mao Tse-tung was the child of peasant farmers. Though not especially poor, he did have an insight into the problems faced by the vast majority of the Chinese population. It also allowed him to speak to the ordinary people.

experienced standing army augmented by additional regular troops raised by normal recruitment methods. The top echelon of commanders were extremely loyal to Chiang Kai-shek, and were indoctrinated with traditional methods of warfare. These emphasized tactics that had been used in World War I, along with the application of heavy firepower to achieve a victory.

Despite American advice to the contrary, and without taking the time to retrain their forces, the KMT advanced rapidly into Manchuria.

However, the Nationalist style of warfare required the support of industry and commerce, which was available only in the cities. As the KMT was pushed away from the urban areas, a disintegrating support chain meant that the combat effectiveness of its forces fell off rapidly.

This was largely a result of Japanese actions rather than those of the Communists. The Japanese took control of the major ports and cities along the eastern and southern coasts, pushing the KMT inland and forcing it to fall back on local resources. Some Western assistance was available, largely airlifted in, but by the time of the Japanese surrender the Nationalist forces were very ill equipped and had been reduced to the status of an armed rabble.

Despite American advice to the contrary, and without taking the time to retrain their forces, the KMT advanced rapidly into Manchuria. The goal was to gain control of the cities of Manchuria, a predictable aim given the conventional thinking of the KMT leadership. At first, things went well. Bringing their new firepower to bear, the KMT was able to sledgehammer the Communists out of the region south of Harbin and the Sungari River. However, a sledgehammer is a poor weapon with which to tackle a swarm of bees, and after regrouping during one of the many truces, the Communists began to infiltrate back into the region and launch harassing attacks.

LOGISTICAL PROBLEM

One of the main problems faced by the KMT was that the main logistical link for these forces was a single railway. Large numbers of troops had to be deployed to protect it, and this dispersed manpower and exposed small groups to attack. By January 1947, the KMT was in control of many cities of Manchuria, but coming under increasingly serious attack outside them.

Having occupied the cities, the KMT then had to hold them. This was a huge drain on manpower, indeed, more than could be afforded. The Communists made the task more

TYPE 96

Type: Light Machine Gun

Calibre: 6.5mm (0.256in)

Length overall: 1054mm (41.5in)

Length of barrel: 552mm (21.75in)

Weight: 9.07kg (20lb)

Muzzle velocity: 730m (92395ft) per second

Rate of fire, cyclic: 550rpm

Feed: 30 round box

The fragmented political structure of China, as much as its outdated military forces, allowed the Japanese to overrun much of the country in the 1930s. Both the Communists and the KMT fought the invaders.

difficult by launching raids and ambushes using weaponry obtained from the Japanese. The situation rapidly stagnated, with the KMT trapped in the cities by Communist control of the countryside and also by their own mindset. They were gradually ground down, with the Communists gaining more weaponry with every garrison they overran.

The answer was to withdraw or at least to try to clear the surrounding countryside of Communist forces, but the KMT were wedded to the concept of positional warfare and lacked both the manpower and the will to conduct difficult counterinsurgent operations in the countryside. The overextended forces were thus gradually depleted while the Communists gained prestige from their victories. The cities remained under KMT control, but the attitudes of the people were gradually changing. The Communists were winning the war in small and apparently insignificant stages.

RAILWAY SEVERED

Late in 1947, Communist forces severed the rail lifeline to the south, cutting off the garrisons. These were still powerful enough to make a direct attack suicidal, but they lacked the capability to project power. Some were evacuated to bolster others, which remained effectively under siege while the Communists consolidated their hold on the surrounding rural population. One of the most important cites in the region was Mukden, heavily garrisoned by KMT forces. Cut off in hostile countryside, the city was supplied by air and subject to strict rationing. The Communists, understanding the importance that their opponents placed on the city, made threatening movements towards it to attract KMT attention, but struck at Chinchow instead.

With their supply line cut and the situation deteriorating rapidly, the Nationalists decided to pull out of Manchuria at last. Some forces drove eastwards, hoping to be evacuated by

The Chinese Civil War was a bitter conflict in which mass executions of enemy sympathisers were carried out. This was more commonly a Nationalist policy, as the Communists preferred trying to convert prisoners to their cause.

sea. Others decided that defection to the enemy was a better option. Forces around Mukden, representing the main concentration of KMT military capability, were badly disrupted by an attack on their HQ, which left them leaderless.

A breakout was attempted in late October but was turned back, and the city's 200,000 defenders surrendered soon after. The Communists were by this point able to take on the Nationalists in the field on their own terms. Indeed, by the end of the year the Communists had captured so much Western equipment from the KMT, and had so greatly worn down their strength that they actually outnumbered their enemies in both manpower and heavy equipment.

The KMT defence of Manchuria collapsed by the end of November

NATIONALIST FAILURES AT CHINCHOW

Chinchow was an important strategic base and supply centre for the Nationalist forces, and its loss would be a disaster. Forces from Mukden were ordered to its relief in September 1948, but an offensive mindset was sadly lacking. A smaller force than intended was sent, and set off later than it was supposed to do. Nor was the movement of other troops ordered to assist well coordinated. The campaign went awry from the start and was completely wrecked when Nationalist forces in Chinchow defected to the Communists.

1948, and the Communists began to drive southwards with their main forces. Raids, harassment and the gradual takeover of the countryside went on unabated in keeping with Mao's principles, and this increased the Nationalists' problems by draining manpower throughout the country. However, the campaign was now moving towards its decisive phase.

The Nationalists concentrated their forces at Xuzhou. The city was well defended and stood on a vital rail nexus. Its loss would effectively rob the KMT of their ability to operate on the North China Plain. Both sides knew that this was the pivotal point of the war. The initial Communist drive on Xuzhou, in November 1948, was repulsed but the city soon became surrounded. A breakout was made southwards in the direction of Suzhou, which was also encircled. The breakout force, numbering over 300,000 men, was badly disorganized. The situation was exacerbated by Chiang Kai-shek's insistence on sending personal orders to divisional commanders in an attempt to micromanage the situation. As a result, there was little coherent strategy and the force was dragged to a standstill by Communist attacks. Cut off and surrounded, it was forced to surrender on 10 January 1949.

After defeating the KMT at Xuzhou, the Communists pushed south. By 20 January, they had reached the Yangtze River, where they paused to regroup. Chiang Kai-shek now resigned and his vice-president, Li Tsung-jen, moved the Nationalist government south away from the immediate threat.

In the meantime, Chiang Kai-shek made preparations to transfer the apparatus of government to Formosa, modern Taiwan.

Negotiations between the Nationalists and the Communists came to nothing, and in April 1949 Communist forces crossed the Yangtze. They were by this time operating as a conventional army with heavy artillery support. The Nationalist defence fell apart and nearby cities were occupied almost without resistance.

Throughout the summer and autumn of 1949, the Communists advanced without meeting serious opposition, consolidating their hold on the country. The Nationalist

Mukden was important enough that the Russian and Japanese armies fought over it in 1905. It was heavily garrisoned by the Nationalists, but by the time the Communists attacked they possessed the ability to defeat their enemies.

Left: The Communists used lenient treatment of prisoners as a political tool. This paid off; many soldiers chose to switch sides, and troops who knew they would be well treated were more inclined to surrender than fight to the last.

Above: The Yangtze River was a significant obstacle for the Communist forces. They wisely halted for a time to prepare for the crossing, by which time they had become a conventional army, complete with artillery and engineers.

government moved to avoid capture, finally relocating to Taiwan on 8 December 1949. In the meantime, the People's Republic of China was established in Beijing on 1 October, with the last Nationalist holdouts surrendering or being reduced within a few weeks.

The Nationalists' campaign into Manchuria proved to be their undoing. By fixating on the conventional goal of seizing control of the cities, they allowed themselves to be drawn into a situation where they could not win without changing their doctrine. The cities were not the key to defeating the Communists, who were not forced to fight for possession of them. As Mao had predicted, they fell into his hands once the fighting capability of the Kuomintang had been destroyed.

To a great extent, the two sides were fighting very different wars. The KMT was conducting conventional operations against an unconventional enemy and never had a realistic chance of success, even though by the normal yardsticks applied to such things they appeared to be winning. The Communists, on the other hand, worked quietly towards eventual victory without becoming distracted by the need to win battles for their own sake.

FRENCH INDOCHINA

Even as civil war raged in nearby China, the same principles of warfare were being implemented against a colonial power elsewhere in Southeast Asia. Great changes were sweeping through the region in the wake of World War II. The prestige of the Western powers, many of which still

The Chinese Communists were not interested in the capture of cities for its own sake, though they would fight for strategic objectives if necessary. Defeating the Nationalist armies enabled them to take control of the cities.

held colonial possessions in Southeast Asia, had been seriously dented and a new sense of nationalist feeling was emerging in many former colonies.

In many regions, communism had taken hold. The Western powers had never been fond of communist groups, but in the dark days of World War II they had accepted whatever allies they could. They armed and trained many of the groups who, after the war, became enemies.

France had obtained large areas as colonial possessions in the 1860s to 1880s, creating the region known as French Indochina and superimposing a colonial government over existing states and kingdoms. German defeat of France in 1940 resulted in the colonial administration being cut off and lacking support, making it easy for the Japanese to overrun the region.

VALIDATION OF INSURGENT METHODS

Mao's victory in the Chinese Civil War validated his thinking on this style of warfare, and prompted many others to use similar methods in subsequent campaigns. Where a more conventional enemy has failed to change its methods to deal with the threat, Mao's principles have brought success to apparently overmatched insurgent forces all over the world.

At the end of the war, France tried to regain control of its colonial regions, but rapidly ran into opposition. Groups formed to fight the Japanese occupation now stood against French reoccupation. Those who had fought and suffered for their independence were disinclined to meekly accept the reintroduction of foreign rule. Among them were Ho Chi Minh and Vo Nguyen Giap, who were both communists.

Various groups, many of them non-communists, had grouped together under the title of the League for the Independence of Vietnam in 1941. This group's rather lengthy name became shortened to Viet Minh, and under that title the league operated against the Japanese, gaining considerable experience of guerrilla operations. Japanese surrender left the Viet Minh in control of the northern part of the country, and a government was formed in September 1945 with its capital at Hanoi. However, the Western powers decreed that the region would be given back to France, and by 1946 French troops were in control of the southern part of the country, with the Viet Minh restricted to a fairly small region in the north.

As Ho Chi Minh set about rallying political support, his military commander, Giap, orchestrated the withdrawal of his forces to safe areas. These troops were experienced regulars and became the core of the resistance to French rule. In the meantime, light French forces occupied Hanoi.

CAMPAIGN TO FREE INDOCHINA

In February 1950, the campaign to free Indochina from French occupation began. Initial operations were modest, in keeping with Mao's proven doctrine. Outposts were targeted for sudden attacks made by concentrated forces, which dispersed when superior forces intervened, such as at Dong Khe, where a French parachute battalion was quickly sent to assist the defenders.

Giap used a preferred tactic of insurgents by using one attack to draw a response that could then be ambushed. A second attack on Dong Khe cut off the garrison of more northerly Cao Bang and forced it to abandon its position. During its subsequent retreat, the garrison was attacked and destroyed, while forces moving up to reinforce those under attack were also ambushed.

The resulting string of defeats cost the French several thousand troops and led to the abandonment of other forward bases. It was made possible by a policy of trying to cover too much ground with too few men, leaving small forces strung out and vulnerable in isolated positions. In some ways, Giap's early operations in the north of the country resembled the situation in Manchuria in 1946–7, albeit on a smaller scale. However, Giap now made a strategic error. Possessing large amounts of captured French equipment and with his core of regulars intact, he believed that the time had come to implement the third stage of insurgent warfare as theorized by Mao, bringing the campaign to a decisive close by entering open battle against the enemy with what amounted to a conventional army.

In January 1951, Giap launched a coventional offensive into the Red River Delta at Vinh Yen, aiming to take Hanoi. This played to the enemy's strengths, not his weaknesses, since French defences had been set up to defeat just such a attack. Giap was repulsed this time, and again in March and May. The French had

French troops in Saigon. The Japanese shattered the myth of Western superiority in World War II and the surrender of France to the Axis further dented their prestige, making regaining control of former colonies considerably more difficult.

secured the Red River Delta with a flexible system of defences. The outer layer comprised fortified outposts, with a mobile reserve of armour and infantry available to respond to an incursion. The effectiveness of the system now prompted the French to return to the offensive.

Seeking to eliminate Viet Minh bases, French forces, spearheaded by paratroops, advanced into the highlands. Giap responded by cutting off the supply lines to these forces and forcing them to withdraw. It became apparent that the French could not exert control over these regions without deploying massive manpower, which was not available, and over the next months the Viet Minh gradually consolidated their control over the region outside the delta fortified zone.

This was not acceptable to the French, who struck at Viet Minh supply centres in October 1952. Most of the available mobile forces were assigned to this mission, which was successful against very light resistance. However, once again the French became overstretched and had to withdraw. They were ambushed several times en route and suffered heavy losses before fighting their way back into the delta.

The Viet Minh response was quicker than anticipated, and the idea dawned on the French commanders that they could draw their enemies into a set-piece battle around Dien Bien Phu. The base was fortified and heavily garrisoned in the hope that the Viet Minh would attack and batter themselves to pieces on its defences.

Dien Bien Phu could be resupplied only by air, which proved increasingly costly as the Viet Minh obtained anti-aircraft guns from China and deployed them in the surrounding hills. Artillery pieces were also manhandled up the hills into places where conventional wisdom said a gun could not go.

Surrounded by five divisions of Viet Minh regulars – whose numbers had been gravely underestimated – the base came under constant shelling from 31 January 1954. As the outer defences were pushed in, the guns crept closer until the airstrip itself came under fire in early March. This made resupply even more hazardous.

Ho Chi Minh. In his youth, he developed a dislike for the French colonial administration and the Vietnamese monarchy. He later travelled worldwide, educating himself, before returning to Vietnam and becoming a revolutionary leader.

The siege of Dien Bien Phu continued for eight weeks, during which time the main strong points and outlying positions were gradually taken. The cost was high, but as each strong point was evacuated the perimeter shrank and the attackers were able to concentrate more forces against the others.

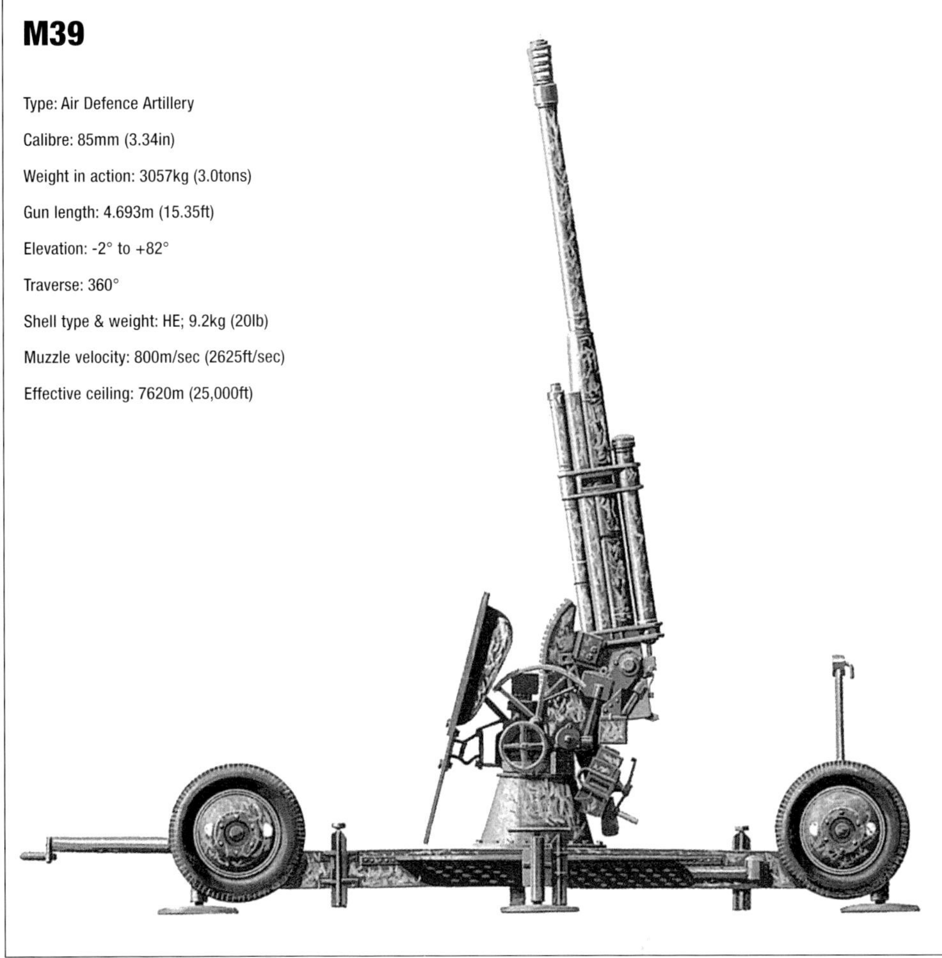

SIEGE WARFARE TECHNIQUES

Several massed charges were made, but these often failed and were always very costly. Giap now implemented siege-warfare techniques, using trenches to encroach upon the defenders under cover of artillery fire. The French responded with air strikes but were not able to impair the Viet Minh artillery or their siege works.

The French base at Dien Bien Phu was protected by a series of strongpoints. The outlying positions were reduced first, enabling the Viet Minh to position their artillery within range of the airstrip and to support attacks on core positions.

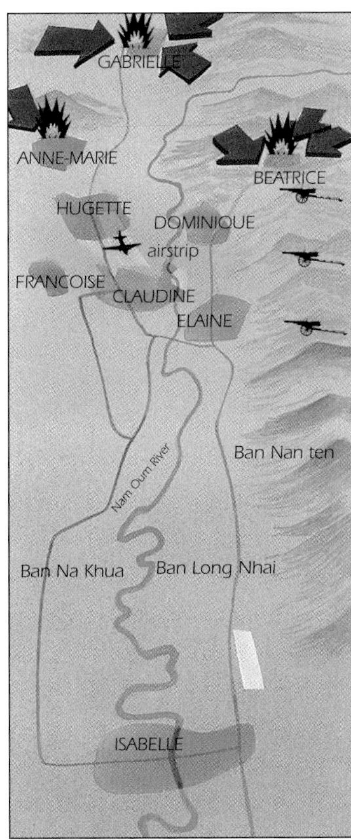

First wave of Viet Minh attacks March 1954

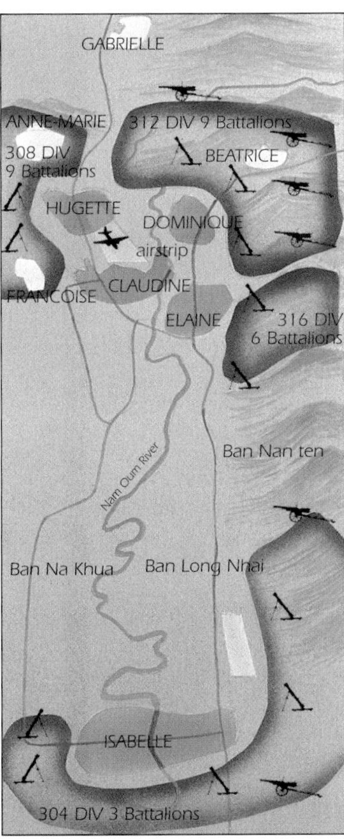

Situation 15 April 1954

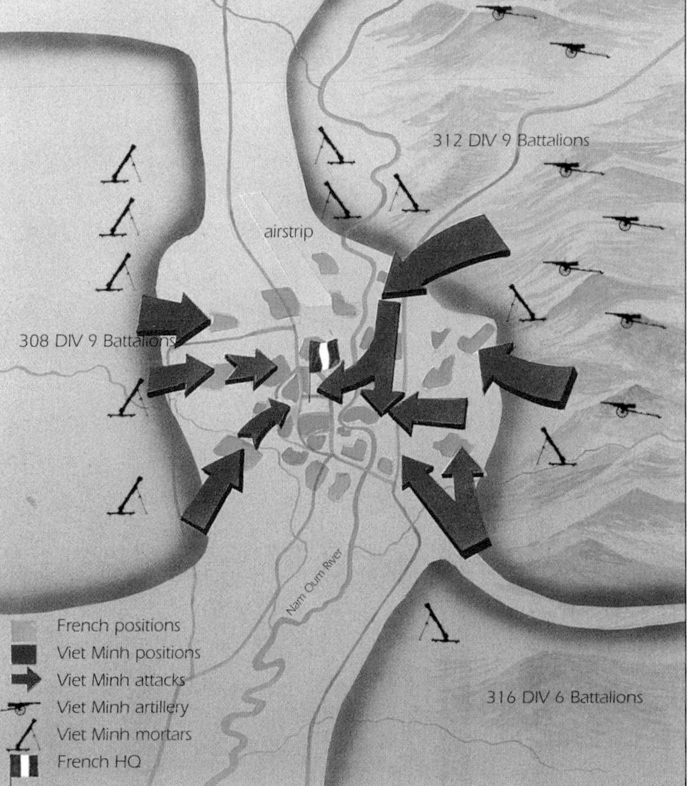

The French Surrender May 1954

The use of helicopters brought a new dimension to counterinsurgent warfare, allowing casualties to be evacuated and supplies brought into remote areas. However, slow-moving helicopters were more vulnerable to ground fire.

Reinforcements were brought in and the supply lifeline was kept open, albeit at grave cost, but eventually the weakened defenders were forced into a small perimeter, which was assaulted from all sides beginning on 1 May. Within a week, the survivors were forced to surrender.

The war in Indochina was dictated by logistics rather than firepower. The French were already at the end of a supply chain stretching halfway round the world, and once supplies reached Indochina they had to be moved through hostile terrain along predictable routes. On more than one occasion, garrisons were withdrawn and the gains that had been made in an operation were abandoned due to an inability to keep the troops supplied in the field.

Road and river transport were easy to ambush. Losses among trucks and barges restricted the logistics capability available for future missions. Air transport was obtainable in limited quantities, but most of the aircraft available were outdated. There were other problems too; airlifted supplies had to be landed on an airstrip or else had to be paradropped into difficult terrain, which made it difficult to collect items that might be scattered all over the countryside. At Dien Bien Phu, many airdrops ended up in Viet Minh hands due to the difficulty of parachuting containers into a small perimeter.

Giap deliberately countered French logistics efforts, obtaining anti-aircraft guns to impose losses on transport aircraft. He understood that a convoy ambush did not only prevent supplies reaching the troops in the combat zone but also reduced the overall capability of the French to keep their forces supplied.

The Viet Minh forces in the field were mainly infantry and thus fairly easy to supply, especially since they were able to capture much of what they needed from outposts and convoys they overran. Most of the rest came from China and were marshalled at the remote town of Bac Kan before being distributed.

REGAINING CONTROL OF THE COUNTRYSIDE

Viet Minh control of the countryside was correctly identified as a serious problem, and a new plan was formulated to regain the initiative. A forward base was to be set up and used for sweeps into the surrounding country, which would gradually clear it of opposition. The site chosen was Dien Bien Phu, which was secured by a paradrop.

The Viet Minh supply chain relied mainly on manpower, but large numbers of trucks were also available. They were used for the rapid build-up of forces around Dien Bien Phu. The French were not able to seriously impair the Viet Minh supply chain, though some attempts at air interdiction were made.

THE NUMBERS, AND THE REALITY

The defenders at Dien Bien Phu lost about 7000 men to the 20,000 or more lost to the Viet Minh, but the numbers do not tell the whole story. The Viet Minh could afford to take such casualties while the French had lost many of their best units. The set-piece battle had indeed occurred, but the French had lost it.

FRENCH DEFEAT

After the defeat at Dien Bien Phu, the French were forced to grant their former colonies in Vietnam, Laos and Cambodia independence. Vietnam was divided between the Communist Democratic Republic of North Vietnam and the Republic of South Vietnam, which was friendlier to Western powers. The French defeat came about for similar reasons to the communist victory in China. Both sides were fighting very different styles of war and while the French were seeking conventional victories in the field, the Viet Minh were gradually moving towards political control of the country. Again, conventional forces possessing tremendous firepower were defeated by highly motivated but far less well equipped insurgents. The main reason for this was

French troops at Dien Bien Phu. The plan to set up a forward base and use it to drive the enemy from the countryside was sound in principle, but the insurgents' possession of large quantities of artillery and anti-aircraft guns turned the base into a trap.

Above: Victorious Viet Minh troops conducting an informal victory parade. Although the war in French Indochina was an insurgent conflict in terms of the methods used, many of the troops under Giap's command were uniformed.

Left: As the perimeter at Dien Bien Phu was gradually driven in, it became impossible to resupply the garrison by air. A final breakout attempt about 1700 men failed. The remainder became prisoners.

AN END TO TRADITIONAL METHODS

Both in Indochina and in China, the insurgents presented the conventional forces with a new form of warfare they were not prepared for. Dealing with unconventional threats of this kind would require a shift in methods and even perceptions on the part of the authorities. Competent insurgents had to be defeated on their own terms; traditional methods no longer worked.

that the Viet Minh were able to maintain a secure area from which to operate, and into which the French could not effectively penetrate. To deal with the insurgents, the French would have had to get into the jungle and fight them on their own terms, but few units were capable of trying this and it was never seriously attempted. Instead, reliance on vehicles and heavy equipment restricted the French to roads and static bases, which were exposed to ambush and difficult to keep supplied.

THE MALAYAN EMERGENCY

The British were also pushed out of their Southeast Asian colonial possessions during World War II. When the Japanese overran Malaya in 1942, the British continued to provide what support they could to local groups resisting the occupation. The most important of these was the Malayan Communist Party (MCP), which already had an organizational structure in place at the time of the invasion.

A sandbagged police post in Malaya. The use of reserve forces and a well-armed police force for security duties freed the army for offensive operations against the insurgents. Reliance on local forces and police also demonstrated trust.

The MPAJA engaged in some low-level resistance operations against the Japanese but had no experience of large-scale combat when the war ended in 1945. The British returned to Malaya soon after, and there was no real chance to try to establish a local government. Instead, the MCP accepted recognition as a legitimate political party in return for dissolving and disarming the MPAJA.

In fact, large amounts of MPAJA weaponry were cached against future need, and the MCP went back to purely political activities for the time being. Over the next three years, the Communists became increasingly powerful among the Chinese population, some of which was disadvantaged compared to the Malays. The Communists found some support among the native Malay population, but were opposed by the United Malayan National Organization, whose membership was

LEGITIMACY FOR THE MALAYAN COMMUNIST PARTY

The MCP enjoyed considerable support among the Chinese population in Malaya, not least due to its denouncement of the Japanese invasion of China. Other smaller groups were brought in to create the Malayan People's Anti-Japanese Army (MPAJA). Some weapons and advisors were provided by the British, effectively recognizing the MCP as the legitimate leadership in the struggle against the Japanese invaders.

primarily Malay. The population of Malaya in 1948 was about five million, of which about 40 per cent were of Chinese origin and roughly 50 per cent Malay. Most of the remainder came from India. Some of the Chinese were integrated into Malayan society and quite well off, but there were over half a million who were anything but. These people had fled the Japanese and settled wherever they could, living by subsistence agriculture on marginal land they had unofficially occupied. Communism had much to offer such people.

In 1948, communism was spreading in many regions and communist insurgents were successfully operating against government forces in China and Indochina.

SPREADING COMMUNISM

In 1948, communism was spreading in many regions and communist insurgents were successfully operating against government forces in China and Indochina. Insurrection broke out in Burma, Indonesia and the Philippines at more or less the same time, possibly prompted by Moscow. Although conditions there were less than ideal for a revolution, Malaya followed suit.

The two main problems faced by the Malayan Communists were opposition from the majority population and the lack of a suitable cause to rally the population. The latter resulted from the fact that the British had already offered Malaya independence and, since other nations including India and Pakistan had been granted it, most people considered that the offer was credible. Communist claims that they were trying to secure Malayan freedom lost some of their appeal given that they were declaring an intent to fight for something that was already being offered for free. In reality, the Communists were fighting for control of the country once it became independent.

The second problem was that the Chinese population primarily supported the MCP. Its military arm was termed the Malayan Races' Anti-British Army (MRABA) and later the Malayan Races' Liberation Army (MRLA), yet its membership was almost exclusively Chinese. The Malayan Nationalists, some of whom had been opposed to the British, now aligned themselves that way in response to what they saw as a threat from the Chinese population.

The Communist campaign opened with attacks on British plantation owners. Three estate managers were killed on 16 June 1948. A small group of young Chinese men approached their targets, looking like any other men seeking a job, and shot them at close range.

Within two days, a state of emergency was declared and the

BREN Mk I

Type: Light Machine Gun

Calibre: 7.7mm (0.303in)

Length overall: 1156mm (45.5in)

Length of barrel: 635mm (25in)

Weight: 10.03kg (22.12lb)

Machine velocity: 744m (2440ft) per second

Rate of fire, cyclic: 500rpm

Feed: 20 round curved box magazine

> The insurgents, who had rearmed their field force with the weapons stashed in 1945, were capable of small-scale operations, yet they were able to kill hundreds of civilians.

government began taking steps to contain the problem. Some fairly tough measures were implemented, including forced relocation, restrictions on movement and internment without trial, yet these were successfully presented as being for the protection of the population and were generally accepted. Although the military took the lead in fighting the guerrillas, the normal civilian administration remained in force. At the beginning of the emergency, the British had six Ghurkha and three Infantry battalions stationed in the country, plus a small amount of artillery. There were also forces based in Singapore. This was entirely insufficient to deal with a large-scale insurgency in a country like Malaya, which was mostly covered in jungle with small coastal plains and a mountainous spine.

REASSURING THE POPULATION

The first necessity was to provide a measure of security and reassurance to the population. The police force was not well equipped for this role and lacked confidence, so initially most of the available troops were assigned to guard duties and, critically, training up forces to take over the security role.

The willingness of British and Malay army troops to enter the jungle and engage the insurgents on their own terms deprived them of an area into which they could safely retreat.

House-to-house searches were conducted in villages suspected of supporting the insurgents, and there were stiff penalties if evidence was found. In areas that had been cleared of guerrillas, no searches were conducted.

Security came from several sources. Police units were rearmed and augmented by the recruitment of a Special Constabulary and Auxiliary Police Force. Training provided by the military gave the police confidence that they could carry out their duties and deal with an attack at least long enough for the army to arrive.

A Home Guard was recruited to protect the plantations, with the owners and managers leading their workforce to protect their mutual livelihood as well as their safety. The good relationship between the British and the Malays was important here, as those who made their living on the plantations saw that their best interests lay in working together against the insurgents. The MCP had never really succeeded in gaining a foothold among the plantation workers and few saw a Communist rising as desirable.

Meanwhile, Malayan troops were raised and reinforcements brought in from other British territories, gradually increasing the amount of troops that could be deployed on offensive operations and as a mobile reserve. This was an important function, since knowing that a relief force would come to their assistance was critical to the morale of personnel manning police posts and other isolated positions.

Such measures provided physical security against guerrilla attacks and freed soldiers for more aggressive action, but could not by themselves win the war. Victory required first of all the retention of the loyalty of the population and, secondly, the elimination of the insurgents, either in combat or by persuading them to surrender.

The early stages of the struggle were demoralizing for the authorities and the population in general. The insurgents, who had rearmed their field force with the weapons stashed in 1945, were capable of only small-scale operations, yet they were able to kill hundreds of civilians and destroy many plantations.

To make the guerrillas' task as hard as possible, the authorities attacked their logistics by removing sources and routes of support. The Royal Navy undertook patrols to prevent supplies reaching the insurgents by sea, but there was little attempt at this anyway.

A mixed patrol of British and Malay troops fords a river in the jungle. Most patrols found nothing and were not only hard work but also stressful and dangerous. However, they were necessary to maintain control of the countryside.

Most of the guerrillas' support came from within Malaya itself, from villages and individuals intimidated into providing supplies or aligned with the guerrillas.

The authorities took bold and risky steps by implementing detention without trial. Although undemocratic, such a measure allows suspects to be held by civilian authorities despite the intimidation of witnesses by the insurgents. Other measures included a system of 'collective responsibility' whereby all residents of a village were considered to have a responsibility to inform the authorities of insurgent supporters or activists in their midst. To encourage this, a system of designating settlements 'White', 'Grey' or 'Black' was implemented.

Identity cards were introduced and tied into a system that made them both vital to daily life, such as for movement and obtaining food, but also granted benefits to card-carriers, making it desirable to have one.

HARSH PUNISHMENTS

Punishments were harsh for those supporting the insurgents. Possession of communist documents carried a 10-year prison sentence. Stockpiling food for the guerrillas was also harshly punished and possession of an illegal weapon carried the death penalty. This was routinely commuted if a suspect provided good information about his fellows. Another source of information was the practice of searching any dwelling without a warrant.

This might have caused resentment under other circumstances but it was presented in a positive manner.

REDUCING SUPPORT FOR THE INSURGENTS

Villages that supported the insurgency were designated Grey or Black, depending on the level of support and were subject to increasingly strict controls on movement and activities, including curfews that might allow people to be abroad for just two hours a day. Villagers were encouraged to believe that turning in Communist sympathizers was in their interest, because their village would eventually be declared 'White', and therefore free from restrictions, as support for the insurgents was curtailed.

Villages designated 'White' rarely saw such things; the designation was a statement of trust as much as anything else. Those that betrayed the trust and failed to self-regulate by informing on Communist supporters would find themselves redesignated Grey and subject to intrusive searches, movement restrictions and the like.

These measures were effective in reducing – and, in some areas, crippling – support for the guerrillas within the majority Malayan populace, but the dispossessed Chinese squatters continued to provide most of what the insurgents needed. They were less amenable to persuasion that it was in their interests to turn in sympathizers, and it became clear that other measures would have to be tried.

> Punishments were harsh for those supporting the insurgents. Possession of communist documents carried a 10-year prison sentence.

The solution was the brainchild of Lt-General Sir Harold Briggs, who came up with the idea of resettling the squatters into purpose-built villages, where they would not only be subject to government control but would genuinely be better off. Since many of them supported the insurgents as a route to a better life, they were likely to withdraw their support if this was already provided by the government. Even if they did not do so, then at least the squatters would now be located somewhere the authorities could control them.

The Briggs Plan involved building almost 150 'New Villages' and moving the squatters into them. This was not without problems; guerrillas interfered with the process wherever

The resettlement programme had at times to be carried out forcibly, and the insurgents attacked the personnel taking part as well as the settlements they created. However, the resettled squatters were genuinely better off.

they could and attacked the villages from time to time. Many of the squatters were suspicious of the government's motives and also resisted in various ways. However, their new living conditions really were much better than those they had experienced before and a gradual shift of allegiance took place.

Despite these measures, the situation was very serious in the middle of 1951. With the Korean War ongoing, there was little British manpower available to react to a sudden upsurge in insurgent attacks.

The killing of Sir Henry Gurney, the British High Commissioner, was a significant blow and came at a low point in the campaign. However, the tide was beginning to turn and measures implemented were beginning to pay off.

> As 1952 dawned, the authorities began taking the war to the insurgents in earnest. British troops were willing to go into the jungle for up to four weeks at a time.

In October the British High Commissioner, Sir Henry Gurney, was ambushed and killed by guerrillas.

Gurney's replacement was General Sir Gerald Templer, who had held both operational command and intelligence posts. Templer's arrival can now be seen as the turning point of the campaign, though he was not personally responsible for many of the changes that occurred. The Briggs Plan was taking effect and more troops had been made available, including SAS units, which was a big help. Just as importantly, the increased capabilities of the local security forces freed more of the available manpower for offensive operations. Templer ordered the Home Guard formations to be issued automatic weapons, a gesture of trust that could have backfired horribly but instead bolstered confidence and loyalty. Multi-racial battalions were raised within the Malay army.

TAKING THE WAR TO THE INSURGENTS

As 1952 dawned, the authorities began taking the war to the insurgents in earnest. British troops were willing to go into the jungle for up to four weeks at a time and fight the guerrillas in their own environment. More importantly, they had learned the skills of jungle warfare and were able to find the insurgents' bases to attack them. No longer could the guerrilla units strike and then withdraw to a secure area to rest and train. Now they were subject to attack, often without warning. This forced the larger concentrations of guerrillas to break up, greatly reducing their effectiveness.

The authorities fought two campaigns – against the Malayan Communist Party and the guerrillas themselves – side-by-side. The MCP provided command and communications, and ensured that the guerrillas received support from loyal villages. Without them the

Jumping out of a aircraft into the canopy of a jungle known to be inhabited by hostile guerrillas requires skilled, brave men. The SAS did more than fight the insurgents directly; they also obtained the assistance of the tribes.

fighting units had no orders and no information to choose their own targets, and also found obtaining food and supplies difficult.

Tactics against the guerrillas themselves were fairly conventional but geared towards small-scale actions in the jungle. As well as the fairly obvious tactic of sending patrols into the jungle to search for evidence of enemy activity, the British used more subtle gambits such as dropping off small parties from a larger patrol, who would then hide in ambush on a trail that insurgents were thought to use.

The SAS was also instrumental in obtaining the assistance of tribesmen living in the wild interior of Malaya. They were offered inducements to find and report on guerrilla concentrations, and in many cases they were entirely willing to attack them. A great many guerrillas died from blowpipe ambushes, especially in the latter stages of the conflict. Tribesmen were also brought in from Borneo and put their expertise to work, guiding patrols through the Malayan jungle.

In addition to breaking up the guerrilla concentrations and making

USE OF AIR-MOBILITY IN MALAYA

SAS units developed a technique of parachuting into the jungle canopy, enabling them to deploy into remote areas. Another trick was to use helicopters to put a force across the line of retreat of a guerrilla unit making an attack. Other forces would try to repulse them, but in any case the guerrillas would be ambushed on their way back to base, often after they thought they were safe.

European and Malay soldiers pose with flags captured from Communist guerrillas during the insurgency. The authorities were successful in driving a wedge between the guerrillas and the Communist party officials.

operations increasingly hazardous for them, the authorities used psychological warfare as well. Word of mouth, loudspeakers on aircraft and leaflets airdropped into the jungle promised guerrillas fair treatment to those who were willing to surrender.

Large amounts of cash were offered to any guerrilla willing to lead troops to an insurgent camp or to persuade his fellows to turn themselves in, and many of these Surrendered Enemy Personnel – or SEPs, as they became known – decided that they liked this form of capitalism a lot better than being a communist living hand-to-mouth in the jungle.

Meanwhile, the Malayan Communist Party was under attack. Its members were being forced to relocate out of the villages and into the jungle to avoid being informed on and captured. A deliberate attempt was made to cut off food supplies to the Party members, forcing them to take risks to obtain basic supplies. Several were caught or killed this way, and the same methods also trapped many guerrillas.

At the same time, a wedge was being driven between the MCP and the guerrilla fighters, whose lives were increasingly hazardous. A clear date for Malayan independence was set, nullifying any claims of fighting for freedom. The guerrillas were increasingly led to believe that it was the Communist Party that was forcing them to remain in the field, risking their lives fighting a meaningless war that they could not win.

In the meantime, captured Party members were offered money for every guerrilla they could bring in – either by inducing him to surrender or luring him into an ambush. Since the whole insurgency was highly compartmentalized, only Party members acted as liaison between guerrilla groups and thus word did not get out that a given Party official had turned coat and was now working for the authorities. Increasing mistrust between Party officials and the guerrillas led to an ever-increasing willingness to betray one another, and to a collapse of the insurgency.

VICTORY IN MALAYA

The state of emergency was formally lifted in 1960, in a free and independent Malaya. Most of the New Villages are today successful towns populated by prosperous citizens. This was an important factor in the ending of the insurgency. By giving the squatters what they needed – a better life – the authorities took away their desire to fight for it and thus their support for those who wanted to oppose the government for their own reasons.

The Malayan insurgency was beaten by a combination of effective military action and a clear strategy of winning over the hearts and minds of the population. Rather than seeking victory in body counts or repelled attacks, the government fought the war in the only place it could be won – in the attitudes of the population.

By 1955, the insurgents were dispersed in the jungle and expending far more effort on trying to survive in their environment than on fighting the war. Talks were opened and the MCP was offered an amnesty but demanded renewed recognition as a legal political party. This was turned down and the campaign continued, though by now it was obvious that the authorities had the upper hand. In fact, the Special Branch of the Malayan Police Force knew both the identity and the approximate location of almost every remaining guerrilla fighter, along with a good estimate of the weaponry available to the units still in the field.

The Federation of Malaya was granted independence from Britain in 1957. Although the insurgency was not entirely beaten, the new government was able to refuse any compromise with the Malayan Communist Party.

Independence was granted in 1957, by which time the MCP had decided to retreat to Thailand. Some successfully crossed the border and escaped while the remaining Party and guerrilla bands were hunted down or starved into surrender.

The military component of the campaign is an excellent example of how to win a low-intensity conflict. Large-scale operations achieved little, though occasionally a guerrilla base was sufficiently well pinpointed that it could be suddenly bombed from the air. On the whole, riflemen on the ground, who learned to penetrate the guerrillas' chosen environment and attack them there, fought the campaign.

The military combination of making the guerrillas' task harder by creating rear-area security forces and taking the fight to them reduced their morale while political measures turned the tide of public opinion against them. Neither the political nor the military dimension alone could have defeated the Malayan Communist Party, and it was here that the Malayan campaign differed from, say, Indochina. The authorities did not try to fight the war they wanted to; they fought the one they needed to, and they won it.

MAU MAU OATHS

One of the key features of the Mau Mau revolt was the use of extreme and bloody oaths to bind members. These were taken very seriously; the Kikuyu believed that terrible things would befall them if they broke their word.

The Mau Mau targeted the loyal or uninvolved Kikuyu more than the white farmers, attacking some and forcing others to swear oaths against the government. Many attacks were brutal, with atrocities such as the hacking to pieces of about 100 people at Lari routine.

THE MAU MAU UPRISING

When the British colonized what is now Kenya in the late nineteenth century, they obtained much of the land they settled from the Masai and Kikuyu tribes by purchase. However, a grave misunderstanding arose from these deals. The settlers thought, reasonably enough, that they were buying the land since that is what they had offered to do. However, as they did not observe the rituals pertaining to such a purchase, the Kikuyu owners, equally correctly, assumed that the Europeans were leasing the land and that it would be returned when the Kikuyu needed it.

Both groups lived in close proximity and relative harmony for many years, but shortly after World War II the Kikuyu, whose living standards dropped as a result of post-war economic factors, became unhappy with the situation. The settlers, for whom the purchased land was the only home they had ever known, refused to give it back. Both

The Mau Mau uprising began as a dispute between some of the Kenyan tribes and the white settlers, both of whom had entirely legitimate reasons for believing that the other was being unreasonable.

Obtaining information about the Mau Mau was at times very difficult. Uninvolved tribes knew little, while those who might have useful information were discouraged from talking to the authorities by the threat of retribution.

sides had good reason to believe that the land was theirs and that they had behaved correctly. This led to a major grievance and, eventually, to open conflict. The troubles really started in late 1952, after a period of escalating violence. Several people were murdered, property was burned and cattle were killed or maimed as word reached the authorities that an organized insurgency was forming.

In October 1952, the governor of Kenya declared a state of emergency and British troops were flown in to try to contain the situation. A raid that freed them and captured a stock of weapons undid an initial roundup of suspects.

More British troops were brought in, but they needed time to adjust to their new role. Their inexperience at counterinsurgency warfare was compounded by a lack of familiarity with the forested uplands of Kenya. One regiment accidentally ambushed its own commanding officer and killed him soon after arriving in the country.

However, countermeasures began to be put in place. Experience in Malaya showed how the civil administration could function even amid a military emergency. The country was divided into zones, with prohibited areas within which the army was permitted to assume a wartime stance and shoot on sight. This limited the insurgents' movements somewhat. However, the Mau Mau obtained supplies from

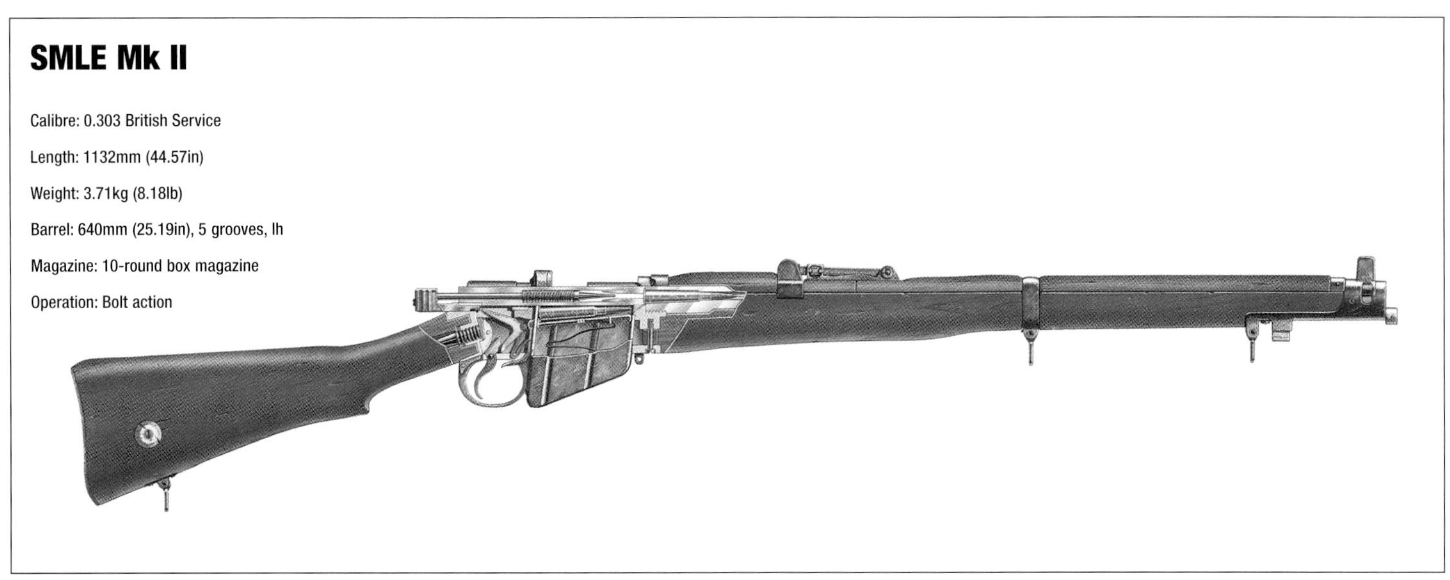

many sources, although weapons were more difficult to come by. Some firearms were stolen, while some were improvised using, among other things, door bolts, while traditional weapons such as spears, knives, clubs and strangling ropes were widely used.

Mau Mau oaths and reprisals frightened many tribespeople into support or at least silence, but support and information were forthcoming from among the Kikuyu, who also provided manpower to assist the army in its 'cordon and sweep' operations. These involved some units forming a 'stop line' or cordon to close off an area while others advanced through it conducting searches.

As yet more British troops arrived in 1953 and onwards, it was possible to mount denser sweeps. These resulted in arrests and skirmishes as well as the occasionally running battle with larger Mau Mau groups. The longest of these lasted four days and resulted in almost 150 insurgents killed or captured.

Most actions were small-scale affairs in which the skill and motivation of riflemen and junior officers were the decisive factor. The high quality of British infantry and the men of the King's African Rifles enabled them to take on the insurgents in their own environment with considerable success.

In April 1954, a cordon and sweep operation was launched in the capital, Nairobi. Almost total surprise was achieved and the Mau Mau support network in the city was more or less eliminated. This disrupted communications and logistics for the forces in the field. Meanwhile, in the countryside villages were encouraged to turn in Mau Mau supporters, mimicking tactics used in Malaya. One effective measure was the use of government witch doctors to de-oath Mau Mau supporters, coupled with an amnesty in return for information.

The Kikuyu Guard was formed to protect their own people, and issued

Searching suspects is time-consuming and can result in ill-feeling among the population, but it is necessary to prevent the free movement of insurgents and to restrict their ability to bring weapons or explosives into any given area.

firearms by the government. Many Kikuyu hated and feared the Mau Mau, and the gesture not only enabled them to resist intimidation but also increased loyalty to a government that was willing to trust them. The constant patrols and sweeps in the countryside did not result in large numbers of 'contacts' and even fewer casualties among the Mau Mau, but they did prevent them from settling down in safe areas. By 1955, the Mau Mau had suffered heavy losses and was losing support among the population in general. However, they were not defeated and had changed the goal of their campaign. Instead of ejecting the whites, they were now seeking to inflict sufficient damage that the government had to grant concessions, and there was a chance that this might happen.

One way to find and eliminate the Mau Mau gangs was to act on information provided by surrendered enemy personnel, as in Malaya. However, an ingenious new twist was tried. The gangs were infiltrated by 'turned' former Mau Mau members who were willing to form 'pseudo-gangs'. These then fed information back to the government.

Sometimes white officers, wearing the most basic of disguises, accompanied the pseudo-gangs, and occasionally the pseudo-gangs acted directly. More often they provided information, which was used judiciously to prevent its origins being suspected. The earlier sweeps had worn down and broken up the Mau Mau into smaller groups; the pseudo-gangs enabled the authorities to find and destroy them.

FAILED MAU MAU REVOLT

By late 1955, troops were being sent home, while the remaining gangs were harried across the countryside and gradually run down by small forces acting on good intelligence. The state of emergency was lifted in 1960, by which time the insurgency was broken. The Mau Mau were prevented from winning by fairly conventional patrolling and sweeps, but they were finally penetrated and broken by the pseudo-gangs. The Mau Mau revolt failed because it failed to establish the broad popular base necessary for a successful revolution. This was largely due to effective government measures to support and protect loyal groups. The use of witch doctors to de-oath Mau Mau was also important; it demonstrated an understanding of the people whose attitudes would dictate the course of the insurgency.

Measures taken to enable the tribes to protect themselves against the Mau Mau encouraged more people to offer assistance to the authorities. Large numbers of Kikuyu assisted in sweeps of the countryside.

The Resurgence of Conventional Warfare 1950–1970

After the end of World War II, there were suggestions that the use of nuclear weapons had brought the age of conventional warfare to a close. However, within five years many of the combatant nations were involved in another large-scale conflict. Most of the wars of the 1950s and 1960s were fought with tactics, and indeed often with hardware, dating from the 1939–45 period.

THE KOREAN CONFLICT

The Soviet Union threw its might against Japan, driving rapidly into Korea from the north at the end of World War II. As in Europe, stop lines were agreed, with the Soviets taking the surrender of Japanese forces in the north and US troops landing to secure the south.

Wrangling over the fate of Korea failed to achieve much. The Soviets, following the same practice as in Eastern Europe, encouraged the formation of a pro-Soviet government in the region they occupied while the UN supervised elections in the remainder of the country. The result was a communist state in North Korea and a pro-West democracy in the south, divided along an arbitrary line at the 38th parallel. Both states maintained that they were the legitimate government of all Korea.

In 1948–49, US and Soviet troops pulled out while the two Korean governments engaged in propaganda warfare. Border incidents were frequent, and raids were at times launched further into hostile territory.

US troops firing a recoilless rifle. This light artillery weapon was very useful in Korea. Light enough to be manhandled up a hill by infantry, it provided useful short-range fire support.

The United Nations was quick to condemn the invasion of South Korea and voted to take action against the People's Republic of North Korea. The United States had already begun rushing troops into South Korea.

Eventually the decision was made to reunify the country by force, and on 25 June 1950 the forces of North Korea crossed the border and drove on Seoul.

The South Koreans were in poor shape to resist. Their army was lightly equipped with surplus US weaponry, and was quite small. Four infantry divisions guarded the border and four more, all of them under strength, remained in reserve. The North Koreans, on the other hand, had 10 infantry divisions, most of which were at full strength and better supported with artillery than their southern counterparts. More importantly, the North Korean divisions were built around a core of experienced troops who had fought alongside the Soviets or in China. In addition, the North Koreans had a brigade of about 150 T-34 tanks supplied by the Soviet Union.

The attack came as a strategic surprise. Many South Korean troops were away on leave and the remainder were wholly unprepared to resist the attack. They also lacked weapons that could stop the spearhead of excellent T-34 tanks. All they had were bazookas that had been supplied by the United States, and these were simply not up to the job.

The North Koreans advanced on three axes, moving towards the

STRATEGIC POSITION OF KOREA

Korea itself is a peninsula jutting out from the coast of Asia towards Japan, with a spine of mountains running down almost the entire length of the east coast. While not rich in industry or resources, it does occupy a strategic position. This is one reason why Korea has been fought over several times in the past.

capital, through the central highlands and down the narrow east coast plain. The latter included an amphibious outflanking movement that showed the influence of Soviet thinking. This was hardly surprising because the Soviets had been training the North Korean army for half a decade. Support from the United States was immediately forthcoming, and a United Nations' resolution soon after called for action to support South Korea. However, there was nothing that could be done in time to prevent the fall of the capital.

Surviving South Korean forces were pushed southwards in disarray. US Naval units were now moving in the direction of Korea and supply deliveries had been authorized, yet US General MacArthur's personal assessment of the situation was that without the deployment of significant US ground forces there was no way to stop the North Korean advance. On his own authority, he took the bold step of ordering the naval and air bombardment of North Korean forces and targets north of the border.

UNPREPARED TROOPS

MacArthur was given command of the nearest available troops. They were not really combat-worthy, having spent several years on 'soft' occupation duties in Japan. There was no alternative but to send them into action immediately, however, so three divisions were landed at Pusan in the south-eastern corner of the peninsula and began moving up to contact.

These units did the best they could, aided by the rallied remnants of the South Korean army. They slowed but could not halt the advance, and were pushed back towards the port of Pusan. By early August 1950, the US and South Korean forces were holding a small area known as the Pusan Perimeter. Their position was shaky at best but they clung on long enough for additional forces to arrive. These initially came from the US and the British Commonwealth, though several other nations contributed forces.

Under the command of General Douglas MacArthur, US forces were rushed into South Korea in time to prevent total defeat, and he subsequently masterminded the extremely risky but ultimately successful Inchon landings.

WEAPONRY IN THE KOREAN WAR

Most of the equipment in use by both sides was left over from World War II, or had been in development during the war. As a result, the overall standard of weaponry was very high, since it had been designed to meet the needs of a major conflict against a well equipped foe and tested in battle. South Korean units were under-equipped compared to the international contingent, resulting in relatively heavier casualties.

Initially North Korean T-34s proved very hard to disable; many anti-tank weapons were entirely ineffective against them. However, once US armoured units began to arrive, the balance was restored. An improved bazooka with a much bigger warhead provided the infantry with a means of defence and was especially effective in close-quarters urban fighting. The UN forces also deployed increasing numbers of tanks. It had initially been felt that armour would not be useful the local terrain, but the North Korean army's use of tanks changed this opinion.

Only the United States, Britain and the Philippines contributed armoured forces, but infantry and support units came from many nations. Some sent a single company; others deployed battalions and larger formations. The presence of the smaller contributions had a mainly moral effect. A single company of infantry could not achieve much, but it demonstrated that the nations taking the brunt of the fighting had the committed support of other UN countries.

Facing growing international strength, the North Koreans made a final drive to try to push their enemies into the sea, but this was repulsed and gradually the Pusan Perimeter was consolidated. By September 1950, UN forces were ready to go over to the offensive. The UN counterstroke, masterminded by General MacArthur, was audacious to the point of recklessness. MacArthur had been considering an amphibious landing since the first week of the war, hoping to distract North Korean attention. This developed into a plan to retake Seoul and thereby sever the supply line of the North Korean forces fighting in the south.

PROBLEMATIC PLAN

There were some significant problems with the plan. The assault force would have to land at Inchon, which meant dealing with outposts situated on islands off the coast and overcoming the problem of reefs in shallow water off the landing site. There were no suitable beaches so the landing was to be made against harbour walls, which were to be scaled with ladders.

The enterprise looked dangerously suicidal, but MacArthur was able to convince his superiors that it could be done. There was one positive factor: since an amphibious landing at Inchon was obviously impossible, performing one there would certainly achieve surprise.

US X Corps undertook the landings, a formation created for the purpose. It comprised a Marine

M40

Type: Self-propelled artillery

Crew: 8

Powerplant: one Continental nine-cylinder radial piston engine developing 294.6kW (395hp)

Weight: 36,400kg (80,080lb)

Range: 161km (100 miles)

Armour: up to 12.7mm (0.5in)

Armament: one 155mm (6.1in) gun

Performance: maximum road speed 38.6km/h (24mph); fording 1.067m (3ft 6in); vertical obstacle 0.61m (2ft); trench 2.26m (7ft 5in)

Dimensions: length 9.04m (29ft 8in)
width 3.15m (10ft 4in)
height 2.84m (9ft 4in)

Division and an Infantry Division, which had been strengthened with South Korean troops. Some of the latter were little more than militia who had been given sketchy training.

The shipping that provided logistical and fire support came from several nations, including the United States, Britain, France, Australia, Canada, New Zealand and South Korea. Civilian vessels were chartered to carry supplies. In all, 230 ships took part in the operation, which landed about 70,000 troops and supported them in place.

After a diversionary operation near Kunsan on 12–13 September, the Inchon landings went ahead, on 15 September. Despite being planned in extreme haste and facing enormous challenges, the assault achieved success. This owed much to surprise and the exploits of an advance party put ashore to report on water conditions.

The landings were preceded by heavy naval bombardment to suppress shore defences. It was possible to continue this more or less constantly, but the window of opportunity for a landing was much more narrow. Only at the very highest tide could landing ships reach the target areas, limiting

Although US forces from Japan were first to come to the assistance of South Korea, British and Commonwealth troops soon arrived, and eventually a large multinational force was deployed to Korea.

> Facing growing international strength, the North Koreans made a drive to push their enemies into the sea, but this was repulsed and the Pusan Perimeter was consolidated.

The Inchon Landings were carried out in the face of almost every conceivable difficulty. Many of the transport ships were in poor condition, having been unexpectedly called from reserve. Merchant ships were chartered as support.

the landings to a three-hour slot in the morning and another in the evening.

A marine battalion was put ashore on the island of Walmi-do on the morning tide, clearing the flank of the main invasion force, which made its landings in the evening. The initial landings on Walmi-do were entirely unopposed and though some resistance was put up after the marines got ashore, the island was quickly secured. This was just as well because, until the evening high tide, there was no way to land more troops or even to rescue the survivors if the assault failed.

The main landings that evening were met with some opposition but were able to push inland onto the hills above Inchon. By 1.30 a.m., the road to Seoul had been cut.

During the next day, the marines and the infantry that followed them ashore had secured a lodgement and was bringing in supplies. By 22 September, Seoul had been retaken. The North Korean army retreated northwards as MacArthur had predicted, allowing the UN forces around Pusan to push forwards and link up with the amphibious units holding Seoul.

CHINESE FORCES IN KOREA

The Chinese forces deployed in Korea were largely composed of infantry recruited from the rural population. Naturally tough and hard working, these peasants-turned-infantrymen were capable of long marches and required little logistic support. One reason for this was the absence of tanks or heavy equipment. There were no anti-tank guns or artillery pieces larger than a mortar in most formations. Satchel charges and grenades were issued for use against tanks.

Small arms were issued according to whatever was available and a great variety of arms was carried. This was inefficient in many ways, but it did allow larger forces to be equipped than otherwise.

Throughout the remainder of September and early October, it seemed that the war was won. UN forces pushed the North Koreans across the border and pursued them deep into their own territory. However, the situation rapidly changed when China took an active involvement in the war. This caught the UN forces by surprise, driving them back towards the 38th parallel.

The situation rapidly changed when China took an active involvement in the war. This caught the UN forces by surprise, driving them back towards the 38th parallel.

Having recently fought through the Japanese occupation and the Chinese civil war, the Chinese had a body of experienced personnel to draw upon, and a strong presence of Communist political officers also contributed to morale. The Chinese divisions had very little 'tail', and required only about one-tenth as much in the way of supplies as an equivalent UN force, though this did mean that they had to forage to some extent, which reduced their combat capability. Much of the logistics train supporting Chinese forces was composed of peasants who simply carried the supplies to the front and then returned for more. A significant amount moved by rail and here, too, the peasant worker played an important role. Work gangs were

The US Marine landings on the island of Walmi-do were a success. With no prospect of reinforcements or evacuation for several hours, the attack was an all-or-nothing proposition.

CHINESE TACTICS IN KOREA

The Chinese lacked sophisticated equipment but were skilled at infantry operations. Among their favoured tactics was a sudden concentration in overwhelming force, usually by secret night marches, followed by a rapid attack from several directions. Infiltration by small parties was another favoured gambit, allowing a position to be taken under fire from an unexpected direction.

stationed close to the rail lines and quickly repaired any damage caused by air raids.

China's entry into the war posed a problem for both the United Nations and the US government. Should the war now be restricted to Korea or should China be treated as a belligerent and attacked? MacArthur argued for the latter, believing that only a decisive defeat of China could secure victory.

However, there were fears that a direct attack on China might lead to further escalation and even war with the Soviet Union. It was thus decided that the war would be limited in scope, and in the resulting furor MacArthur was dismissed.

Having been forced south and after losing Seoul for a second time, the UN forces rallied and began to advance northwards again, retaking the capital in March 1951. However, this advance was now halted by a

Much of the war was fought in the countryside, but urban battles did occur. The capture and defence of cities was a job for the infantry, who had to clear buildings and streets one by one in the face of counterattacks and sniper fire.

M4A3 SHERMAN

Type: Infantry tank

Crew: 5

Powerplant: one Ford GAA V-8 petrol engine developing 335.6 or 373kW (400 or 500 hp)

Weight: 32,284kg (71,024lb)

Range: 161km (100 miles)

Armour: 15–100mm (0.59–3.94in)

Armament: one 76mm (3in) gun; one 7.62mm (0.3in) coaxial machine gun

Performance: maximum road speed 47km/h (29mph); fording 0.91m (3ft); vertical obstacle 0.61m (2ft); trench 2.26m (7ft 5in)

Dimensions: length with gun 7.52m (24ft 8in)
width 2.68m (8ft 9.5in)
height 3.43m (11ft 2.875in)

powerful counterattack launched at the Imjin River.

'HUMAN WAVE' ATTACKS

The Chinese used the enormous manpower at their disposal to launch 'human wave' attacks, sending forward wave upon waves of troops, who rushed in small groups from cover to cover. The plan was always to maintain a general forward movement, with the survivors of a shattered wave joining the next as it passed through them. Only the most motivated troops could successfully make such an attack, but the Chinese managed it on many occasions. Indeed, UN forces found that the only way to halt a wave attack was to lay down so much firepower that the attackers were all disabled.

> Having been shoved south and losing Seoul for a second time, the UN forces rallied and began to advance northwards again, retaking the capital in March 1951.

Wave attacks therefore represented an appalling cost to the Chinese, but they worked and enabled the ill-equipped Chinese to take on the UN forces with a reasonable chance of success.

A renewed Chinese offensive was launched in April and May 1951, but failed to achieve decisive results. UN forces were able to inflict sufficient casualties to stall the campaign, and the war eventually settled down into a bitterly contested stalemate. Peace talks began, and both sides tried to occupy terrain or win battles to strengthen their bargaining position. This led to battles for possession of otherwise irrelevant terrain features such as Pork Chop Hill.

It was during the static period of the war that the worst casualties occurred. Battles were fought for political reasons connected with the peace negotiations rather than in an attempt to win the war in the military context. This would seem like a criminal waste of lives, but for one critical factor. By this point, it was clear that the UN could not win the war by purely military means. Attempting to do so would require attacks on China, and that particular option had already been rejected.

The only hope of a successful outcome lay in a favourable conclusion at the negotiation table. All wars are fought with a goal in mind, and that goal is almost always political. Therefore, if the taking of a militarily trivial map coordinate advanced the negotiators' position, it was indeed worthwhile in the overall context of the war.

Although the threat of nuclear bombardment was a factor in making the Chinese seek a settlement, it was used more to set an upper limit to the violence that would be permitted than anything else. The UN forces were willing to fight a conventional campaign but eventually a line was

The arbitrary division of Korea at the 38th Parallel into Western and Soviet zones of influence was caused by mistrust between the allies at the end of World War II. The result was an armed standoff that led to war.

drawn – if the Chinese wanted to push the issue and let the fighting drag on, for years longer, the United States was prepared to respond with an escalation of their own, raising the stakes to a level that their opponents could not match. Korea was the first 'limited war' in that sense. Korea also demonstrated that large-scale battles of the kind fought in World War II were not a thing of the past. They may have been limited by the threat of nuclear weaponry, but international warfare was still a viable concept.

YEARS OF WAR BUT NO CHANGES

As the peace talks dragged on and the casualties mounted, Dwight D. Eisenhower replaced US President Truman. Determined to bring the war to a close, Eisenhower threatened to use whatever means were necessary, which included attacks on Chinese targets and even nuclear weapons. At this time, China had no nuclear weapons of its own and no chance at all of delivering one to the distant United States. The result was an armistice signed in July 1953, which partitioned the country along the 38th parallel. Nothing had changed despite years of war.

SUEZ AND THE SINAI

In the years after World War II, profound changes took place in the world. The establishment of Israel as a homeland for the Jewish people was one; the British retreat from empire was another.

Jews and Arabs had lived side by side for centuries in what is today Israel, usually in peace. Indeed, much of what is often imagined to be an ages-old conflict actually dates back to the activities of Nazi-supported anti-Jewish activists in the twentieth century. There was some friction in the region, of course, and this was made much worse when thousands of refugees began to arrive from Europe.

The establishment of a Jewish homeland was more or less forced upon the region.

It is hard to see what else could have been done, but the result was a tiny Jewish state surrounded by hostile Arab nations determined to rid the world of it. There were legitimate grievances on all sides and the Jewish people, having recently suffered the horrors of the Holocaust, were not inclined to tolerate any future threat.

BRITAIN DISENTANGLES

Meanwhile, the British were beginning to disentangle themselves from their former colonial holdings. Some states became independent peacefully. Indeed, many remained part of the Commonwealth, which benefited all concerned. In others, the transition was more turbulent. However, despite the fact that Britain was ceasing to be a colonial power, the Suez Canal remained vital to her strategic interests.

Britain's involvement in Egypt dated back many years. British troops had occupied Egypt in the 1880s to protect the canal and the country remained an important British fleet and military base into World War II. British troops began to pull out of Egypt only in 1954.

However, two years before that, King Farouk of Egypt was deposed by Colonel Gamal Abdel Nasser, who was now determined to re-establish Egyptian prestige and to place himself at the head of Arab affairs on the world stage. He therefore decided to ally his nation with the Soviet Union, which brought the advantage of access to stocks of Soviet military equipment. This provoked economic sanctions from Britain and the United States.

A few weeks after the last British units had departed from Egypt, President Nasser announced the nationalization of the Suez Canal, which seriously endangered British strategic interests. The emergence of a military dictator who seemed to have big plans was considered a threat by many observers in Britain, who wanted him deposed. Given that the world had only recently emerged from World War II, a conflict that was arguably the result of insufficiently strong measures taken against another ambitious dictator, there was much support for this point of view. The French, too, felt threatened. They had recently lost much of their colonial empire and were now engaged in dealing with a rebellion in Algeria. In an attempt to portray Nasser as the head of the Arab world, Radio Cairo had been claiming that the revolt in Algeria was led and inspired from Egypt. These claims were untrue, but that may not have been known at the time. Thus, action against the instigator of their troubles suited French interests.

Britain and France decided to act against Nasser, but could not do so immediately. First it was necessary to redeploy to airbases in the region fighters that could deal with newly

Colonel Gamal Abdel Nasser was one of the leaders of the 1952 revolution in Egypt, which overthrew the monarchy and created a republic. He pushed through a number of economic and industrial reforms.

THE ISRAELI MILITARY SYSTEM

The Israeli army was based on a system of national service, which ensured that a large segment of the population had some military experience. After their service, personnel passed into reserve and could be called up to quickly create a sizable military force considering the small population of Israel. Maintaining large forces in the field would cripple Israel's economy so the emphasis was placed on offensive action to achieve a decision quickly.

Hardware was mostly equipment dating from World War II, and came from the United States, Britain and France. Sherman tanks provided the main armoured striking force. These were backed up by infantry riding half-tracks and supported by British 25-pounder field guns.

acquired Egyptian MiG jets, and to retrain the parachute units who would spearhead the operation. The latter had been serving as elite infantry for some time and so were not at full readiness for what was theoretically their main role. Thus while there was a window of opportunity for success in July 1956, the operation did not begin until late October.

ISRAEL TAKES DECISIVE ACTION

Meanwhile, Israel felt increasingly threatened by Egypt and saw an opportunity to take decisive action. In a statement in October 1956, the Egyptians declared that they would lead a coalition of Jordanian and Syrian forces, plus their own, in any future war with Israel, and more or less stated that they planned to do so at a time of their choosing.

Israel was thus faced with a very clear threat. By humbling Egypt, self-appointed leader of the Arab world, Israel could perhaps deter future aggression. A pre-emptive strike was the only way for Israel's small armed forces to defeat their much larger neighbours, and with two major powers also planning to attack Egypt the opportunity seemed too good to pass up.

The Egyptians had considerable forces along the border with Israel, which were partially equipped with modern Soviet weaponry. However, their strategy was one of static defence, with little in reserve for a mobile counterattack. Training levels and doctrinal weaknesses made it difficult to organize one anyway.

On 29 October 1956, Israeli forces entered the Sinai Peninsula. This was not valuable in itself, but did offer access to the Suez Canal. A parachute assault captured the east end of the strategic Mitla Pass. This was one of

This could be a scene from World War II rather than a decade later. The Israeli armed forces were largely armed with World War II-era equipment obtained from the United States and the wartime Allies.

Tanks and armoured cars of the Israeli Defence Force during the advance into the Sinai. Mobility played an important part in Israeli tactics during the war, enabling tough positions to be bypassed or attacked.

the few practicable routes across the region, which was mostly desert.

On 30 October, other parachute units, acting as an elite infantry spearhead, pushed across the central desert route. After breaking what resistance they encountered, they linked up with their colleagues at Mitla, but were unable to push through and open a route to the Canal's southern end at Suez. At the same time, armoured forces began traversing the northern routes across the desert. Stiff resistance was encountered at Abu Aweigila, which was eventually outflanked and bypassed, and at El Arish, about halfway across the peninsula.

On 31 October, with the paras still trying to force the Mitla Pass, an infantry force moved down the south-eastern coast towards the port of Sharm el Sheikh. The next day, Egyptian forces began pulling back from the Sinai to defend Egypt from the expected Anglo-French landings.

The Israelis were still pushing forward, but the Egyptian order to withdraw made their task much easier. Some armoured skirmishes broke out, but the Egyptians were more interested in getting to the canal than fighting the Israelis in the desert, so nothing decisive was achieved.

The Israeli advance continued for a time and then, by 3 November, it more or less came to a halt. The only exception was at Sharm el Sheikh, which was taken by infantry and paratroops moving down from the Mitla Pass. Sharm el Sheikh was under Israeli control by 5 November, by which time the Egyptians were under attack from a different direction.

France and Britain had issued an ultimatum on 30 October to both combatants, which included a demand that their troops be permitted to occupy areas critical to the protection of the canal. There was never any chance of the ultimatum being accepted, and so, just two days later, the British and French made their move.

British soldiers from 3rd Battalion, the Parachute Regiment, at El Gamil airfield during the Suez invasion. The practice of using paratroops ahead of a seaborne invasion or ground assault was well established.

The attack opened with air strikes by carrier-based air units and others flying out of Malta and Cyprus. This continued from 31 October to 4 November. Paratroops began landing in Egypt on 5 November but by this time international protests began to be heard. Nevertheless, seaborne forces came ashore on 6–7 November.

The British and French deployed 500 aircraft and 130 warships. The vast majority were British, as the French had not rebuilt their forces to pre-war levels after losing most of them in World War II. Among the British forces were aircraft carriers converted to the 'commando carrier' role, using helicopters to put forces ashore. This was a relatively new concept, which has been used many times since. Helicopters allow an assault 'over-the-beach', meaning that forces can fly inland and deploy near their targets rather than having to assault a beach from landing craft.

> With Port Said more or less under control, attempts were made to clear the blockships sunk in the harbour mouth and thus enable supplies to be unloaded directly at the port.

There was nothing new in using airmobile troops to seize objectives ahead of a ground assault, though it had failed at times in the past. The original plan had called for paradrops at strategic points all along the canal, but as international pressure increased the plan was amended. The new version, among other things, required the paratroops to hold their objectives unsupported for longer than had originally been envisaged, conjuring up worrying visions of the battle for the Rhine bridges at

Arnhem in 1944. However, the operation opened well. The British struggled stoically through the limitations of their training and equipment while the French, who had better retained their readiness, conducted a textbook airborne assault against the bridges at Raswa. Their troops dropped directly onto a defended target through anti-aircraft fire and captured the objective for a handful of casualties. The airfield at Gamil was quickly taken by British paratroops, who then ran into determined resistance and were forced onto the defensive.

The British paratroops were supposed to have advanced into Port Said and captured it. Even though they had not managed to do so, the garrison commander there was sufficiently rattled that he asked for permission to surrender. This was denied, and the defenders distributed arms to the civilian population as they prepared to meet the inevitable assault. This was put in by seaborne troops the next day, covered by light naval gunfire. Heavier guns were available but were not permitted to fire in the hope of reducing collateral damage. The first forces ashore were Royal Marine Commandos, followed by Centurion tanks. These were able to link up with the French forces at Raswa but did not have the numbers to take Port Said.

CONTROL OF PORT SAID

With Port Said more or less under control, attempts were made to clear the blockships sunk in the harbour mouth and thus enable supplies to be unloaded directly at the port. While this was going on, a mixed force of British tanks and French paratroops pushed south until they ran into resistance. By then, dark had fallen and the force halted for the night, not knowing that a ceasefire had been proposed by London.

With the possibility of a ceasefire in the offing, it was important to grab as much territory as possible for use as bargaining chips and to avoid being in a bad position if negotiations broke down. Sending out infantry and paratroops in commandeered local vehicles, the British and French expanded their gains as much as possible in the last hours of the operation. There was no opposition other than continued harassment in Port Said.

Militarily the operation was a success, but politically the situation

CONTRASTING APPROACHES TO THE OPERATION

British Commandos landed by helicopter largely carried out the task of pacifying Port Said. Fiercest resistance came from snipers; most of the armed civilians simply got rid of their weapons as soon as possible. The town was not completely under control at any point in the operation, though this was mainly due to an unwillingness to risk civilian casualties. In contrast, French troops tasked with the capture of Port Fouad on the far side of the canal had no such reservations and simply smashed all resistance with overwhelming firepower.

AMX-13

Type: Light tank

Crew: 3

Powerplant: one SOFAM eight-cylinder petrol engine developing 186kW (250hp)

Weight: 15,000kg (33,000lb)

Range: 400km (250 miles)

Armour: 10–40mm (0.4in–1.57in)

Armament: one 75mm (2.95in) gun; one 7.62mm (0.3in) machine gun

Performance: maximum road speed 60km/h (37mph); fording 0.6m (1ft 11.7in); vertical obstacle 0.65m (2ft 1.7in); trench 1.6m (5ft 3in)

Dimensions: length 6.36m (20ft 10.3in)
width 2.50m (8ft 2.5in)
height 2.3m (7ft 6.5in)

UPHEAVALS IN FRANCE

The French fared worse than the British. Bogged down in the Algerian revolt, the French army felt betrayed by the decision to send it into Suez and then accept a ceasefire that threw away the fruits of its labours. Two years later, a revolt in the army led to the replacement of the French government with a new system headed by General Charles de Gaulle as President. Named the Fifth Republic, this system remains the current form of government in France.

was very different. Opposition from many world powers, notably the United States, resulted in pressure that could not be ignored. The United Nations passed a resolution requiring all nations involved to withdraw to their start lines, and even within the British parliament there was division and heated debate.

The operation failed to reopen the Suez Canal and cost the British government a vast amount of money both in military spending and other costs. The UN resolution did allow for a peacekeeping force to be deployed in the Sinai region, which contributed somewhat to stability in the region for a while, but otherwise nothing really changed except in Egypt, where Nasser's prestige rose ever higher. This was partially due to successfully placing the emphasis on resisting the Anglo-British operation and playing down the defeats at the hands of the Israelis.

For Israel, there were immediate benefits. The threat of being crushed by an Egyptian-led Arab coalition receded rapidly, and although the ceasefire agreement required the Israelis to leave the Sinai Peninsula they had established that they could defend themselves if necessary. However, it was not long before conflict began once again.

THE SIX-DAY WAR

It can sometimes seem odd that a given area might be fought over several times in different centuries, but there are solid reasons for this.

The Suez operation was doomed from the start by the political climate. Despite achieving their military objectives, the British and French troops were forced to pull back and depart empty-handed.

Multiple-launch rocket systems. Egypt favoured such systems, having obtained quantities from the Soviet Union. Although inaccurate and incapable of sustained fire, they are excellent for preparing the way for an assault.

Geography does not change, after all, and the routes that are appropriate for armies to take often remain the same over the centuries. Military forces, as well as commercial and economic transport, can take only certain routes.

From that perspective, it is not hard to see why certain places have been the site of more than one battle. The routes taken by Israeli forces advancing into the Sinai in 1967 were more or less the same as in 1956. An appraisal of the local geography also casts light on some of the reasons for the conflict.

Israel was surrounded by hostile powers that openly talked of joint action to exterminate the Jewish state, and there were good reasons to believe that the threat was real. Since the 1956 attack on Sinai, a UN peacekeeping force was in position, and theoretically provided a measure of security on that flank. When, amid rising tensions in May 1967, Egypt demanded that this force be withdrawn, matters came to a head.

> Israel was surrounded by hostile powers that openly talked of joint action to exterminate the Jewish state, and there were good reasons to believe that the threat was real.

Egyptian army units moved into Sinai in strength, and at the same time Egypt closed the Straits of Tiran opposite Sharm el Sheik to Israeli shipping. This effectively cut off Eilat, Israel's only port with access to the Indian Ocean. Arguments broke out about whether or not the closure constituted a blockade and was therefore an act of war. Egypt's stated position was that the blockade was irrelevant; the question was simply one of when and how to bring about the destruction of Israel.

If the threat was as serious as it sounded, Israel could not hope to survive if she awaited attack. The Arab nations around her were in the

process of forming a unified command structure, and Israel was faced with a stark choice. If she did not mobilize for war, she would be quickly overrun in any attack. Yet a mobilization would destroy the economy unless the troops were stood down and back at work within two weeks. There was one other option. Israel could gamble everything on her only two advantages. The first was that she occupied a central position between her enemies and could, in theory, lunge against first one then the others. The second advantage complemented the first. Events in 1956 had validated the concept of rapid armoured assault as the tool of decision, and the Israeli army had been reorganized accordingly.

The wreckage of disabled and abandoned vehicles litters a road in the Sinai. It is a fact of modern warfare that the victorious side can salvage vehicles from the battlefield, sometimes even putting them back into combat.

The enemies of Israel had placed her in a position where she had no choice but to strike first, yet for various reasons they did not believe that she would do so. Thus the Israeli attacks that began the Six-Day War, as it became known, achieved a level of surprise that should simply have been impossible.

It was necessary to hit Egypt first. Forces were left covering the other frontiers, but these were relatively

ISRAEL'S LACK OF STRATEGIC DEPTH

Most nations have a certain amount of depth to them. That is, in the event that they are invaded, there are natural barriers to slow down the enemy and allow sufficient room for defenders to fall back, trading space for time to prepare an effective response. Israel had neither terrain barriers nor strategic depth. Indeed, an armoured strike from Jordan, at the narrowest point of Israel, could reach the Mediterranean Sea in less than an hour, effectively severing the country in two.

small to enable maximum effort to be thrown westwards into Sinai. If the Israelis failed to win a decisive victory there – and fast – the other fronts did not matter anyway.

The war opened with an all-or-nothing air attack to suppress the Egyptian Air Force. Virtually the entire Israeli Air Force was committed to the strike, which achieved almost total surprise and smashed the Egyptians on the ground. As quickly as the planes could be turned around, they were sent back to finish the job. Egypt's allies had air forces of their own but with the largest and best-equipped force out of the fight Israel had air superiority, which was exploited in the days to come.

The ground assault followed soon after. Its aim was to use the classic tactics of breakthrough and exploitation to wreck the Egyptian army. Armoured spearheads were to smash holes in the line and to cut the enemy lines of supply, overrunning headquarters and causing maximum confusion.

Although the Egyptian forces, especially the artillery, fought back hard, the armoured spearheads were able to quickly achieve their objectives. However, in so doing they tended to outrun their supports, which sometimes became bogged down fighting their way through units that had been disrupted but not destroyed by the armour. This weak coordination caused some needless losses but did not prevent success, which meant that the same mistake would be repeated in later conflicts.

With the Egyptian Air Force out of the picture, Israeli air units were available to give maximum support to the advancing ground forces, often taking the place of the artillery that had been left behind by the speed of the advance. Helicopters were used to land paratroops behind the main enemy positions. This was especially

Motorized transport enabled the Israelis to advance quickly and to keep their forces supplied. Animal transport, still common use at the start of World War II, had disappeared from the battle zone by this time.

Tanks throw up dust as they manoeuvre; obscuring the situation and risking clogged air intakes. The vehicle in the foreground is a US M3 half-track. Large numbers of these useful but anachronistic vehicles were used by the Israelis.

effective at Abu Aweigila, where the paras were able to get in among the Egyptian artillery.

The main thrust was across the Sinai Peninsula using much the same routes as in 1956, but a force was also sent southwards to take the port of Sharm el Sheik and remove the blockade of Eilat. A paradrop and units of Israel's small coastal navy accompanied this.

By 8 June, the Egyptian army was in full flight, abandoning heavy equipment and artillery as it rushed headlong towards the safety of the Suez Canal. Several hundred tanks were lost, and even more artillery. By the time the remnants rallied behind the canal, seven divisions had more or less ceased to exist. Once the Egyptian collapse began, units were pulled out of the fighting there and sent racing north and east towards Syria and Jordan. An initial defensive stance was planned in these areas, but there were gains to be made that would greatly benefit Israel. If the West Bank region of Jordan could be taken, the river itself would provide a natural frontier. The same was true of the Golan Heights facing Syria. But first any attacks coming from those directions would have to be contained.

JORDAN AND SYRIA UNPREPARED

Fortunately, the decision to strike first had paid dividends. Jordan and Syria were not ready for a massive combined attack into Israel. Indeed, although both nations had treaties with Egypt they took some persuading to join the war. Claims by Egypt that her forces were overrunning the Israelis helped convince her allies to join the fighting, when in fact the situation was rather less rosy.

The Jordanian army began with small-scale attacks on 5 June, which were beaten off. The Israelis countered with an encirclement of Jerusalem and eventually captured the city while air units smashed up

FRAGILE EGYPTIAN FORCES

Although the Egyptians had good equipment, including Soviet-made tanks and artillery in large numbers, their forces were somewhat brittle. There was a wide gulf between the educated officer class and the peasant conscripts of the infantry formations, and little trust between them. This contrasted with the motivated and extremely professional Israeli forces. It is perhaps telling that fully one-third of Israeli casualties were officers or NCOs, while casualties among Egyptian officers were virtually nil.

Jordanian forces moving to intervene.

Air supremacy was important in this theatre, and allowed the Jordanians' movements to be greatly impaired while the ground forces wore them down. Although the Jordanian forces, particularly the Arab Legion, put up a stiff fight they were driven out of the West Bank.

Their air force, like that of Jordan, was quickly eliminated but the harsh terrain of the Golan Heights prevented serious damage to ground units.

The Syrians, having swallowed false claims that the Egyptians were already winning the war, began rather cautious operations against Israel with some shelling and relatively minor advances. The truth of the situation began to dawn when Syrian positions and air bases were hit by Israeli air strikes. Their air force, like that of Jordan, was quickly eliminated, but the harsh terrain of the Golan Heights did at least prevent serious damage to ground units. The Syrians then decided to settle for shelling targets over the border from their positions in the heights, and this continued until 9 June, when Israeli forces began driving into the Golan Heights. This was a perilous undertaking, against positions that had been carefully constructed to counter just such an assault.

Although the Syrian positions were indeed very strong, the Israeli assault was extremely aggressive and pressed with great determination along three axes, with heavy air support. Late on the first day, a breakthrough was achieved. On 10 June, the second day of the Israeli attack on the heights, the Syrians fell back just in time to avoid being caught in a classic armoured double-envelopment launched into the Golan plateau. The Six-Day War was a triumph for aggressively handled

Closely watched by Israeli troops, a group of Egyptian civilians wait to be permitted to cross the Suez Canal. Their rapid victory in 1967 over the Egyptian army caused the Israeli armed forces to become dangerously complacent.

END OF THE SIX-DAY WAR

Having gained enough territory to create buffer zones or borders based on natural obstacles, Israel agreed to a ceasefire, which brought the war to an end on 11 June. In just six days, the military of Egypt had been shattered and both Jordan and Syria were now forced to give up strategic territory.

armoured forces with good air support. Unfortunately for Israel it fostered a certain complacency, which would have serious consequences just six years later. For the time being, however, Israel's desperate gamble had paid off. She had achieved the security she needed and could send her citizen-soldiers back to their peacetime jobs.

THE INDO-PAKISTANI CONFLICT

When the British surrendered their colonial empire, two nations were created north of the Indian Ocean. The largest was, of course, India. The second was Pakistan, sometimes described as the world's most militarily absurd state.

As established in 1947, Pakistan consisted of the relatively rich West Pakistan, located northwest of India, and East Pakistan, a much smaller and poorer region separated by the entire width of India. East Pakistan was also surrounded by India, except where it bounded the Bay of Bengal.

Consisting mainly of the floodplains of three great rivers, including the Ganges, East Pakistan was a source of agricultural exports that generated considerable wealth, but which received little of the returns. Meanwhile, West Pakistan was

Agha Muhammad Yahya Khan, President of Pakistan, inherited a troubled political situation from his predecessor. He took measures which, while sensible, were far too late to be effective. When this failed, he turned to harsh methods.

M24

Type: Light tank

Crew: 4 or 5

Powerplant: Two Cadillac 44T24 V-8 engines developing 82kW (110hp)

Weight: 18,371kg (18tons)

Range: 281km (175 miles)

Armour: 38mm (1.5in)

Armament: one 75mm (2.95in) M6 gun; one 12.7mm (0.5in) MG; two 7.62mm (0.3in) MGs

Performance: maximum road speed 55km/h (34mph)

Dimensions: length 5.49m (18ft)
width 2.95m (9ft 8in)
height 2.46m (8ft 1in)

far more important in political terms and was home to the major economic and governmental centres.

Tensions between East and West Pakistan gradually increased throughout the 1950s and 1960s, accompanied by a steadily worsening internal political situation. East Pakistan, whose representatives had previously campaigned for better treatment within the nation as a whole, now began seriously to consider independence.

ELECTIONS

In December 1970, elections were held, but the results were not to the liking of General Yahya Khan, who had counted on holding the balance of power afterward. Instead, a clear majority emerged under the leadership of Sheik Mujibur Rahman. General Yahya offered a deal and when this was rejected he arrested the sheik and imposed martial law in East Pakistan.

The army, which was largely drawn from West Pakistani sources, then began trying to intimidate the East Pakistani people with a campaign of terror and atrocity. It has been estimated that up to one million people were murdered before the population rose up and, with no alternative, tried to fight back.

The army, which was largely drawn from West Pakistani sources, then began trying to intimidate the East Pakistani people with a campaign of terror and atrocity.

Yahya sent reinforcements and stepped up his campaign of terror, which caused hordes of refugees to flee over the border to India. He hoped that the international political situation of the time would allow him to avoid foreign intervention. In this, he was partially successful; the world's larger powers were preoccupied elsewhere, but India was becoming increasingly alarmed.

The refugees flooding into eastern India were overstraining local resources and destabilizing the region. Worse, the Pakistani army had taken to chasing guerrillas over the border into India and was carrying out operations in Indian soil.

There was little love lost between India and Pakistan. In 1965, India had lost territory in a border clash, and now, with Pakistani internal affairs causing serious problems, her leaders decided to act. The first response was diplomatic but a request to the United Nations for assistance yielded nothing useful. That left India with only the military option.

Initial clashes were minor, as Indian army units engaged their Pakistani counterparts only when they penetrated Indian territory. But India had already decided to fight a major campaign and defeat Pakistan. Her preparations became obvious, and in

While there was no question about the outcome in East Pakistan, the Indian army had a fight on its hands in the west. Its armoured forces clashed with their Pakistani equivalents and emerged victorious in the south.

early December 1971 the Pakistani air force launched a pre-emptive strike in the hope of destroying the Indian air force on the ground.

The Pakistanis hoped to re-create the spectacular success of the Israelis against Egypt in 1967, but in the event they failed utterly. Attacking at nightfall meant that many of the strikes missed their targets, which were in any case protected by hardened shelters. This incident marked the beginning of the Indo-Pakistani war.

The Indian intention was to overrun East Pakistan as quickly as possible while preventing forces from West Pakistan from making any significant gains. The Indian army went into East Pakistan from four directions, converging on the capital, Dacca, from all sides. Its axes of attack were dictated by the terrain, which was dominated by large numbers of watercourses. This allowed the outnumbered Pakistani forces to predict where an attack would come from and to set up defences accordingly. However, the Indians were prepared to overcome these measures. Rather than attack the Pakistani forces head on, a policy of infiltration was initially used, slipping

THE FOLLY OF FIXED POSITIONS

Reasoning that the local terrain would force the Indian army to advance along predictable axes, the Pakistani forces in East Pakistan deployed in fixed positions without significant mobile reserves. Although crossing the region's many wide rivers proved a difficult task, the Indians were able to bypass the strongest Pakistani positions and either attack from the rear or cut the supply line. This undoubtedly prevented a great many Indian casualties and caused the Pakistani strategy to unravel.

light units into the rear of the Pakistanis' forward positions.

OPENING ATTACK

The attack proper opened on 4 December, bypassing some strong points and using helicopter-borne troops and paradrops to get behind others. The Pakistani army, which had been deployed to hold rigid positions along the border, found itself outmanoeuvred and fell back from some positions without a fight. Others were reduced in hard fighting. Bogra in the north of the country held out until 14 December.

The Indians made extensive use of amphibious light tanks and bridging equipment obtained from the Soviet Union to get across the many rivers of the region, though not always without difficulty. This, coupled with infiltration tactics, cut off and prevented many Pakistani units from falling back to make a stand at Dacca.

Some forces did make it to Dacca and prepared a defence. However, they were surrounded and defending a city where they had committed tremendous atrocities. After initially refusing an invitation to surrender on 7 December, the Pakistani army offered a ceasefire on 15 December. The Indians demanded unconditional surrender, and the next day this came into force.

Meanwhile, things went little better for Pakistan in the west. The border had been drawn up in an arbitrary fashion, trying to match the borders of historical states in the region, and meandered around considerably. Both sides wanted to straighten the border and perhaps anchor parts of it on terrain features.

Pakistan had 12 divisions available for operations in the west, two of them armoured and the rest infantry. Indian strength is not known but is generally thought to be equal or slightly superior to their opponents. The Pakistanis moved first, advancing on the ground just after their air strike went in. In the Kashmir region in the north, the offensive was mostly held, though gains were made near Chamba before the defence firmed

> The Indian intent was to overrun East Pakistan as quickly as possible while preventing forces from West Pakistan from making any significant gains.

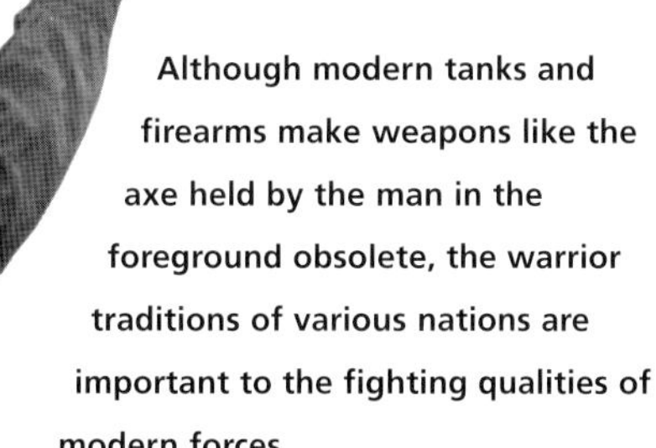

Although modern tanks and firearms make weapons like the axe held by the man in the foreground obsolete, the warrior traditions of various nations are important to the fighting qualities of modern forces.

up. Further south, in the Punjab, a major armoured clash took place, in which the Indians came off best.

Meanwhile, closer to the coast, the Pakistanis ran into real trouble. One of their armoured brigades became stuck in soft sand and was then mauled by the air units that should have been pre-emptively destroyed. Indian forces advanced into the region that had been ceded in 1968 and retook it, along with a considerable amount of Pakistani territory. Much of these gains consisted of worthless desert, and crossing this barrier slowed down the Indian advance. At the time the ceasefire took effect, Pakistani forces were rushing south to contain the incursion.

In the west, both sides lost some territory, but the Indians gained far more than they had lost, and in addition defeated their enemies in most engagements. The result was a redrawn border and the resumption of an armed and hostile confrontation across the border. However, in the west much more had changed. East Pakistan became independent as the modern nation of Bangladesh. Thus the problem of refugees and military incursions was solved for

> West Pakistan had lost its distant territory but since most of the nation's economic and political apparatus remained intact, the consequences were not too severe.

The Pakistani surrender created the nation of Bangladesh from what had formerly been East Pakistan. This did not greatly affect West Pakistan, where most of the nation's economic and industrial strength was located.

Indian troops withdrawing from Pakistan. These two nations have a troubled history. Although the Simla Agreement of 1972 attempted to mitigate tensions arising from territorial gains in the war, relations have rarely been good.

India, and the Pakistani army's reign of terror had been brought to an end. In the west, Indian air support proved very useful, validating the theory behind the pre-emptive air strike even if its execution proved a failure. Operations in the west were fairly conventional, though the possession of high ground usable as artillery observation positions was contested by small infantry forces in very challenging conditions.

ANOTHER LIMITED CONFLICT

The Indo-Pakistani war of 1971 demonstrated another kind of limited conflict; the fighting was brief and ended with West Pakistan largely intact. It had lost its distant territory but since most of the nation's economic and political apparatus remained intact, the consequences were not too severe as to be unacceptable. In some ways this kind of conflict harks back to an earlier age, in which the adage 'grab what you can and sue for peace' applied.

PAKISTAN'S UNTENABLE POSITION

Pakistan was in an appalling military position at the beginning of the war, trying to fight on two widely separated fronts. There was never any real chance to win in the east, though a more effective defence might have been beneficial in subsequent negotiations. In the event, attempting to hold a 'thin, hard crust' of defensive positions around the border proved to be a poor strategy. Once infiltrated or outflanked, these positions became untenable and there was little provision for a mobile defence.

Revolution and Insurgency 1956–1995

One of the basic requirements for a successful revolution or insurrection is that there must be a disaffected segment of the population from which to obtain support. Some revolutionaries, notably Enrique ('Che') Guevara, maintained that the actions of the revolutionaries themselves could create such a group, but this was at best a dubious proposition. As events in South America showed, violence alone cannot create the conditions for a successful revolution.

Where a segment of the population supports one side in an otherwise conventional conflict, it becomes possible for an insurgency to take hold and to work alongside the conventional forces towards a common goal. In some cases, these friendly partisans remained separate and even become hostile once the common foe was defeated. At other times, the insurgents were not only fighting the same foe; they operated as part of the same command structure.

REVOLUTION IN CENTRAL AND SOUTH AMERICA

When Dr Fidel Castro and his followers, who included 'Che' Guevara, landed in Cuba in December 1956, the conditions for a successful revolution were already in place. General Batista, dictator of Cuba, presided over a corrupt regime that had created large numbers of disaffected people. It seemed likely that a few acts of revolutionary violence might be all that was necessary

Soldiers man a machine-gun position dug out of the road surface in a Latin American town. Their bandoliers are an easy way to carry belts of machine-gun ammunition.

Enrique 'Che' Guevara was born in Argentina and had travelled widely in South America when he joined Castro's group in Mexico. After serving in Castro's government in Cuba, he attempted to carry on his revolutionary goals in Congo.

to trigger a general rising. However, the instigators of these acts were quickly captured and most of Castro's band were killed by the Cuban military. Castro and about a dozen survivors took refuge in the Sierra Maestra mountains and started again. All they could do at first was to make pinprick raids, and although recruits came in to join the movement they numbered in tens rather than the thousands that were needed. Castro and his men owed their survival to the corruption and inefficiency of the Batista regime, which removed competent officers in favour of political favourites and sent out a demoralized and ineffective army to find the insurgents.

Batista's army behaved in the same way as the rest of the regime. It was, essentially, a terrorist organization in that fear and brutality were routinely used as a tool and often just for the sake of it. Castro and his men came to be seen as heroes fighting against the evil dictatorship, and steadily gained support among the population.

The rural population of Oriente province where Castro's men operated was alienated by their landlords, who used the army to drive them off their land. This swelled the numbers of insurgents considerably, and by early 1958 the chance to eliminate Castro's band was gone. Although the army still vastly outnumbered them, the margin was not big enough to make up for the almost total ineffectiveness of its formations.

CUBA: CLASSIC INSURGENT STRATEGY

The model used by Castro was typical of rural insurgency: attacks on military outposts to discredit the government and to gain weapons, the destruction of sugar mills and other economic assets, and the use of ambushes against security forces. Although Castro maintained that he came up with his strategy independently of Mao and Giap's thinking, the mode of operation was much the same.

In May 1958, Batista threw 17 battalions of troops, with air support and some armour, into an operation to find and eliminate Castro. In the resulting fiasco, one battalion was shattered and the rest achieved nothing in return for a steady toll of casualties. This encouraged Castro to begin launching raids into other provinces. The raids were wildly successful. The demoralized and badly led Cuban army broke and fled from small groups of insurgents, further discrediting the Batista regime. By December, the eastern end of Cuba was more or less in Castro's hands, and Batista was more concerned with escape than trying to put down the insurrection. Meanwhile, disaffection and resistance to Batista's regime was becoming increasingly open in the countryside and the towns.

Not only did the guerrillas receive information, supplies and recruits from the populace, the latter began actively to obstruct the security forces, draining their resources and, more significantly, their already weak will to challenge the revolutionaries.

TIPPING THE BALANCE

As the balance steadily tipped, Batista's forces made a stand of sorts near Santa Clara. However, even before the fighting started, Batista had given orders for an aircraft loaded with valuables to be kept standing by. On 1 January 1959, he fled the country and a week later Castro and his followers were welcomed into Havana by cheering crowds. It was not so much that the people wanted Castro in power as they wanted to be rid of the corruption and brutality of the Batista regime. The general expectation was that a new era of democracy was about to begin, and the subsequent embrace of communism was not quite what most of them had wanted.

Although the US government was worried by what became known as the 'domino effect', Guevara himself went a long way towards disproving the theory in Bolivia.

EXPORTING REVOLUTION

After the success in Cuba, which owed much to the fact that the conditions for revolution already existed, Guevara drew some dubious conclusions. He theorized that a successful revolution in one country could trigger one elsewhere, and that conditions for a successful revolution could be created simply by the revolution itself.

Although the US government was worried by what became known as the 'domino effect', Guevara himself went a long way towards disproving the theory in Bolivia. Believing that the

Fidel Castro was born in Cuba and became involved with student political groups at university. He was a practising lawyer and a candidate for a seat in parliament when General Batista seized power.

the Andes could be used as a base and that the rural population there would support him, he set about trying to start a new revolution. He was killed by the security forces in 1967.

The Latin American revolutionary Carlos Marighela believed that suitable conditions for an insurrection could be brought about by groups of urban guerrillas or terrorists committing acts of what he called 'revolutionary violence', which would cause the government to crack down and thus make segments of the population unhappy. This in turn would create the disaffected group needed for larger-scale revolution. Marighela also believed that urban guerrillas would pull troops in from the countryside, enabling a rural insurrection to get going.

FROM RURAL TO URBAN INSURGENCY

Attempts to start rural insurgencies failed in several Latin American countries during the 1960s. Most were swatted without difficulty, and it soon became apparent to the survivors that a different approach was necessary. At that time, South America was undergoing a great deal of urbanization and consequent social upheaval, so the urban environment was the logical place to ferment trouble.

MARINGHELA METHODS

Marighela decided to use the same methods Guevara had tried in Bolivia, but in the urban centres. A well

The aftermath of a failed rebel attack on an army barracks near Matanzas, in 1956. The attacking force consisted of 11 insurgents, who were eliminated by the troops who were their intended target.

Not only had the Cuban army previously been a power base for the Batista regime, but its performance in the field had been seriously sub-par. After the revolution, it was necessary to instil both loyalty and increased competence.

armed band of guerrillas would cause disruption and destruction, forcing a government response that would alienate the population. He added one useful feature – every act, whether violent or not, was to be milked for maximum propaganda value. This use of publicity was his main contribution to the theory of insurrection. Marighela's insurrection in Brazil was just one of many going on in the cities of that nation. The result was a confused and ineffective mess of urban revolutionaries who were often at cross purposes. One by one, the insurgent groups were broken and Marighela himself was killed in 1969.

> A well armed band of guerrillas would cause disruption and destruction, forcing a government response that would alienate the population.

In Guatemala, the guerrillas were put down with extreme brutality after engaging in a bloody series of terrorist attacks. In Uruguay, the insurgents used rather different methods. The insurgency started in the countryside

VIVA
AL
EJERC
TO DI
26 de
JU
¡VIVA FIDEL!
¡VIVA!
GOBIERNO REVOLUCIONARIO
URRUTIA
PRESIDENTE
P.S.P.

FAILED REVOLUTION IN VENEZUELA

Urban guerrillas tried their hand in various nations. In Venezuela, the urban campaign was extremely violent and accompanied by a rural insurgency. Despite causing a lot of harm, the guerrillas achieved little. One reason for this was that the president demonstrated that change was possible via democratic means, causing the insurgents to lose support.

A successful insurgency requires the support of a significant segment of the population. The banners borne by these people, which depict Fidel Castro booting Batista out of the country, suggest that this was not lacking in Cuba.

but moved to the towns because more than three-quarters of the population lived there. Violence was used, but the overall aim was to ridicule the government. Many 'attacks' were intended to be harmless and humorous, which attracted positive attention overseas.

URBAN GUERILLA MOVEMENTS

In Argentina, pro- and anti-government urban guerrilla movements turned the streets into a battleground, reducing the country to chaos. Indeed, it became impossible to maintain a stable political base until a military junta seized power in 1976, winning popular support.

Other nations had their share of revolutionary violence but although the effects were at times serious, successful revolutions did not follow. The main reason for this was effective response by the security forces. Those who believed that violence alone could bring about a revolution had missed two important points. In a stable country, the authorities were better able to respond to insurgents than the corrupt and ineffective

Carlos Marighela was a Brazilian Communist. He was successful in triggering government repression which he believed would result in popular disaffection, only to fall victim to a police ambush in 1969.

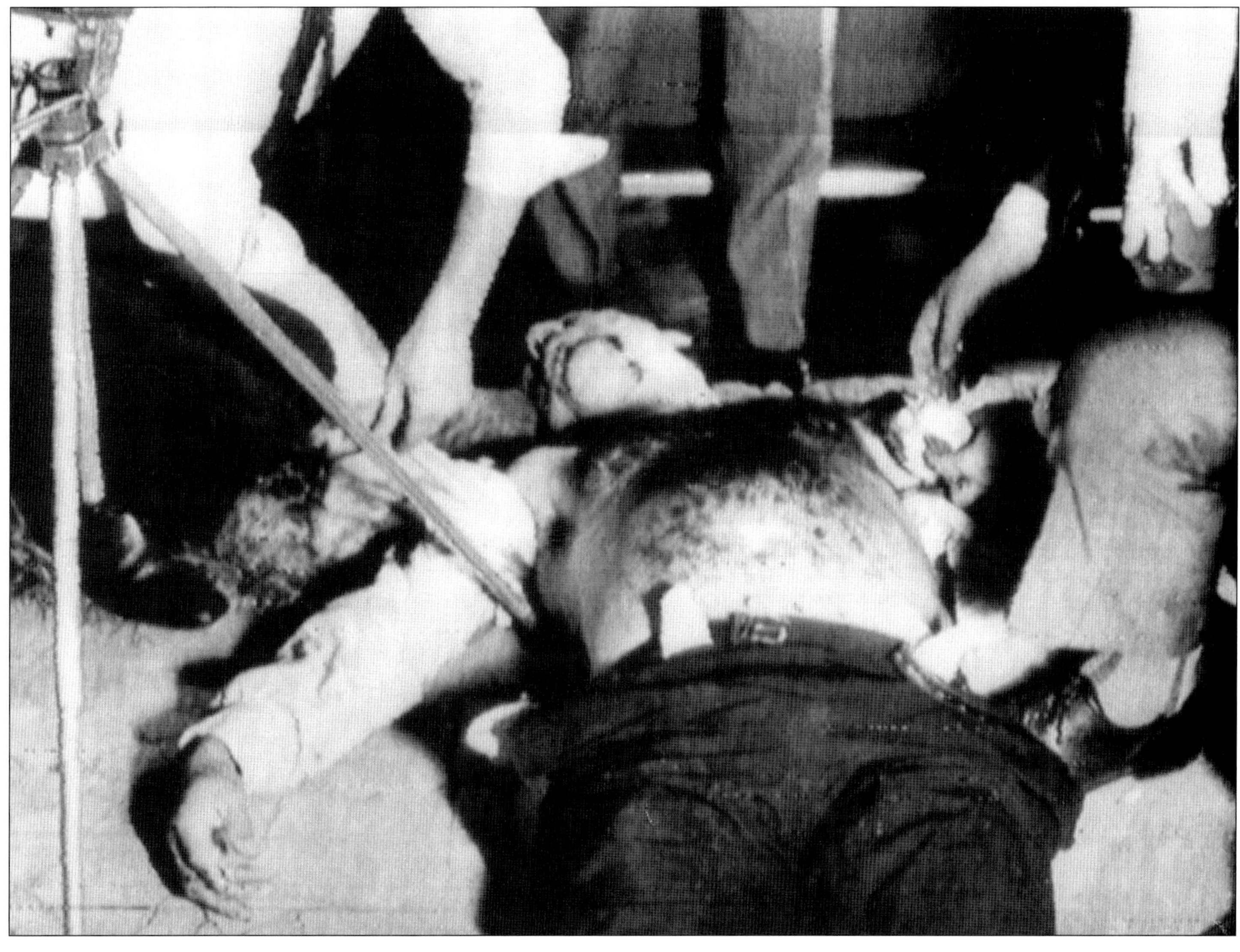

Weapons and flags of Guatemalan guerrillas. Note the image of 'Che' Guevara, who became a symbol of revolution even though he was not actually very successful once he parted company from the more competent Fidel Castro.

Cuban army had been, and in a country without a disaffected social group the insurgents would not only lack support but were likely to be exposed to the authorities. As a result, although the insurgents did indeed force the governments they attacked to crack down and impose repressive measures, these were successfully portrayed as necessary to protect the common citizen from a small minority of troublemakers. In most cases, the repressive measures they triggered were sufficient to cripple the insurgent movement to the point where it was unable to take advantage of any disaffection that might result.

Although disruption was caused and in some cases political change did occur, it rarely created the result the revolutionaries wanted. The failure of some revolutions was due to repression; in other cases, 'softer' methods worked just as well. The common denominator was the simple fact that it is not possible to create successful revolution simply by causing

Although disruption was caused and in some cases political change did occur, it rarely created the result the revolutionaries wanted.

trouble. If the conditions for a revolution exist, as in Cuba, then success is possible. If not, the insurgents are doomed to failure.

INDEPENDENCE AND CIVIL WAR IN AFRICA

The modern nation of Zaire was for many years a colony of Belgium. Then named Belgian Congo, it became independent in 1960. There was an element to the withdrawal of snatching fingers out of the fire, as Congo was beset by internal troubles at the time. Despite a promising start, with elections and a workable national constitution, violence broke out almost immediately.

Whites were targeted and many had to flee or became trapped. This created an immediate need to rescue those cut off in suddenly hostile territory. Belgian paratroops were rushed into Katanga province to protect the white population there, while the situation deteriorated fast. Fearing (with some cause) that the central government was going to align itself with the Soviet Union, the governor of Katanga province

A COMPLEX SITUATION IN THE CONGO

Internal politics in Congo were very complex and were further muddied by the involvement of international mining companies and the political machinations of the big Eastern and Western power blocs. Belgian forces also engaged the various factions, but their actions were mostly directed towards the rescue of Europeans who were trapped or held as hostages in the war zone.

Belgian paratroops secure N'Dhilli airport. Control of airfields allowed the UN to limit access to the country, bringing to an end what had been referred to as 'Soviet Imperialism' by cutting off any chance of support for the Soviet-aligned factions.

declared independence. Central government appealed to both the Soviet Union and the United Nations for assistance. UN troops stationed in Africa and the Middle East were rushed in to try to impose stability. Meanwhile, some Soviet forces were also flown in, and the Cold War became a little warmer as arguments broke out over what the West called opportunistic Soviet imperialism.

Low-intensity fighting took place throughout the country, usually on a very small scale. Ambushes and raids were common, the enemy being engaged by units that were rarely more than a hundred or so strong. The result was indecisive but bloody. Tribal violence was also common since groups formerly held in check by the colonial authorities now came into conflict.

Mercenaries serving in the Congo fought on both sides of this action, and a mercenary force was later used in a failed attempt to depose Mobutu.

That particular issue was solved when UN forces closed Congo's airports to all but UN-sanctioned flights. However, a military coup in September further complicated the situation. A new civilian government appeared in December, claiming to be the successor to the duly elected one that had recently been deposed.

The civil war continued with few interruptions until 1965, by which time the central government had more or less re-established itself and the rebel leaders had mostly fled the country. Elections were held against a backdrop of rebellion and occasional flare-ups of fighting. Almost immediately, General Mobutu deposed the elected government and managed to impose a measure of stability on the situation.

MERCENARIES

Mobutu faced opposition from various directions, including a revolt among his military personnel. Mercenaries serving in the Congo fought on both sides of this action, and a mercenary force was later used in a failed attempt to depose Mobutu.

Mercenaries were widely used in the Congo. The word 'mercenary' has unpleasant connotations to many people, but in truth it means nothing more than a soldier who fights for an organization other than his national government. True, a mercenary fights for pay, but so do all professional military personnel.

The first mercenaries were brought in to protect the Belgian-owned mines and European populations within Congo. They trained and led a gendarmerie, which protected vulnerable groups in the countryside as well as engaging in conventional combat. Most of the mercenaries were withdrawn due to

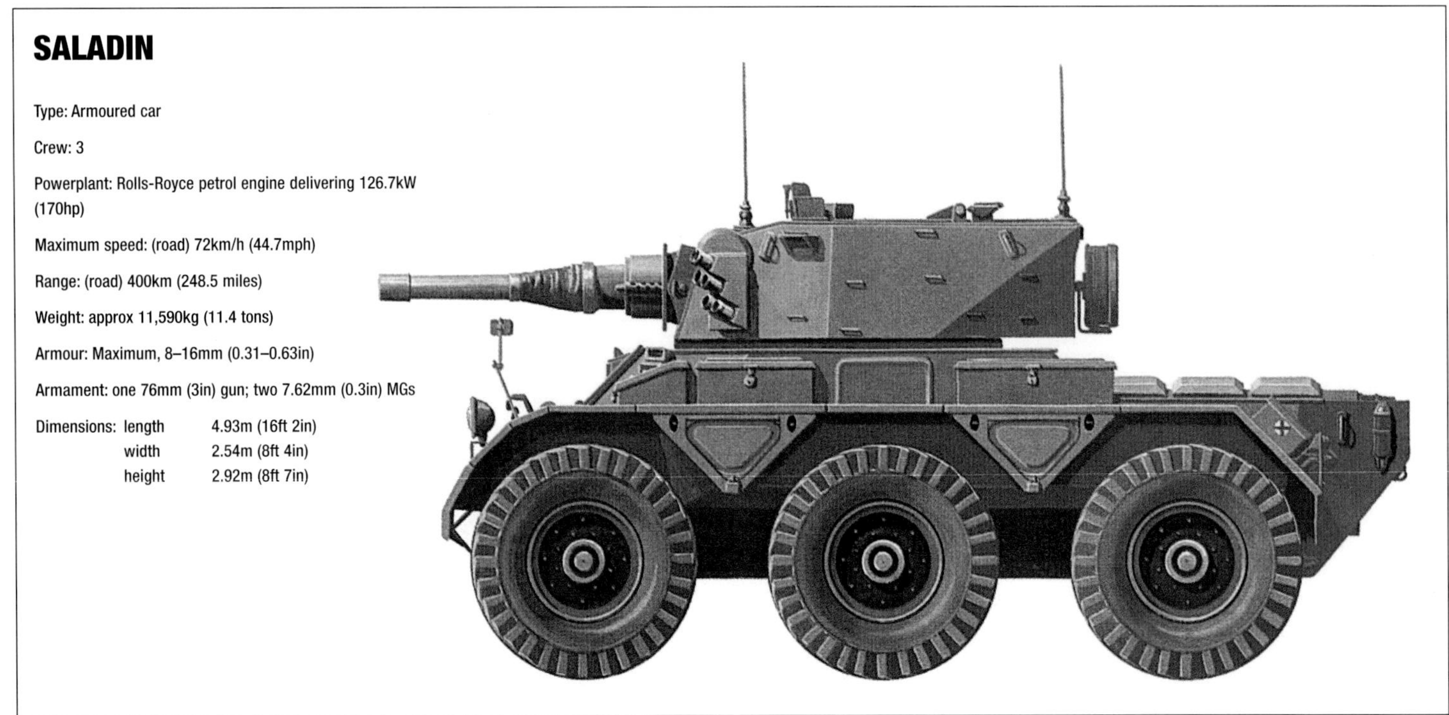

THE POLITICAL SOLUTION FAILS

The Portuguese government tried to remedy the situation by removing the grounds for disaffection. Generous concessions were offered, but the situation was out of control. Within three years, guerrilla warfare was taking place in all three colonies, with insurgents often coming in from neighbouring territories.

UN pressure, but one group played an important role.

In 1964, a force of mercenaries under 'Mad Mike' Hoare was contracted to fulfil a range of assignments. Most importantly, they were deployed to block arms shipments from reaching rebels via the Sudan border, which largely crippled the rebels' operations.

THE PORTUGUESE COLONIES

The situation in the Congo arose from a power vacuum caused when a colonial power withdrew too suddenly and too quickly and left behind a period of chaos. In this, the Congolese situation was different to many conflicts in Africa, in that the usual pattern was one of fighting for independence rather than because of it. The fight for independence of the Portuguese colonies is an example of the latter.

Portugal had maintained colonies in Africa for longer than any other nation, and the nation's neutrality in World War II meant that there was no sudden upheaval to create the conditions for an independence movement. Nevertheless, disaffection gradually increased throughout the 1950s.

Peacekeeping forces from the UN have attempted to protect non-combatants and to maintain order in conflict zones worldwide for many years. Small arms and light armoured vehicles are usually more useful than tanks.

Strikes and civil disobedience increased in intensity, and the measures to control the situation became ever more authoritarian until, in August 1959, troops fired on striking dockers in Guinea. Further incidents followed in Portugal's other African colonies (Angola and Mozambique), until by 1961 northern Angola was in revolt. The insurgents were aided by forces coming across the border from Congo to the north, which had recently become independent. Several thousand people were massacred. The first attacks in Angola caught the authorities by surprise. By the time Mozambique came under attack, containment measures were in place and the

The first attacks in Angola caught the authorities by surprise. By the time Mozambique came under attack, containment measures were in place.

A Portuguese soldier fires a light machine gun from the hip, using his sling to keep the weapon stable in an 'assault position'. The long grass provides excellent concealment, making it very difficult to hit a target.

Many insurgencies have made use of porters. In many cases, people on foot can go places that vehicles cannot. Groups on foot may be slow but they can often move into an area undetected.

INDEPENDENCE AS A COST-CUTTING EXERCISE

The main problem for the Portuguese was one of costs, both financial and in terms of manpower. The commitment required just to hang on to the colonies represented an enormous drain on the economy and many senior military figures became disaffected with the government. In 1974, they launched a coup in Portugal and soon afterwards granted the colonies independence.

insurgents were unable to penetrate far into the country. However, more than half of Guinea was in guerrilla hands by 1970.

CROSS-BORDER OPERATIONS

The anti-Portuguese guerrilla operations were characterized by their cross-border nature. Many of the insurgents spent little time in Portuguese territory but instead dashed a short distance over the border to make an attack and then retreated quickly. Relatively small numbers of guerrillas operated deep in the country or remained there for long. Several different insurgent organizations took part in the fighting. What they all had in common was a desire to create safe areas where they could grow food and 'educate' the local population to their way of thinking. Limited success was achieved, however, and most of the areas the guerrillas could reach were too far from the economic and population centres to achieve major results.

The insurgents' weaponry improved steadily during the campaign, but so did the Portuguese response. After a somewhat shaky start, the Portuguese initiated a strategy of trying to win hearts and minds by improving the lot of the locals in the combat zone. Secure villages were built with schools and hospitals and linked by new roads. Meanwhile, air interdiction was used against guerrilla supply routes.

In the forefront of the ground fighting were paratroop and marine units and infantry who had been trained in US counterinsurgent

The Vietcong were masters at hit-and-run tactics, using mines and ambushes to harass government forces on terms advantageous to the guerrillas. Here a Vietcong guerrilla is seen laying a mine.

methods learnt in Vietnam. By these methods, the Portuguese were able to avoid losing any more ground to the insurgents, but there was no end in sight by the mid 1970s.

US INVOLVEMENT IN VIETNAM

In the period after World War II, one of the top items on the agenda for US foreign policy was to halt the spread of communism. This was both an urgent and a daunting proposition, as communist revolutionary groups seemed to be springing up all over Asia, Africa and South America. Even in Europe certain terrorist organizations seemed to be receiving support from communist nations.

The ejection of French power from Vietnam left the country divided into a communist North and a democratic South. South Vietnam got off to a shaky start but managed to establish itself as a stable state. This was not to the liking of North Vietnam, whose leaders had expected a collapse that would enable them to assume control of the entire country. There was no chance of reunification through democratic means. The South rejected the suggestion of an election, as the North had a larger population and would almost certainly dominate voting. As South Vietnam established its statehood, it received American support. The United States was keen to assist any nation that might otherwise become a communist state. This was not acceptable to the North, which decided to use force. The means were already in place; the Viet Minh organization was inactive but intact. Thus in 1959, conflict broke out again with the resumption of guerrilla warfare. This time, the targets were not French but belonged to the state of South Vietnam.

For the duration of the conflict, guerrilla forces used a network of paths and dirt roads through Laos and Cambodia to move personnel and supplies. Known as the Truong Son Road in North Vietnam, this route was referred to as the Ho Chi Minh Trail in the wider world. Attempts were made to interdict movements along the trail, but these were confounded by both the dense jungle and the intricacies of international relations.

The possession of a fairly safe logistics route was extremely beneficial to the North Vietnamese, enabling operations to be carried out in the far south of the country, which would otherwise have been severely limited.

VIETNAM: IDEAL INSURGENT COUNTRY

Like Malaya, Vietnam was a guerrilla's paradise, with dense jungle interspersed with mountains. Roads had to run through this close terrain, offering countless opportunities for ambush followed by a rapid escape into the jungle. The long border with Laos and Cambodia also gave the guerrillas an advantage in that regular military units could not cross into another country in pursuit or to intercept their movements, whereas insurgent forces did not care whether they had permission or not.

DIFFERENT APPROACHES TO WAR

At the start of hostilities, South Vietnam possessed a conventional

American-trained army equipped to fight a Korea-style conflict. Its most likely opponent was North Vietnam, but the Army of the Republic of Vietnam (ARVN) was not set up to deal with a large-scale guerrilla war. Military thinking of the time was very much influenced by World War II and the Korean Conflict.

There were, broadly speaking, two military forces at the disposal of the north. The term Viet Cong generally referred to lightly equipped guerrillas while a conventional North Vietnamese Army (NVA) also existed. The two organizations were more or less entirely separate but both were developed from the Viet Minh and were made up of the same hardy and experienced fighters that had defeated the French.

North Vietnam approached the war in a Maoist manner, seeking to gain control of the country by gradual stages rather than a decisive military confrontation in the short term. The NVA was held in reserve early on, with Viet Cong guerrillas carrying out a low-level insurgency that gradually gained in scope and intensity.

Part of the initial Northern strategy was to infiltrate as much of South Vietnam as possible, getting communist representatives into as many villages as possible and generating a support base for the Viet Cong. This was countered by a 'strategic hamlet' project similar to that used in Malaya by the British. Such methods have been proven to work in various conflicts before and since, but in Vietnam in the early 1960s it was not enough.

SENSIBLE BUT INEFFECTIVE MEASURES

The Army of the Republic of Vietnam was not really suitable for counterinsurgency operations, so light infantry and civil guard units were raised to provide security and a more flexible response at an appropriate level. This, too, was a sensible measure but a combination of internal politics (including a coup) and North Vietnamese experience of this sort of campaign resulted in a gradual downwards slide for the south.

US ASSISTANCE

It was obvious that unless the Republic of Vietnam received concrete assistance, it would inevitably fall to the Communist North. The United States was already providing support and assistance, but from 1965 US combat troops were deployed and air strikes were made in conjunction with South Vietnamese air units.

In hindsight, it is possible to see the seeds of defeat in the way the United States conducted the war. Operations against North Vietnam itself were hamstrung by political considerations, while air strikes against the northern logistics routes proved ineffective. On the ground, the war became a campaign of attrition, with victory measured in terms of body count.

This approach was flawed. The North Vietnamese could afford to take serious casualties without major political repercussions, but the United States could not sustain even fairly minor losses for long. The war in Vietnam had relatively little popular

Roads in Vietnam ran through thick jungle that could conceal an ambush. Off the roads, it was virtually impossible to use vehicles in most areas and movement on foot was slow and difficult for troops not experienced in jungle operations.

The Army of the Republic of Vietnam (ARVN) was set up to fight a conventional war and was not well suited to counterinsurgency operations. It was rapidly augmented by local defence units and light infantry formations, which were better suited to their tasks.

support in the United States and questions were being asked about why American troops were dying in a foreign war. However, there was one immediate and palpable benefit. The ARVN had been coming off worst in many engagements, and the arrival of American firepower helped to turn this around.

Like the ARVN, US forces in Vietnam relied on the use of massive firepower. This would have worked well against a conventional enemy but was ineffective against the tactics used by the NVA and Viet Cong.

In an attempt to control remote areas of the country, the United States set up forward bases. These were used for patrolling and as firebases to support forces in the field. They were defended with a mix of infantry support weapons, mortars and artillery, and sometimes tanks. The perimeter was protected by barbed wire and anti-personnel mines plus directional Claymore mines. However, the proximity of the jungle to the base perimeter made it possible for snipers to infiltrate close to the base.

Other measures were implemented, sometimes with good effect. Riverine patrols and hovercraft operating on the Mekong Delta were able to reach areas that might otherwise have been inaccessible, and effort was made to rally support among the population. Success was mixed in most quarters, but the Montagnards (a French word meaning 'mountain people') of the central highlands were willing to fight alongside US forces.

Nevertheless, US and ARVN forces were generally successful in the field and it was possible to imagine that they were winning. Benchmarks like casualty figures, raids beaten off and weapon caches captured all pointed to a gradual victory. Of course, the real war was being fought in the hearts and minds of the Vietnamese people, and that was not going so well.

Nor was public opinion in the United States supportive. Anti-war feeling led to deep divisions in society and large-scale protests. A totalitarian country can ignore such things, but a democracy cannot – not if the government entertains any hope of re-election. The Viet Cong were able to exploit this situation. By imposing unacceptable casualties and provoking troops into excessive reactions, the Communists gave ammunition to the anti-war faction in the United States, which eventually led to the withdrawal of US troops.

RULES OF ENGAGEMENT

A range of political considerations, and rules of engagement that changed over time as well as from place to place, hamstrung US forces. Although troops might come under fire anywhere in the country, the acceptable level of response was different as a rule in the north, nearer the border, than in the supposedly friendly south.

THE TET OFFENSIVE

In late 1967, it seemed that the United States was winning the war. Heavy concentrations of troops along the northern frontier of South Vietnam were having some success in keeping the NVA out of the nation, though infiltration remained a problem. This comfortable appraisal was challenged in January 1968 by the Tet offensive, named for the period in the Vietnamese calendar when it was launched.

The Tet offensive was enormous in its scope, and its intentions were more than military. It was the brainchild of General Vo Nguyen Giap, who planned a large-scale conventional attack to coincide with raids by Viet

> The guerrilla war had resulted in a level of security and readiness not encountered in peacetime, meaning that even in 'safe' areas the security forces were reasonably alert.

Cong guerrillas and NVA infiltrators in over one hundred towns and cities. This massive attack was intended to overload the south's ability to respond and to trigger a general uprising in favour of the Communist North.

Despite imperfect timing of the attacks, which was only to be expected given the scale and scope of the operation, the defenders were caught by surprise. Many of the attacks achieved initial success but most were repulsed after a short time. The ongoing guerrilla war had resulted in

Above: The Montagnards ('mountain people'), of the Central Vietnamese highlands were culturally separate from the rest of the Vietnamese people and did not share their politics. Many fought alongside the US Army during the Vietnam War.

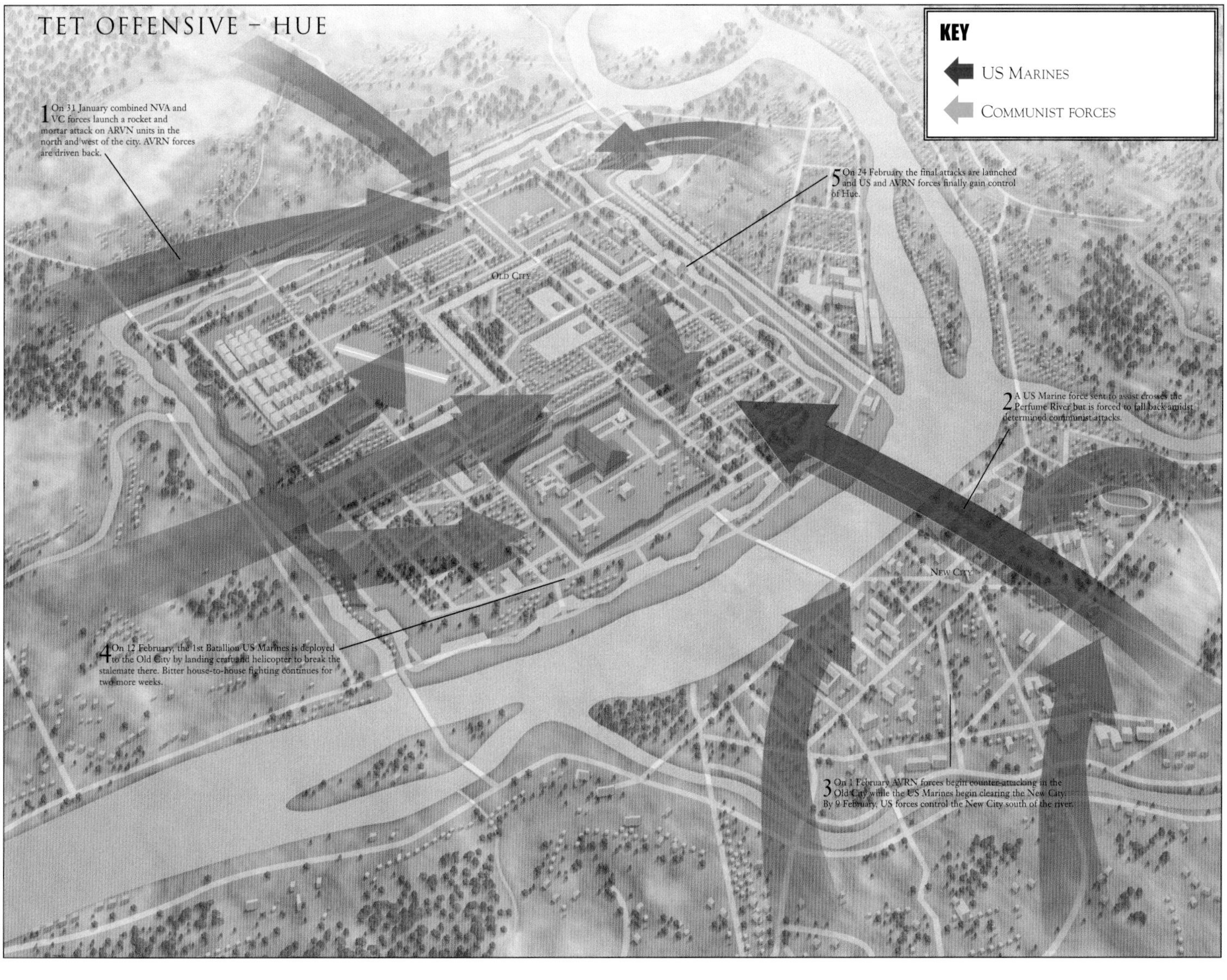

Hue was a priority target for North Vietnamese forces in the Tet offensive. The attacks were initially successful but did not capture the whole city before US and ARVN reinforcements then began the long struggle to retake Hue.

TET OFFENSIVE – HUE

KEY
US MARINES
COMMUNIST FORCES

1 On 31 January combined NVA and VC forces launch a rocket and mortar attack on ARVN units in the north and west of the city. AVRN forces are driven back.

2 A US Marine force sent to assist crosses the Perfume River but is forced to fall back amidst determined communist attacks.

3 On 1 February AVRN forces begin counter-attacking in the Old City while the US Marines begin clearing the New City. By 9 February, US forces control the New City south of the river.

4 On 12 February, the 1st Batallion US Marines is deployed to the Old City by landing craft and helicopter to break the stalemate there. Bitter house-to-house fighting continues for two more weeks.

5 On 24 February the final attacks are launched and US and AVRN forces finally gain control of Hue.

OLD CITY

NEW CITY

US troops scramble to take cover as an attack begins. Even in relatively safe areas, snipers and mortar attacks made life difficult; in the more 'active' areas, firebases and forward patrol bases seemed like islands in a sea of hostiles.

a level of security and readiness not encountered in peacetime, meaning that even in 'safe' areas the security forces were reasonably alert and, more importantly, were not suffering from a complacent mindset.

In Hue, which had once been the capital, fighting went on for about four weeks. Although the attackers had not managed to capture the whole city, they were able to pin down the small forces of ARVN and US troops present into small areas of the city. Reinforcements were pushed in by both sides, until US troops threw a cordon around the city to prevent any more getting in. Even then, a bitter street-by-street campaign was necessary to clear the city of hostiles.

Meanwhile, on the border with North Vietnam, the NVA pressed attacks on the US base at Khe Sanh for two months. Like Dien Bien Phu, the base was surrounded and besieged, and an attempt was made to reduce it by artillery attack. However, the US artillery forces within the base were skilled and equipped well, and were supported by air assets that pounded the North Vietnamese positions. Air resupply was used much more successfully than at Dien Bien Phu, largely because of the much greater numbers and capabilities of the available aircraft.

Eventually the NVA was pushed away from Khe Sanh, and there was a lull while Giap prepared a renewed offensive. This opened in May with more attacks on US bases and an attack on Saigon. There was no element of surprise this time and most NVA forces were met in the field.

A final effort in August did not involve the Viet Cong, who had suffered such massive casualties that

M50 'ONTOS'

Type: tank destroyer

Crew: 3

Powerplant: General Motors 302 V6 petrol engine delivering 108.2kW (145hp)

Maximum speed: (road) 48km/h (30mph)

Range: (road) 241km (150 miles)

Weight: approx 8641kg (8.5 tons)

Armour: 13mm (0.15in)

Armament: Six 106mm (4.17in) recoiless rifles; one 7.62mm (0.30in) machine gun

Dimensions:		
	length	3.83m (12ft 5in)
	width	2.60m (8ft 6in)
	height	2.13m (6ft 10in)

M101 HOWITZER

Type: Towed artillery

Calibre: 105mm (4.13in)

Weight: (travelling and firing) 2258kg (4978lb)

Dimensions: (travelling) length 5.99m (19ft 9in); width 2.16m (7ft 1in); height 1.574m (5ft 2in)

Elevation: -5° to +66°

Traverse: 46°

Maximum range; with M1 projectile 11,270m (12,325 yards) or with M548 projectile 14,600m (15,965 yards)

Rate of fire: 10 rounds per minute

Armour: Maximum, 30mm (1.18in)

Armament: one 57mm (2.24in) gun; six or seven 7.92mm (0.312in) MGs

Dimensions:	
length	8m (26ft 3in)
width	3.05m (10ft)
height	3.3m (10ft 10in)

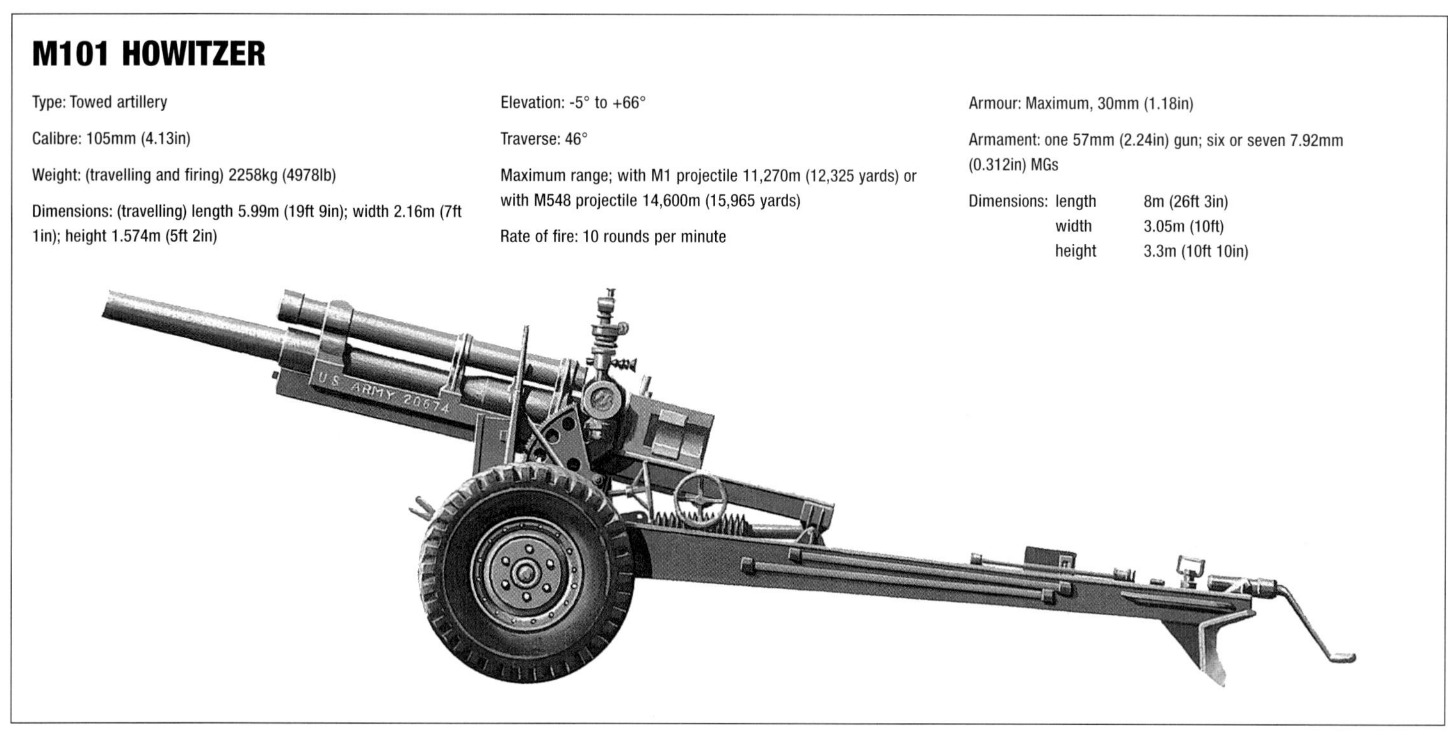

they never recovered. More attacks were made by the NVA in the northern border zone, but for the most part these were beaten off with heavy losses.

CHANGED STRATEGY

The United States moved towards a strategy of enabling the Republic of South Vietnam to cope on its own, against a backdrop of negotiations with the North. US troop commitment was reduced, but at the same time control over the countryside improved. This owed much to the reduced capabilities of the Viet Cong, which was no longer able to conduct effective insurgent warfare.

Ironically, the failure of the Tet offensive robbed North Vietnam of the traditional means of the weaker power – guerrilla groups – and forced a reliance on more conventional methods. This led to an attack across the border in March 1972, which was made by regular NVA units. These were supported by Soviet-supplied tanks and artillery.

Such an offensive was what the ARVN was originally trained and equipped to deal with, and with US assistance it proved equal to the task. Although some gains were made, the invasion was fought to a standstill and eventually repulsed. Again, casualties were very heavy on the NVA side, while the South Vietnamese army remained combat-worthy.

Negotiations restarted between the United States and North Vietnam, since the United States was increasingly suffering from internal problems caused by anti-war activism. Eventually a ceasefire was agreed and US forces pulled out. Subsequent events showed that North Vietnam did not honour the ceasefire but instead rebuilt its forces while slipping more infiltrators into the south.

Once the time was right, North Vietnam launched a new invasion that was beyond the capabilities of the ARVN to halt. The first attacks were made in March 1975 and by the end of April it was all over. The country was reunified under the communist government of North Vietnam.

Despite being largely composed of less-than-enthusiastic conscripts, the US Army was generally effective in Vietnam. Helicopter-mobile troops were used successfully in many operations, with helicopter gunships acting as a cross between flying tanks and mobile artillery in support. Patrols went into the jungle and searched for the enemy, although with mixed success. Overall, the military

OUTCOMES OF THE TET OFFENSIVE

Overall, the Tet offensive was a shattering military defeat for the Communists, who took massive losses for no gain. However, it was not immediately apparent how much damage had been suffered by the North Vietnamese forces. The offensive sparked even more anti-war protests in the United States and shook the confidence of both political and military leadership. The possibility that the war might involve unacceptable costs if it could be won at all led to a move towards a negotiated settlement.

The Soviet intervention in Afghanistan pitted a powerful modern army against a collection of insurgents and rebels. The Soviet political and military leaders must have initially thought that the matter would be swiftly concluded.

component of the war was carried out with skill and determination, and in military terms the US army emerged undefeated.

However, there are two ways to defeat a military force: to destroy its means to carry out combat operations, or to erode the will that drives those operations. It was the latter that led to the US withdrawal from Vietnam. The political climate 'back home' was such that a pull-out became necessary, no matter what consequences this might have for world politics. The 'body count' benchmark used to determine who was winning early in the war can be seen as meaningless with hindsight. North Vietnam suffered 1.1 million dead and another 600,000 wounded, compared to less than 60,000 American dead and just over 300,000 wounded. Yet these casualties were unacceptable. In the final analysis, the US military was defeated in the hearts and minds of the voting public.

POLITICAL CONTROL OF INFORMATION

Vietnam stands as an example of the contrast between totalitarian and democratic nations, and also the consequences of information availability. North Vietnam was able to conceal its casualty figures from the public, who in any case had little ability to influence government policy. In the United States, the figures could not be concealed and the public had a number of ways to influence government policy.

AFGHANISTAN: THE SOVIET UNION'S VIETNAM

Afghanistan consists mainly of rugged wilderness and has seen many clashes of international interests. The population has a long history of opposing foreign intervention.

Britain and Russia became embroiled in Afghanistan during the nineteenth century, but after the departure from India the region ceased to be of much importance to the British. The Soviet Union, however, maintained a continued interest in Afghanistan, and when foreign aid was requested the Soviets were entirely willing to grant it. This prompted the United States to offer an aid package as well, in the hope of countering Soviet influence. However, interest waned and the United States pulled out after a time.

During the 1960s, left-wing influence grew in Afghanistan. A coup in 1973 changed the political climate for a time, but in 1978 a left-wing group within the military launched its own coup and assumed power. Soon after, aid and advisors from the Soviet Union arrived and changes began to take place.

Although the intention was to bring Afghanistan into the twentieth century and the reforms would probably have improved the lives of all concerned, things went badly wrong. An attempt to eliminate peasant debt to the landowners backfired and caused a widespread catastrophe in the rural economy, while Muslim sensibilities were offended by measures aimed at changing the way women were viewed in society.

Overall, the reforms may have been well intended but they were carried out in a heavy-handed manner that caused resentment as well as serious economic damage in an already poor country. Faced with what looked like a threat to their entire way of life, many Afghans decided to resist. The revolt spread rapidly, following a familiar pattern. The government retained control of the major urban centres, but many rural areas came under the control of rebel groups.

The Soviet Union responded by supplying equipment to the Afghan government forces and pushing for a more carefully considered programme of reforms. This might have been carried through successfully but for the actions of elements within the Afghan government who favoured more extreme measures. These ensured their ascendancy by killing the president and putting their own men into important positions.

DIRECT INTERVENTION

With their advisors already coming under attack and the new Afghan leaders determined to pursue a course that would prolong the insurrection, the Soviets decided that direct intervention was the only option. This began in December 1979.

The invasion was made easier by the fact that the Soviet army already had large numbers of personnel in the country who could report on locations and strengths of government forces. Deception operations were also helpful, and under the guise of maintenance the Soviets arranged for the batteries to be removed from large numbers of Afghan army vehicles. Meanwhile, troops were flown into Bagram airbase near Kabul, ostensibly as allies. However, once there they were able to seize control of the

Soviet BTR armoured personnel carriers in Afghanistan. Armed with a turreted machine gun and equipped with firing ports for the infantry carried aboard, these vehicles made effective counterinsurgency platforms.

COSTS OF THE INTERVENTION

The cost, in terms of casualties, was less of a factor in Soviet thinking than it had been in the United States. The Soviet Union was better able to suppress such unpleasant facts and could control dissent with more repressive measures than could be used elsewhere. However, the financial drain and obvious inability to win the war were important, as was international pressure.

installation. This allowed rapid reinforcement by air, and Soviet troops were in control of parts of the capital by the next day.

The Soviets had to fight for control of the presidential palace, however, and this was to have serious repercussions. Up to this point, it was still possible to force through some governmental changes in Afghanistan while a pro-Soviet leader claimed to have asked for help. However, once combat broke out it was inevitable that the invasion would be seen for what it was.

The bulk of the invasion forces arrived overland, moving rapidly along routes secured by paratroopers. Most of the Afghan army was persuaded not to intervene. The situation was very confused, since until very recently the Soviets had been seen as friends and advisors. Some units did resist, but these were pushed aside. The remainder of the army largely dissolved, with many former soldiers ending up in resistance groups.

By the end of January 1980, the Soviets had secured the main routes into the country and were in control of the major cities. However, the anti-government insurrection in the countryside was not much affected, and as the winter came to an end its members turned their attention to the new enemy.

GUERRILLA WAR IN AFGHANISTAN

The anti-Soviet guerrillas in Afghanistan were armed with a wide range of equipment. It ranged from homemade muskets called Jezails, which had been in service since the British were the enemy many years ago, to modern weapons supplied by the United States or captured from Soviet troops. In the towns, stealthy knife attacks were also used.

As always in such situations, the Soviets were more or less able to keep the urban centres under control but could not project power effectively into the wilderness. Since the country's major roads run for many kilometres through rugged mountains, there was no shortage of ambush points. It was relatively easy for guerrillas to halt a patrol or convoy with rocks on the road and then snipe at the crews as they attempted to clear the obstruction. The rough terrain also offered many opportunities to slip away as a response to the attack began.

Protecting the entire length of these mountain roads is impossible, so the Soviets came up with an alternative strategy. Using helicopters to leapfrog units from one high point to the next, the Soviets were able to take control of the high ground as a

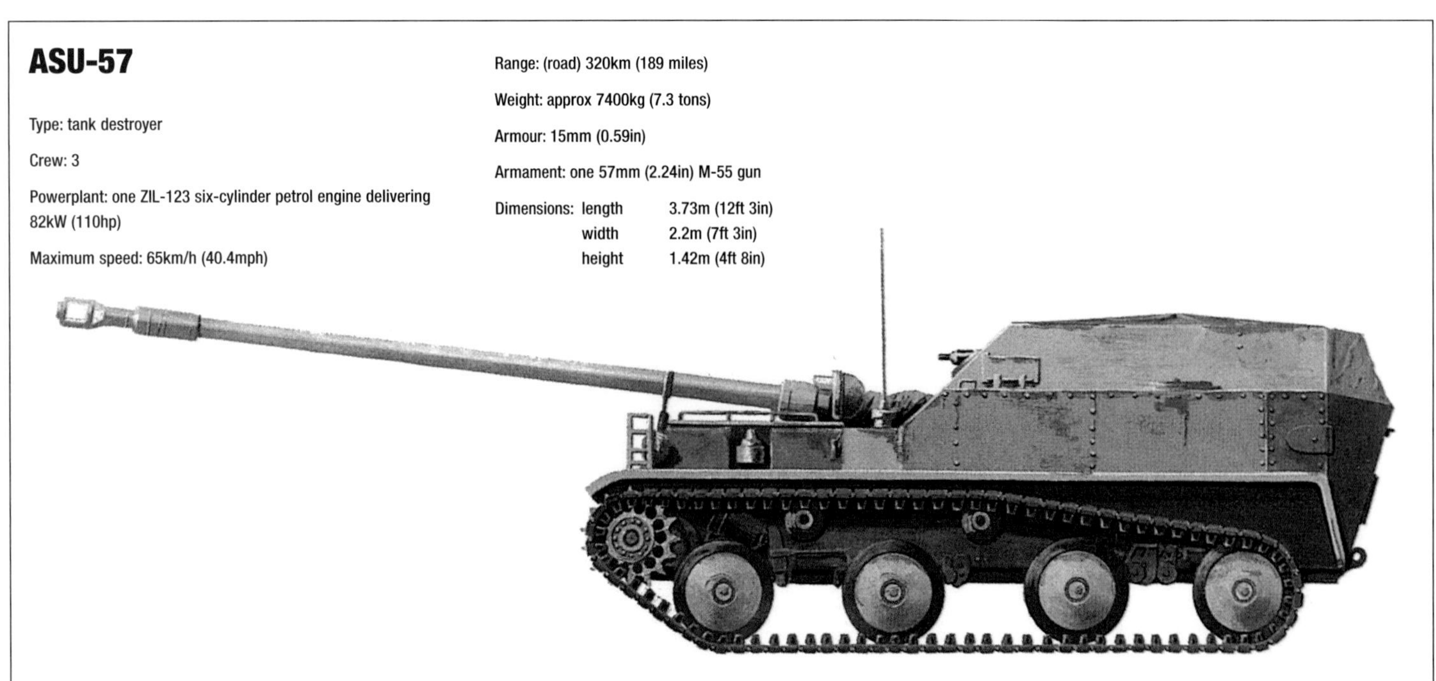

Afghan guerrillas in the mountains. The ancestors of these men fought against British and Russian troops in previous centuries, possibly even using the same ambush points against the few roads through the mountains.

convoy passed it. However, this measure proved very expensive in terms of fuel and wear on machinery, which in turn pushed up the cost of the occupation.

This was the crux of the matter. If the Afghan guerrillas could make the price of occupying their country high enough, the Soviets would be forced to conclude that Afghanistan was more trouble than it was worth and pull out. It was unlikely that this was ever a coherent strategy – the guerrillas belonged to a large number of different groups and factions with a broadly similar aim but no overall command structure.

As a foreign invader, the Soviets had very little local support and no real chance to win hearts and minds. Thus the only real option was to crush the guerrillas by military means. This proved problematical, since just to locate them could be difficult. When a base area was identified, the Soviets would launch an operation against it, sending a large force into the

COLLAPSE OF THE AFGHAN GOVERNMENT

After a period of diplomatic negotiation that shored up the Afghan government's international position, Soviet troops left in 1989. For a time, the Afghan army was able to hold its own against the guerrillas and even win some successes. However, the economic and social damage caused by the conflict was too severe. The government lasted another three years or so before the country collapsed into chaos, leaving much of it in the hands of warlords and creating the conditions that led to the rise of the Taliban in the mid 1990s.

United Nations troops in the Balkans. The international forces were in a very difficult position, trying to impose a peace that apparently nobody wanted.

immediate area and others to cover the flanks. Those guerrillas that tried to fight were met with massive firepower. Most would simply withdraw, however.

The Soviets could do nothing but destroy the bases and try to eliminate the guerrillas' supplies of food and munitions. However, the Soviet forces could not remain in occupation of the area and once they had gone the guerrillas eventually came back.

It was obvious by 1985 or so that the Soviets were fighting a war they could not win. The only way to stop losing was to stop fighting, and that meant getting out of Afghanistan. However, the political damage caused by a retreat would be considerable. The solution was similar to that used by the United States in Vietnam; the Soviets began helping the Afghan government to build up its forces and these gradually took over the role of fighting the guerrillas.

CIVIL WAR IN THE BALKANS

The Balkan region in southeastern Europe has always been troubled. Political, economic and racial differences have prompted many small wars and a few large ones, and the ambitions of larger states have served only to muddy the waters.

At the end of World War II, the various peoples of what became the Socialist Federal Republic of Yugoslavia were united against the German occupation. However, internal tensions were high, with each ethnic group seeking greater influence or wanting redress for the actions of some of the others. Some wanted autonomy, others to dominate the nation overall.

Political wrangling produced no solution, and eventually the states of Solvenia and Croatia decided to secede. Slovenia announced secession on 25 June 1991, to which the federal government responded with force. The level of violence was low, however, and after some minor clashes a truce was agreed, under the terms of which Slovenia agreed not to make any further moves towards independence for three months.

Violence flared up again soon after, when the Serb population in Croatia decided that they did not want to be part of an independent Croatia but preferred to remain within Yugoslavia. They announced their own secession

> Croatia had no army and its territorial forces had been disarmed by the federal authorities, which meant that the rebels were better armed than the Croatian forces.

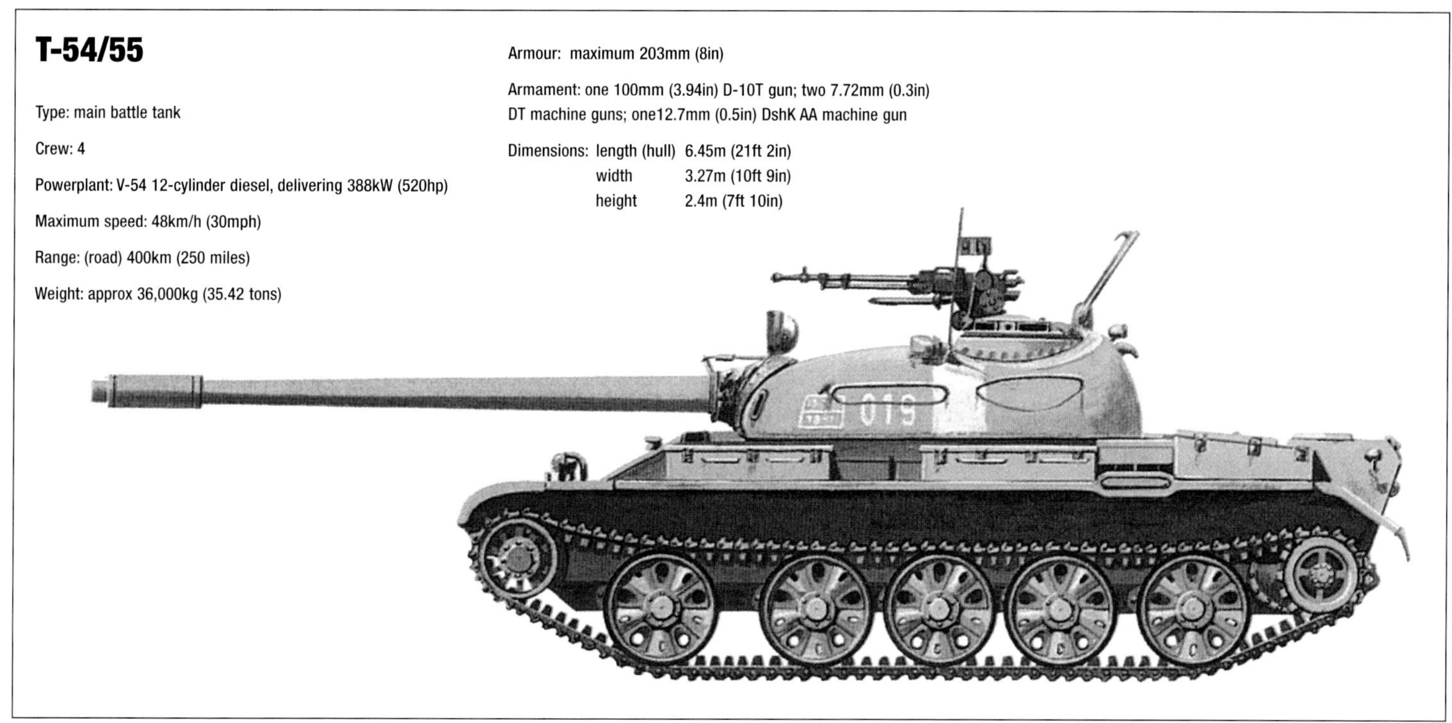

from Croatia. Conflict then erupted, in which the Serb rebels had a distinct advantage. Croatia had no army and its territorial forces had been disarmed by the federal authorities, which meant that the rebels were better armed than the Croatian forces they were fighting.

The fighting spread as other groups became involved. In 1992, Bosnian Serbs came into conflict with Croats and Muslims. Though all were citizens of the same state, ethnic differences and old enmities led to a bloody clash. The fighting was savage and complex, since there were no clear-cut lines of demarcation between the various groups. The Croats and Muslims fought each other at times, at others allying against the Serbs. Croatia formed its own army, using it to retake lost territory and impose a measure of stability. This drove many Serbs to flee, as ethnic cleansing and other atrocities were common during the conflict. This Croatian victory in 1995 allowed a ceasefire to be put in place, which was formalized at the end of the year. Meanwhile, ethnic and political conflict continued in Kosovo and Macedonia, as well as parts of Serbia, until and beyond the end of the century.

RESOLVING INTERNAL CONFLICTS

This sort of internal conflict, between groups who have lived alongside one another for centuries in some cases and have solid claims to territory they occupy, tends to be the bitterest of all forms of war. The cycle of violence is hard to break, especially if atrocities are committed, and there is no simple solution. If a negotiated settlement cannot be found, the only answer is to forcibly impose a solution on those who oppose it, and that inevitably leads to renewed conflict at some time in the future.

At the same time, such conflicts are among the easiest to fight. Small arms are easily available and cheap, and targets may live in the next town over. Where a major war can be ended by crippling a nation's war industry or its logistics chain, bands of highly motivated guerrillas need little support and can be hard to control. No sooner has one group agreed to stop fighting than they are attacked by a faction of another and conflict begins again.

Increasingly, the armed forces of the world are being sent into war zones of this sort, to protect refugees or aid workers or on 'operations in support of peace'. This can be one of the most frustrating – and, indeed, dangerous – of all military tasks as troops on the ground try to uphold a ceasefire or other agreement that nobody seems to want, or find themselves bound by rules of engagement that seem to place them in greater danger or force them to allow insurgents to do as they please not far away.

There is little glory to be had in peacekeeping, and the risks are no less than in a large-scale conventional conflict. But the task is a necessary, if thankless, one.

Modern Conventional Warfare 1973–1991

It has been said that 'defeat promotes innovation; victory breeds complacency', and there is much truth in this adage. However, it is rare for a war to go so well that no lessons need be learnt from it. Most militaries emerge from their latest conflict with at the very least some food for thought. However, the lessons learnt are not always the right ones.

After World War I, British tank designers tended to build well protected vehicles with good obstacle-crossing capability but relatively light armament for use in trench warfare. In many cases, these designs did not cope well in combat against other tanks. Similarly, the Israeli Defence Force drew from its experiences in 1967 the conclusion that unsupported tanks could charge through almost any opposition, and that the Arabs did not make good fighters. However, later conflicts demonstrated that these conclusions were, at best, dubious.

Towards the end of the twentieth century, it may have seemed that any future conflict would be highly asymmetric and that dealing with guerrillas was the future of warfare. Perhaps the 'Grand Threat' of massed armoured formations no longer really existed. Perhaps the day of the tank was past and it was time for armies to begin re-equipping with lighter vehicles better suited to a security role.

As it turned out these, too, were dubious assumptions. Large-scale warfare was still a likelihood, and an army that could fight and win a major battle

Iraqi infantrymen equipped with Soviet small arms, including the assault rifles of the AK series and an RPG-7. The latter might be able to damage a tank of the 1980s.

An Egyptian amphibious vehicle crosses the Suez Canal, heading for one of the ramps created by using high-pressure hoses to wash away the banks. This innovation greatly reduced the time needed to move forces across the Canal.

remained an essential form of life insurance for its parent state.

THE YOM KIPPUR WAR

Having been twice defeated by rapid Israeli advances through the Sinai Peninsula, Egypt's armed forces had been forced to rethink their strategies. They were also faced with a major problem in any renewed conflict with Israel. The Israelis now held the Sinai and were positioned behind the Suez Canal, offering a formidable obstacle to the armoured assault that would be needed to break into their positions.

Renewed war was highly likely, as Israel occupied territory taken from both Egypt and Syria. Both wanted their land back but had stated that they would not negotiate with nor even recognize the existence of Israel. The Israelis had no alternative but to assume that an attempt would be made to crush them once again, and accordingly built strong positions behind the Suez Canal, named the Bar-Lev line after the general that presided over their construction.

The static defences were backed by mobile armoured reserves for a counterattack. There was, however, a note of complacency in Israel's planning. The collapse of the Egyptian army in 1967 and the lack of offensive spirit shown by the Syrians in the same conflict suggested that any aggressive action by either would be ham-fisted, timidly executed, or both. This was a very dangerous assumption, yet the statement was made more than once that any Israeli soldier was worth several Arabs.

The Egyptians, however, knew they were up against one of the best armies in the world, well equipped and strongly dug into good positions. The Israelis were also fighting for their very survival, which would add desperation to their determination if their enemies looked like winning.

With no illusions about the difficulty of the task they faced, the Egyptians prepared well. New weaponry was obtained from the Soviet Union, including man-portable guided anti-tank missiles and amphibious assault equipment. Just as importantly, the Egyptian army developed new techniques to solve the problem of crossing the canal.

The Israelis knew that it would take a long time to demolish the sandy banks of the canal with bulldozers in order to make a ramp for tanks to climb up. What they had not anticipated was the Egyptians' use of high-pressure hoses to wash away the banks far faster than they could have been excavated. This allowed the Egyptians to attack the fortifications beyond the canal much earlier than the Israelis had planned for.

An Egyptian tank and crew. Large quantities of armoured vehicles, anti-armour missiles and air defence equipment had been recently provided by the Soviet Union, along with advisors to train troops in the use of these weapons.

Perhaps most importantly, the Egyptians practised excellent operational security and deception measures, concealing their preparations under the guise of exercises and routine movements. By making provocative gestures and then allowing tension to dissipate, they were able to manipulate Israeli thinking to some extent. As a result, any warning signs that were spotted tended to be downplayed in the belief that such things had happened before and nothing had come of it.

The Egyptians practised excellent operational security and deception measures, concealing their preparations under the guise of exercises.

The Egyptian attack surprised Israeli forces with its suddenness and efficiency. The initial Israeli response in the Sinai was overconfident, resulting in unnecessary losses from Egypt's newly obtained infantry anti-tank missiles.

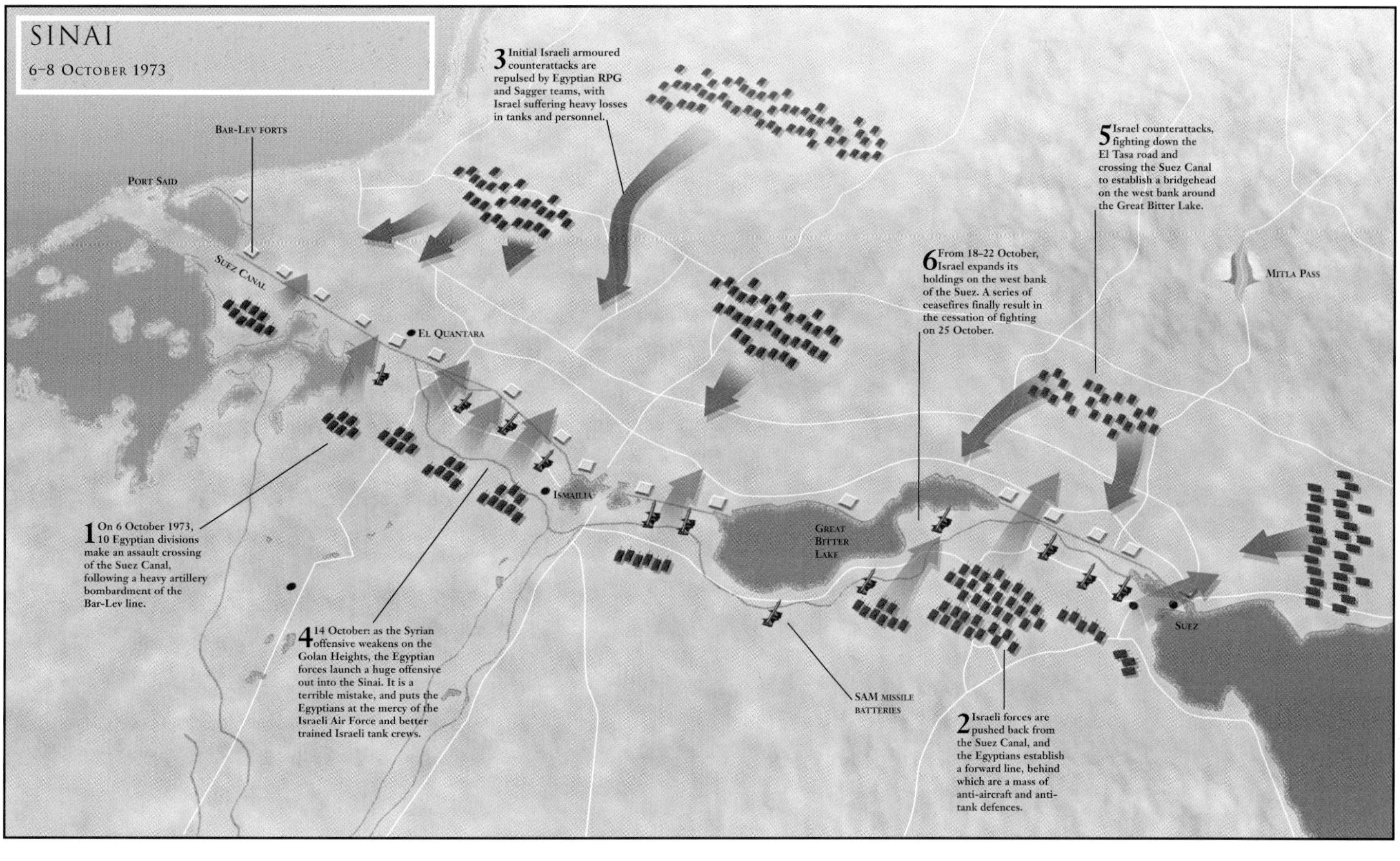

SINAI
6–8 October 1973

Bar-Lev forts
Port Said
Suez Canal
El Quantara
Ismailia
Great Bitter Lake
Suez
Mitla Pass
SAM missile batteries

1 On 6 October 1973, 10 Egyptian divisions make an assault crossing of the Suez Canal, following a heavy artillery bombardment of the Bar-Lev line.

2 Israeli forces are pushed back from the Suez Canal, and the Egyptians establish a forward line, behind which are a mass of anti-aircraft and anti-tank defences.

3 Initial Israeli armoured counterattacks are repulsed by Egyptian RPG and Sagger teams, with Israel suffering heavy losses in tanks and personnel.

4 14 October: as the Syrian offensive weakens on the Golan Heights, the Egyptian forces launch a huge offensive out into the Sinai. It is a terrible mistake, and puts the Egyptians at the mercy of the Israeli Air Force and better trained Israeli tank crews.

5 Israel counterattacks, fighting down the El Tasa road and crossing the Suez Canal to establish a bridgehead on the west bank around the Great Bitter Lake.

6 From 18–22 October, Israel expands its holdings on the west bank of the Suez. A series of ceasefires finally result in the cessation of fighting on 25 October.

A crippled tank destroyer, originally obtained from the Soviet Union. The Arab-Israeli wars often pitted Western equipment against the Soviet equivalents, although much of the hardware was from earlier generations.

Meanwhile, the Syrians were also preparing to attack. Troop movements towards the border were spotted and caused some concern but the strategic analysis was that Syria would not attack without Egyptian cooperation, and the Egyptians were not about to attack. This opinion began to change as warnings came in from various quarters, and on 5 October 1973 the Israeli leadership finally decided that an attack was imminent.

The timing was disastrous. The following day was Yom Kippur, the holiest day of the year, and much of the army was stood down. A partial mobilization order was issued and the difficult decision of whether or not to launch a pre-emptive strike had to be quickly addressed. Normally Israel's defensive strategy relied on such a strike to break an offensive before it could be launched, but the political situation was complicated. Israel at the time relied greatly on US aid and could not afford it to be withheld, which was a possibility if the Israelis were perceived as having started the conflict. Thus the decision was made to let the enemy strike first and then deal with the consequences. Shortly after this decision was made, the United States made its position clear – no aid would be forthcoming if Israel launched a pre-emptive strike.

THE SYRIAN ATTACK

The Syrian army vastly outnumbered the Israeli defenders at the time of the attack, having about 1300 tanks to oppose 180; there were similar disparities in other areas. As helicopter-borne troops struck at Israeli observation points, the massive Syrian force rolled forwards. For Israel, the situation was utterly desperate, and the response was appropriate to the circumstances.

All Israeli reserves were sent to the Golan Heights. As the reservists arrived, they were formed into scratch units and sent up to join the fighting. As soon as a suitably trained man was available to fill every seat on a tank, it went forward. Secondary armament was not fitted, in order to save time in getting the tanks to the front. This remarkable piece of corner-cutting got men and equipment into the fight faster than anyone could have predicted, though in a very disorganized manner. In any case, there was a 15-hour period during which the troops of the Israel Defense Force (IDF) in the Heights were forced to fight as best they could without reinforcement. Their best was very good indeed. Records show that the entire IDF tank strength in the Golan Heights came into action – not one tank failed to fire its weapons at the enemy, and the air force offered what support it could although the terrain was not well suited.

Despite their best efforts, the Israelis were pushed back and sustained heavy casualties. Some units lost their commanders and became broken up but simply fought on wherever they found the enemy. Others started out as orphans and simply joined the action on their own initiative. The most famous of these was Lieutenant Zvika Greengold, whose tank arrived in action solo and found itself opposing a major Syrian advance down an otherwise unguarded route.

Greengold attacked alone until other forces joined the fight, and then engaged in a spectacular rampage that earned his tank the title of Zvika Force as it plunged from one action to another. Although wounded when his tank was knocked out, Greengold found another and kept on fighting. He is thought to have gone through six tanks during the battle, while taking part in dozens of combats.

Greengold's was not the only tank fighting in this manner; his actions perhaps demonstrate the spirit that motivated the Israeli solider in those hours. In a confused and deteriorating situation, with the prospect of annihilation following defeat, there was no other option than to fight as hard as possible and to hope that if everyone else did the same, victory might somehow be secured amid the chaos.

> The Israelis advanced a little further into the Golan Heights, reaching a point where the Syrian capital of Damascus was within artillery range of Israeli positions.

A DESPERATE SITUATION

The situation remained desperate in some areas, notably near Nafah where the IDF 7th Armoured Brigade had lost its senior commanders and was fighting a disjointed defensive action as ad-hoc sub-units. However, by 8 October the arrival of reinforcements and the stubborn defence of engaged units had blunted the Syrian offensive to the extent that counterattacks could be made.

By 10 October, the Israelis had pushed their Syrian foes back over the pre-war border and now had to make a difficult decision. Should they assume a defensive stance and send troops to Sinai, where matters were not going well at all, or should they push on?

A Soviet-supplied SA-2 Guideline anti-aircraft missile. Determined not to allow a repeat of 1967, when the Israeli Air Force was able to smash up ground forces more or less at will, the Arab nations obtained modern air defence technology from the Soviet Union.

OUTDATED ISRAELI STRATEGY

Israeli doctrine of the time was overconfident and worked on the assumption that charging at the enemy with tanks would scatter them. This had worked in the past, but the Egyptians were ready now. As the attacks developed, they ran into the fire of tanks and artillery as expected but also infantry-launched guided missiles. These rather primitive weapons were available in large numbers and were highly effective across the open terrain of the desert. There were many of them for every tank, and those that got closer were then attacked by infantrymen armed with Soviet RPG-7 unguided anti-tank weapons.

It was decided that an advance into Syria was vital for long-term strategic reasons. Forces sent to Sinai would take several days to make their presence felt, and in the meantime a ceasefire was possible. If that happened, the Israelis would find themselves in the position of having been beaten by the Egyptians in the south without having made any gains in the north. That was not acceptable; they needed to show a victory. So the Israelis advanced a little further into the Golan Heights, reaching a point where the Syrian capital of Damascus was within artillery range of their positions. They were unable to make further gains, and were pushed back somewhat by counterattacks, but they would not be ejected from Syrian territory during the remainder of the conflict.

One reason for the Israeli setback was the arrival of a force from Iraq, which moved faster than anticipated and launched an attack before its arrival was noticed. Nevertheless, the IDF hung on to most of its gains for the remainder of the war, which was important in negotiations afterwards.

BREAKING THE BAR-LEV LINE

Meanwhile, the Egyptian army had a good plan and carried it out effectively. Their attack opened with shelling of the Bar-Lev positions and several assault crossings of the Canal. These were made between the Israeli fortifications and were conducted with great skill. The Egyptians were across the Canal and established on the far side before the Israelis could react. Once there, they quickly overran many of the fortifications, which were relatively lightly held.

Neither the canal nor the forts slowed the Egyptians down anything like as much as the Israelis had hoped. However, they reacted quickly. In just three days, 6–8 October, some 23 counterattacks were launched, most with the aim of preventing the fall of a strong point or pushing a bridgehead back into the Canal. However, these ran into unexpected problems.

The Israeli counterattacks caused serious casualties, but they did not succeed in pushing the Egyptians back. Matters were not helped by the disjointed nature of the attacks, or by the fact that there was little combined-arms cooperation. This meant that the Egyptian build-up was able to continue in accordance with the plan.

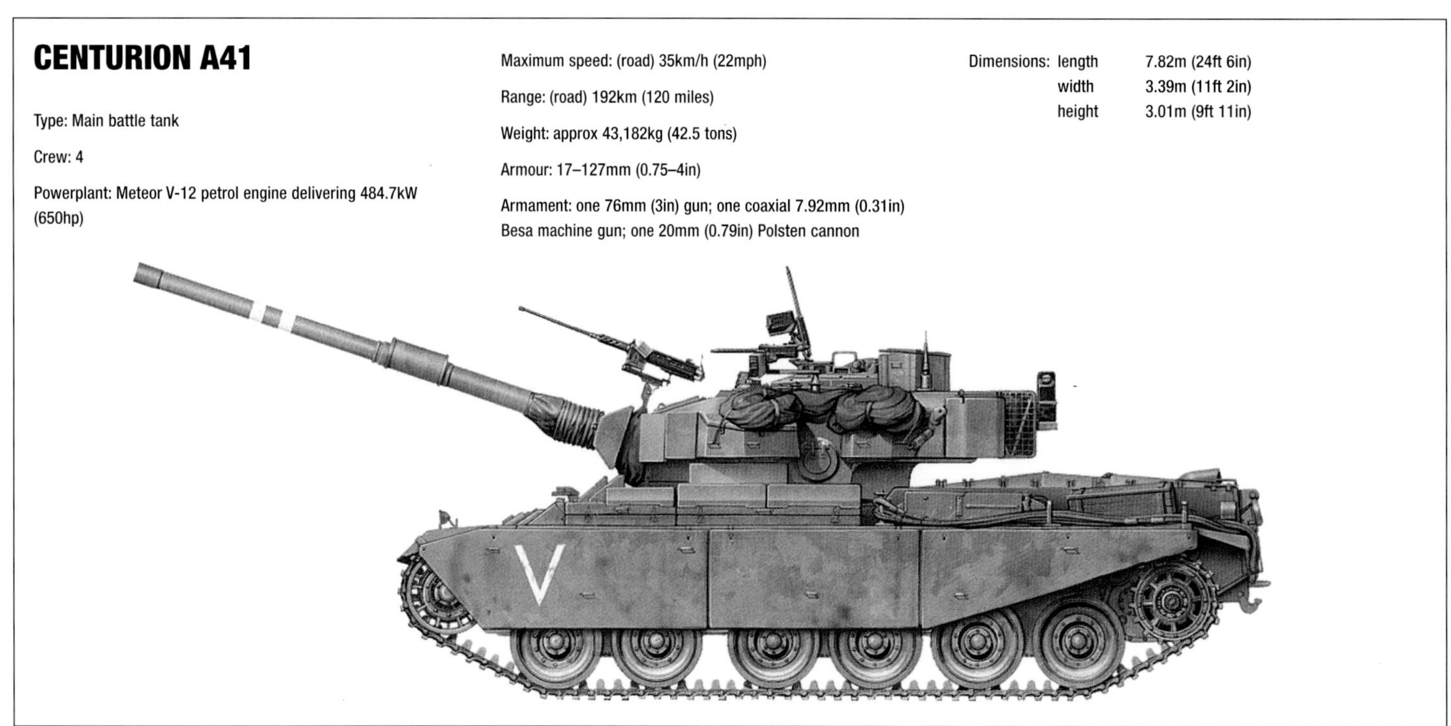

CENTURION A41

Type: Main battle tank

Crew: 4

Powerplant: Meteor V-12 petrol engine delivering 484.7kW (650hp)

Maximum speed: (road) 35km/h (22mph)

Range: (road) 192km (120 miles)

Weight: approx 43,182kg (42.5 tons)

Armour: 17–127mm (0.75–4in)

Armament: one 76mm (3in) gun; one coaxial 7.92mm (0.31in) Besa machine gun; one 20mm (0.79in) Polsten cannon

Dimensions: length 7.82m (24ft 6in)
width 3.39m (11ft 2in)
height 3.01m (9ft 11in)

Among the problems faced by the Israelis in 1973 was the fact that some Syrian tanks were equipped with infrared night fighting equipment, and their Israeli opponents were not. This gave the Arabs a significant advantage.

The Egyptians were careful not to advance too far. They wanted to remain within the coverage of their Soviet-supplied anti-aircraft missile defences, which were effective in preventing the Israeli Air Force from smashing up the Egyptian formations as it had done in the past. The limited advance was also part of a plan to lure the Israelis into a battle of attrition that would play to the Egyptians' strength in terms of both manpower and equipment. However, with the Syrian attack in the north showing signs of failure, further attacks had to be considered.

MOBILE OPERATIONS

By 10 October, the Israelis had ceased making disjointed counterattacks and were assuming a more defensive posture. The Egyptians had managed to push considerable forces across the Suez Canal and were now in a position to advance out of their bridgehead. This was not the original intention, but the situation in the Golan Heights seemed to require it.

Correctly predicting an Egyptian attack, the Israelis prepared to meet it rather than trying to carry out an advance of their own, and when the Egyptian offensive opened on 14 October it ran into trouble.

Advancing across the open desert terrain, the Egyptians ran into the fire of hull-down Israeli tanks, which were now properly supported by infantry. The latter were particularly effective in suppressing Egyptian infantry anti-tank weapon positions by 'hosing them down' with machine-gun fire. Since these weapons were manually guided, a gunner who was wounded or who flinched from a near miss would not hit his target.

As each assault failed, an armoured flanking force advanced to inflict further casualties on the wavering Egyptians, and as the enemy advanced out of the coverage of his anti-aircraft weapons the Israeli Air Force was able to attack much more effectively.

The decision not to pre-empt was also paying off at last. US military aid had begun to arrive, including guided

> US military aid had begun to arrive, including wire-guided missiles. These were put to use against Egyptian armour and proved effective.

At the end of the Yom Kippur War, an entire Egyptian army was cut off by Israeli forces. The only supplies that could reach it, including food and water, were those permitted access through Israeli checkpoints.

infantry anti-tank weapons in the form of wire-guided missiles. These were put to use against Egyptian armour and proved effective.

As the Egyptian attack disintegrated, the Israelis began to advance. No longer overconfident and now making excellent use of combined-arms combat tactics, they were able to advance to the Suez Canal and to get some forces across at the Great Bitter Lake. Bridging equipment was in short supply, but gradually more forces were pushed across the canal as the Egyptian lodgement on the east bank of the Canal was gradually reduced.

The Israeli advance on Ismailiya, on the west bank of the canal, was halted only by flooding the land around it, and by 20 October the Egyptian forces on the east bank of the canal were in serious trouble. At the end of the war, they were cut off; with their backs to the canal, and running short of water.

MOVES TOWARDS PEACE

A ceasefire was proposed, but implementing it proved problematical. Officially the ceasefire began on 22 October, but there were numerous incidents in the next few days. The ceasefire prevented a planned Syrian resumption of hostilities, and peace talks were opened.

THE CEASEFIRE

This made for a huge change in the political climate. Egypt had always refused to negotiate with Israel or even acknowledge her existence; direct talks were a de facto recognition of Israel as a nation state.

Political factors were at work elsewhere. From the decision not to pre-empt to the imposition of the ceasefire, the influence of other world powers and the United Nations were a factor. Pressure from the United States to accept a ceasefire was, at least

The Mitla Pass has been a factor for armies moving through the Sinai for centuries. It lies on one of the few practicable routes across the peninsula and can be a significant obstacle to an advancing army if strongly held.

in part, applied in response to the Arab states' oil embargo on the United States itself.

This illustrates a major factor in modern warfare; not only must battles be fought and won on the ground but one eye must also be kept on the wider political situation. Foreign pressure may force a ceasefire at an inopportune moment. Equally, gains made in war serve as useful bargaining chips in subsequent negotiations.

The fact that Israel had an entire Egyptian army cut off and deprived of even drinking water was a significant factor in Egypt's willingness to negotiate. Had that army simply been smashed in combat, its value to Israel would have actually been less.

THE IRAN-IRAQ WAR

In 1980, Iran and Iraq were two very different sides of the same coin. Both were Islamic states, but Iraq was a

PT-76

Type: Light amphibious tank

Crew: 3

Powerplant: one V6 six cylinder diesel, delivering 179kW (240hp)

Maximum speed: (road) 45km/h (28mph); (water) 10km/h (6.2mph)

Range: (road) 280km (174 miles); (water) 65km (40.4miles)

Weight: 14,000kg (13.78 tons)

Armour: 5–17mm (0.197–0.67in)

Armament: one 76.2mm (3in) gun; one 7.62mm (0.3in) machine gun and sometimes one 12.7mm (0.5in) antiaircraft machine gun

Dimensions: length 6.91m (22ft 8in)
width 3.14m (10ft 4in)
height 2.255m (7ft 5in)

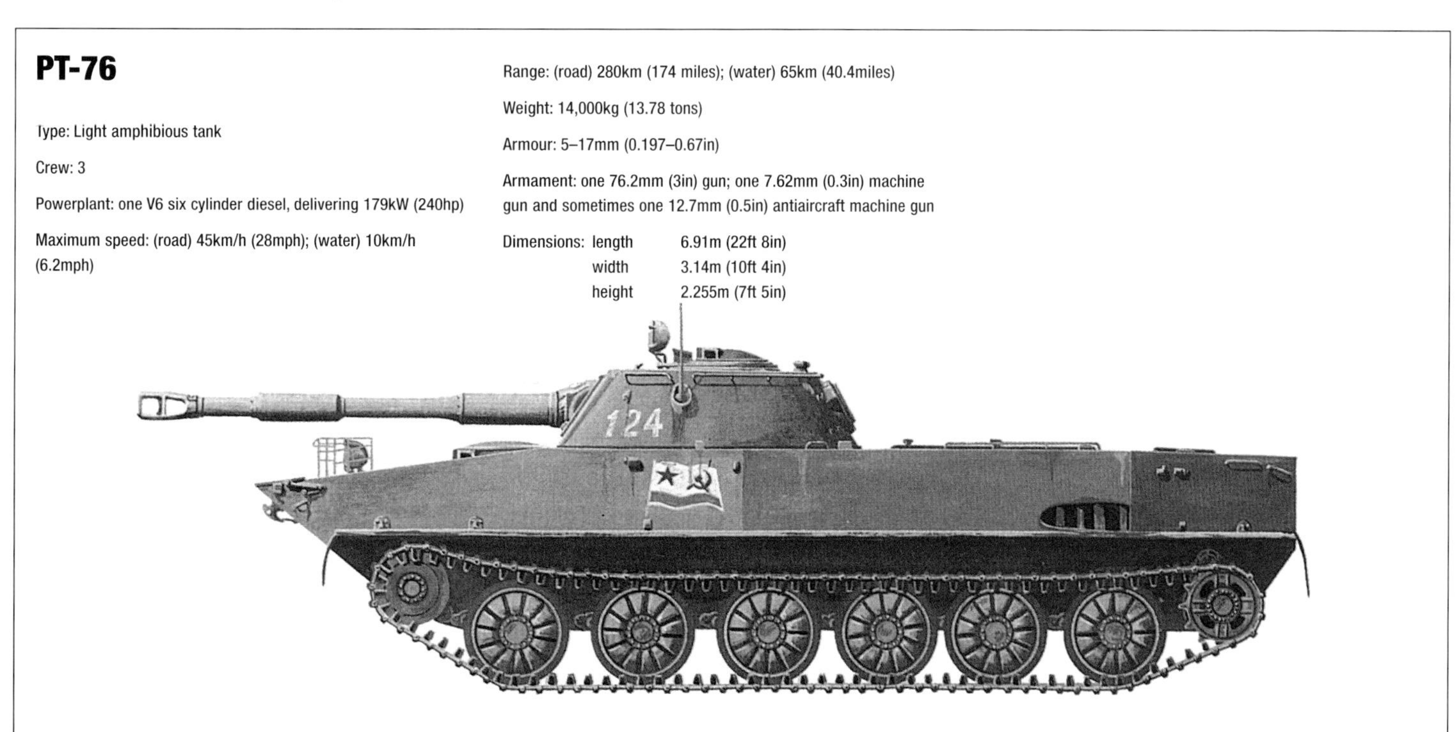

virtual dictatorship whereas Iran had recently overthrown its leader, the Shah, and set up an Islamic republic. There was an official government under President Abolhassan Bani-Sadr, but in practice the nation was ruled by the senior religious leaders, of whom the Ayatollah Khomeini was the most prominent.

Saddam Hussein made a number of demands and engaged in military posturing to demonstrate his serious intent. His demands went unmet.

Iran and Iraq were well equipped with modern weapons. The Iranians, under the leadership of the Shah, had been friendly with the West, enabling them to acquire large stocks of military equipment from Britain and the United States. However, a great deal of technical support was needed for this equipment and this had always been carried out by the suppliers rather than Iranian personnel. The overthrow of the Shah brought a new anti-Western stance to Iranian politics, which meant that her modern weapons were lacking necessary support and a significant proportion was therefore out of service at the beginning of the war.

Iraq had obtained an impressive arsenal from the Soviet Union, though much of the equipment was obsolescent. Iraq's relationship with her equipment supplier had also gone downhill in recent years, though not so radically. This was less of a problem as Soviet equipment was simpler and easier to care for in the first place.

With Iran in chaos, it seemed like an opportune moment for Iraq to take advantage of the situation. Saddam Hussein made a number of demands and engaged in military posturing to demonstrate his serious intent. His demands went unmet.

Both nations began sponsoring rebellion and sabotage within each other's territory, and artillery exchanges occurred. War did not break out immediately, however. It was not until 12 September 1980 that serious military action was taken. This came in response to an Iranian attack on villages near the border.

The Iraqi response followed a well-thought-out battle plan. Moving forces into position to block any counterstroke and launching

The overthrow of the Shah of Iran resulted in the creation of a republic, but in practice the nation was dominated by clerics led by the Ayatollah Khomeini, whose hatred of Saddam Hussein was a factor in the Iran-Iraq conflict.

Soviet-made BTR APCs positioned behind hull-down earth mounds for protection. The Iraqis made extensive use of dug-in armoured vehicles in their conflict with Iran. The tactic was repeated with less success during the Gulf War.

diversionary raids, Iraq then sent armoured formations into Iran. Initially these were able to advance without opposition.

CLEAR AIMS

Iraq had clear aims in the early stages of the war. These involved capturing territory that had long been claimed by Iraq, including the huge oil refinery at Abadan and the port of Khorramshahr. For political purposes, the intent to fight for limited objectives was clearly stated. It was thought that the invasion would fragment Iran's already chaotic internal political situation, enabling a new government to emerge. Finding itself in a difficult position, this new government would be willing to make peace.

In the event, Iran's government did not fall, and the small forces in Khorramshahr put up a desperate fight that cost the Iraqis dearly and resulted in considerable destruction. Iraqi forces reached Abadan in mid October and beat off a small-scale counterattack, but the fighting went on for some time thereafter.

REASONS FOR THE WAR

There were many reasons for a clash between the Iran and Iraq. Disputes over territory and borders had been ongoing for well over a century, and there was a very personal hatred between Khomeini and Saddam Hussein, president of Iraq. Hussein was worried that the recent revolution in Iran might spread to his country, since the majority of people in Iraq were Muslims of the Shia sect, as was Khomeini. The Iraqi ruling elite, on the other hand, were members of the Baathist sect.

However, the Iraqis now had another problem. They had advanced through desert and floodplains, and needed to secure their line of communications before bad weather made the temporary roads unusable. Thus the towns of Dezful and Ahvaz, which were among the objectives at the start of the war, were shelled but not assaulted. Susangerd, which had been bypassed, had to be dealt with to ensure its garrison did not harass the Iraqi supply lines.

The Iraqi army had entered the war with limited aims and using only a small part of its strength. However, as it became apparent that Iran was not going to fall apart obligingly, more divisions were called forwards. These initially became engaged with small

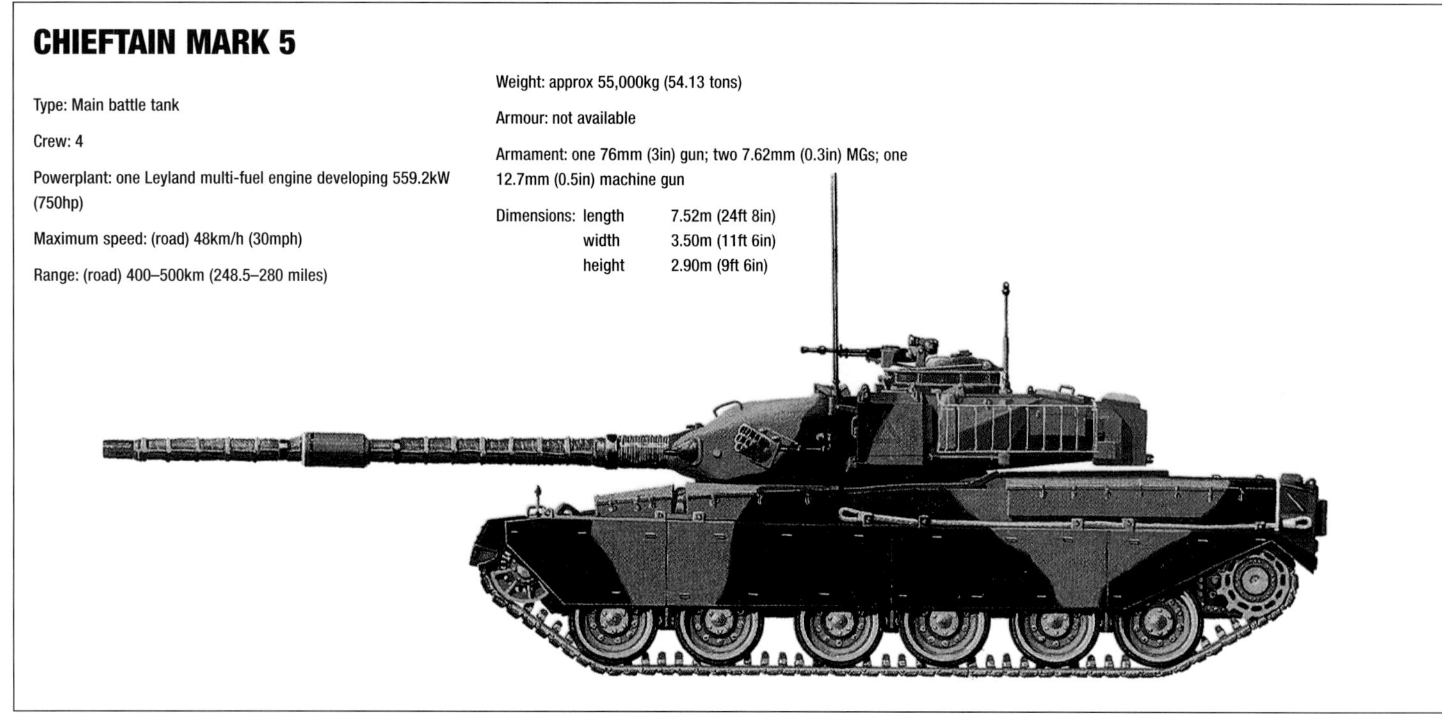

forces that had remained behind when the main Iranian army formations withdrew eastwards. No major counterattacks materialized, and the Iraqi advance continued, though with a curious lack of urgency.

In particular, the Iraqi army was reluctant to become involved in urban combat. The fighting that took place at Khorramshahr had resulted in disproportionate casualties considering the Iraqis' advantages in numbers and hardware, and it had become obvious that their troops lacked the skills for effective urban warfare. Thus the Iraqi army, virtually unchallenged in the field, preferred to shell towns rather than enter them.

Two segments of the Iranian army distinguished themselves during this stage of the war. One was the infantry of the stay-behind parties and the segments of the army that became cut off. These men put up determined, even fanatical, resistance and made the Iraqis even more reluctant to enter urban zones.

> The Iraqi advance came to a standstill and stalemate ensued. Large numbers of Iranian volunteers came forwards to fight and were able to wear down the Iraqi army.

The other highly effective force was the Iranians' tank-busting helicopters. These were American-made AH-1s equipped with guided missiles. Using the terrain for cover, they executed 'pop-up' manoeuvres to shoot, then departed the area swiftly. Although effective, their attacks were little more than a nuisance, as there was no force available to exploit the situation.

The Iraqi advance eventually came to a standstill and stalemate ensued. In Iran, large numbers of volunteers came forwards to fight against the invaders and these, although badly trained, were able to wear down the Iraqi army. By the middle of 1982, a series of somewhat disjointed counterattacks had retaken much of the lost territory.

The Iranian army, despite problems keeping its equipment serviceable, returned to the fray in support of the mobs of volunteers. With good air and artillery support, and accompanied by tanks that were highly effective even if their crews could not get the best from them, the volunteers made massed human wave attacks. These were costly, but they inflicted serious casualties on the Iraqis and gradually pushed them out of the territory they had gained.

Both sides were struggling by this point to maintain their more advanced weaponry, creating what has been described as a 'balance of incompetence' that limited the capabilities of both sides. On the whole, the Iraqis were more effective in combat, but they were in hostile territory and facing fanatical resistance, and it was clear that there was no prospect of a victory in any foreseeable future.

The Iraqis pulled back to the border, where strongly fortified positions awaited. An attempt was made to negotiate peace, but Iran made demands that Iraq would not even consider. Meanwhile, Khomeini stated that he wanted to replace Saddam Hussein's regime with an Islamic republic. An attack into Iraq followed soon after.

IRANIAN OFFENSIVES

The Iranians opened their campaign with an offensive towards Basra, second city of Iraq, but almost immediately ran into problems. The Iraqis were no longer in exposed or hastily fortified positions but had occupied fortifications that had been built before the war in great strength. Impeded by minefields, obstacles and barbed wire, the Iranians were shelled as they approached and then engaged by machine guns and tanks in fortified firing positions.

Worse, for the Iranians, was the disintegration of combined-arms support. The inevitable friction of war had rendered large amounts of the army's hardware unserviceable, and poor relations between the religious leaders and the army meant that the support which existed in theory was not always available. The solution was to make human-wave assaults with little or no support, sending groups of fanatics rushing into minefields to trigger them and thus opening a path for those that followed behind.

The war had taken on some aspects of World War I, with massed infantry assaults trying – and failing – to breach a fixed defensive line. Gas warfare, another concept dating back to World War I, was also introduced. The Iraqis made extensive use of chemical weapons, which the vast majority of Iranian troops had neither the training nor the equipment to counter.

Despite the failure of human wave attacks to breach the Iraqi defences, the tactic was repeated over and over, with five large-scale offensives in 1983. These were mostly carried out by ill-trained militia, though they did have some support from the Iranian army. Little success was achieved in return for massive casualties, but still Khomeini refused to even consider negotiating. In an effort to force a settlement, Iraq began bombarding Iranian cities.

THE WAR OF THE CITIES

An ultimatum was issued: if Iranian attacks did not stop, Iranian cities would be attacked. This was ignored,

The commander's machine gun atop this Iraqi tank can be used for anti-personnel work and defence against minor threats. Against the human-wave assaults thrown in by Iran in the latter years of the war, it was highly effective.

however, so Iraqi air and missile forces began strikes against 11 Iranian cities in February 1984. The Iranians responded with strikes of their own, beginning the first 'war of the cities'. A major ground assault was also launched.

The ground campaign was under army control, although only one-fifth of the 250,000 men involved were regulars. The remainder were militia, including boy soldiers whose main function was to draw fire and detect mines by stepping on them.

Although initially repulsed with massive losses, the Iranian attacks gradually forced their way into the Iraqi defence line and captured some territory. The Iraqi counterattack, supported by both mustard gas and nerve agents, was beaten off after retaking only part of the lost territory.

The campaign wound down by the middle of March 1984, and most of the remainder of the year passed in stalemate. Attempts were made to influence the course of the conflict by other means, such as attacks on tankers in the Persian Gulf. These had taken place since 1981, but they escalated in 1984, and attacks on neutral ships now became commonplace.

The bombing of cities and attempts to disrupt the oil trade did not seriously affect the outcome of the war. However, the United States in particular was resolved that Iran must not be permitted to win. Aid to Iraq was stepped up as a means of preventing the export of Iran's revolution. This further reduced the chances of Iran breaking through the border defences.

Although initially repulsed with massive losses, the Iranian attacks gradually forced their way into the Iraqi defence line and captured some territory.

An Iranian oil pipeline destroyed by bombing. Both Iran and Iraq attacked one another's oil-exporting industries as a means of reducing the opposition's ability to support the war.

The Iranian armed forces started the war in possession of large numbers of British-made tanks that were more than equal to the task of engaging the Soviet-made vehicles of the Iraqi army.

After a long period of stalemate characterized by air and missile attacks on cities, Iran launched a renewed bid for victory in 1987. This began with a drive on Basra, which was broken in Iraqi fortifications. A second attempt, directed at Kirkuk, threatened to be more successful. However, the limitations of the Iranian forces were such that they could not exploit a breakthrough nor establish a good holding position quickly, so only small gains were made.

Iran was sufficiently encouraged by the success it had achieved that it now chose to reject a UN resolution calling for a ceasefire and return to the prewar borders. This had unfortunate consequences because in April 1988 Iraqi forces attacked into the captured territories and retook them, also pushing into Iran.

Suddenly the UN ceasefire resolution seemed more attractive, but now it was the turn of Iraq to reject its terms. The offensive was continued, and managed to make little headway in the face of determined resistance. With no real prospect of victory, Iraq finally agreed to the UN resolution, and in August 1988 both sides agreed to return to the prewar borders.

Both sides suffered very serious casualties in the eight-year war, which resulted in no change to the borders of either country. The Iran-Iraq war was one of the bloodiest in the second half of the twentieth century, and one of the few occasions in which chemical weapons have been used.

THE FALKLANDS WAR

During the course of the twentieth century, Britain had withdrawn from many of her colonial territories. Among those that remained were the

IRAQI USE OF CHEMICAL WEAPONS

Iraq escaped much in the way of condemnation for its use of nerve and irritant gases against Iranian forces, although the UN did issue a statement that it was 'concerned' about the use of these weapons, which are prohibited and have been since 1925. Poison gas was also used in Iraq against the Kurdish minority, but in spite of the fact that this was common knowledge little was done at the time to prevent it or to punish Iraq's leaders.

Troops of the Argentinean army en route to the Falkland Islands. The cream of the army, the mountain troops, were held back for political reasons and to guard against incursions by Chilean forces.

Falkland Islands, a fairly unimportant group of islands located in the distant South Atlantic. Possession of the islands had been disputed by Argentina for many years, but the population, who were almost entirely of British descent, had voted to remain part of the United Kingdom.

Recovery of the Malvinas, as the islands are called in Argentina, was one of the goals of the Argentinean government, a military junta under General Leopoldo Galtieri. Galtieri's regime was facing considerable internal trouble and he now decided upon the seizure of the islands as a propaganda coup to distract the populace from economic and social troubles at home.

WARNING SIGNS

There were warning signs that something might be about to happen, but even if the British government had reacted earlier it would not have been possible to get reinforcements to the islands in time to make any difference. As it was, the raising of the Argentinean flag on South Georgia by scrap metal merchants dismantling an old whaling station was seen in London as somewhat silly rather than threatening.

A detachment of Royal Marines stationed at the capital, Port Stanley, made up the only British troops in the Falklands. This force was never intended to be enough to repel an invasion, but it was enough of an

FLAWED STRATEGIC ASSUMPTIONS

Galtieri and his advisors were sure that Britain would not fight for the Falklands, and in any case was probably not capable of doing so at the end of a supply line that was thousands of kilometres long. Subsequent events proved both theories wrong, but confidence was high in March 1982 as preparations for the invasion were made.

armed presence that fire would be exchanged in the event of an attempt to annex the islands. While there might be some ambiguity about a situation where an undefended territory was grabbed, shooting at British military forces was a definite act of war. A force of 22 marines and one officer were sent from Port Stanley to South Georgia. Their orders were to dislodge the scrap merchants and send them home, but three days after their arrival on 23 March a company of Argentinean troops arrived. The badly outnumbered marines could do no more than observe the intruders, and were forced to surrender when the main force at Port Stanley did so.

Argentinean troops began landing on East Falkland, near the capital, on 2 April 1982. Now there was no longer any doubt as to their intentions. The marines were ordered to make a token 30-minute resistance and then surrender. The governor, Rex Hunt, knew there was no chance of a successful defence, and he would not to throw away lives needlessly. However, the gesture of defiance was important in political terms.

> The raising of the Argentinean flag on South Georgia by scrap metal merchants dismantling an old whaling station was seen in London as somewhat silly.

Thus, when Argentinean forces suggested that the garrison surrender, the offer was rejected. The defenders were mostly Royal Marines, assisted by a handful of naval personnel and about 30 members of the Falkland Islands Defence Force, who were essentially volunteer militia. Other citizens tried to impede the invasion in various ways.

MAIN INVASION FORCE ADVANCE

While Argentinean commandos tried to neutralize the marine barracks (which turned out to be empty), the main invasion force, which included amphibious APCs, was advancing on Port Stanley. It was engaged by a section of marines using disposable light anti-tank weapons and a Carl Gustav recoilless rifle.

Other forces attacked Government House, resulting in a fierce firefight that went on for considerably longer

For the Argentine army, getting troops ashore in the Falklands was not a major problem. Less than one hundred effectives were present to resist them, and there was no real chance of preventing a landing.

than the planned 30-minute defence. Finally, the governor began to negotiate a surrender, which came into effect at 9.30 a.m. The marines were taken to Argentina as prisoners while the Falkland Islands Defence Force volunteers were simply disarmed and released.

The Argentinean forces were under orders to avoid unnecessary casualties during the assault, for various reasons. Not the least was the hope that Britain might not react to a bloodless, or almost bloodless, occupation. After all, the Falklands were far away and of little importance. There had been no British casualties; the Argentineans had lost one killed and two wounded. Galtieri's junta had reason to hope that matters might rest there.

BRITISH RESPONSE

The British response took most observers by surprise in terms of both scale and efficiency. By 5 April, a naval task force was assembling. A powerful escort of naval ships, including two aircraft carriers, would accompany amphibious warfare vessels and civilian ships loaded with troops and equipment. On 7 April, the force sailed for its assembly point at Ascension Island, more than halfway to its destination. In the meantime, British attack submarines took up station off the Falklands to enforce an exclusion zone intended to prevent reinforcement of the islands' garrison.

There was no declaration of war by either side. The Argentinean position was that they were simply reoccupying territory that had always been theirs, while the British treated the matter as a piece of old-fashioned colonial policing to a great extent. A declaration of war was undesirable for other reasons, too. It was possible that the whole matter might be resolved by a show of force and some tricky negotiations, and a state of war meant that there was further to climb down for whichever side chose to give up the islands. In the event, neither was prepared to even consider it.

The Falklands consist of two large islands (East and West Falkland) and a great many smaller islands, few of which were important to the campaign. West Falkland was not significant; most of the main settlements and the capital were all located on East Falkland and it was there that the issue would be decided.

Only the northern half of East Falkland was important to the campaign. The southern half,

British troops guard prisoners taken in the fighting for the Falkland Islands. Although the Argentinean forces were mainly made up of ill-trained conscripts unprepared for their task, many Argentinean units put up a stubborn fight.

One of the few British armoured vehicles sent to the Falklands, this Scorpion is correctly termed a Combat Vehicle Reconnaissance (Tracked) Fire Support. Previous generations would probably have just called it a light tank.

connected only by a thin isthmus occupied by the towns of Darwin and Goose Green, contained little of any value and no major settlements. It was control of the towns that would decide ownership of the islands; there was no point in garrisoning an expanse of desolate moorland.

Thus although the land area was quite extensive and the mass of islands rather complex, the campaign's aims were fairly simple. Argentinean forces were in possession on the northern half of East Falkland and would have to be attacked there. Operations elsewhere were only useful if they supported that aim.

On 21 May, the first British troops from the task force went ashore on the Falkland Islands. A special forces raid on 14 May, in which SAS troops landed on Pebble Island and destroyed Argentine aircraft stationed there, preceded the landings. These were mainly Pucara ground-attack aircraft, which could otherwise have been used to support the ground battle.

Air and sea power greatly influenced the land campaign that followed. Naval supremacy was quickly established by the British, whose nuclear submarines were able to keep the Argentine navy bottled up in port and unable to intervene against the British task force. However, Argentine submarines and, more significantly, the Argentine Air Force attacked the British fleet. Although the submarines were unable to achieve anything, air attacks sank several navy and logistics ships, depriving the forces ashore of most of their transport helicopters among other vital supplies. The logistics ships obtained some protection by anchoring in San Carlos Water, between East and West Falkland. The area became known as 'bomb alley' with good reason; air attack became commonplace and several ships were lost.

> It was control of the towns that would decide ownership of the islands; there was no point in garrisoning an expanse of desolate moorland.

One of the first requirements for the ground forces was to establish a supply base ashore and to get army Rapier air defence missile batteries onto high ground over San Carlos Water. This would give additional protection to the vital logistics ships.

Lack of transport was a problem in the campaign, forcing a return to traditional methods. Here, heavily-laden British infantry 'yomp' (or 'tab', depending on their regiment) across the moorlands.

Once the beachhead was secure, the daunting task of removing the Argentinean army from the islands could begin.

According to conventional wisdom, the task was impossible. The Argentinean army had landed over 10,000 men and benefited from time to prepare its positions. The British had only about 9000 troops and a handful of tanks. These were light Scorpion and Scimitar armoured reconnaissance vehicles, whose low ground pressure enabled them to cross the kind of boggy terrain that would defeat heavier vehicles.

However, the British troops were qualitatively far better than their opponents. An all-volunteer force with high morale and excellent training, they included a significant proportion of elite units – Royal Marines, the Parachute Regiment and special forces, including Special Air Service (SAS) and Special Boat Service (SBS) detachments.

The Argentineans had, for their part, left many of their best units at home. Their elite mountain troops were watching the Chilean frontier in case of hostilities, and the best army units tended to also be the most politically reliable. These were kept back to suppress opposition to the junta, while most of those sent to the Falklands were composed of low-status conscripts, many of whom had very little experience.

On top of this, there was a big divide between Argentinean officers and men. Officers had a tendency to find themselves comfortable, warm billets in the towns and to all but abandon their troops, who were poorly supplied even if some of their equipment was actually superior to that issued to their opponents. Argentinean boots were found to be much more waterproof than British ones, for example.

A POSITIONAL STRATEGY

Due to the low capabilities of the Argentinean ground forces, their commander, General Mario Menendez, chose a positional strategy. Most of his forces were deployed around Port Stanley with detachments holding the other towns. Other than some resistance by forces that happened to be nearby, there was no real attempt to repel the landings at San Carlos Water.

One reason for this was the difficulty of moving overland in the Falklands. The Argentineans, who only had to hold on to the islands to win the war, did not see the need to brave the difficult conditions. With temperatures of -20°C (-4°F) recorded and with high winds blasting over a barren landscape of rocks and moorland, it is not hard to see why. Besides, there was a possibility that additional British troops might assault Port Stanley directly if the defence was weakened.

In fact, direct assault had been ruled out as impossible. Instead, the British strategy was to clear the flanks and then advance overland on Port Stanley. Initial operations were against Goose Green in the south and Douglas in the north. Having lost

> To add to their troubles, the BBC announced that British troops were advancing on Goose Green – to which, fortunately, the enemy did not react.

many transport helicopters aboard the container ship *Atlantic Conveyor*, the British had no choice but to 'yomp' across the islands on foot, carrying what they needed.

Thus the troops set out overland across cold moorland, some men carrying 54kg or even 63 kg (120–140lb) of gear, with the intention of fighting a battle at the far end. Previous training on British moorland was of some help, though in the end it was sheer physical fitness and a 'can do' attitude that carried the men to their destination.

CONTROVERSIAL REPORTING

To add to their troubles, the BBC announced that British troops were advancing on Goose Green – to which, fortunately, the enemy did not react. This and other pieces of reporting that gave useful information to anyone who happened to be listening caused a certain amount of controversy both during and after the war. There were even calls for senior BBC officials to be prosecuted for treason. Journalists accompanying the troops were not blamed by their armed companions; their lives were also endangered by the release of sensitive information. A little more

Despite an announcement by the BBC that forces were advancing on Goose Green, the defenders were not well prepared to face an attack by the Parachute Regiment. After putting up a fight on the approaches to the town, they surrendered.

than 500 British troops of the Parachute Regiment, supported by three artillery pieces, attacked Goose Green, which was defended by over 700 Argentinean troops. Some of the latter were of above-average quality; the majority were conscripts with little training. The Argentineans put up determined resistance on the approaches to the town, eventually causing the paras' assault to stall.

As the paratroopers tried to get moving again, their commanding officer, Colonel 'H' Jones, attempted to lead an assault on a machine-gun position. He had done this before on exercise and had been declared dead by umpires on several occasions. This time, it happened for real. Jones was posthumously awarded the Victoria Cross but in reality the overall commander of the force had no business behaving like a lieutenant.

After a stiff fight, the paras were able to force the Argentine positions. Some of the defenders fled as the assault approached them; others had to be eliminated with grenades or even bayonets. Once the positions before the town were taken, the airfield was overrun. Like that on Pebble Island, the airfield had been used by Pucara support aircraft and its elimination reduced the enemy's support capabilities.

The defenders of Goose Green surrendered soon after, freeing the paras to advance eastwards as the southern half of a pincer attack heading for Port Stanley. In the meantime, the communities of British citizens at Goose Green and Darwin had been liberated and large stocks of Argentinean supplies captured.

The northern arm of the pincer, comprising mainly paratroopers and marines supported by four tanks, was now advancing across country towards Douglas and Teal Inlet. Several skirmishes were fought along the way. Some were with Argentinean special forces patrols dropped off by helicopter; others with minor forces deployed in the region.

INTENSIFIED RESISTANCE

As the two arms of the pincer began to converge, resistance intensified. Most of the Argentinean force was deployed on the high ground around Port Stanley, and forcing these positions was an arduous business. The artillery put down its heaviest bombardment since World War II, but in the end the advance on Port Stanley was infantry warfare in the old style. Each position had to be suppressed, assaulted and eliminated before the attackers could move on.

The rugged terrain of the Falkland Islands, coupled with the cold conditions, proved a significant but surmountable obstacle to the British forces. One British soldier commented that the Falkland Islands were 'just like home'.

Although the Argentinean forces possessed a number of armoured vehicles, they played little part in the fighting for the islands. Some were used in the initial landings.

Here, as elsewhere in the campaign, some Argentinean officers deserted their men, but overall the Argentineans put up a determined fight, with small parties holding out long after the main force had been driven back. One by one, however, these positions were broken and the enemy driven back, to mount a last stand on Mount Tumbledown.

MOUNT TUMBLEDOWN

Tumbledown stood above Port Stanley; there were no more strong natural positions to which the Argentineans could fall back. It was, however, a very tough obstacle. The assault would have to be made uphill over hard going, in the face of fierce opposition. A heavy bombardment was put down to soften up the positions, and on the night of 13/14 June 1982 the final assault went in.

The assault on Tumbledown was carried out by the Scots Guards with support from the Royal Marines and Gurkhas plus four tanks of the Blues and Royals. The attack met extremely determined resistance and several times British and Argentinean units became pinned down in close contact, close enough for the combatants to shout abuse at each other as they exchanged fire.

Gradually, the assault ground its way forwards. Bunkers were destroyed with anti-tank weapons or assaulted with bayonets and grenades, and eventually the last resistance was broken. By then, it was morning; fighting had been going on all night.

The fall of Tumbledown and the surrounding high ground made it obvious that defeat was inevitable. The remaining forces in and around Port Stanley surrendered on 14 June 1982. Six days later, the South Sandwich Islands, part of Britain's possessions associated with the Falklands, also surrendered, bringing hostilities to a close.

Most observers suggested that Britain could not retake the Falklands, and would not even try. In doing both, the British armed services showed that many elements of war on a grand scale, which seemed to have had their

Tumbledown stood above Port Stanley; there were no more strong natural positions to which the Argentineans could fall back. It was, however, a very tough obstacle.

Argentinean prisoners are disarmed by their captors after the battle of Goose Green. Weak strategy on the part of the invaders allowed the British forces to advance in stages, defeating each settlement garrison before moving on.

day, were still vital. The battle for the Falklands was an amphibious operation on a strategic scale, while most engagements were infantry affairs, usually with close support from relatively small amounts of artillery.

In addition to reaffirming the need for close artillery/infantry cooperation, the Falklands war was characterized by extensive use of infantry rocket and missile weapons, such as the MILAN guided anti-tank missile, the 66mm (2.59in) Light Anti-Tank Weapon and the 84mm (3.3in) Carl Gustav Recoilless Rifle. There were no tanks to shoot these weapons at, yet they proved their worth in many other ways, engaging troops in buildings and bunkers, and even a small naval vessel.

Today, light guided and unguided weapons of these sorts are routinely used as 'bunker-busters', but in 1982 the concept was considered novel. Criticism was levelled at the use of the expensive MILAN missile against enemy bunkers, but this was answered by the fact that it costs far more to train a good infantryman, and a missile does not leave behind a widow.

The Falklands Conflict caused a rethink of British defence policy, particularly concerning the navy. The army could not have won its battles without the protection, transport, logistics and support provided by naval forces, and the ability to project power onto land at great distances was again shown to be vital. In other areas,

> Having rebuilt his forces after the war with Iran, Saddam Hussein of Iraq turned his attention southwards in the direction of the small but rich nation of Kuwait.

US troops arrive in the Middle East as part of Operation Desert Shield. The first priority was to prevent any further Iraqi aggression, then to build up forces for the eventual ejection of the invaders from Kuwait. This phase took much longer than the actual ground campaign.

current thinking was found to be correct. Extensive use was made of special forces raiding parties and reconnaissance missions, and these proved their worth on every occasion.

THE GULF WAR

While it was being fought, the Iran-Iraq war was referred to as 'The Gulf War', but this title was later used for the campaign against Iraq by an international alliance known as the Coalition. This conflict is now usually termed the 'First Gulf War' since a second, similar, conflict took place in the early years of the twenty-first century. In many ways, these three separate conflicts are all intertwined; without the Iran-Iraq war, the others would probably not have taken place.

Having rebuilt his forces after the war with Iran, President Saddam Hussein of Iraq turned his attention southwards in the direction of the small but rich nation of Kuwait. The reasons were largely financial; Iraq had ended the Iran-Iraq war with large international debts, much of which were owed to Saudi Arabia and Kuwait. The latter had recently increased her production of oil, which

The Coalition plan for the ground campaign was to make a left hook, breaking through the Iraqi positions and rolling them up towards the sea. The speed and firepower possessed by Coalition armoured forces made the operation a success.

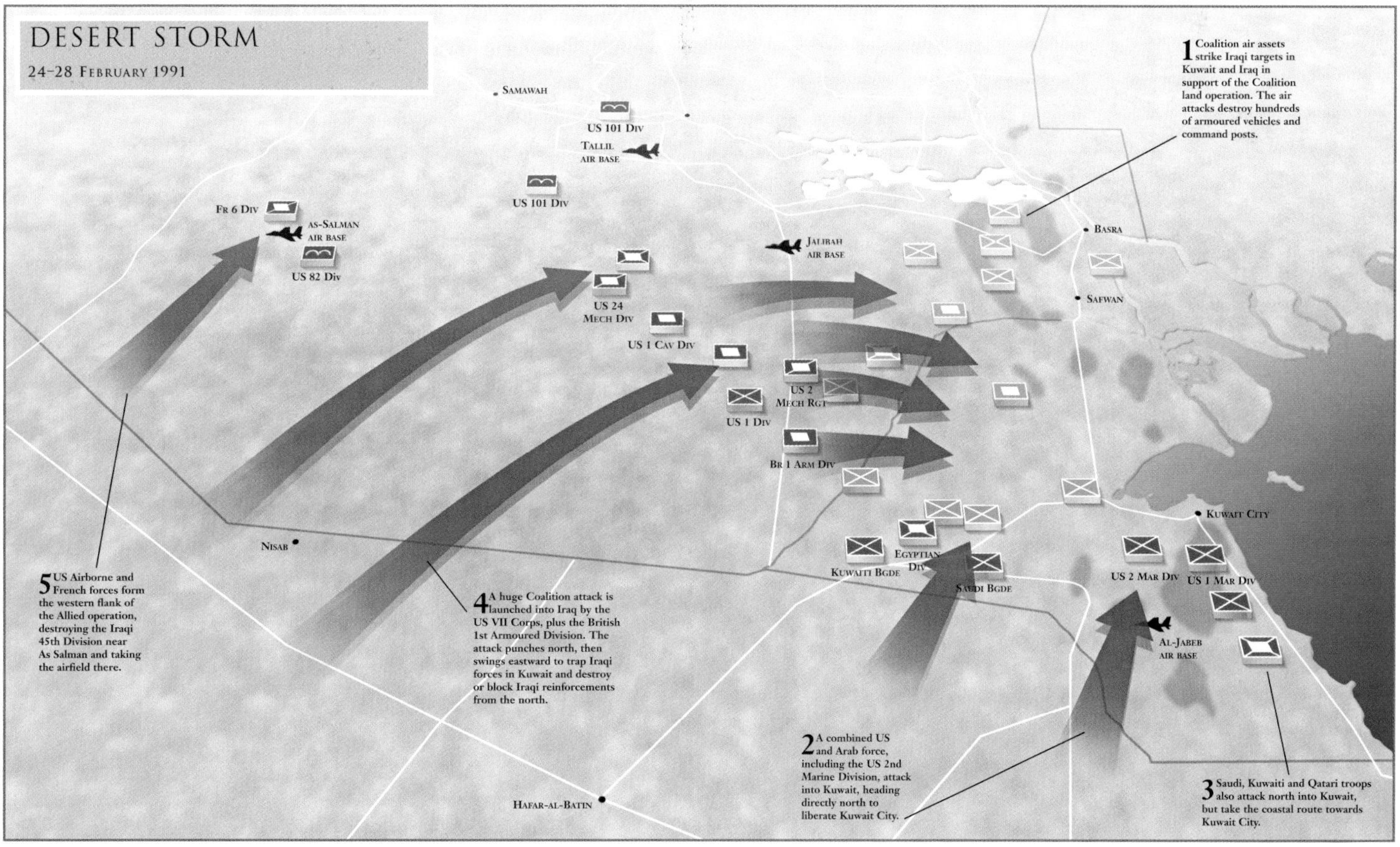

DESERT STORM

24–28 February 1991

1 Coalition air assets strike Iraqi targets in Kuwait and Iraq in support of the Coalition land operation. The air attacks destroy hundreds of armoured vehicles and command posts.

2 A combined US and Arab force, including the US 2nd Marine Division, attack into Kuwait, heading directly north to liberate Kuwait City.

3 Saudi, Kuwaiti and Qatari troops also attack north into Kuwait, but take the coastal route towards Kuwait City.

4 A huge Coalition attack is launched into Iraq by the US VII Corps, plus the British 1st Armoured Division. The attack punches north, then swings eastward to trap Iraqi forces in Kuwait and destroy or block Iraqi reinforcements from the north.

5 US Airborne and French forces form the western flank of the Allied operation, destroying the Iraqi 45th Division near As Salman and taking the airfield there.

Samawah
US 101 Div
Tallil Air Base
US 101 Div
Fr 6 Div
As-Salman Air Base
US 82 Div
Jalibah Air Base
US 24 Mech Div
US 1 Cav Div
US 2 Mech Rgt
US 1 Div
Br 1 Arm Div
Basra
Safwan
Kuwait City
Nisab
Kuwaiti Bgde
Egyptian Div
Saudi Bgde
US 2 Mar Div
US 1 Mar Div
Al-Jabeb Air Base
Hafar-al-Batin

The Gulf War was a huge undertaking from the point of view of logistics as well as troop involvement.

pushed the price down. This harmed the Iraqi economy, which depended heavily upon oil revenue. Relations between Iraq and Kuwait deteriorated and Iraqi troops began moving towards the Kuwaiti border.

In July 1990, responding to international pressure, Iraq agreed not to invade Kuwait without a renewed attempt at negotiations. However, the invasion went ahead on 2 August 1990. Kuwaiti forces were vastly outnumbered and at a low state of readiness. Iraqi preparations had largely been seen as posturing of a sort Saddam Hussein was known to favour when involved in a dispute.

Four divisions of the Republican Guard, the cream of Iraq's ground forces, made the invasion. A spearhead of special forces and elite units in divisional strength was sent ahead in helicopters to seize Kuwait City. These suffered losses from the Kuwaiti air force, which was then mostly able to escape to Saudi Arabia.

The nearest Kuwaiti forces engaged the Iraqi advance and imposed some delay, though they never had any chance of halting the greatly superior force. Other elements of the army were ordered to flee to Saudi Arabia and took part in the war later. The invasion was complete within two days, leaving Iraqi forces almost unopposed in possession of Kuwait.

This not only wiped out Iraq's debt to Kuwait but placed its formidable economy at the disposal of Saddam Hussein. However, the United Nations Security Council and the Arab League were both opposed to the invasion and passed resolutions condemning it as well as demanding the withdrawal of Iraqi troops from Kuwait.

PROFESSIONALS STUDY LOGISTICS

Getting forces into Iraq was a significant logistical challenge for the United States. Fortunately the need to deploy rapidly anywhere in the world had been foreseen and fast container ships were ready to transport quantities of equipment wherever they were needed. More importantly the system was exercised regularly and could be carried out efficiently.

President Bush addresses U.S forces during Operation Desert Shield. Behind him is the A-10 Thunderbolt which was one of the most effective aircraft ever to fly. It was armed with a 30mm (1.18in) tank-killing cannon.

OPERATION DESERT SHIELD

There was concern that Iraqi forces might next move on Saudi Arabia. This would give Iraq control of much of the world's oil, an outcome that was desirable to no one but Saddam Hussein and his government. There were other plausible reasons to assume that an invasion was planned, as Iraq also owed a great deal of money to Saudi Arabia. Fears grew when Saddam Hussein began to speak out against Saudi Arabia.

On 6 August 1990, the UN imposed economic sanctions on Iraq, and the next day US forces began moving into Saudi Arabia to take up defensive positions. This was the beginning of Operation *Desert Shield,* intended to protect Saudi Arabia from invasion.

There was a period where Saudi Arabia was vulnerable. Sufficient forces could not be deployed to resist an invasion until sometime in October, though naval air power was available to disrupt an Iraqi advance

> In November 1990, the United Nations demanded that Iraqi troops withdraw by 15 January. Iraq responded by offering a series of counterproposals.

Although self-propelled artillery is common in today's military forces, there is still a place for more traditional towed guns. The main problem they face is counter-battery fire, which SP guns can avoid by using 'shoot-and-scoot' tactics.

long before that. Meanwhile an international alliance was forming. Although the USA provided 75 per cent of the ground troops deployed, some 34 nations were represented, some in considerable force.

In November 1990, the United Nations demanded that Iraqi troops withdraw by 15 January. Iraq responded by offering a series of counterproposals. The politics of the period were complicated by the fact that Israel was coming under SCUD missile attack from Iraq and naturally wanted to act. However, several nations hostile to Israel had aligned themselves with the Coalition against Iraq. A compromise was reached whereby Israel would remain neutral in return for an effort by Coalition special forces to locate and destroy the missile launchers.

By January 1991, Operation *Desert Shield* was complete. Sufficient Coalition forces were in place to prevent an invasion of Saudi Arabia, but these could not remain deployed forever. With three days remaining to the withdrawal deadline, the US government authorized the use of military force to remove the invaders from Kuwait, and the rest of the Coalition followed suit.

STRATEGY: THE ART OF PLAYING TO YOUR STRENGTHS

It is not always possible to predict which advantages will be decisive. Superior weaponry did not win the war in Indochina for the French, and numbers were not enough for the Arab allies fighting Israel in 1967. Making best use of the advantages that exist, and creating new ones, while offsetting those of the enemy, is what strategy is all about.

OPERATION DESERT STORM

It has been rightly said that winning a battle or a war is all about the accrual of advantage. Sometimes this is the result of a sudden masterstroke. More

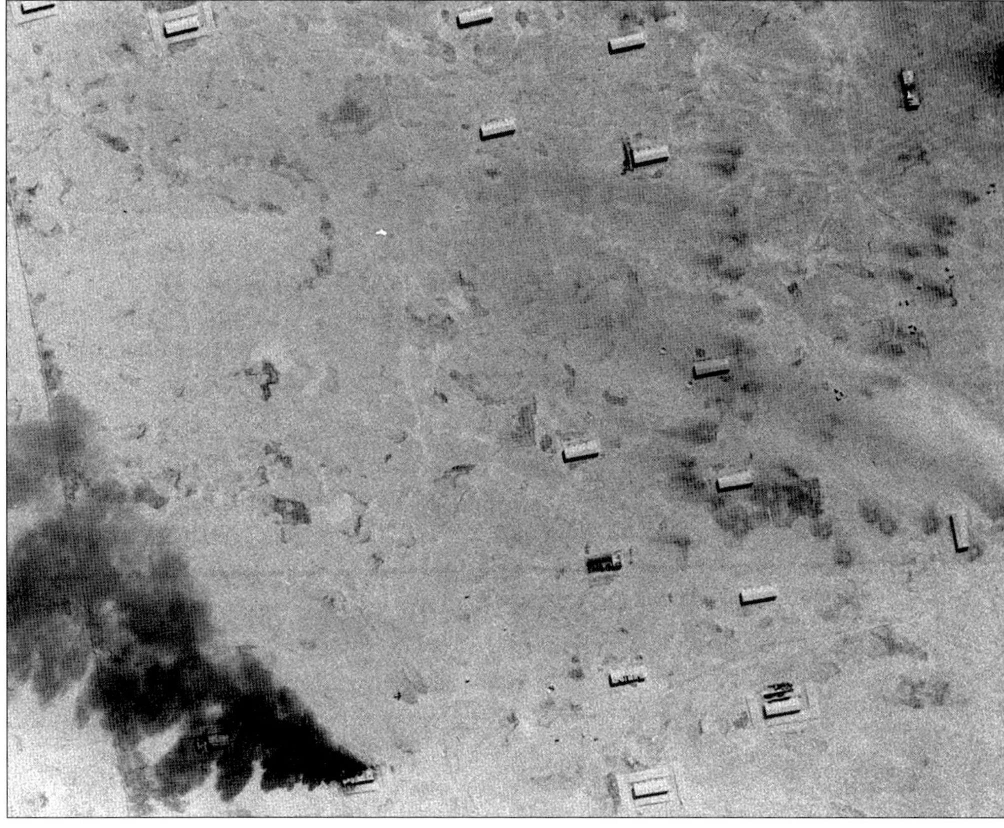

Attacks on Israel using SCUD missiles threatened to force Israeli retaliation, which would have had significant political consequences for the Coalition. This launcher site has been destroyed by air attack.

often, advantages are won gradually until the balance is tipped in favour of one side. Some advantages are territorial, such as the possession of a critical terrain feature. Some are technical, such as the possession of superior weaponry or better protection than the enemy. Some are the result of training or doctrine, or political alliance-building.

The Coalition facing Iraq had advantages in terms of training and equipment, but all the same it faced a daunting foe. Iraq at that time had one of the largest armies in the world, with about 5000 tanks and 500 self-propelled guns, mostly of Soviet origin. There were over 40 divisions, though many were not at full strength.

The majority of the army consisted of conscripts whose training and morale were not good, and it was conscript divisions that now held Kuwait. The Republican Guard had been withdrawn and was held in reserve. It was a formidable force and would be used to confront the Coalition if military action proved necessary. Saddam Hussein promised the world the 'mother of all battles' if the Coalition decided to fight.

However, the Coalition had no intention of fighting the powerful Iraqi army on its own terms. Instead, Coalition forces set about accruing all the advantages they could obtain before embarking on the ground campaign. The Iraqi army was

CHALLENGER 1

Type: Main battle tank

Crew: 4

Powerplant: one liquid-cooled diesel engine developing 1200hp (895kW)

Maximum speed: (road) 55km/h (35mph)

Range: (road) 400km (250 miles)

Weight: 62,000kg (61.51 tons)

Armour: not available

Armament: one 120mm (4.72in) gun; two 7.62mm (0.3in) machine guns; two smoke dischargers

Dimensions: length 11.56m (35ft 4in)
width 3.52m (10ft 8in)
height 2.5m (7ft 5in)

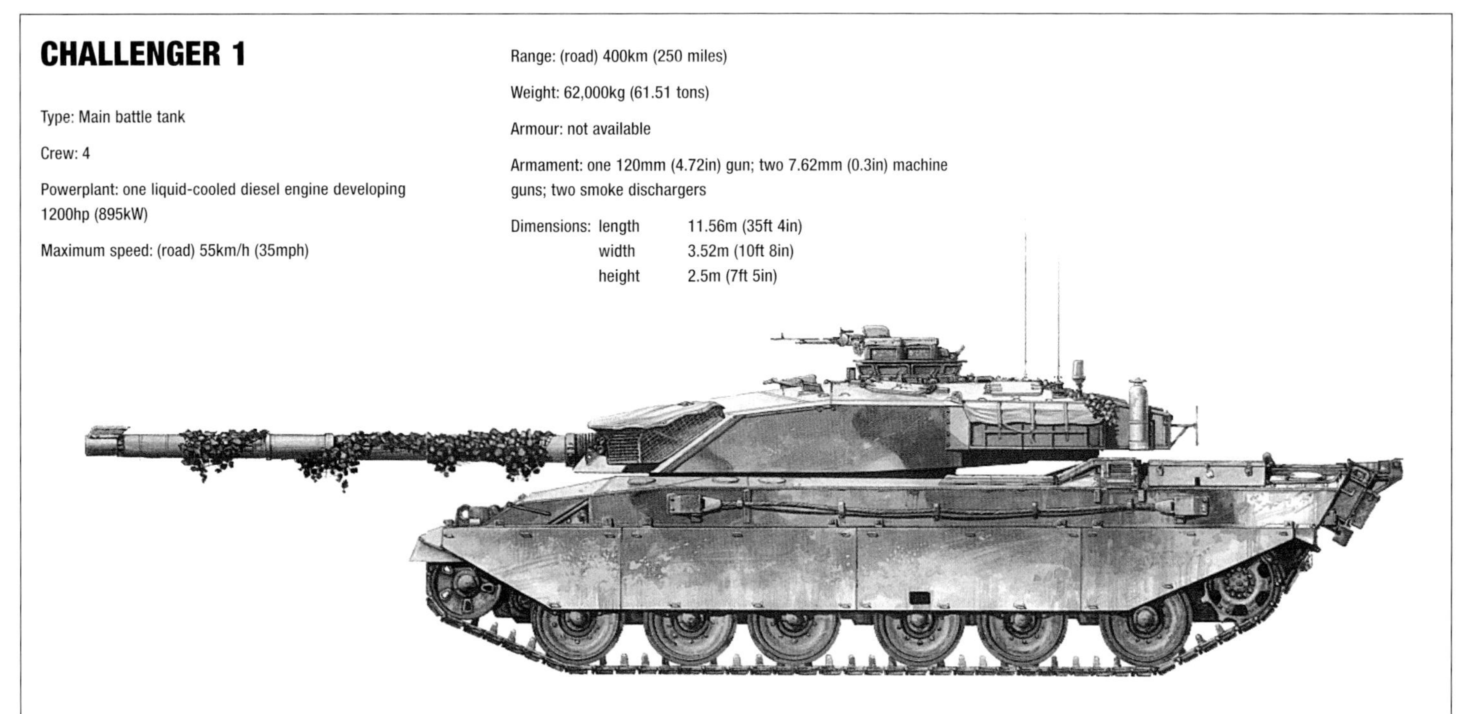

powerful, but its effectiveness could be greatly reduced by 'crumbling' it in a massive air campaign. Thus on 17 January 1991 Operation *Desert Storm* began, with air and missile attacks against Iraqi forces and command facilities.

After reducing the air defences, the priority was to cripple command and communications facilities. This severely limited the capabilities of the units in the field. Communications are vital to any force but the Iraqi army was used to close control from Baghdad, and its commanders were uncomfortable operating without it.

With their capabilities dwindling daily, the Iraqis had to do something. An attack into Saudi Arabia was launched and actually took the city of Khafji. However, Coalition ground forces with US air support quickly ejected the invaders.

The Gulf War was, in many ways, the pinnacle of armoured warfare. Once the ground offensive began, fast-moving Coalition armoured forces were able to hook into the enemy rear with surprise and heavy firepower.

EFFECTS OF THE AIR CAMPAIGN

The overall ability of Iraq to support its military forces was also reduced by the destruction of bridges, power stations and the like. Attempts to find SCUD launchers using special forces troops, who would then call in air strikes to destroy them, were less successful. Iraqi missiles did relatively little damage throughout the conflict, however.

OPERATION DESERT SABRE

By the middle of February, the Iraqi army was at least halfway to defeat. Demoralized by constant air attack and deprived of supplies by strikes against the logistics 'tail' that supported the fighting 'teeth' units, the remaining ground units were not in a condition to undertake a major battle of manoeuvre. Their positions were well known to the Coalition and plans had been drawn to take advantage of the situation.

Saddam Hussein suggested that Iraq was willing to withdraw from Kuwait but added a number of unacceptable conditions, including reparations for damage caused by Coalition air attacks. On 21 February, he announced that Iraq was ready to fight the ground war, and two days later the Coalition offensive opened.

US and British armoured forces spearheaded the ground assault, codenamed Operation *Desert Sabre.* Their Abrams and Challenger tanks proved impervious to everything the Iraqis fired at them, and their on-board electronics allowed first-shot kills on the move at ranges of 3km (1.8 miles) and more. The Iraqi armour facing them was of an older generation and lacked night sights, laser rangefinders and ballistic computers. Doctrine was also inadequate, with many tanks simply dug in as fixed bunkers.

With its right flank and rear secured by joint Coalition forces and the more lightly equipped French

Wreckage on the 'Highway of Death'. The collapse of Iraqi forces in Kuwait resulted in a rush northwards up the only available road in whatever vehicles could be appropriated. Given time, these forces could have rallied to fight.

acting as a mobile flank guard, the spearhead launched its main attack on 24 February 1991. The plan was to bypass major centres of resistance and get into the Iraqi rear, making a left hook eastwards and enveloping the defenders. Airmobile forces were thrown well forward to keep the enemy off balance. Meanwhile, US marines and Coalition forces attacked towards Kuwait City, encircling the city. The plan called for Arab forces to undertake the actual liberation of the Kuwaiti capital.

Some Iraqi units put up a stiff fight. Others, demoralized and caught by surprise, simply collapsed as soon as the ground offensive approached them. Those that fought inflicted few casualties on the Coalition forces; their equipment, training and motivation were simply not up to the task imposed on them.

Republican Guard units, with their better equipment and higher morale, were targeted for destruction. These formations, along with the better

> With its right flank and rear secured by joint Coalition forces and the French acting as a mobile flank guard, the spearhead launched its main attack on 24 February 1991.

A captured Iraqi S-60 anti-aircraft gun. The 57mm (2.24in) gun can be manually aimed but is normally used with radar direction, and poses a hazard to aircraft within 6000m (6560 yards). It was once a standard Warsaw Pact weapon.

regular divisions, represented the main threat of a counterattack against the Coalition forces. These forces proved harder to break but simply could not match the firepower of the Coalition spearhead. When the Medina Division of the Republican Guard tried to ambush a US armoured division, it was roughly handled and lost over 200 tanks for minimal Coalition casualties.

By 26 February, Iraqi forces in Kuwait had largely collapsed. Vast numbers of vehicles were fleeing northwards up the only road to Iraq. This vast bottleneck made an unmissable target for aircraft and helicopters, and massive casualties were inflicted on the Iraqi army, turning the retreat into a chaotic rout. The road became nicknamed the 'Highway of Death'.

Kuwait City was liberated on 27 February, and on the same day a

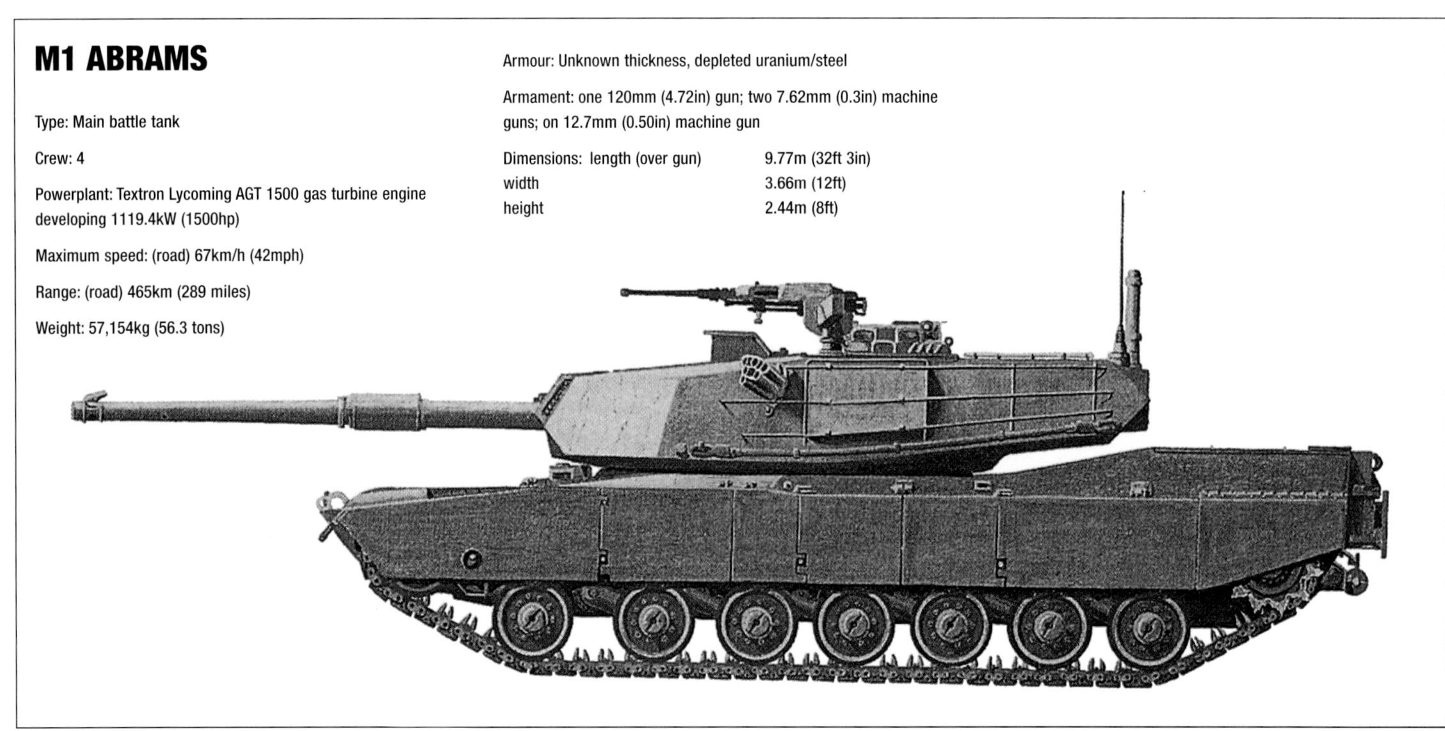

M1 ABRAMS

Type: Main battle tank

Crew: 4

Powerplant: Textron Lycoming AGT 1500 gas turbine engine developing 1119.4kW (1500hp)

Maximum speed: (road) 67km/h (42mph)

Range: (road) 465km (289 miles)

Weight: 57,154kg (56.3 tons)

Armour: Unknown thickness, depleted uranium/steel

Armament: one 120mm (4.72in) gun; two 7.62mm (0.3in) machine guns; on 12.7mm (0.50in) machine gun

Dimensions: length (over gun)	9.77m (32ft 3in)
width	3.66m (12ft)
height	2.44m (8ft)

ceasefire was announced after just 100 hours of combat operations. The decision whether or not to chase the shattered Iraqi army north and overthrow Saddam Hussein was a tricky one, but it was decided to remain within the bounds of the UN mandate, which was to liberate Kuwait from Iraqi occupation, not to engage in an offensive war against Iraq.

Although the Gulf War did not entirely deal with the problems posed by Saddam Hussein and his regime, it did fulfil its objectives and the overall goal of liberating Kuwait, at a very small cost in Coalition lives. This had as much to do with doctrine and strategy as with technology, though the two went hand in hand.

The Iraqis obligingly tried to fight a traditional war in the open, enabling the Coalition to use conventional tactics to defeat them. The technological gap between the two forces was such that the Iraqi army simply could not beat the Coalition forces even if it had not been ground down almost to the point of defeat by the air campaign. The Iraqis were strong in conventional terms, and tried to play to their strengths. The Coalition forces were stronger in that area, so in the end the Iraqi army played to the greater strength of the enemy and paid the price.

The Gulf War was the final major land conflict of the twentieth century, but the manner in which it was conducted would be familiar to Sun Tzu, the ancient Chinese military thinker who said that a wise general wins first and then goes to war. In truth, the Gulf War was won before the ground assault opened.

Although the Gulf War did not entirely deal with the problems posed by Saddam Hussein's regime, it did fulfil its objectives and the overall goal of liberating Kuwait.

A Kuwaiti soldier after the Iraqi withdrawal from his home country. Some commanders wanted to push on into Iraq and depose Saddam Hussein, but the UN remit for the war was simply to liberate Kuwait.

The Complex Battlespace – Warfare in the 21st Century

At the beginning of the twentieth century, warfare could be said to take place in two dimensions. Forces moved over the surface of the ground or tunnelled a little under it. This situation had been much the same throughout history, but all that changed in the space of a few years.

Observation balloons had been used for some decades but their effectiveness was very limited. Powered flight took combat into a third dimension as aircraft flew and fought above the battlefield. Combat zones became wider and deeper as airmobile troops or air strikes became capable of reaching previously inaccessible places.

A fourth dimension was created by the use of the electromagnetic spectrum for communications and information gathering, while electronic warfare served to prevent the enemy from making use of this information.

As air power and electronic warfare became increasingly vital to the conduct of ground operations, the concept of a 'battlefield' faded away at some point in the middle of the twentieth century. Although the term had not yet been coined, it came to be understood that wars were being fought in a complex battlespace consisting of the terrain of the battlefield plus the air above and around it and the electromagnetic spectrum in the general vicinity.

Other considerations also became increasingly important. The political dimension, in terms of

The workings of a gun would be familiar to an artilleryman of 1914, but its range and accuracy when firing in conjunction with advanced communications and GPS assistance would astound him.

Communications intercepts, radar jamming and other information-gathering have a direct impact on combat operations even if the personnel manning these systems never sight the enemy with their own eyes.

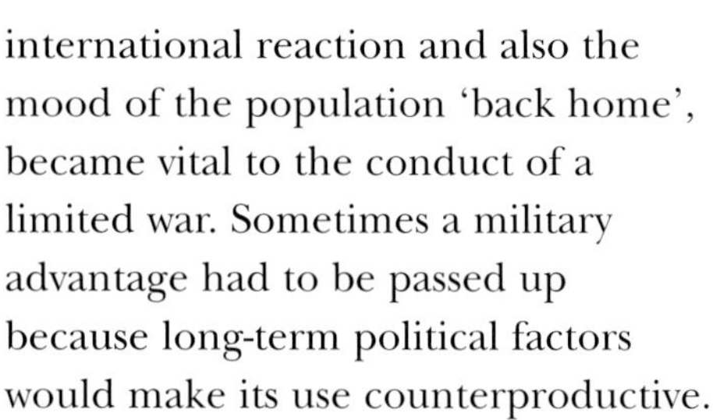

international reaction and also the mood of the population 'back home', became vital to the conduct of a limited war. Sometimes a military advantage had to be passed up because long-term political factors would make its use counterproductive.

As an example, in the Gulf War Iraq launched missiles at Israel in the hope that Israel would respond with military force. Although this would bring yet another nation into the Coalition, it might well cause Arab nations hostile to Israel, who were already contributing more than Israel was likely to, to leave the alliance.

All-out wars have become far less common since the middle of the twentieth century, at least between major industrial powers. Those that have occurred have been limited by various factors, and victory has tended to go to those that successfully played the political as well as social angles.

It has been shown that a force that loses no battles and suffers very low casualties can be forced to withdraw and effectively lose the war by an opponent who is being, in the military context, mauled. The mobility of information makes it ever more possible to manipulate the political component through the media.

This adds yet another dimension to the conduct of military operations. In a war zone, people will inevitably get hurt, and some of them may not be directly involved in the conflict. Images of civilian casualties may provoke an outcry and while this does mean that it is more difficult to get away with committing atrocities, it is also possible for the opposition to manipulate the situation by either faking incidents or laying the blame where it does not rightly belong.

MAJOR CONFLICT POSSIBLE

The possibility that a major conflict, with tank brigades clashing in massed combat, cannot be discounted and wise governments prepare for such an

US infantrymen make use of lightweight, portable communications equipment. Depending on circumstances, they can request air or artillery support, reinforcements or casualty evacuation, or report a lack of enemy contact.

The last major conflict of the twentieth century was characterized by mass use of tanks; a concept that did not exist before 1917. It is not possible to predict the changes over the next century.

eventuality. However, as a rule the battlespace has become ever more complex and the focus tighter. Military operations have become enmeshed with political, economic and social considerations, and troops have to adapt to rapidly changing conditions in an environment where they may be surrounded by friendly, or at least non-hostile, people.

This has always been the case to some extent, of course. However, in recent years a 'gentleman's war' with very little civilian involvement, such as that fought in the deserts of North Africa in 1941–43, has become all but impossible.

To paraphrase US military thinking, modern forces may find themselves protecting aid workers, rendering humanitarian assistance, securing their own bases and local infrastructure, dealing with insurgents and engaging in a major firefight involving armoured vehicles all within a three-block radius and all at the same time.

This 'three-block war' concept is a difficult challenge to confront, but it is a realistic appraisal of the needs of modern warfare. The 'Grand Threat' may re-emerge at any time, forcing the military to confront hordes of tanks, helicopters and infantry, and this capability must never be lost. But in the vast majority of cases it is small units of infantry, led by junior officers, who will have to deal with extremely complicated situations while trying to ensure that their actions do not make the situation worse in the long run.

> The possibility that a major conflict, with tank bridges clashing in massed combat, cannot be discounted and wise governments prepare for such an eventuality.

And so, at the dawn of the twenty-first century we return to the fundamental concept of fighting wars – that despite advanced weapons, technology and the eternal march of progress, it is still the training and skill of the ordinary soldier that makes all the difference.

Index

Picture Credits

Art-Tech/Aerospace: 14, 21, 24, 57, 68, 69, 78, 79, 82, 84, 86, 87, 95, 96, 99, 101, 102, 104, 106, 108, 109, 111, 114, 116-118(all), 137, 144 147(all), 159, 167, 176, 179, 180-182(all), 185, 190, 192, 197, 203, 236, 237, 241-245(all), 280, 286, 287, 289, 291, 292, 296-301(all)

Art-Tech/MARS: 50, 65, 66, 90, 92(top), 100, 103, 105, 110, 113, 115, 130, 131, 133, 136, 148, 149, 155, 193, 213, 215, 220, 221, 238, 240, 252, 261, 269, 294, 295, 302

Cody Images: 6, 13, 17, 20, 23, 28, 30-34(all), 36, 46, 49, 51, 56, 58, 77, 135, 164, 166, 199-202(all), 204, 206-209(all), 212, 214, 217, 218, 222, 223, 246, 248-251(all), 256-258(all), 260, 263-268(all), 270, 272, 273, 275, 278, 281-283(all), 285, 288, 293

Corbis: 62, 184, 187, 188, 191, 198, 210, 219, 235, 254, 255

Will Fowler: 76

Getty Images: 61, 93, 195, 259

Getty Images/Popperfoto: 63, 72, 94, 107, 126

Library of Congress: 40, 74

Mary Evans Picture Library: 8, 9, 15, 22, 45, 75

Bertil Oloffson/Krigsarkivet: 10, 25, 29, 37-39(all), 43, 44

Photos.com: 19, 48, 59, 60

Photos 12: 54, 55(bottom), 64, 71

Public Domain: 216

Süddeutsche Zeitung: 12, 26, 27, 41, 42, 47, 52, 55(top), 73, 88

Ukrainian State Archive: 92(bottom), 119, 120, 122(both), 124, 125, 128, 138, 140-143(all), 150, 151, 172, 183

US Department of Defense: 35, 89, 129, 132, 134, 154, 156-158(all), 160, 161, 163, 165, 168-171(all), 173-175(all), 186, 224, 226, 227, 229-232(all), 234, 276, 303-315(all)

All Artworks courtesy of Art-Tech/Aerospace